But Also Good Business

But Also Good Business
Texas Commerce Banks and the Financing of Houston and Texas, 1886–1986

WALTER L. BUENGER
JOSEPH A. PRATT

Texas A&M University Press COLLEGE STATION

Library of Congress Cataloging-in-Publication Data
Buenger, Walter L. (Walter Louis), 1951–
  But also good business.
  Bibliography: p.
  Includes index.
   1. Texas Commerce Bank—History. 2. Banks and
banking—Texas—History. I. Pratt, Joseph A.
II. Title.
HG2613.H654T4913 1986   332.1′2′097641411   86-40215
ISBN 0-89096-280-4

Manufactured in the United States of America
FIRST EDITION

To Barbara Eaves,
and in memory of Carole Knapp

Contents

viii   *Contents*

Illustrations

Figures

Tables

PREFACE

This book was written under an exemplary arrangement between the authors and Texas Commerce Bancshares, Inc. It began in late 1981, when Ben F. Love, the bank's chairman and chief executive officer, decided that a centennial history of the institution should be written. He sought a history that was professionally written and academically legitimate, not one which would be perceived as a public relations work. The search for authors led to Joseph A. Pratt, a business historian, and Walter L. Buenger, a historian of Texas and the South. After a summer of preliminary research and interviews, the authors signed a contract with Texas Commerce to complete the study.

This contract contained several key provisions. The authors were given complete editorial control and the copyright of the manuscript, with the company retaining the right to review the manuscript and to recommend changes at the authors' discretion. Points of disagreement with the authors, if any, were to be indicated in explanatory footnotes. The contract also stipulated that the authors would have full access to the records of the organization while specifying that several categories of information available for background research would not be available for publication. These restricted areas included material pertaining to matters currently under litigation and other proprietary information, which if published might adversely affect the current operations of the bank. This aspect of the contract raised a particularly sensitive issue, since the authors intended to study Texas Commerce's lending activity while concluding with an overview of the history of the institution in recent decades. To indicate that the company and the authors accepted and agreed upon the focus of the book to be written, the contract also included an appendix which set forth a preliminary chapter outline. Finally, the contract established a target date for publication in 1986 and stipulated the financial assistance to be provided by the bank to enable the authors to meet this target date while also holding full-time appointments at Texas A&M University. This assistance can be summarized as follows: Texas Commerce provided funds for release time from teaching duties for one semester and four summers for each author. Further, the company provided a professional archivist for part-time work in organizing records and paid for research assistance and research expenses.

The writing of the contract proved time-consuming and at times frustrating, as the lawyers for both parties reduced what seemed like simple, straightforward agreements into legally appropriate language. Yet in retrospect, the time absorbed in negotiating a contract proved quite well spent. By anticipating possible areas of conflict and reducing agreements about such issues into a legally binding document, the two parties laid the basis for a smooth working arrangement in which each knew and accepted the rules. The writing of the contract also set a standard of mutual respect and cooperation which has been a hallmark of this project.

From the preliminary negotiations forward, the authors sought to write more than an institutional history. They wanted to place Texas Commerce in its region, to trace its role in financing the growth of the economy. Texas Commerce readily agreed to this focus and helped the authors gain access to a wide range of individuals and records connected to its history. Long-standing customers, directors and former directors, major participants in the Houston economy, and employees and former employees all were interviewed. The list of interviews in the bibliography is testimony to Texas Commerce's assistance. The authors also had the benefit of a series of interviews conducted by William Allison, an employee of Texas Commerce, done in the early 1970s in anticipation of writing a history.

Written records were abundant—sometimes too abundant. Both authors remember their shock at seeing 25,000 boxes of uncataloged paper in the organization's off-site storage center. Other records, however, were more easily used. Several officers had carefully preserved their papers. The *Directors' Minutes* of most of the predecessors of TCB–Houston were still extant. Minutes of loan committees, bound volumes of statements of condition for all Houston banks from the 1920s to the 1960s, and complete records regarding major mergers were also available. More records turned up as news of the project spread among those connected to Texas Commerce.

Photographs also proved abundant. Most of the photographs which appear in this book were located in the bank and have been collected in the TCB Archives. Mrs. Gainer B. Jones, John E. Whitmore, and E. O. Buck donated photographs from their personal collections.

Will Rice College at Rice University allowed us to photograph their portrait of Will Rice. John van Beekum of the *Houston Chronicle* took that photograph and the photographs of the drawings of past executives used in the book. He also reproduced older photographs and in doing so improved the quality of the illustrations.

In sifting through and acquiring photographs and written records, in conducting the host of oral interviews, in working out the exact contractual arrangements, and in a myriad of other ways the authors were greatly aided by Barbara Eaves, an assistant vice-president of TCB–Houston. From its conception Eaves backed the history project and did all she could to smooth the way for the sometimes cantankerous authors. Without her the project would never have been completed on time. We owe her a special debt.

Marshall Tyndall, executive vice-president, oversaw the project and was of great help to the authors. Whether new office space was needed or a particularly difficult problem had to be solved, Tyndall did his best to help.

The support and encouragement of Ben Love has also been essential. Love, who wrote a history of National Bank of Commerce when he first joined Texas Commerce in 1967, sent a clear message throughout the organization that the authors were to have complete access to records and people. For his own part, he freely gave time from a busy schedule for interviews while meticulously observing the agreement that the authors were to exercise editorial control.

Others at Texas Commerce also helped. John E. Whitmore, a former chairman of the board, gave freely of his time and knowledge. E. O. Buck, retired officer, and Lloyd Bolton, a vice chairman of TCB–Houston at the time of the writing, increased our understanding of oil lending and real estate lending, respectively. The legal staff, people in financial accounting, those in the records section, and many others all have our thanks. We gratefully acknowledge all those employees interviewed by us. Once a draft of the manuscript had been completed, numerous specialists within the bank reviewed sections of it for accuracy. Love, Tyndall, Eaves, Whitmore, Buck, Marc Shapiro, James Cochrane, R. Bruce LaBoon, and Lee Straus read and commented on the entire manuscript.

Outside Texas Commerce we also incurred many debts. Our lawyer, Claude D. Davis of College Station, represented us in the contract negotiations. Robert A. Calvert, a colleague at Texas A&M, first told us about the possibility of writing a history of Texas Commerce and later conducted interviews. Larry D. Hill, another colleague at A&M, read the entire manuscript in an earlier form and gave us many useful comments. Louis Marchiafava, of the Houston Metropolitan Research Center, also read and improved the manuscript. Donald Fraser, of the Finance Department at Texas A&M, provided useful comments on the chapters dealing with recent events. Carole Knapp entered on a word processor and printed countless versions of the manuscript. Her speed and accuracy saved us much time. Nancy Boothe, the director of the Woodson Research Center at Rice University, organized our archives and put together the biographical sketches of current and former officers in Appendix B. Those interviewed who were not employees also gave freely of their time and we thank them. William D. Berry generously shared his knowledge of real estate in the Houston area. Jim Glass drew the figures and maps and designed the book; his work has added clarity and beauty to it.

Our wives, Suzy Pratt and Vickie Buenger, both assisted on the project. The former has balanced our books, paid our bills, and figured the tax implications of this project. The latter has helped with the research, assembled material for tables and figures, prepared Appendix A, and assisted in the assembling of an archives. They have our thanks and our love.

Of course, mention of the model working arrangement we have enjoyed with Texas Commerce and of the help we have received from numerous individuals in no way negates our responsibility for what appears on these pages.

But Also Good Business

CHAPTER 1

Introduction: A Century of Growth By a Bank and Its Region

*In 1931 two Houston banks stood at the brink of failure, but finan-*cial contributions from the city's major banks and industrial corpora-tions averted disaster. Jesse Jones, chairman of the board of National Bank of Commerce of Houston and soon to be head of the Reconstruc-tion Finance Corporation under President Franklin D. Roosevelt, or-chestrated the rescue effort. When the crisis had passed, Houston's financial institutions remained standing, shaken but sturdy. Panic had been prevented; runs on banks had been stemmed. The regional banking system had survived, largely intact. When asked about these events, Jones observed that the cooperative actions of those who con-tributed to the rescue effort were "patriotic acts, but good business as well."[1] His words reflected an attitude toward banking which Jones shared with his counterparts in other Houston banks: What was good for their region was good for their banks.

Texas Commerce Bank, and the holding company it formed, was created by the merger of National Bank of Commerce and several of the other Houston banks involved in the 1931 episode. While pursu-ing its primary business of taking deposits and making loans, Texas Commerce helped finance a century of regional development. This his-tory examines the "patriotic" contributions of a profit-seeking con-cern; it discusses the intertwining of a region's economic needs with an institution's ambitions.[2]

The region served by Texas Commerce has not remained static over the past 100 years. During this time Houston grew dramatically as improvements in transportation and communications integrated more and more of the surrounding area into the economic life of the city.[3] At the same time, the trade area of Houston expanded. The city's merchants, bankers, and manufacturers steadily extended their influ-

Table 1.1   Population Growth in Houston, 1870–1980

Year	Total Population, Houston	Percentage Increase in Decade
1870	9,382	76
1880	16,512	67
1890	27,557	62
1900	44,633	76
1910	78,800	75
1920	138,276	111
1930	292,352	32
1940	384,514	55
1950	595,163	57
1960	938,219	31
1970	1,232,802	29
1980	1,595,138	

SOURCE: Michael T. Kingston (ed.), *The Texas Almanac and State Industrial Guide, 1984–85*, p. 349.

ence over the commerce of a wide section of Texas and Louisiana. Several of the region's products, notably cotton, oil, and oil tools, entered national and international markets. As businesses headquartered in the city became more involved in this larger economy, Texas Commerce grew from a small bank primarily for local merchants into a major Texas bank active throughout much of the world.

In response to increasing demands for banking services, Texas Commerce often expanded through mergers and acquisitions. A history of the institution therefore encompasses the history of numerous predecessor banks. The family tree of the organization's lead bank, Texas Commerce–Houston, reveals two particularly large branches: National Bank of Commerce (NBC) and Texas National Bank (TNB). NBC was long controlled by Jesse Jones, one of the most prominent Houston businessmen and civic leaders in the first half of the twentieth century. Founded in 1912, NBC acquired two smaller banks during the banking crisis of 1930–31, but otherwise it grew without relying on mergers until 1964, when it merged with Texas National Bank.[4] TNB was itself the result of the merger in 1953 of South Texas National Bank and Union National Bank, two organizations whose impact on the financial and civic affairs of Houston was particularly strong in the years before World War II. Of these two banks, South Texas had the older lineage. It was formed in 1912 by the merger of Commercial National and South Texas National and until 1949 was called South Texas

Figure 1.1. Texas Commerce Bank–Houston's family tree.

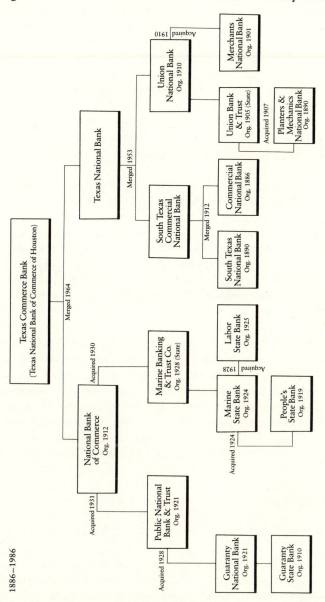

SOURCES: Bill Logan, The Houston Heritage Collection of National Bank Notes, 1863 through 1935; *Houston Post*; *Houston Chronicle*.

Commercial National Bank (STCNB). Commercial National was organized in 1886 and is the oldest of the Texas Commerce predecessors. Among the leaders of Commercial National and later South Texas Commercial National was Captain James A. Baker, a prominent lawyer and businessman. The primary ingredients for success at Captain Baker's bank as well as NBC and Union National were close contact with a limited number of important accounts and an established reputation for integrity and safety. All three banks had only a small number of employees who could be supervised in a highly centralized management system. The merger of 1964 thus brought together banks with long and similar histories. They had in common close ties to the business elite of Houston and an orientation toward the commercial customer.

This 1964 merger created an institution which since has remained one of the largest banks in Houston and one of the four largest banks in Texas. The evolution of the organization took a new direction in 1971, when the management of Texas Commerce Bank–Houston organized a bank holding company, Texas Commerce Bancshares, which acquired TCB–Houston and then other member banks throughout Texas.* By 1986 Texas Commerce Bancshares had 70 member banks in cities in all parts of the state, and it had become one of the 25 largest banking organizations in the United States.

Throughout its century-long existence, Texas Commerce helped finance economic development, and this critical function is the first of four primary topics of this history. Like commercial banks in other cities, Texas Commerce specialized in corporate business, extending short-term credit primarily to local businesses and prominent businessmen. Texas Commerce was broadly involved in the day-to-day economic life of its region through account relationships with companies and individuals active in the many types of business enterprises found in a major city. While financing the commerce and the construction

---

* Authors face a potentially confusing question of nomenclature in discussing the history of an organization made up of numerous once-separate parts. To avoid the endless repetition of phrases such as "Texas Commerce–Houston and its predecessors" and "the numerous ancestor banks of Texas Commerce," we have used the much simpler designation "Texas Commerce" to refer to all of the banks which are currently a part of Texas Commerce–Houston. At times, of course, precision has required the use of the former name of a predecessor bank, but when there seemed little danger of confusion, we opted for the simpler "Texas Commerce" instead of the cumbersome "Texas Commerce and its predecessors." In the holding company era after 1971, "Texas Commerce" or "TCBK" designates the entire banking organization, while "TCB–Houston" designates the Houston bank which originally organized the holding company.

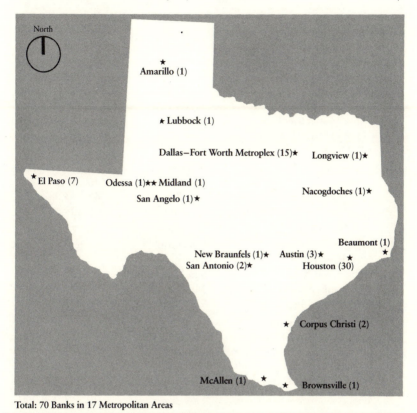

Map 1.1. Texas Commerce Bancshares, 1986.

generated by its rapidly growing region, however, the bank became deeply involved in two industries—cotton and oil—which gave Houston and its banks a distinctive pattern of development. Cotton and oil have ebbed and flowed in importance. The significance of cotton lending diminished in the 1930s, and oil lending increased after that point. In turn, oil lending declined in the 1960s, only to increase in importance in the 1970s and again decline in the 1980s. Despite this ebb and flow, cotton and oil lending take on an added significance in the history of Texas Commerce because they established the bank's identity within the national financial system.

Cotton and oil lending as well as other financing functions are closely dependent upon a second major topic of this history, the place of the bank in the banking industry and the changing nature of that industry. As Figure 1.2 suggests, for many years Texas Commerce and

Table 1.2   The Top Twenty-five Banks in the United States, December 31, 1984

Name	Headquarters	Total Assets
1. Citicorp	New York	$150,586,000,000
2. BankAmerica Corp.	San Francisco	117,679,502,000
3. Chase Manhattan Corp.	New York	86,883,018,000
4. Manufacturers Hanover Corp.	New York	75,713,707,000
5. J. P. Morgan & Co.	New York	64,126,000,000
6. Chemical New York Corp.	New York	52,236,326,000
7. Security Pacific Corp.	Los Angeles	46,117,443,000
8. First Interstate Bancorp.	Los Angeles	45,543,888,000
9. Bankers Trust New York Corp.	New York	45,208,147,000
10. First Chicago Corp.	Chicago	39,845,731,000
11. Mellon Bank Corp.	Pittsburgh	30,602,815,000
12. Continental Illinois Corp.	Chicago	30,413,791,000
13. Wells Fargo & Co.	San Francisco	28,184,124,000
14. First Bank System	Minneapolis	22,437,746,000
15. Crocker National Corp.	San Francisco	22,322,223,000
16. Bank of Boston Corp.	Boston	22,078,819,000
17. Marine Midland Banks	Buffalo, N.Y.	22,055,697,000
18. InterFirst Corp.	Dallas	21,617,000,000
19. RepublicBank Corp.	Dallas	21,594,769,000
20. Norwest Corp.	Minneapolis	21,345,800,000
21. Texas Commerce Bancshares	Houston	20,732,000,000
22. MCorp	Dallas	20,697,000,000
23. Irving Bank Corp.	New York	18,982,403,000
24. First City Bancorp. of Texas	Houston	17,318,567,000
25. NCNB Corp.	Charlotte, N.C.	15,678,599,000

SOURCE: *Fortune* (June 10, 1985).

the other Houston banks lacked sufficient resources to serve as primary sources of credit for major corporations whose needs were filled by money center banks. Houston banks have gained slightly on the money center banks and now are somewhat better able to handle large loans. Even at their smallest, however, Texas Commerce's predecessors were much bigger than the country banks of the state. It was true as well that, for most of their history, NBC, Union National, and STCNB were larger than most other Houston banks and had a significant share of the city's banking business. The position of Texas Commerce in the national, state, and local banking industry determined what type

Figure 1.2. Changes in the relative size of deposits of the average of the top three banks, 1900–80. *

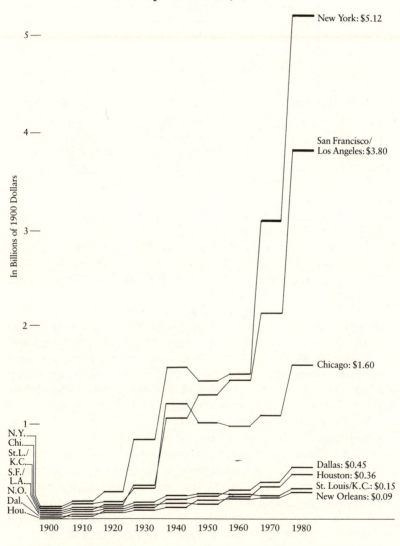

SOURCES: *Moody's Bank and Finance Manual; Fortune; Business Week.*
* After their creation, holding company deposits are used for their headquarters city.

of loan the bank could most easily make, and changes in its position altered its pattern of lending.

Significant changes in the operations of the bank also came in response to new federal and state regulation, and the third primary topic addressed in this book is the impact of regulatory changes on banking. In three periods Texas Commerce and its predecessors have faced sweeping regulatory changes which required basic adjustments in the banks' operations. Between 1905 and 1912, a state banking system was organized in Texas, and the Federal Reserve was created by the national Congress. The 1930s witnessed a wave of security-based banking reforms aimed at restoring confidence in financial institutions badly shaken by the Great Depression. During the 1970s, the reforms of the 1930s were modified, allowing for greater competition among financial institutions. At the same time, the creation and spread of bank holding companies active throughout Texas marked a sharp departure from the state's historic limitation of a bank's operation to a single location. Throughout the past hundred years, bank regulators have sought to strike a balance between the desire for a stable, secure banking system and the desire for a competitive, efficient one. As the regulatory pendulum has swung back and forth between these often conflicting goals, bankers have faced the difficult challenge of managing amid regulatory uncertainties.[5]

While working within regulatory constraints, Texas Commerce and its predecessors sought greater size, profitability, and security. Pursuit of these goals often required significant institutional change, and the analysis of such change is the book's fourth primary topic. Larger size helped ensure greater profitability and security and was obtained either by attracting new customers or through mergers. Profitability and security were also influenced by the organization and attitudes of the bank's management. Sudden increases in size through mergers placed particular strain on managers.[6] The merger process and the managerial adjustments required by sustained growth are the most important aspects of institutional change examined throughout this book.

Four closely related topics—the financing of regional development, the changing position of Texas Commerce in the nation's financial system, the impact on the bank of swings in banking regulation, and institutional change—thus provide the focus for this history. Although the narrative which follows moves through a century of change in chronological order, it seldom strays far from these primary topics.

One organizational device which has proved useful in sorting out the bank and the region's history has been the shifting of the focus of the narrative from external to internal affairs in alternating chapters.

The chapters dealing with external forces paint a portrait of the evolving economy in which the bank operated. They generally cover a decade or more of lending patterns and changes in the banking industry. Taken together, they provide an overview of a century of growth in and around Houston while also tracing the evolution of the banking system as a whole. In contrast, the chapters on the internal affairs of Texas Commerce focus on the strategy and structure of the bank, including its reactions to regulatory change. These chapters tend to include more detail about specific managers and the choices they made in guiding the bank; they generally also cover fewer years than do the external chapters. The external and internal chapters take the reader from a bustling late-nineteenth-century town to a sprawling late-twentieth-century city; from a small new bank trying to establish a permanent foothold in southeastern Texas to a statewide organization of seventy banks trying to secure a place for itself among the established money center banks.

CHAPTER 2

The Rise of Houston and Its Banks, 1886–1914

Development into a modern economy came later to Texas than to most other parts of the United States. As late as 1880 the state had no city with a population of more than 25,000 and none of the financial or manufacturing capacity common to larger cities. Instead the state was handicapped by the legacies of the pre-1880s era: an agricultural economy dependent upon ill paid labor, a poor transportation system, lack of credit, and semicolonial status within the nation's economy. By the early 1900s, however, a few larger cities had begun to emerge in the state. One of these cities was Houston, situated at the point where, as its promoters claimed, "the railroads meet the sea." [1]

Railroads, the sea, cotton, and lumber account for the rise of Houston. Throughout the post–Civil War period and into the early twentieth century railroad construction dominated the economic life of the area, creating demands for lumber and for workers. By 1886, however, enough track was in place to make a difference in the cotton and wholesale trade. Transportation problems from Houston to the sea also began to be resolved. As transportation improved, the cotton trade passed from the hands of the cotton factor, who sold the cotton for the grower, to the cotton dealer, who purchased the cotton and put together large lots to be resold to the manufacturer. The volume of cotton passing through Houston and the efficiency of its movement increased. Cotton dealers also expanded into the related cottonseed oil and wholesale-grocery industries. The burgeoning lumber industry, which was stimulated by railroad construction, and the need to repair and maintain the machines and facilities used in transportation added to the manufacturing base of the city. By the start of World War I, improved transportation and the growth of closely related industries had transformed Houston into a center of commerce and the site of limited manufacturing.

Bankers both benefited from and assisted this maturation of the economy. They held deposits for the railroads and led the fight for improved connections to the sea. Their primary business came to be short-term loans to cotton dealers. By providing vital services in a credit-hungry and still developing region, bankers made a handsome profit for their stockholders. Indeed, one measurement of the economic upsurge and growing maturity of the Houston region after 1886 was the increase in national banks from one at the start of that year to five at the close of 1890. Of those five banks in 1890, three, Commercial National, South Texas National, and Planters and Mechanics, eventually became part of Texas Commerce. With the emergence of modern Houston began the intertwining of the region's economic development and the institution that became Texas Commerce.

Such a rapid increase in the number of banks in Houston reflected a level of economic growth that would have been impossible before the 1880s. Cultivation of field crops, primarily cotton but to a limited degree sugarcane, dominated the Gulf Coast economy before 1886. Livestock and lumber added some variety. The economy revolved around the growth, harvesting, and sale or exchange of these raw materials. Wholesaling of groceries and manufactured items was limited to the immediate region. Most of these manufactured items were imported, and local manufacturing produced only such items as wagons and wheels, which aided the flow of cotton, sugar, lumber, cattle, and hogs out of the region. In this extractive economy very little capital was directed towards securing the trade of a larger region or towards more lucrative forms of manufacturing such as the production of cotton cloth. Indeed, except for a few merchants, Houstonians seldom had enough capital to justify the existence of a bank.[2]

Even so, as long as world demand for cotton, sugar, lumber, and livestock remained high, limited prosperity was possible and city leaders dreamed of better things. From Houston's founding in 1836 to the 1870s, these dreams were thwarted by a transportation system confined to shallow rivers, muddy roads, and short, unconnected railroads. Transportation between Houston and the interior almost stopped in periods of peak rainfall or excessive drought. Rain turned the roads into seas of mud, but did fill up Buffalo Bayou enough to float cotton down to the Gulf of Mexico. Drought improved the condition of the roads but made Buffalo Bayou too shallow to transport the region's products to the sea. Because of these seasonal interruptions and the slowness of transportation, the predictable, continuous, and inexpensive movement of goods was impossible.[3]

Transportation problems spurred an interest in railroad building in the 1850s. Railroads did not depend upon the weather, and they could haul large and bulky cargoes at low rates. Unfortunately, they were also expensive to build. That pointed to another major limiting factor on the Texas economy. Throughout the nineteenth century, Texans could rarely scrape together enough surplus capital for large scale investments. There were a few exceptions to this rule in the Houston area. Brazoria County planters, many of whom were among the richest men in antebellum Texas, took some of their profit from sugar and cotton and together with $75,000 from their county government built a railroad from Columbia to Houston. Yet without public aid even these planters did not have the funds to construct the fifty miles of track connecting the two cities.[4]

By 1861 and the start of the Civil War, Texans along the Gulf Coast faced a classic economic problem. Generations of Texans and their southern forbears owned slaves, purchased land, and grew cotton. In the short run, such investments yielded the best return for the moderate amounts of capital available to most Texans. The trap, however, was that the habits of slavery and cotton growing and their alluring profitability precluded substantial investments in transportation and manufacturing. Such investments might have ended exclusive reliance upon a few exports out of the state and broadened the distribution of income.[5]

Perhaps Texans would have slowly accumulated surplus capital and invested in manufacturing, but the Civil War stopped such advancement and introduced an era of more severe problems. For at least twenty years after the war the Gulf Coast suffered from the declining profitability of small and medium-sized farms, more serious capital shortages than those that existed before the war, a federal monetary policy that discriminated against the region, and the boom-or-bust economic development of that era. By specializing in food crops or raising livestock, yeoman farmers increased their level of profitability from 1850 to 1860, but this was seldom the case thereafter. The postwar construction of railroads financed by investors from outside the state made cheap foodstuffs available, gave an advantage to the larger stock raisers, and usually left cotton as the only viable crop for Texas farmers who wished to be part of a market economy. As more and more farmers in Texas and in other places in the world grew cotton and as the transportation links connecting Egypt, India, and the American South to Europe and the North improved, cotton ceased to be a commodity in virtually limitless demand. Instead, from 1865 onward there was often more cotton than the market would bear. As a result, only the larger and more efficient producer could make a profit in farming over the long run. By 1886 it was clear that the city, not the farm, was the place for the average person to rise in the world.[6]

Economic development in Houston and other urban centers, however, was hampered by serious capital shortages. Land, slaves, currency, and cotton in storage traditionally had served as the major forms of capital. Only cotton emerged from the war with its value near intact, though that value fluctuated. Slaves were freed, resulting in massive capital losses. Roughly one-third of the capital in Texas in 1861 was in the form of slaves. That was gone by the close of 1865. Confederate currency and Confederate national and state bonds were also worthless at the end of the war. Without slaves to work the land and without capital to buy new acreage, landowners watched land values plummet.[7]

Complicating the capital shortage was the monetary policy of the U.S. government. In an effort to ensure a strong currency, a substantial proportion of paper money was removed from circulation in the postwar years, and the growth of money in circulation generally lagged behind the growth rate of the economy. The supply of money was much less than the demand. This scarcity of money favored those with money to lend but hurt regions in need of capital because over the lifetime of a loan the value of the dollar increased, and lenders had no incentive to make loans in unfamiliar areas. This meant that industrialists and financial institutions in the established Northeast held the upper hand in their dealings with capital-short states such as Texas. Although long on natural resources and desire for development, the Houston area needed investment capital to develop new industries.

To make matters even worse, the Texas economy was battered by a series of economic recessions in the late nineteenth century. Cotton prices fell sharply in the late 1860s. There was an extended recession in the mid-1870s and a briefer recession in the mid-1880s. Each recession tightened credit, worsening the existing shortage of capital.[8]

Another factor which limited economic growth was the low level of consumer spending. As should be expected in an export-dominated agricultural economy in which almost one-third of the population was poor, newly freed slaves, income distribution was very uneven. Large planters, cotton brokers, lawyers, insurance men, ranchers, and mercantile elites made substantial fortunes in the period from 1865 to 1890. Small farmers and workers in the lumber industry, many of whom were former slaves, lived barely above the subsistence level. They were trapped at that level by a heritage of racial prejudice, lack of capital, and an increasingly competitive economy which forced their earnings lower. Certain workers in Houston were slightly better off, particularly artisans who owned their own tools, but jobs as unskilled laborers were scarce in an economy which lacked major industries.[9]

Banks were both victims and villains in the pre-1886 Houston-area economy. By discounting notes, issuing currency, and circulating checks, banks made more money available for circulation. Loans from banks increased the availability of credit. In the nineteenth century, however, both private and national banks catered almost exclusively to the cotton trade and to the major merchants. As the *Houston Post* pointed out in 1886, "National banks do not allow interest to depositors, and in fact generally refuse the small sums that are brought to them by workingmen." Moreover, banks lent money for no more than 90 days and did so only in the form of personal notes. There was no mortgage money available for long-term capital investment in Houston. Not only custom prevented the paying of interest to small depositors and the making of mortgage loans. Dealing with small deposits and the ordinary citizen involved considerable risk. The three banks that tried it in Houston before 1890 failed. Many that tried it after 1890 also failed. Making long-term loans demanded more money than Houston banks could provide while continuing to service the day-to-day needs of commerce. New York and other money centers were the primary sources for long-term and more extensive lines of credit.[10]

In part, this dependency upon out-of-state financial centers grew out of the history of banking in Texas. Before the Civil War, except for a bank chartered by Mexico on the eve of the Texas Revolution, there were no government-chartered banks in Texas. State law forbade additional incorporation of banks, and no federal law existed to supersede that of the state. To ease wartime credit problems and stabilize the banking system, however, the U.S. Congress passed banking acts in 1863 and 1864. These laws established the current national bank system, and they were applied to Texas when federal authority was re-established over the state in the summer of 1865. A bank which had a specified amount of capital determined by the size of the community in which it was to be located and a charter approved by the comptroller of the currency could open for business in Texas. In 1866 the First National Bank of Houston, with $100,000 in capital stock, became the first publicly chartered bank organized in the city.[11]

There had been private banks in Houston long before 1866. The laws of Texas could not eliminate the needs for short-term credit to carry farmers over from the time their cotton was harvested until it was sold and the need to arrange for the payment for cotton. Oftentimes this payment came from New York or some other distant point. Quite naturally banking functions drifted into the hands of the merchant or cotton factor who not only handled the transfer of funds but also advanced funds or merchandise to the planter awaiting payment for his crop. Gradually some of these merchants and cotton factors began to specialize in banking. Both Thomas W. House and Benjamin Armistead Shepard were carrying on an active banking business before the Civil War. Shepard bought control of First National in 1867 and operated under a national charter, but T. W. House and Company continued to act as an unincorporated bank until 1907.

Such banks, operating without charters from any level of government, were quite common before 1907. Private banks had the advantage of no government limitations on their loans and deposits and the further advantage that no minimum capitalization was required for them to begin business. As long as they could maintain public confidence, they could do a thriving business. Indeed, in 1880 at least 85 unincorporated banks were operating in Texas, and they were a more influential force in the economy than the state's 14 national banks.

As the scale of banking grew larger, however, banks regulated by the United States or by the state of Texas gained substantial advantages. National banks could issue currency. Their high initial capitalization inspired confidence in their stability, and government supervision assured the public of their soundness. By 1893 there were 222 national banks in Texas and only 133 private banks. The number of private banks continued to increase, however, until the period 1905 to 1910. The establishment in 1905 of a state banking system with low capitalization requirements diminished one of the advantages of private banks. The Panic of 1907 caused the bankruptcy of the House bank, one of the state's premier private banks, and weakened numerous other private banks. In comparison, the panic severely damaged few state or national banks. Public confidence in private banks waned, and their numbers declined after 1907. Many converted to state or national banks. Others ceased doing business altogether. In the 1920s, state law made it difficult to organize a private bank. An unregulated bank had come to be seen as an unsafe bank. The era of private banking had passed.[12]

Public skepticism about all banks was deeply ingrained in Texas. Most early-day Texans were followers of Andrew Jackson and believed with him that large banks would inevitably transfer their significant economic power into political power. Many Jacksonians had nothing against smaller banks, and were often interested in setting up a banking system in which easy entry into the industry and extensive competition balanced the power of banks. Like Iowans and citizens of a few other agricultural states, Texans went a step further by banning incorporated banks in their Constitution of 1845. Subsequent constitutions of 1861 and 1876 carried the same ban on state-chartered banks. This ban on banks stemmed as much from pragmatic experience as from ideology. Texas immigrants had been hard hit by the Panic of 1837, which had forced the closing of banks across the South and had made the profuse notes issued by those banks worthless. In the 1840s the rapid establishment of banks and their equally rapid failure gave witness to the risks of banking. By the mid-1870s banks were associated with the economic exploitation which Democrats alleged pervaded the era of Radical Republican domination. Careless overexpansion of banking was seen as one cause of the Panic of 1873. To most Texans, banks were a big business which could rob the common man of his democratic rights and impoverish the unwise investor or depositor. Either reason justified their banishment.[13]

This public hostility toward banks deserves scrutiny because it long shaped the evolution of the Texas banking industry. While the origin of this prejudice is reasonably clear, the explanation of its persistence is less so. At the Annual Convention of the Texas Bankers' Association in 1889, the main topics were the need for a state banking system and public attitudes toward banks and bankers. James Everett McAshan, who during the next year helped found South Texas National Bank, proclaimed:

> Antagonism to Banks must be due, first to ignorance, and second to the fact that old State Banks of former days, issuing floating millions of dollars of paper currency, which at its best was not current beyond the bounds of its native State, and most of which was never redeemed, brought the honorable profession of legitimate banking into disrepute, and the present constitutional prohibition of Texas against the chartering of Banks no doubt had its origin in these two causes.

Another speaker at the convention asked the pertinent question: "Is not the fierce opposition of Texas to the establishing of Banks one of tradition and not of reason?"[14]

Tradition and the bad record of antebellum state banks indeed played a continued role in prejudice against banks in Texas, but there were other reasons. Until the 1930s bank failures were common enough to remind Texans that banks could be seductive robbers of hard-earned funds. For those investors and depositors who lost money the old hostility had renewed meaning. Certainly, the ability of Democrats in Texas to taint anything associated with the Republicans as exploitative and elitist also played a role in the persistence of antibank attitudes. Banks also came to be associated with cities and with the economic control cities exerted over the post-Civil War Texas countryside. Yeoman farmers, who usually voted Democratic and who made up the bulk of the population, had instilled in them during the 1870s and

1880s a prejudice against banks and the power they could wield in society. The Populist movement, which attracted many of these same farmers to its cause in the late 1880s and early 1890s, reinforced this attitude. In that era, banks were closely linked to railroads and to the large cotton dealers. These groups were particular targets of Populist ire and were depicted as manipulating the economy to their advantage and the farmers' disadvantage. This image of banks as agents of big-city outsiders who enter a community to manipulate its economy to their own advantage has most influenced the ongoing attitude of Texans toward banks. Even after the state ceased to be dominated by farmers, Texans continued to favor small locally owned banks and to insist on unit banks which carried out their business at one location. For most of the nineteenth century, such sentiment caused Texans to prohibit any type of state banking system.[15]

For a brief moment in the history of nineteenth-century Texas, however, the state softened its attitudes toward banks. From 1869 to 1875, while Republicans governed the state and the Constitution of 1869 was in effect, a few state banks were chartered. Requiring less capital stock than national banks, these banks and savings institutions were intended to provide essential banking functions to a broader segment of society and aid economic development by increasing credit and savings. State banks organized in Houston were Houston Loan and Trust, Houston Savings Bank, and City Bank of Houston. Also organized in this era was Houston Land and Trust Company, but it did not offer a full range of banking services. Fewer than twenty banks opened for business across the state before the Constitution of 1876 restored the traditional ban on state banks. These banks were too small and too few to have much impact on the state's economy. Most either failed or merged with national or private banks. Of the state-chartered institutions in Houston in the Reconstruction Era, only Houston Land and Trust survived into the twentieth century.[16]

In fact, all the state-chartered banks except Houston Land and Trust were gone by 1886. That year marks a convenient dividing point in the economic history of Houston, since it witnessed the beginning of a rapid increase in the number of national banks and the establishment of the regional headquarters and machine shops of the Southern Pacific Railroad in Houston. Both the increase in banks and the arrival of major railroad companies suggested that a new economy was emerging in Houston.

In the old pre-1886 economy, cotton went by rail to Saint Louis or by ship to New York; money and manufactured goods came in from the same places. Local manufacturing and service industries had only a limited market because only a few consumers could afford their goods and services. When these concerns attempted to expand their markets, as did Houston-area producers of textiles and canned beef, they failed because they lacked sufficient capital, experience, access to transportation, organizational skills, and modern machinery. Even the short-term loans demanded by the agricultural export business could be supplied by New York and Saint Louis banks. Some have described this situation as a colonial economy dominated by outside manufacturers and financiers.[17]

Outside domination did not preclude increased prosperity. As the demand for cotton in the industrialized world rose in the early 1880s, the Houston region's economy improved. But the improvement was limited. Wealth remained concentrated in a few hands, while large sections of the population remained poor. Outsiders controlled investment capital, and industry was scarce. Downward swings in the commodities market brought staggering economic setbacks to the region. In 1890, the *Houston Post* trumpeted: "Cities like Houston must not wait for outside capital to build manufactories and make them great; they must put their own shoulders to the wheel." Yet words alone could not alter Houston's dependent position.[18]

It is difficult to imagine the Houston area beginning to break out of its dependency upon agricultural exports and outside capital without railroads. Railroads did four basic things. First, railroad construction provided jobs, increasing the circulation of money in the region and starting a ripple of buying and selling that by 1890 had created the highest level of overall prosperity since the 1850s. Second, railroads allowed more efficient and extensive transportation into and out of the city and thereby increased the volume and profitability of the merchandising of cotton and the wholesaling of goods. Third, railroad construction and the transportation it provided once completed stimulated the lumber industry, which offered a new source of employment. Fourth, when railroad companies located their regional offices and centered their rail systems in Houston, the city gained a long-term increase in jobs and an advantage in the struggle to wrest regional hegemony from Galveston.[19]

Railroad construction moved ahead with startling speed in the last quarter of the nineteenth century. By 1900 Texas contained 10,000 miles of track, almost all of which had been laid since 1876, when the new state constitution authorized large land grants to railroads. Most of this track was in the eastern half of the state, and its construction created great demands in the Houston region for workers in construction and related fields. Workers came from Germany and from the small farms of the region. They in turn created demand for food and drink. It was no accident, for example, that the city's first major brewery began business in the 1880s.[20]

As thousands of miles of track were built in Texas and organized into efficient connecting lines, the marketing of cotton and the wholesaling of goods imported into Texas passed into the hands of larger and more efficient concerns. Firms such as Wm. D. Cleveland & Co. took advantage of the latest improvements in transportation and communication to steadily increase the flow of cotton into and out of Houston. A little less than half a million bales left Houston in 1885. That figure had doubled by 1892. By increasing the scale, speed, and reliability of their transactions, Houston's cotton merchants increased their profits. Wholesaling followed much the same pattern. By increasing the speed and scale of their transactions, Wm. D. Cleveland; F. W. Heitmann and Company, which distributed sawmill and railroad machinery and hardware; and J. N. Taub, which specialized in cigars and loose-leaf tobacco, made substantial profits and provided more jobs. In the case of Carson, Sewall and Company, Wm. D. Cleveland, and a few others, the cotton dealer was also a wholesale grocer, and the railcar which brought cotton to Houston took back groceries to rural counties. Growth into complementary ventures and growth in scale allowed the most efficient use of storage and transportation facilities and brought increased prosperity.[21]

The East Texas lumber industry also benefited enormously from the huge demand for crossties and heavy bridge beams created by railroad construction while also creating demands of its own. Companies like F. W. Heitmann had new customers for its sawmills. Railroads had a steady cargo of yellow pine and cypress. Lumber had its own wholesalers and manufacturers like M. T. Jones, who manufactured sashes and doors and sold lumber wholesale across the United States. Jones's success was due to the vertical integration of his enterprises and to economies of scale made possible by improved transportation and communication. Around 1886, Jones came to own or control timberlands, mills, and wholesale distributorships. Current knowledge of the market gained from the telegraph and inexpensive, predictable shipment by rail allowed Jones to adjust the harvesting and milling of timber so that he could maintain a rapid and near-continuous flow from the forest to the customer. Since demand remained high, Jones and others who used the same techniques prospered.[22]

By the mid-1890s, Houston was a major rail center with over one hundred passenger and freight trains leaving and entering daily. Keeping these trains and their tracks in smooth working order and handling all the clerical and managerial duties required nearly 5,000 workers. That was one-eighth of an urban population of roughly 40,000. Both directly and indirectly, then, the railroads had an enormous influence on the Houston area, and it was no coincidence that new banks rapidly emerged as Houston was integrated into a nationwide rail system. Railroads meant that Houston banks had more customers and that those customers did a greater volume of business.[23]

Railroads also contributed mightily to Houston's rise to dominance within its region. Galveston was Houston's major competitor, and the island city's obvious advantage over the inland city was that it fronted directly on a harbor. Houston was roughly fifty miles from the sea, and before the dredging of the ship channel oceangoing vessels could not reach Houston's docks. As late as 1890, the advantage of its harbor meant that Galveston had a larger population and more and larger banks than Houston's. It, not Houston, was the cotton-exporting and financing center of Texas. But by 1900 the jobs, impetus to trade, and increase in capital provided by the rail system radiating out of Houston had moved it ahead of Galveston in population and volume of trade.[24]

Galveston, however, still had the advantage of its harbor. In fact, after the entrance to the harbor was dredged to a depth of twenty-five feet in 1896, oceangoing vessels could tie up at the Galveston docks. Before that time, freight had to be placed in shallow-draft vessels and lightered out to vessels anchored in the roadstead outside the bar blocking Galveston Bay.

Before 1896 Houston's shippers competed on an almost equal footing with their Galveston counterparts by using Buffalo Bayou. During the 1870s and 1880s the bayou was dredged to a depth of about ten feet from just outside Houston to Galveston Bay. Freight barges ran from the railroad terminals near Harrisburg to the waiting ocean vessels outside the bar. Before 1896 the same three-step-process—railroads, shallow-draft vessels, deepwater ships—was used out of Galveston and Houston. After 1896 moving freight out of Galveston required only two steps.

In 1896 Houstonians quickly launched their effort to restore the balance between their city and Galveston. Civic leaders set their sights on persuading the U.S. Congress to approve the funding of construction of a twenty-five-foot-deep channel from Houston to Galveston Bay. By 1897 they had entertained a delegation from the Rivers and Harbors Committee of the U.S. House of Representatives and had secured an engineers' report that said that a twenty-five-foot channel was possible and would be relatively inexpensive. After several years of political bickering in Congress and debate over the proper head of navigation on Buffalo Bayou, construction of a turning basin for the ship channel began in 1906. Improvements to the channel had slowed by 1908, but the next year Houstonians took advantage of a state law to form a navigation district empowered to sell bonds for the improvement of the bayou. With the revenue from the bonds Houstonians offered to pay half the cost of dredging to twenty-five feet. This offer convinced Congress to increase its funding for the ship channel, but the appropriation was contingent upon Houston first coming up with its share of the cost. In January, 1911, Harris County voters approved the creation of the navigation district and the sale of $1,250,000 in bonds. Congress appropriated its half of the needed funds, and in 1912 construction on the deepwater channel began. Work was completed in September, 1914. Once again Houston had the same transportation costs as Galveston's. Equal transportation costs and the devastating effects on Galveston of the hurricanes of 1900 and 1914 moved Houston far ahead of the island city in population and volume of trade.[25]

Houston Banks and the Financing of the Ship Channel, 1911

Houston bankers played a prominent role in the quest for better water connections to the Gulf. They realized that water was the cheapest way to transport bulky cotton bales and that the cotton trade was the lifeblood of the Houston economy. In 1897, for example, William Bartlett Chew, president of Commercial National Bank, and Charles Dillingham, president of South Texas National Bank, joined other prominent Houstonians in journeying to Washington to lobby members of Congress for increased funding for the channel. Bankers were also among the group who developed the plan for the joint local and federal funding of the channel, and bankers long served on the Board of the Harris County Navigation District and on the Houston Harbor Board.

The most important contribution of bankers to the construction of the ship channel, however, was their purchase of Harris County Navigation District bonds issued in 1911. The bonds proved difficult to sell, and it appeared that Houston would not be able to raise the $300,000 needed to match the federal appropriation for 1912. Jesse H. Jones, a director and major stockholder of Union National Bank, and William T. Carter, another director and major stockholder in

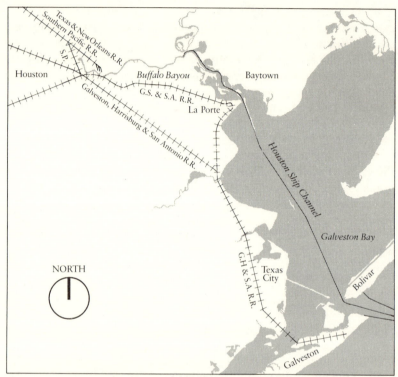

Map 2.1. Houston Ship Channel and Railroad Connections, 1920.

Union, played a prominent role in persuading the banks to buy navigation district bonds. They had little trouble convincing the president of
their bank, Jonas S. Rice, to go along with their plan. His brother,
Horace Baldwin Rice, was the mayor of Houston and a long-time promoter of the ship channel. Dillingham and Chew were still the presidents of South Texas and Commercial National, and the presidents of
the other major banks had also supported the idea of a ship channel.

In October and November, 1911, First National Bank, Commercial
National Bank, Houston National Exchange Bank, Union National
Bank, South Texas National Bank, Bankers' Trust, and Houston Land
and Trust Company agreed to purchase jointly $750,000 of the bonds.
The rest of the bonds were purchased by the city and county govern-
ments or were sold to investors. With the money raised, work on the
ship channel began the next year.

SOURCES: South Texas National Bank, *Directors' Minutes* 2 (October 26, 1911): 140; 2 (November 10, 1911): 142–50; Marilyn
McAdams Sibley, *Port of Houston: A History*, 137–38.

Long before the opening of the ship channel in 1914, however, the scale and organization of the cotton trade altered to the benefit of the city and its bankers. Improvements in the rail connections out of Houston and the dredging of Buffalo Bayou to ten feet in the decade before 1886 set the stage for these major changes. Gradually the rail lines were integrated into a nationwide system that offered regularly scheduled and frequent service. Similar service was offered by barges and ocean steamers. These improvements in transportation were accompanied by construction of telegraph lines that gave Houstonians access to current market news. As already noted, the number of bales of cotton shipped out of Houston increased from half a million to one million from 1885 to 1892. In the three years before the opening of the twenty-five-foot channel in 1914, an average of over three million bales moved through Houston each year.[26]

This increase in cotton shipments was not simply the result of improved transportation and communication. It was also the result of changes within the cotton industry. Before the 1880s cotton factors handled much of the cotton trade, acting as the agent of the grower or rural merchant who purchased cotton from the small farmer. Usually the factor sold the cotton for the best available price and took a percentage as a fee. Cotton factors also often purchased groceries for the farmer or rural merchant and sometimes extended credit.

In the 1880s, however, the cotton dealer began to replace the cotton factor. The dealers purchased the cotton from the farmer or rural merchant and then sold that cotton to manufacturers. For a time companies like T. W. House or Wm. D. Cleveland were both factors and dealers. But it soon became clear that dealing cotton yielded greater profit than factoring cotton. This higher rate of profit allowed the dealer to offer the grower a higher price than the factor could offer. This was especially true because the factor subtracted a commission from the price he received for the merchant's or planter's cotton.

Higher profits for the cotton dealer came from economies of scale and expansion into cotton by-products. Cotton dealers collected cotton in large lots, compressed and stored it, carefully watched the market, used futures to hedge against loss, and sold at the most advantageous time. Gradually the major companies established agencies in Europe or the Northeast to improve their access to cotton spinners. In general, the larger the amount of cotton handled and the bigger the company, the greater degree of efficiency and profitability. Cotton dealers also moved into the ginning of cotton and the purchase of cottonseed. The seed was pressed into cottonseed oil, and by the 1890s the oil was being used in several food products. The cake left after processing was used as cattle feed or fertilizer. Business was most profitable if done on a scale large enough to keep the processing equipment in constant use. Thus cotton dealers were encouraged to offer a higher price for ginned cotton if they were also able to buy the seed.

While a higher volume of cotton and cottonseed ensured greater profit, it also created a greater need for credit. Since cotton factors did not purchase cotton or cottonseed and had a steady income from their commissions, they needed little credit. Instead they lent money. Cotton dealers, on the other hand, required much more capital to buy and store cotton and cottonseed. Most dealers tried to speed the cotton to the mills as soon as possible, reducing the time they required credit. But starting in August when the year's crop first entered the market and continuing through December, their credit needs surged. Acquiring the necessary capital to profit as a cotton dealer was simplest for the well-established cotton factors. A few local factors were wealthy enough to begin purchasing cotton aggressively without borrowing money. Others had access to credit advanced by major European or American mills. Some had well-established business contacts with bankers in England or the Northeast which often led to extensive lines of credit. As transportation and the cotton trade improved, large cotton firms from outside the state began to do business in Houston and brought with them their own sources of credit. Geo. H. McFadden and Bro., a major east-coast firm, for example, was doing business in Houston by the mid-1890s. Even well-established firms, however, often turned to local banks for short-term credit. Such credit was all the more essential for firms without recognized names and established contacts. Houston banks began to lend from a few thousand to in excess of $100,000 as early as 1890. By 1900, short-term credit at a local bank became a prerequisite for a cotton dealer's prosperity.[27]

In fact, as early as 1886, cotton dealers, railroad companies, steamship companies, and the Houston banking industry had entered into a mutually beneficial arrangement. None could prosper without the others. Steam lines and railroad companies made possible the rapid movement of large quantities of cotton. This allowed the cotton dealer his necessary volume of business. In turn, the rail and steam lines needed the cotton dealer because his cotton was their major freight. They profited because the cotton dealers packed their railcars and ship holds with cotton on a regular basis. Cotton dealers could not function without credit. They needed banks. Banks needed cotton dealers because they were their safest and most profitable loan customers. Banks needed a source of funds to lend to cotton dealers. Railroad companies and steam lines needed a place for their deposits to meet their payrolls and a place to invest their profits safely. Banks provided both. Railroads and steam lines provided the money to banks to loan to cotton dealers. In the process they ensured that cotton dealers would be able to pay them to haul freight. This circle of mutual need and mutual benefit in the cotton trade lasted from the 1880s until the 1930s.[28]

The close and mutually beneficial relationship among cotton dealers, cotton transporters, and the Houston banking industry of the late nineteenth century is well illustrated in the history of the members of the Texas Commerce family from 1886 to 1901. Managers, owners, and directors from all three enterprises were closely tied. Indeed, a manager of one was usually a director or owner of another. From that vantage point they were able to monitor closely the increased profit of all three primary areas of Houston's economy.

Even before the mid-1880s Houston's banks and the cotton trade were closely linked. The most prominent local bankers had all begun their careers in the cotton trade, which had long been the mainstay of their banks. In 1886, with the founding of Commercial National Bank, the first Texas Commerce predecessor, the ties between cotton and banking increased. Two reasons probably account for the importance of cotton men in founding the bank. First, cotton factors faced a decline in their method of doing business and banking offered them a lucrative alternative in which their experience in the cotton trade proved valuable. Second, banks had not kept up in number or size with the growing business of the Houston-Galveston area. As credit needs expanded, cotton merchants were forced to go outside the region to secure loans. Usually only the largest and safest firms had access to such outside credit. Continued growth of the cotton trade, therefore, depended upon either outside credit or the building up of local sources of credit.[29]

By 1886, Houston's cotton merchants and other businessmen saw dependency upon outside credit as detrimental to the overall growth of the economy not only because loans from out of the region might be difficult to obtain but also because the absence of banks cut down on the circulation of currency. Until the 1930s national banks issued bank notes which served as currency. The amount in notes that a bank could place in circulation was governed by the amount of U.S. bonds owned by the bank and on deposit with the comptroller of the currency in Washington, D.C. When bond prices went up in 1886, Benjamin A. Shepard, who owned over 90 percent of the stock of First National of Houston decided that his bank should cease issuing notes. That meant that if a new bank could afford to keep a substantial amount of its capital tied up in bonds in Washington, then even if it took a small loss on the bonds, because it could issue currency it stood a good chance of attracting major customers who needed to convert notes on New York banks or other forms of commercial paper into currency to make their payroll or buy the raw materials they needed.[30]

The absence of sufficient banking facilities also made it difficult to transfer funds to the countryside where cotton was purchased and from the cities of the Northeast and Europe where it was sold. After the failure of two state-chartered banks earlier in 1886, Houston's only banks were the First National Bank and T. W. House. The two state banks had helped finance the cotton trade, and their absence coupled with the increasing volume of that trade made possible by better transportation created an acute need for a new bank. As the editor of the *Houston Post* wrote the day after the organization of the Commercial National Bank on May 19, 1886, "The demands of Houston's trade made the establishment of another bank an absolute necessity, for, since the collapse of the City and the Saving bank the facilities of those remaining have been severely taxed to accommodate the needs of trade."[31]

Given the opportunity for profit and the need for another bank to help handle the cotton trade, it was not surprising that a new national bank was organized in May, 1886, and that many of its original officers, directors, and stockholders were connected with the cotton trade. Henry Gardes, a New Orleans cotton dealer and banker, supplied over 50 percent of the $200,000 in capital of the Commercial National Bank. Gardes was an original director and the first president of the bank. Members of the cotton firms Carson, Sewall and Wm. D.

William Bartlett Chew was one of the many early-day bankers who began his career in the cotton business. Born in Kentucky, Chew moved to Jefferson, Texas, in 1868, when that river port became a booming center for the export of cotton from northeast Texas by way of the Red River. Chew worked for various grocery and cotton firms in Jefferson and married Virginia Schluter of that city. In 1881 he moved to Houston and took over the cotton department of Carson, Sewall, and Company. When Commercial National bank was organized in 1886 he became a director and officer of the bank while he was still a partner in Carson, Sewall.

Chew became president of Commercial National in 1891 and served in that office until 1912, when the bank merged with South Texas National Bank. He then served as president of the new South Texas Commercial National Bank for two years before retiring from the bank. From 1924 to 1931 he was again a director of South Texas Commercial National.

While Chew devoted much time to his bank, he was never just a banker. The cotton business occupied much of his attention. He stayed with Carson, Sewall for several years. Then for a time he had his own firm, W. B. Chew and Company. At the time of his retirement from the bank he was president of Gordon, Sewall & Co., the successor of Carson, Sewall, and president of the Merchants' Compress Company. Chew also had an interest in various dry-goods, streetcar, railroad, and real estate companies.

Like other prominent Houstonians, Chew took part in several cooperative efforts to boost the economy of his city. He was an officer of the Houston Cotton Exchange and Board of Trade from 1902 to 1914. He was also involved in the effort to deepen and widen Buffalo Bayou into a waterway that would allow oceangoing vessels to reach the city. All in all, he was a good example of a man of talent who moved to Houston from one of the small towns of the Texas countryside and who made a sizable fortune while helping his adopted city grow.

Chew was famous for his fine handwriting and he wrote the first page of the Commercial National Minute Books reproduced in Appendix C. John G. Dreaper, who went to work for Commercial National in 1902 at age eighteen, remembered Chew as "a stickler for correctness in everything" and described his handwriting as "beautiful, like steel engraving."

SOURCES: Commercial National Bank, *Directors' Minutes* 1 (May 19, 1886): 1; Interview with John G. Dreaper by William Allison, Allison Papers, TCB Archives. Also see Mrs. Henry Fall (ed.), *The Key to the City of Houston*, 183–84; South Texas Commercial National Bank, *Directors' Minutes* 1 (January 13, 1914): 185; Houston *Post*, January 4, 1914; August 18, 1932; *The New Encyclopedia of Texas* 1: 262.

Cleveland were original stockholders. William B. Chew, of Carson, Sewall, was another original stockholder and director.

Other original directors and stockholders benefited indirectly from the cotton trade. Eden L. Coombs, a director and next to Gardes the largest stockholder, was a real estate developer and owned an opera house. His businesses depended upon the prosperity brought to Houston by cotton. Martin Tilford Jones, Adam Clay, and Conrad Bering, three other original directors and stockholders, were wholesale clothing and dry-goods merchants. Jones and Bering would soon be prominent in the lumber business, but in 1886 their sales were tied to the prosperity brought to the region by the cotton trade.[32]

Ties between railroads and banks in Houston were not as well established as those between the cotton trade and banks, but such ties also increased with the founding of Commercial National in 1886. The improved transportation provided by railroads, of course, aided business in general and thereby increased deposits and demand for loans at Houston banks. Beyond the improvements in transportation, however, railroad companies were important to banks because they were the first large corporations to do business in the Houston area. In the 1880s and 1890s the banking industry in Houston was far different than it would be after the creation of a state banking system in 1905 and the Federal Reserve in 1913. Custom and the evolution of the enforcement of the National Currency Act of 1863 and the National Bank Act of 1864 dictated that national banks could make only short-term loans, usually of 90 days or less, and that these loans could not be secured by real estate. Banks obtained most of their funds from demand deposits of corporate customers but also obtained funds from deposits by other banks and from profits on bonds and other investments. Small savings accounts were not common but interest was occasionally paid on deposits by other banks or on large certificates of deposit. Because of these habits and restrictions, bank customers were few and were usually major commercial firms and the wealthy elite. Railroads themselves were such major customers.[33]

Railroads had good incentives to ensure that banks prospered. Not only did the cotton trade need bank services, but so too did the wholesale trade. Cotton filled the railcars going into Houston and dry-goods and other trade items filled them going out. Railroad companies needed the checking-account services of a bank to pay their several thousand employees, and those employees needed the bank to cash their checks. The ties between Commercial National and Southern Pacific offer an excellent example of the role of railroads in banking. John Dreaper recalled that when he started working for the bank in 1902, it had a railroad teller and "a lot of railroad business." That business predated Dreaper's arrival at the bank and continued after his retirement. From 1886 to 1964, Commercial National and all of its successors enjoyed an extremely close relationship with Southern Pacific and its associated company, Union Pacific. As was almost always true of a bank's best customers, representatives of these lines sat on the bank's board of directors.

In 1886, the final original director of Commercial National was the bank's vice-president, Edward Pinckney Hill. He was the Texas attorney of the Southern Pacific Railroad and had been an organizer of Houston Land and Trust Company. Hill's inclusion on the board indicates both his own wealth and the influence of Southern Pacific, which in 1886 was opening a large machine shop in Houston. Hill, born in Bastrop, Texas, in 1838, moved to Houston in the 1870s and became the first of many lawyers who represented the Southern Pacific on the board of Commercial National. In fact, Hill was the bank's president from 1889 to 1891 and after that was again a vice-president. When he retired from the bank in January, 1897, he was replaced as vice-president by James A. Baker, a partner in the law firm which represented Southern Pacific and Union Pacific in Texas for many years. Joining Baker from his law firm on the bank board in 1900 was Robert Scott Lovett, who stayed on the board until 1916 after he had already become chairman of the board of directors of Union Pacific and Southern Pacific. Once in place, the tradition of a reciprocal relationship between the bank and Southern Pacific did not die until the merger of National Bank of Commerce and Texas National in 1964. This early and lasting connection to one of the major corporations active in the region provided the foundation for Commercial National's expansion.[34]

Building on its close ties to Southern Pacific and to local wholesalers and cotton dealers, Commercial National got off to a healthy start. By March, 1887, the bank had over $220,000 in deposits and $277,441 in loans. It kept $50,000 in U.S. bonds on deposit in Washington and was therefore able to issue substantial currency. By 1889 the bank had almost $270,000 in deposits in comparison to $875,000 at the much older First National. From the beginning Commercial National was a profitable venture and one that helped the cotton, railroad, lumber, and wholesaling businesses. It should be noted, however, that it was profitable only because it initially attracted enough outside capital to operate at an efficient size and because it concentrated on large commercial accounts.[35]

Railroads and the greater volume and new methods of the cotton trade did not instantly revolutionize the banking industry in Houston. No more national banks were established in the city until May, 1889, when Houston National Exchange Bank was chartered. Houston National never became part of the Texas Commerce family, but two Houston banks formed the next year eventually merged into the Texas National branch of the bank's family tree.[36]

By far the most significant of these two predecessor banks was the South Texas National Bank, organized in May, 1890. As its name implies, this bank aimed to capture the business not just of Houston but of a greater region. To this end the original stockholders subscribed $500,000 of capital stock instead of the $200,000 minimum required by law. Fred K. Rule, a Kansas City broker, supplied $300,000 of this capital and gradually sold that amount of bank stock, but the rest of the stock was subscribed by area capitalists. Managerial control of the bank always remained in local hands.

Lumber interests instead of railroads supplemented the omnipresent cotton trade in this bank. Between 1886 and 1890 the lumber industry grew rapidly and by the 1890s was second in importance only to cotton in the regional economy. Lumbermen were added to the circle of mutual dependence that included bankers, cotton dealers, and representatives of transportation companies. Railroads which purchased lumber products for construction and which hauled lumber products had the most in common with lumber companies. Many cotton dealers, however, were also involved in lumber and banks quickly assumed a relationship with lumber companies similar to that with the railroads. The lumber industry required a degree of manufacturing and accelerated the industrialization of the Houston region. M. T. Jones Lumber Company, for example, manufactured sashes, doors, blinds, and other lumber items needed in the building trades and employed 100 operatives at its Houston mill in the 1890s. In this era most lumbermen did not need loans from banks because demand for their products was high and the cost of starting business was low. But like the much larger railroad companies, they needed banks to handle the deposits required for their payrolls. Banks also proved a safe investment for lumbermen's profits and offered them opportunities to branch out into other businesses. M. T. Jones, who had been an original director of Commercial National, resigned from that board to become a major stockholder and president of South Texas. Caesar Lombardi, also a prominent lumberman and a partner in Wm. D. Cleveland & Co., was another large stockholder and director.

Other original directors of South Texas National were real estate developers H. F. MacGregor and Sam Allen. The inevitable lawyer was O. T. Holt, who was later mayor of Houston. H. B. Sandborn was a prominent area retailer, and Charles Dillingham was a wealthy cotton dealer. The only professional banker in the group was James Everett McAshan.[37]

Another of the original stockholders in South Texas National Bank was Daniel Ripley. Ripley was the owner of the Daniel Ripley Steamship Company, and just as the ties between Commercial National and Southern Pacific illustrate the relationship between banks

James Everett McAshan
1857–1916

James E. McAshan was one of the first prominent Houston bankers who devoted his entire career to the banking business. He was born in Fayette County, Texas, but spent most of his life in Houston. His father, Samuel Maurice McAshan, moved the family to Houston in 1865 when he became associated with T. W. House in both cotton and banking. He later started his own cotton business, but the younger McAshan went to work for the House bank in 1872.

James McAshan participated in most of the early state banking associations and was a frequent contributor to their journals. He wrote several articles on improved banking techniques, and he liked to think of himself as an intellectual as well as a banker.

The McAshans were long prominent in Houston banking and in the cotton trade. James's father was in partnership in the cotton trade with his brother-in-law C. S. Longcope. Longcope was a founder and the first president of the Houston Cotton Exchange and Board of Trade. James, like his father and his uncle, held important positions in the Houston business world. From 1890 to 1912, he was the chief operating officer and a director of South Texas National. From 1912 to 1915 he was a director and vice-president of South Texas Commercial National. His son, Samuel Maurice McAshan, was president of South Texas Commercial National from 1927 to 1941. His grandson Harris McAshan filled the same position from 1948 to 1953 before serving as president of Texas National Bank from 1953 to 1959. Harris McAshan's brother, also named Samuel Maurice McAshan, was, like his great-grandfather, involved in the cotton business and rose to become chairman of Anderson, Clayton & Co.

Looking back, the third Samuel Maurice had this to say about his grandfather James Everett:

> Everybody in the family believed that he would have been a happier man if he had not been a banker, because the inclination of his nature was toward scholarship rather than toward business. He had gone to college in Huntsville, Texas, and all his life read serious literature, including books in French. He chose for his wife the daughter of Houston's superintendent of schools, Dr. Smith, one of the few men in the Houston of a century ago who could have been called learned. He wrote articles for newspapers and banking magazines. Today we would call James McAshan an intellectual and there

would be occupations open to him as such. But things were different in the rough-hewn world of Houston a century ago.

Despite his grandson's disclaimers, McAshan was a good banker and one of the first to study his profession seriously. Indeed, he was one of the first in Houston to consider banking a profession and not a sideline. McAshan tried to encourage a sense of professional ethics and pride in his fellow bankers. Sometimes, however, his erudition stood in the way of his message as witnessed by this excerpt from a speech which he gave before a meeting of Texas bankers in 1888:

> Banking is a very ancient institution. There doubtless were public depositories for money when Demosthenes and Cicero were making their age of the illustrations unrivaled for eloquence. Doubtless there were places of safe deposit in Herculaneum and Pompeii when those first rude tremors of the earth were felt, and those first blinding showers were seen, so brilliantly described by Pliny.

Such a speech better suited an age schooled in the classics than now, but even so McAshan must have seemed a novel combination of banker and scholar.

Like other bankers of his time, McAshan was involved in varied business endeavors and in projects for civic betterment. He was an original trustee of Rice University and was vice-chairman of its board until his death. He was also president of Merchants and Planters Oil Company. But more than W. B. Chew or other contemporary bank executive officers, he was primarily a banker, and as such he set an example for those like his son who were to be even more devoted to the profession of banking.

SOURCES: Interview with Samuel Maurice McAshan by William Allison, TCB Archives. Also see McAshan Family File, Allison Papers, TCB Archives; South Texas Commercial National Bank, *Directors' Minutes* 2 (August 19, 1914): 265–67; (April 19, 1916): 113; 10 (May 5, 1949): 129–32. Interview with James E. McAshan by William Allison, TCB Archives; "A Tribute to the Memory of Harris McAshan, 1906–1962," TCB Archives; *Texas Bankers Record* 4 (September 1914): 47–49; Max H. Jacobs and H. Dick Golding, *Houston and Cotton: Commemorating Seventy-five Years of Leadership and Progress as a Cotton Market*, 21.

---

and railroads, his company's long association with South Texas National and its successor illustrate the relationship between banks and steamship companies. Ripley moved to the Houston-Galveston area from Alabama in the 1880s and worked for the Houston and Texas Central Railroad. By 1893 he had organized his steamship company.

His specialty was the shipping of cotton, and in 1911 he became a cotton broker as well as a shipper. As his business expanded, he both borrowed money from South Texas and purchased bank stock. Ripley also kept his deposits at the bank. In 1909, in recognition of his stock ownership and his value as a customer, he was made a director. In 1917 he became an inactive vice-president. At the time of his death in 1921 he was the bank's largest stockholder. The next year his wife Edith joined the board of South Texas Commercial National, becoming the first woman to serve on the board of any Texas Commerce predecessor. The Ripley company continued to prosper during the 1920s and Edith Ripley continued to buy bank stock. She remained a director until her death in 1934. For forty-four years Daniel and Edith Ripley were stockholders, directors, or officers of South Texas and its successor. Throughout that time they were also among the bank's most important depositors and loan customers.[38]

The other predecessor of Texas Commerce founded in 1890 was Planters and Mechanics National Bank. As the name implies, it aimed to serve not only the traditional agricultural interests of the region but also the increasing number of railroad mechanics and other workers in the city. Until 1905 it was the only bank in Houston that actively sought small savings accounts and women's accounts. Among its major stockholders were timber tycoon John Henry Kirby, leading retail merchants E. L. Coombs and Louis Tuffly, cotton dealer and dry goods wholesaler Felix Halff, and insurance man J. M. Cotton. Capital stock in this bank totaled only $200,000, and it was seldom as financially sound as Commercial National or South Texas National. Perhaps its financial problems stemmed from its attempt to be the little man's bank. Workers in railroad machine shops, cottonseed-oil mills, and lumber mills grew in number in the 1890s, but the distribution of income in the Houston region still was uneven, and industrial workers had relatively little money to deposit in banks. The bank also depended almost solely on local money and therefore was probably undercapitalized. The Houston region had not yet escaped dependence on outside capital.[39]

From 1890 until 1901 no more banks were chartered in Houston. It took time to consolidate the economic gains made possible by improved transportation, and the depression of the mid-1890s disrupted trade. At the turn of the century, however, Houston banks and the Houston economy entered another period of growth. Much of this growth was made possible by increased population and by the ability of a greater percentage of this population to buy consumer goods.

Retailers were the most obvious beneficiaries of the rise of the consumers. Improved rail transportation helped clothiers, jewelers, and others stock a greater variety of lower-priced wares. Better-paying

jobs brought these items within the price range of a growing number
of Houstonians. Just as the workingmen had Planters and Mechanics
serving their banking needs, the retailers soon had a bank targeted on
their needs. In June, 1901, Merchants National, another Texas Commerce predecessor, was founded by George Washington Brackenridge,
a wealthy San Antonio banker and developer who owned almost all of
the bank's capital stock of $250,000. Merchants National was rela-
tively prosperous, but was occasionally attacked for its out-of-town
ownership.[40]

The organization of Merchants National in 1901 brought to a
close the earliest era in the history of Texas Commerce. From 1886 to
1890 necessity and the chance for profit led cotton dealers, steamship
operators, railroad representatives, and lumbermen to establish and
operate banks. As railroad machine shops, lumber mills, and cottonseed oil mills added greater manufacturing capacity to the local economy, the number of industrial workers rose. The number of clerical
workers at the cotton companies and railroad companies also increased
with the volume of trade. The cotton industry provided opportunity
for small businessmen to gain greater wealth. With time, service- and
consumer-oriented sectors of the economy also developed. The founding of Merchants National in 1901 was a symbol of the new maturation of the economy—an economy that was market-oriented and included manufacturing, professional services, and retail trade as well
as agriculture and wholesale trade. From 1886 to 1901 a modern
economy emerged in Houston, and as it did, the number of banks
increased.

The year 1901 also offers an appropriate point to stop to examine
another facet of the Houston economy that was destined to dwarf all
others: oil. Beginning in 1895 with the discovery of significant quantities of oil at Corsicana and increasingly after the discovery of the
massive Spindletop field in 1901, railroads hauled oil along with
lumber and cotton. Petroleum would be a major force in the growth
of twentieth-century Houston, but at the turn of the century it was
only beginning to be of importance. Oil like lumber made the most
profit for men who controlled production, refining, transportation,
and distribution and who adjusted these processes according to current market conditions. One of the oilmen who integrated the various
stages of the industry was J. S. Cullinan. When he moved the headquarters of the Texas Company to Houston in 1908, others followed.
A new stimulant to the economy and a new set of bank investors and
customers were added to the region. Perhaps the key point, however,
was that the Houston economy had begun to mature before oil became

important. Oil was simply another element in the building of a modern economy.[41]

Even agriculture in the Houston region had begun to change by 1901. It was more mechanized, diversified, and dependent upon scientifically improved crops. It also brought greater prosperity to the area. The introduction of rice culture was the most significant example of this change. Like so much else the story of rice in Texas was intimately tied to railroads. Railroad companies owned large blocks of land along the Gulf Coast, and they sought additional freight for their lines. Touting the cultivation of rice was an easy way to promote the sale of low-lying coastal lands and to increase the tonnage hauled. The industry was also helped by the introduction of new strains of rice around 1900. Wheat was already moving through Houston by 1900, and the new crop added to the city's grain trade. Local rice farmers needed large pieces of equipment from local implement dealers. Supplying that equipment added to the region's economy and the wealth of bank directors. F. A. Heitmann, a director of South Texas National, and Conrad Bering, a director of Commercial National, for example, expanded the offerings of their hardware companies to include the large equipment needed for the efficient cultivation of rice.[42]

The evolution of a modern economy was not without cost or critics, and the weighing of these costs and the words of the critics would have much to do with the further development of Houston banks. After 1901, the predecessors of Texas Commerce were as affected by changes in law and regulation as they were by economic conditions. The changes brought about by improved transportation and the development of large-scale businesses most immediately benefited economic elites while hastening the decline of small farms. They also made Texans more subject to business cycles. The Panic of 1893, for example, which hit railroads hard, would have had less impact on earlier-day Texans. It is not surprising, therefore, that in the late 1880s the Populist movement emerged in Texas as a protest against the new economic order. Populists were a complex group, but it is clear that they rejected a world dominated by the elites and corporations which controlled most of the early Houston banks and railroads. Constant themes of the Populists were the need for the creation of small postal savings banks and the need for easier credit. They often attacked national banks and called for their abolition. These attacks on the monied interests were particularly strong in Texas, where ideology and practical experience made rural Texans, in particular, skeptical of all banks. Yet by 1900 the apparent necessity of banks for economic progress led to repeated calls for a change in the state constitution which would allow the develop-

ment of a state-chartered banking system. These state banks were intended to be small and locally controlled. Once introduced, the call for
small banks oriented toward the common man remained a theme for
public discussion even after the waning of the Populist party in the late
1890s.[43]

In part this call for smaller banks remained in politics because
it was picked up by such emerging Progressives as Thomas B. Love,
of Dallas. Banking reform also continued to attract the attention of
populist-oriented followers of William Jennings Bryan. Professional
bankers saw the opportunity for profit presented by state-chartered
banks which enjoyed public confidence and joined in the call for the
creation of a state banking system. Gradually opponents of the monied
interests, Progressives, and bankers worked out their differences on
the structure of the proposed system and won over the public. In 1904
voters of the state passed a constitutional amendment removing from
the Texas Constitution the prohibition against state-chartered banks.
In 1905 the call for reform culminated in the state legislature's enact-
ment of a state banking law. In August, 1905, Union Bank and Trust
became the first state bank chartered under this new law, and years
later it too joined the Texas Commerce lineage.[44]

Union Bank's creation was a noteworthy milestone. Texans had
begun to change their minds about banks. More Texans realized that
banks were necessary for economic progress, and they were willing to
sacrifice their old antibank principles for that progress. They wanted,
however, to retain local control of their banks. Union was noteworthy
in this regard, too, for as Table 2.1 illustrates, it was one of the first
major banks organized almost entirely with local money. Texas banks
and Houston banks were making some progress toward ending depen-

---

Table 2.1   Major Sources of Funding for Houston's New Banks,
1886–1905

Bank	Year Organized	Orginal Capital Stock	Major Source
Commercial National	1886	$200,000	New Orleans
South Texas	1890	500,000	Kansas City
Planters and Mechanics	1890	200,000	Houston
Merchants National	1901	250,000	San Antonio
Union	1905	500,000	Houston

SOURCES: *Directors' Minutes;* Bill Logan, *The Houston Heritage Collection of National Bank Notes, 1863 through 1935;* Planters and Mechanics File, TCB Archives.

dence on outside capital. Yet a quick look back at Figure 1.2 reveals that Houston banks still trailed far behind New York banks in this era. If the goal of Houstonians was economic independence, they had far to go.

After 1905 the Houston economy continued to grow. The ship channel opened in 1914. Cotton and lumber passed through Houston in greater quantity. Fledgling manufacturing enterprises in cottonseed oil, lumber, and petroleum added to the wealth and population of the city. By 1910 that population stood at 78,800 as compared to 27,557 in 1890. Houston seemed well on its way to becoming a city with an economy driven by industry as well as agriculture and trade. The emergence of a more modern economy, however, was far from complete, and its rewards did not seem evenly distributed. In 1905 the rest of the economy was far ahead of the banking sector and banking drew its share of criticism in Houston as well as in the state as a whole. A few years earlier John Henry Kirby wrote in the *Houston Post*:

> One serious drawback to Houston's progress has been the ultra-conservatism of her bankers. There are notable exceptions to this rule, but those who have been abreast of the times and who have undertaken to make the institutions with which they are connected useful to the community are not those who are managing the largest banks. There is often great scarcity of money in the community, when merchants and manufacturers find it difficult to control sufficient cash upon which to operate their business and when at the same time the vaults of the banks of the city are literally bursting with money.[45]

Kirby may have been correct in insisting that bankers were too conservative and had money which they did not use for the betterment of Houston. Yet bankers faced real constraints. Their experience had taught them that aggressive banks which catered to consumers and smaller businesses usually failed. Indeed, Kirby's own Planters and Mechanics experienced difficulty. Moreover, local banks did not have easy access to the large sums of money needed by the city's major businesses and entrepreneurs. Until the city's financial institutions matured, financiers in New York, Saint Louis, Chicago, New Orleans, and Kansas City retained a hold on the growth of Houston.

CHAPTER 3

Creating a New Banking Order

After the surge in the number of bank foundings from 1886 to 1890,
few new banks were opened in Houston until the early twentieth century, when the improved health of the Houston economy and the creation of a state banking system in 1905 accelerated the establishment
of banks. By early 1907 the number of banks in Houston had hit a
pre-1920s peak. At that time there were eight national banks, two state
banks, three private banks, and two savings banks. Five of these fifteen
banks ultimately merged to form Texas National Bank. Those five were
Commercial National, South Texas National, Planters and Mechanics
National, Merchants National, and Union Bank and Trust. The Panic
of 1907, however, ended the rapid increase in numbers, and there was
a precipitous decline in the years that followed. By 1912 mergers and
acquisitions had reduced the predecessors of Texas National to two:
Union National and South Texas Commercial National. Despite the
decline in total numbers illustrated in Figure 3.1, some new banks entered the industry in the years immediately after the Panic of 1907.
One of these, founded in 1912, was National Bank of Commerce, the
other major branch of the Texas Commerce family tree. By 1914 the
most important ancestors of Texas Commerce were in place as part of a
new banking order more suited to the region's needs.[1]

The history of these Texas Commerce predecessors as well as the
other Houston banks was a playing out of the need to balance public
accessibility and accountability with the need for size and stability.
Many of the demands placed upon banks grew from the economic
changes discussed in the previous chapter. As transportation and communication improved the linkage of Houston with the rest of the world,
the volume and speed of goods passing through the city increased. Cotton factors became cotton dealers with increased need for credit.

Figure 3.1. Number of banks in Houston, 1889–1919.

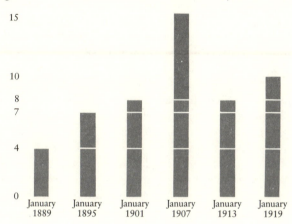

SOURCES: *The Industries of Houston: Her Relations as a Center of Trade, Business Houses, and Manufacturing Establishments*, 14; *The Industrial Advantages of Houston, Texas, and Environs*; *Houston Post*; *Houston Chronicle*.

Wholesalers increased the size and range of their business. Oil and lumber added to the wealth of the region. To service the growing financial needs of commerce, lumbermen, wholesalers, oilmen, and cotton dealers took portions of their profits and established new banks. Both the tendency to merge in search of size and stability and the proliferation of banks reflected the surging growth of the Houston economy.

These economic changes called into question deeply rooted social and political values, including the long-standing public opposition to the concentration of control over money in a few hands. Many Texans saw this as detrimental to political democracy because money could be used to buy political power, and detrimental to economic democracy because control of credit could be used to limit the upward mobility of the middle class. In this view, bankers were monied aristocrats who enriched and empowered themselves at the expense of the rest of society. While acknowledging that banks were essential for economic growth, those who viewed them with suspicion insisted upon government regulation. One of the primary reasons behind the establishment of the Texas state banking system in 1905, a system which banned branch banking and had low start-up costs, was to encourage the creation of more small banks and thereby prevent elites from controlling credit. This sentiment of Texans reflected a broader national concern with the concentration of power in banking which fostered the creation of a decentralized Federal Reserve System in 1913. In both cases, one goal of regulation was to democratize the control of money.

Among bankers and established businessmen, however, the primary goal of this era was not to increase the number of banks but to increase their stability. The best guarantees of stability seemed to be large size and prudent management. But even a bank as large and as traditionally well managed as T. W. House and Co. went bankrupt in the Panic of 1907. After the panic, the search for stability turned to regulation by the state and nation. Through the actions of the Federal Reserve System or through the administration of the state guaranty fund, imprudently managed banks would be brought into line and banks weakened by economic conditions beyond their control would be eased through difficult times. The upshot was that bankers became part of a more tight-knit professional community with fixed rules. They were part of a new banking order called into being by a maturing Houston economy and by state and federal regulation.[2]

This new banking order encompassed several previously existing cooperative arrangements. One of the centerpieces of collective action by banks was the Houston Clearing House. Organized in September, 1890, the clearing house facilitated the use of checks and sped up the flow of money. In later years, when a panic caused unusual demands to be placed on the money in Houston banks, the Clearing House Association often acted to ease the demand and to restore public confidence in the banks. Another instance of cooperative action by members of the clearing house was the purchase of bonds for the improvement of the ship channel in 1911. Perhaps the most significant activity of the Clearing House Association was its sponsorship of schools which taught bankers the emerging techniques of professional banking. Such private associations increased the efficiency and stability of regional banking through collective action and the spread of professional standards of bank management.[3]

Cooperative action went beyond the banking circles of Houston and stretched out across the state of Texas. In 1884 the state's bankers founded the Texas Bankers' Association and held their first annual meeting in Lampasas Springs. By the early twentieth century the association was also putting out a monthly magazine. In their annual meetings and in their journal, the Texas Bankers' Association attempted to educate bankers about modern banking practices and to make them aware of legislation that might affect them. The journals also included frequent essays encouraging cotton farmers to diversify and other articles on attracting manufacturing to the state.[4]

Table 3.1   Relative Importance of Deposits from
Correspondent Banks, June, 1908

Bank	Total Deposits	Bank Deposits	Percent
Commercial National	$2,377,517	$1,395,212	58.7
First National	3,795,921	993,363	26.2
South Texas National	2,705,435	822,794	30.4
Union Bank and Trust	4,592,174	1,097,413	23.9

SOURCE: *The Texas Banker* 7 (June 1908): 23.

Houston banks placed numerous advertisements in the journal and published reports of the annual conventions. These advertisements made good business sense because deposits from banks across the state made up a high percentage of the total bank deposits in the pre–World War I years. As Table 3.1 shows, in 1908, deposits from outlying banks made up almost 60 percent of the total deposits in Commercial National and were a significant percentage in other Houston banks.

Three factors explain this high percentage of deposits by outlying banks in Houston banks. First, Houston was fast becoming the center of the Texas cotton trade, and money paid to farmers and rural cotton merchants for the crop often remained on deposit in Houston banks to pay for the goods and services of Houstonians. Second, deposits from outlying banks could earn a higher rate of return in Houston banks than in banks at home. One consistent source of capital for the building up of Houston was these deposits from rural banks. Third, both before and after the advent of the Federal Reserve, Houston banks lent money to rural banks and provided necessary collection and exchange services. In return rural banks kept compensating balances in Houston banks.

As Table 3.2 shows, the importance of deposits from other banks declined with the growth of the Federal Reserve System. Yet these deposits remained high in banks such as South Texas Commercial National, which were deeply involved in the cotton trade. Besides adding money to the Houston economy, deposits from outlying banks linked the fortunes of Texas banks. A Houston bank's failure could also cause its rural bank depositors to fail. Nothing added more to the need for a secure banking system or added to the calls for well-regulated banking practices than the close relationship between city banks and country banks.[5]

Table 3.2   Change in Importance of Deposits from
Correspondent Banks, 1914–25

| | *Percent of Total Deposits* | |
Bank ·	1914	1925
South Texas Commercial National	33.1	30.8
Houston National	19.7	26.6
First National	32.2	25.3
Second National (Lumbermans)	25.4	20.9
Union National	30.0	11.3
National Bank of Commerce	41.9	5.9

SOURCES: *Texas Bankers' Record* 3 (February 1914): 44; Statements of Condition, December 31, 1925, TCB Archives.

One of the most important attempts to gain stability by state regulation was the Texas Guaranty Fund Law, passed in 1909. This law required all state banks to pay up to 2 percent of their average daily balance into a state fund which would be used to protect all noninterest-bearing and unsecured deposits in member banks. As an option to the guaranty fund, state banks could elect to join the Bond Security System, in which a bond or insurance policy in an amount fixed by the state commissioner of banking protected deposits. This bond plan was also open to private and national banks operating in the state, but few chose to join.[6]

On September 1, 1910, the Guaranty Law together with the option to join the bond plan went into effect. The Guaranty Law provided that no state bank could own more than 10 percent of the capital stock of another bank. It also required frequent inspection by the office of the state commissioner of banking, made provisions for the commissioner to take charge of a bank declared insolvent, and in other ways limited the prerogatives of a state bank. These new state limits on their activity together with the cost of paying into the guaranty fund angered the directors of the Union Bank and Trust, the largest bank in the state-chartered system. President Jonas S. Rice and the rest of the directors believed that the resources of their strong and stable bank should not be used to support weak banks across the state. Acting before the Guaranty Law went into effect, they converted Union to a national charter in March, 1910. Union's movement out of the state banking system illustrated the Guaranty Law's greatest weakness, the fact that it required the most secure banks to subsidize the cost of deposit insurance for less stable banks.[7]

Texas was the fourth state in the nation to establish a guaranty fund. Eventually another half-dozen states passed similar laws, all of which were precursors of the Federal Deposit Insurance Corporation, created in the 1930s. The Guaranty Law attempted to resolve the difficulty of having numerous banks which ensured the public's access to money and at the same time having stable banks. The law was endorsed by carriers of the Populist tradition, such as William Jennings Bryan, who spoke in favor of the bill before the state legislature. Early versions of the bill were drafted by Thomas B. Love, a leader of the Progressive wing of the state's Democratic party and at the time the banking commissioner of Texas. Such widespread support led to a resounding call for deposit insurance in the state Democratic convention of 1908.[8]

These theoretical underpinnings of the guaranty fund had been present since before the turn of the century. What brought the need for a guaranty fund into sharp focus was the failure of numerous banks during the Panic of 1907. Unlike the earlier Panic of 1893, the Panic of 1907 hit Houston-area bankers hard. May, 1907, witnessed the beginning of a gradual decline in the money available for loans and business financing in the United States, but that gradual decline accelerated sharply in September, 1907, as frightened depositors withdrew their funds from banks. To complicate matters further, English bankers had reduced credit available to American businesses. This resulted in a precipitous drop in business activity and an equally sharp upturn in unemployment. Banks across the country failed as depositors lost confidence and demanded their money. The situation would have been much worse if the U.S. government had not deposited $25 million in New York City banks and if J. P. Morgan had not organized a pool of about $35 million to further protect these banks. The government also increased the currency available to banks across the country. Despite these measures, southern banks were particularly hard hit, and a large number of them failed.

Few Houstonians would have anticipated that T. W. House and Company would be among those to fail. It had been in existence since before the Civil War and for most of those years had been the largest bank in the city. The bank had always been deeply involved in the cotton trade, however, and that led it into close association with English bankers and rural Texas bankers. The House bank held deposits from rural banks and used those deposits to finance the movement of cotton to English mills. The sharp decline in money in circulation in September and October occurred at a point when the House bank had lent money to cotton dealers and factors but before it had received payment from England. Country bankers panicked and demanded their deposits. Unable to obtain its usual line of credit in New York or England and with most of its funds tied up in the cotton trade, the House bank did not have enough cash, easily collectible loans, or securities to meet the withdrawals of its depositors. The bank was also hurt by a lack of frequent examination by federal or state authorities, which would have tended to limit the percentage of deposits used as loans. Finally, as a private bank, it was unable to hold U.S. currency bonds, which were used to back currency issued by national banks. In the Panic of 1907 the bonds were made much more easily available to provide a quick influx of cash for national banks. As a result of the House bank's difficult position and lack of safeguards, its managers were forced to declare bankruptcy late in 1907.[9]

While exposing the vulnerability of private banks, the Panic of 1907 also demonstrated to many influential bankers and politicians the need for reform of the U.S. banking laws. The reform movement culminated some years later in the Federal Reserve Act of 1913, which increased participation by the federal government in banking, solidified the leading position of New York in the U.S. banking system, and provided other features of a central bank. Eventually it facilitated the movement of money without the use of currency. U.S. Representative Carter Glass of Virginia and other designers of the Federal Reserve Act sought to soften public criticism of centralized banking by creating a system in which much of the power over day-to-day operations was in the hands of twelve regional Federal Reserve banks scattered across the country.[10] Houston bankers had good reason to be disappointed that Dallas and not Houston became the seat of their regional Federal Reserve Bank. The Reserve Bank helped make credit more easily available and facilitated the transfer of funds and payment of accounts. In part because of these advantages a few Dallas banks quickly grew to be the largest in the state. Larger banks and the presence of the Reserve Bank increased the importance of Dallas in the cotton and wheat trade and in the distribution and wholesaling of merchandise. Dallas, which was virtually the same size as Houston in 1900, had a lead of 20,000 in population by 1920. The establishment of a Houston branch of the Dallas Federal Reserve Bank in 1919 and the overall advantages of the Federal Reserve System benefited Houston bankers. Houston typically had many more banks than Dallas. Yet, as Table 3.3 shows, the Federal Reserve System helped Dallas with its few large banks gain parity with and for a time surpass Houston in total bank deposits.[11]

Even before the founding of the Federal Reserve System, Houston banks began to recover from the troubles of 1907. Not all of the banks

Table 3.3   Total Bank Deposits, Dallas and Houston, 1905–30

End of Year	Dallas	Houston
1905	$ 22,000,000	$ 27,000,000*
1910	27,500,000	33,600,000
1915	34,300,000	42,100,000
1920	94,400,000	85,200,000
1925	148,100,000	134,800,000
1930	162,300,000	167,500,000

SOURCES: Statements of Condition, TCB Archives; *Dallas Morning News; Texas Bankers' Journal; Dallas Times Herald.*
* This figure includes a $5 million estimate of the deposits of T. W. House, whose deposits were described as being as large as those of any other bank in the city but were never officially reported. The top two government-chartered banks in Houston had deposits in excess of $5 million.

that became part of the Texas Commerce family survived the panic, however. Two banks, Planters and Mechanics and Merchants National, came into the family unwillingly because they never recovered from the currency drain of 1907. Their story offers an instructive parallel to that of their more stable cousins.

Planters and Mechanics was one of the more aggressive and innovative of Houston's banks. Besides financing the traditional cotton trade, its directors and officers made repeated attempts to gain the business of railroad mechanics and other wage earners. The bank had a long-standing and well-established savings department, which paid 4 percent interest on deposits. In 1900 one of its advertisements pointed out that "a mechanic saving twenty cents daily would be worth $11,000 at old age." The same advertisement insisted that "a shoemaker saving but fifteen cents a day would be lastingly grateful with nearly $8,000 to retire on." Such aggressive marketing of their services to small-scale savers was a new departure for Houston banks. Indeed, Planters and Mechanics took special pride in assisting public virtue by encouraging the habit of saving. According to the bank:

> Laboring men and women who are able to lay aside a small amount daily or weekly will find Planters and Mechanics Bank the most convenient and effectual means of accomplishing that end. Could young men form habits of saving as fixed as those of smoking and drinking, it would mean *independent manhood* infinitely increased. A dollar foolishly spent is gone forever and leaves nothing but a sting behind and leads to poverty and degradation.[12]

The history of Planters and Mechanics reveals some of the difficulties with this innovative approach. Under the direction of President James A. Patton and Cashier Octavius C. Drew, who were experienced bankers, Planters and Mechanics turned a modest profit for its stockholders. It was harder hit than most other Houston banks by the Panic of 1893, however, and thereafter changed presidents much more often than was the rule among Houston banks. Gradually John Henry Kirby, who was rapidly emerging as a dominant force in the Houston area economy, became the major stockholder and in 1901 president of the bank. Day-to-day management of the bank rested in the hands of Frank A. Reichardt, who was also treasurer of Kirby Lumber Company. Kirby's attempts to expand his lumber company ran into financial difficulties, and Kirby Lumber Company was put into the hands of receiver Jonas S. Rice from 1904 until 1909. Perhaps the distractions of his lumber business caused Kirby to neglect his bank, which was hit hard by the Panic of 1907. Although it never closed its doors and always had enough money to pay off its depositors, the cotton brokers and businessmen of Houston began to lose confidence in the bank. Kirby had the resources to see the bank through a slow period. Unfortunately Reichardt, who had succeeded Kirby as president, had been ill for some time, and Kirby was too busy to attend to bank business. Kirby, Reichardt, and the other directors, including Horace Baldwin Rice, the mayor of Houston and brother of J. S. Rice, chose to have their bank absorbed into Union Bank and Trust in November, 1907. This was very much a friendly takeover. Besides being the receiver of Kirby Lumber and the brother of H. B. Rice, J. S. Rice was the president of Union Bank and Trust.[13]

Two factors led to the demise of Planters and Mechanics after only a seventeen-year existence. First, the bank seldom had the full-time attention of an experienced bank manager. During its first few years under President Patton and Cashier Drew the bank prospered. From 1894 to 1899 under Dr. Thomas J. Boyles, a busy Houston physician and hospital owner, the bank lost ground. The bank's next president, John H. Burnett, was almost seventy years old when he took office. Kirby was president from 1901 to 1906 but had little time for the bank. Frank A. Reichardt was a good businessman but was not an experienced banker. George Hamman, who later went on to a profitable career in business and banking, became cashier in 1906, but it was already too late. During its seventeen years the bank had five presidents. Commercial National Bank and South Texas National in those same seventeen years had only two presidents each. Frequent changes in leadership and lack of direction and professional banking skills in that leadership plagued Planters and Mechanics.[14]

•   Second, the bank never grew to a size that inspired confidence and allowed stability. Despite frequent advertisements in newspapers and bankers' journals its deposits, capital stock, and surplus did not increase as fast as those of First National, South Texas National, Commercial National, or Union. For example in October, 1907, it had $1.5 million in deposits, while two-year-old Union had $3.5 million. Whether this was due to weak management or to the bank's orientation toward small accounts remains unclear. What is clear is that by 1907 the storm that caused barely a ripple at Commercial National, South Texas, and even the newly organized Union Bank and Trust hit Planters and Mechanics hard. A multitude of banks worked well enough when times were good, but economic difficulties caused the downfall of weaker banks.[15]

Merchants National was another local bank hit hard by the Panic of 1907. In 1904, George W. Brackenridge, of San Antonio, sold his holdings in the bank, which amounted to four-fifths of the total stock, to I. H. Kempner, of Galveston. Although Brackenridge and Kempner made substantial fortunes in other ventures, their tries at Houston banking were less successful. This was especially true during the Panic of 1907, when Kempner claimed that the frequent withdrawals made by his customers stemmed from rumors of "the insincerity of non-resident majority ownership." Deposits dropped from over $4 million in early 1907 to $2 million in 1908. In the latter year control of the bank's stock passed to Jesse H. Jones. Jones was also a stockholder in Union Bank and Trust, and in 1910, when Union National was organized, that bank purchased Merchants National.[16]

Both Planters and Mechanics and Merchants wound up being part of Union National, a bank whose phenomenal early growth was shaped by state and federal regulation. At the turn of the century, state banks around the country offered investors attractive alternatives to national banks. In Texas, state banks had savings departments which paid interest on small deposits. As the Houston working class increased, so did the potential for small deposits. State banks could also be combined with trust operations, a choice then forbidden to national banks. Unlike national banks, state banks could make loans with real estate as collateral and had less stringent restrictions on the size or term of their loans. In Texas, state banks could lend up to 25 percent of their capital and surplus to a single individual or company, whereas national banks were limited to only 10 percent. There was also virtually no limit on the amount a state bank could lend on cotton secured by warehouse receipts. National banks, on the other hand, had to stay within the 10 percent limit on cotton loans until 1919, when the limit was changed to 25 percent. Of course, national banks were usually much larger than state banks and therefore could make larger loans. Such was not the case at Union Bank and Trust, whose capital and surplus were greater than those of most national banks in Texas. The opportunities that state banks offered help explain why innovative businessmen like J. S. Rice and Jesse Jones joined reformers in urging the creation of a state banking system in Texas, and why they joined with other businessmen to found Union Bank and Trust, a state bank large enough to enjoy fully the special advantages of Texas banking laws.[17]

State banks in Texas had another advantage: for the first few years of the existence of a state system, it was possible for directors of a national bank also to be directors of a state bank. Thus the early officers and directors of Union Bank and Trust were drawn almost exclusively from the officers and directors of already established banks. Among the first officers and directors of Union were W. B. Chew, president of Commercial National, and Charles Dillingham, president of South Texas. J. S. Rice, the president of Union, was a director of Commercial National. T. W. House, Jr., head of the House bank, was a vice-president of Union. Directors of the bank who also served on the boards of Commercial National or South Texas included W. M. Rice, W. T. Carter, C. H. Markham, and J. M. Dorrance. Also on Union Bank and Trust's original board was Jesse Jones, who later owned Merchants National. Other directors of note included Thomas H. Ball; his law partner Frank Andrews; R. H. Baker, a railroad promoter; and E. M. House, brother of T. W. House, Jr. Ball was a former U.S. congressman. Andrews, Baker, and E. M. House played prominent roles in the Texas Democratic party from 1895 to 1905. Without exception, Union's organizers were drawn from the financial, social, and political elite of the city and the state.[18]

Union was the first state bank chartered under the 1905 law. Because of its head start, its location in Houston—a central point in the shipping of cotton—and the influence and wealth of its directors, who provided the bank with a capital and surplus of $625,000, the bank grew very rapidly. From 1905 to 1910 it was the largest state-chartered bank in Texas and was a correspondent bank helping finance the cotton trade for many of the state banks in the interior. The bank actively sought reserve funds from other state banks and lent them money as needed. It enjoyed excellent connections with banks in Dallas, where J. S. Rice served as vice-president and director of Guaranty State Bank and Trust, the second largest state bank in Texas. It also served other state banks as a collection center for money paid to them in Houston.[19]

One of the purposes behind the creation of state banks in Texas was to provide more places for Texans to save money, and, like Planters and Mechanics, Union put a high premium on its savings department. By 1908 depositors had over $1 million in savings accounts in Union and were drawing 4 percent interest compounded semiannually. Its advertisements that year claimed that "for the convenience of its Savings Department patrons, who, by reason of their occupation, are not able

Jonas Shearn Rice
1855–1931

William Marsh Rice, Jr.
1857–1943

At the turn of the century no Houstonians could claim a more distinguished lineage than the patrician bankers and businessmen Joe and Will Rice. Their mother, Charlotte M. Rice, was the daughter of Horace Baldwin, an early-day mayor of Houston, and the niece of Augustus C. Allen and Charlotte Baldwin Allen, who helped found the city of Houston. Their father, Frederick A. Rice, helped build the Houston and Texas Central Railroad and was a prominent merchant whose tenure in the city dated from 1850 to his death in 1901. Frederick's brother William Marsh Rice was for many years one of the richest men in Texas, and it was his bequest that led to the founding of Rice University. Joe and Will's younger brother H. Baldwin Rice followed in his grandfather's footsteps, serving as mayor of Houston from 1905 to 1913.

J. S. Rice began his business career working for his father's railroad, the Houston and Texas Central. With his brother Will he entered the lumber business in 1881 and remained active in it the rest of his life. From 1904 to 1909 he directed the affairs of Kirby Lumber Company while that enterprise was in receivership. He also was extremely active in real estate and for many years was president of the Great Southern Life Insurance Company. In 1905 he became president of Union Bank and Trust and remained with Union either as president or as chairman of the board until his death.

In 1887, Rice married Mary J. Ross, the niece of Civil War hero and Texas governor Lawrence Sullivan Ross. This family tie along with the many prominent friends of his father and uncle gave Joe Rice great po-

litical advantage over other bankers and businessmen. In his own right
he was a friendly and outgoing man who worked diligently for the
Democratic party. He was a member of what fellow organizers of
Union Bank and Trust, Frank Andrews and E. M. House, called "our
crowd," a small group headed by House and his chief lieutenant,
Andrews, which controlled the governor's office and state patronage
from 1895 to 1905. Rice benefited from this control of patronage and
was superintendent of the Texas prison system from 1899 to 1902. It
was no accident that in 1905 this experienced businessman and well-
connected politician received the first state-granted charter under the
new banking law.

Joe and Mary Rice had three daughters, Laura Rice Neff, Lottie Rice
Farish, and Kate Rice Farish. All three daughters married into promi-
nent families, and many of their descendants still own stock in Texas
Commerce.

Will Rice was never as active in banking and politics as his brother
Joe, but they served together on the Board of Directors of Commercial
National and then of Union. Will's business activities were more directly concerned with lumber and oil. Like John Henry Kirby and
W. T. Carter, Will Rice made a fortune in lumber between 1880 and
1920. He took some of that money and invested in bank stock. When
the timber began to play out, Rice began to explore for oil on his
timberlands. During most of his business career, he was a trustee of
Rice Institute, as the school was then called. Will Rice never married,
and at his death in 1943 much of his estate passed to the school named
for his uncle.

Will and Joe Rice offer a clear picture of the role and function of
Houston's elite during the city's first period of substantial growth,
1885 to 1930. Their family and friendship ties gave them access to the
leading financial and political figures in the state and city. These connections and their own talents enabled them to accumulate large fortunes. Once in positions of wealth and power, they became part of
a network of interlocked boards of directors or governing bodies of
Houston's major banks, businesses, social clubs, civic groups, and educational institutions. They and other members of this elite provided
the financial, political, and civic leadership of early-twentieth century
Houston.

SOURCES: Houston Press Club, *Men of Affairs of Houston and Environs: A Newspaper Reference Work* (Houston, 1913): 18, 38, 52;
The New Encyclopedia of Texas (Dallas, 1926), 1: 230–31, 358;
Union National Bank, *Directors' Minutes* 2 (March 17, 1931): 172–
73; Biographical Files, TCB Archives; Edward M. House to Frank Andrews, June 18, 1901, in James A. Tinsley (ed.), *Letters from the
Colonel: Edward M. House to Frank Andrews, 1899–1902* (Houston,
1960): 9–10.

to make deposits during the regular banking hours, this institution has inaugurated the practice of remaining open each Saturday from five to eight p.m., that all may share equally the profits accruing from a modern system of right treatment of the public." [20]

Buoyed by the acquisition of Planters and Mechanics, Union seemed in 1908 to be well established as the premier state bank in Texas. The Panic of 1907, however, had led to tighter regulation of both state and national banks amid a heightened concern over the concentration of power over the nation's financial system. Such concerns had led in 1906 to the insistence by state regulators that directors and officers of national banks could not also be directors and officers of state banks in Texas. Both Joe Rice and his brother Will resigned from the board of Commercial National in March of that year. Such concerns also lay behind the passage of the Texas Guaranty Fund Law. In turn, the guaranty fund and the chance to acquire Merchants National led to the creation of Union National. [21]

By the end of 1910 the deposits of the newly created Union National were $10 million, a figure that ranked it in a tie with First National for leadership among all Houston banks. By 1924, however, First National had twice the deposit figure of Union, and South Texas Commercial National had a $10 million lead over third-place Union, whose record as a national bank never matched its phenomenal record as a state bank. The bank's management struggled with the tighter loan regulation of a national bank. Indeed, the Minute Books of Union are filled with letters from the U.S. comptroller of the currency asking the bank to explain dubious loans. When R. M. Farrar became president of Union in 1924, he reacted to the bank's history of loan problems by making Union the most conservative bank in the city and eschewing growth in loans for safety's sake.

Government regulations seem to have shaped Union's early prosperity and subsequent decline. Taking advantage of its central position in the state system from 1905 to 1910, the bank enjoyed rapid growth. After 1910, however, Union's managers had a difficult time adjusting to the rules under which national banks operated. They were consistently either too lax or too stringent in their interpretation of federal regulation. [22]

In addition to its troubles with federal regulatory bodies, Union had problems with its officers. Over the summer of 1910 it was discovered that the vice-president of the bank had embezzled almost $8,000 over the preceding four years. He resigned and repaid the bank. This information never became public, but it disrupted the administration of the bank, which had rested in his hands. It was an ill omen of things to come. [23]

Another shakeup in leadership occurred because of disputes between two of the bank's major stockholders, William T. Carter and Jesse Jones. According to Earl V. Dreyling, in 1917 Carter became convinced that Jones was trying to pad his own pocket at the expense of Union National Bank. Dreyling, who worked for Union at the time, recalled that Carter told Jones: "Jesse, I don't want to be on the same board of directors with you. Either you buy all my stock in the Union National Bank or I will buy all of yours." Jones elected to sell his stock to Carter, whose family then joined the Rice family as the dominant stockholders in Union Bank. James M. Rockwell, a friend and busi-

---

William Thomas Carter
1856–1921

William Thomas Carter was one of the richest lumbermen in East Texas. He was born in Tyler, Texas, and his father was also in the lumber business. Carter started out as a small manufacturer of sawed lumber, but in the 1880s, after the arrival of the railroad made possible large-scale lumbering, he acquired more and more timberland. He proved particularly adept at designing and building larger and more efficient sawmills to satisfy a growing demand for lumber. Like such contemporaries in the lumber business as Jesse Jones and R. M. Farrar, Carter supplied various lumber products for the wholesale and retail trade and built some residential and commercial properties in Houston. What set Carter apart, however, was his ownership or control of about 200,000 acres of timber. This access to timber and his efficiency as a sawmiller spurred the steady growth of W. T. Carter and Brother, the Carter-Kelly Lumber Company, and the W. T. Carter Lumber and Building Company.

Carter moved to Houston from East Texas in 1903, and he and his family were soon among the city's elite. He was active in many civic endeavors and played his expected role in such activities as the improvement of the Houston Ship Channel. Carter shipped much of his lumber over the Southern Pacific lines, and one telling illustration of his family's place in Houston was the close connection between the Carter family and the law firm which represented the Southern Pacific, Baker & Botts. W. T. Carter's brother, Clarence Leon Carter, was a partner in Baker & Botts until his death in 1936. Two of the daughters of W. T. Carter's daughter Lena Carter Carroll married partners in the firm, John P. Bullington and Dillon Anderson.

His other children and grandchildren also became prominent in social, business, and civic endeavors in Houston. Perhaps the most interesting of these was his daughter Frankie Carter Randolph, who was a leader of the liberal wing of the Democratic party in Texas and national committeewoman from the state in the 1950s.

Banking solidified this family's position among Houston's elite, while providing a good investment. Carter took surplus funds and after moving to Houston in 1903, purchased bank stock. He was a stockholder of South Texas National and served as a director of the bank from 1906 to 1908. He was also a major stockholder and director of Union from its inception in 1905 until his death in 1921.

By the time Union National was organized in 1910, Carter owned 260 shares of stock in Union Bank and Trust. One of his daughters owned another 40 shares. Carter's was the second-largest block of stock owned by an individual, behind the 265 shares owned by Will Rice and ahead of the 219 shares owned by Joe Rice. Those shares, added to shares owned by their brother David Rice and the related Neuhaus and Lummis families, gave the Rice family group about 20 percent of the 5,000 shares of Union Bank and Trust. By 1953 and the merger of Union and South Texas, the family of W. T. Carter owned or controlled 2,355 shares of a total of 10,000 shares. Descendants of the Rice family group owned fewer than 200 shares of stock.

The influence of W. T. Carter in Union was less obvious than that of Jesse Jones at National Bank of Commerce, but it was equally important. The role of Aubrey Leon Carter in the bank offers a good example of the Carters' low-profile approach. Aubrey Carter was the son of W. T. Carter and upon his father's death became the managing partner in W. T. Carter and Brother. At that time he also became a director of the bank, but was never an active officer. In the 1920s the Carter family and other major stockholders purchased from the bank about $500,000 in poorly performing notes and real estate loans that had been repeatedly criticized by bank examiners. At about the same time, Aubrey Carter moved the office of W. T. Carter and Brother to the Union National Bank Building, where he kept in daily contact with the operations of the bank. When Union became a part of Texas National Bank and moved into a new building, Aubrey Carter and W. T. Carter and Brother moved with it. Until his death in 1956 he remained a director of Union and then of Texas National. Other members of the Carter family who helped manage Union and its successors were R. D. Randolph, Dillon Anderson and Winston Carter.

SOURCES: Stockholders File, TCB Archives; *New Encyclopedia of Texas*, 408; J. Lester Jones, *W. T. Carter and Bro.*, 7–18; Interview with Walter G. Hall by Chandler Davidson, Walter L. Buenger, and Louis Marchiafava, November 19, 1979, Walter G. Hall Papers, Rice University (typescript), 40–44; Interview with Tom Carter by Walter L. Buenger and Joseph A. Pratt, April 2, 1986, TCB Archives; UNB, *Directors' Minutes* 1 (April 1, 1924): 21–27.

ness associate of Jones, also sold his stock and resigned as a director. Squabbles among the major stockholders and the disruption of the leadership of the bank caused by those squabbles could not have been good for business, but it was perhaps of more long-range importance that the managers and owners of Union National remained suspicious of Jesse Jones and his associates for the next forty years.[24]

Jones's departure from Union in 1917 did not mean that he was out of banking, for in October, 1914, he had become a director of the National Bank of Commerce. Jones had been an original stockholder of the bank when it was formed in 1912, and his close associate N. E. Meador had been an original director. Because of his wealth, Jones probably had a major voice in the National Bank of Commerce from its beginning. He certainly had an established record of investing in new and struggling banks. He was involved with Planters and Mechanics Bank, Merchants National, Central Bank and Trust Company, National City Bank, and Union before becoming involved with National Bank of Commerce. In each banking venture he made a profit.[25]

Besides N. E. Meador, other original directors of the National Bank of Commerce were H. S. Filson, F. W. Fraley, J. M. Logan, O. T. Holt, R. D. Collins, J. W. Reynolds, Arch McDonald, G. A. Kelley, J. A. Hulen, J. L. Hudgins, E.A. Blount, A. M. McFadden, Charles Schreiner, S. Samuels, C. J. Von Rosenberg, James H. Adair, Thomas Flaxman, Edwin Hobby, A. H. Whited, and Jeff N. Miller. Holt, a lawyer, former mayor of Houston, and former director of South Texas National, was the president. Logan, a former national bank examiner, was the cashier.

Like other bank boards, the directors of NBC were primarily local cotton merchants, lumbermen, rich investors, and representatives of railroad companies. Filson, Reynolds, and Kelley were chief executives of area lumber companies. Samuels, Adair, and Hudgins were cotton men. Miller, Blount, and Von Rosenberg styled themselves capitalists and owned significant blocks of stock. Whited and Hulen were railroad executives. In a foreshadowing of things to come, Fraley was an oilman. McFadden was a rancher, investor, and cattle dealer. They were elected to the board in recognition of their stock ownership or to firm up ties between the bank and their enterprises. They were also expected to give advice on loans in their areas of expertise.[26]

A few of the directors did not fit this pattern. One of the most interesting exceptions was Charles Schreiner, of Kerrville, Texas. Schreiner was a wealthy banker, rancher, and mohair dealer. Houston banks were still attracting outside capital, but as in the case of George Brackenridge and Merchants National, this capital was increasingly supplied from other Texans who recognized the growth potential of the Houston area. Schreiner stayed on the board until 1922 but seldom took an active role in the management of the bank. In fact, his interest in the Houston bank may simply have been to firm up the correspondent banking relationship between his Kerrville bank and NBC.[27]

Another exception was Arch McDonald, editor of the *Houston Chronicle*. From its formative years forward, National Bank of Commerce was closely associated with the *Chronicle*. After McDonald, later editors M. E. Foster and W. O. Huggins were also bank directors. The reason for this close association was Jesse Jones's ownership of the *Chronicle*. Jones acquired a half interest in the newspaper in 1908 before he purchased total ownership in 1926. After that, it was standard practice for the chief official of the *Chronicle* to be on the board of National Bank of Commerce. J. H. Creekmore continues that tradition in the 1980s with Texas Commerce.[28]

National Bank of Commerce started business in the building just vacated by the Commercial National Bank and struggled a bit its first few years. President Holt died in February, 1913, and Cashier Logan soon left. One of Holt's political supporters, former alderman and cottonseed-oil merchant Gus S. Street, took over as president. In 1914, Street left, and Jesse Jones, who was purchasing the bank's stock at a rapid rate, secured the appointment of his associate, R. M. Farrar, as president. Farrar remained as president until 1921, and his leadership brought stability and profitability to the bank.[29]

In addition to the creation of National Bank of Commerce, the year 1912 witnessed another event of importance in the evolution of Texas Commerce and the Houston banking industry: the merger of Commercial National and South Texas National to form South Texas Commercial National. This merger resulted from what the *Texas Bankers' Record* called "the romance of two royal houses," and was the first major merger in the history of Houston banking. Before 1912 strong banks had acquired smaller, weaker banks, but this merger combined two of the city's largest and most stable banks. South Texas, upon liquidation, had $500,000 in capital stock, $4,000,000 in deposits, and $7,500,000 in total assets. Commercial National had $500,000 in capital stock, $3,500,000 in deposits, and $6,500,000 in total assets.[30]

These two banks had more than size in common. In 1905, as has already been pointed out, officers of each had been among the organizers of Union Bank and Trust. Both banks had been leaders in the sale of bonds for the Houston Ship Channel. Both pursued cautious lending policies and counted among their customers the major cotton merchants, lumbermen, railroad companies, and wholesalers of the city. Several officers had worked in both banks. The most important of these was Beverly D. Harris, the cashier of Commercial National from 1907 to 1908 before moving to South Texas National. Harris was selected to oversee the daily management of the new bank. John M. Dorrance had also been a director and officer of Commercial National until he became a director of South Texas in 1909.[31]

Common business and civic endeavors, shared officers and directors, and similarities in their business philosophy and major customers had long united the two banks, preparing the way for their merger. A more immediate cause of the merger, however, was that after Beverly Harris and John Dorrance left Commercial National in 1908, the growth of deposits and assets slowed. This slight decline probably began in the fall of 1907, when several correspondent banks failed, causing Commercial National's profits and deposits to slip. The bank never seemed to recover fully. It had long been one of the most profitable banks in the state, and it remained a healthy concern in 1912. But as its rate of growth slowed, interest in a merger rose. The bank's president, W. B. Chew, was also president of the cotton brokerage firm Gordon, Sewall and Company and had many other business interests. The fact that he was over sixty years old and wanted to reduce his work load provided further incentive for consolidating with South Texas and turning over management to Harris. Knowing the talents of Harris and realizing that their bank was slightly larger, directors of South Texas probably assumed that their people would dominate the affairs of the new bank. Rivalries between the newly merged banks, however, seem to have been minimal.[32]

Both banks sought the strength to match the growing Houston economy and to compete with the two largest Houston banks, First National and Union National. Competition among banks in Houston appears to have intensified after the turn of the century. Previously banks tended to fail or lose business because they were poorly managed, not because of a scarcity of opportunities. Problems associated with the Panic of 1907, however, demonstrated that there was probably not enough low-risk business to go around, and there were certainly not enough competent bank managers available. Smaller banks, lacking major customers and substantial earnings, were forced to make riskier loans and employ less experienced managers.

The panic also brought about the acquisition of Planters and Mechanics by Union Bank and Trust, and catapulted that bank into the number-one spot among Houston banks. As Table 3.4 demonstrates, this position of leadership was reinforced by consolidation with Mer-

Table 3.4 Growth in Deposits in Houston Banks, 1904–14

End of the Year	Planters and Mechanics	Merchants	Union	Commercial	South Texas National	First National
1904	$ 753,366	$1,999,902		$3,532,850	$1,622,364	$ 3,666,357
1905	1,200,000	2,800,000	$ 1,111,000	4,550,000	2,800,000	4,600,000
1906	1,169,669	4,042,464	2,750,564	5,253,970	1,893,454	5,000,000
1907	1,500,000 *	3,500,000	3,799,400	3,831,554	2,087,305	4,302,552
1908		2,051,523	5,162,868	4,259,753	3,050,634	4,949,359
1909		2,902,841	6,706,549	3,469,153	2,993,693	4,765,686
1910		2,902,841 *	10,000,000	3,855,159	4,982,772	6,723,759
1911			8,577,276	4,727,594	5,537,643	8,400,230
1912			10,628,483	13,178,868 †		11,905,119
1913			7,980,055	9,382,314		9,873,874
1914			6,257,823	7,277,105		8,490,256

SOURCES: Statements of Condition (where possible, December statements), TCB Archives; *Annual Report of the Comptroller of the Currency: Texas Bankers Journal.*
* Acquired by Union (deposits are those at time of acquisition).
† Merged to form South Texas Commercial National Bank.

chants National in 1910. To meet this competition, South Texas National organized a savings department in 1910; it had earlier recruited Harris to run its business. Commercial National was less aggressive and innovative, and as a result its deposits grew very slowly after 1908. One sure way to gain parity with Union and the equally fast-growing First National was to merge. More than ego was at stake in this quest for size. With memories of 1907 still lingering in their minds, the managers of South Texas National and Commercial National realized that over time a smaller bank could not sustain loan quality, maintain high earnings, and retain the most talented managers. This could be disastrous when the economy turned downward.[33]

This first major merger set a pattern that was followed in mergers in the 1950s and 1960s among the banks that now form Texas Commerce. The two banks were of a similar nature. There was a management succession problem at Commercial National, where growth had slowed from a previous high level. Greater size was needed by both banks to match the expanded economy and to keep up with their major competitors. This size was also essential to the continuation of the tradition of stability.

Negotiating the details of consolidation and integrating the two banks went fairly smoothly. Both South Texas and Commercial National stockholders agreed that the two old banks would be liquidated and the new bank would acquire their assets. A new charter was issued in 1912 for South Texas Commercial National, the former owners of South Texas and of Commercial National each owning one half of the capital stock of $1,000,000. Most stockholders simply traded one share of South Texas or Commercial National stock for one share of South Texas Commercial National since the figure of $1,000,000 was arrived at by adding together the $500,000 in capital stock in each of the old banks. A few liabilities and some matching assets were retained by the liquidators of the two old banks, but most of the assets and liabilities went to the new bank. South Texas's larger, more modern bank building became the home of the new bank. Commercial National's people moved into their new quarters along with their records and their cash on March 2, 1912, and on that date the two banks began to operate as one.[34]

Beverly Harris, vice-president and cashier of South Texas Commercial National, was a highly professional, competent banker—perhaps too competent for Houston, because within a few years he moved on to a New York bank. But as one colleague described him, he was "dictatorial and bossy." Those personality traits had caused friction with W. B. Chew when Harris had worked at Commercial National. In 1912, however, Chew, although the president of the new bank, became less active in its management. Harris's position was also bolstered by the creation of the position of chairman of the board. That office was filled by Charles Dillingham, the former president of South Texas. The board over which Dillingham presided contained all the former directors of South Texas and Commercial National. With Harris as the primary force in the bank and a solid group of directors and top officers, the new bank got off to a good start. Deposits dipped from their 1912 level in 1913 and 1914 as the Houston economy slowed, but by 1917 the bank was enjoying record profits and deposits.[35]

Of course, even the best of mergers have unexpected problems, and the 1912 merger of South Texas and Commercial National proved no exception. John Dreaper, who became the chief teller of the new bank after working for Commercial National for ten years, recalled that "at the end of the third day of consolidated operations, somebody found that we were short about $75,000. You can bet there was a scramble then. The men of both banks worked all evening. Those outside experts were working, too, but they were no help, because they didn't know a damned thing about banking." A bookkeeping error caused by the difficulty of integrating two different bookkeeping systems had caused the shortage, but before that was discovered, Harris was fuming: "There were tears of anger in Bev Harris's eyes and he said: 'Somehow this bank has lost $75,000, and I am going to wire New York to send down here to Houston the best damned auditors in the country.'" The auditors were not needed, nor were the experts hired by the bank to work out the details of the merger. Dreaper and other employees discovered the error and allowed everyone to go home for a good night's sleep.[36]

Harris's impulse to wire New York for assistance illustrates another feature of Houston banking. Just as rural banks in Texas were dependent upon Houston banks, Houston banks were dependent upon New York banks. Before World War I much of the cotton destined for foreign mills went from Houston to New York, and goods for the wholesale and retail trades went from New York to Houston. Deposits from Houston banks were often made in New York banks to facilitate this trade. New York banks also paid attractive interest rates for money on deposit and were a safe place for Houston banks to invest surplus capital. If Houston banks needed a loan, collection and exchange service, or some specialized service, they naturally turned to New York banks. This dependence upon money-center banks by Houston banks was altered by the advent of the Federal Reserve System, but in this era it never totally disappeared.[37]

In fact, the Federal Reserve System caused problems for Houston bankers because it forced them to move away from traditional practices. The Federal Reserve did not emerge fully developed in 1913. Ideas about the system evolved from at least 1907 to 1913, and interpretation and application of laws governing the system evolved from 1913 into the 1920s and beyond. In effect, from 1910 bankers confronted constantly changing regulations which played an increasingly important role in the operations of their banks.[38]

In January, 1914, national banks were required and all other banks were asked to accept or reject membership in the Federal Reserve System. South Texas Commercial National, Union National, and National Bank of Commerce became members and purchased stock in their regional Federal Reserve Bank. Each member bank was required to buy stock in the amount of 6 percent of their capital stock and surplus. The Federal Reserve then went about the business of facilitating exchanges between banks and regulating the amount of currency in circulation. With the new laws, however, also came heightened interest by federal regulators in the routine operation of banks.[39]

South Texas Commercial National, for example, was questioned repeatedly about loans made with cotton or farmland as collateral.

These controversies usually arose when the Federal Reserve applied new rules that were contrary to long-standing practices among Houston banks. The cotton trade, which presented huge seasonal demands upon Houston banks, was a special target of federal regulators. Houston banks had traditionally extended large lines of credit and overdraft privileges to their established customers in the cotton business. As the directors of South Texas Commercial National put it in 1914 in a letter to the deputy comptroller of the currency: "In meeting the annual burden of moving this crop, this bank has been called upon at times to furnish locally as much as $4,000,000 to $5,000,000, in addition to loans made to our bank correspondents over the State, in connection with the cotton movement." At that time the cotton trade remained the single most important part of the bank's business. In the same letter the directors of South Texas Commercial National begged the deputy comptroller to clarify the rules concerning overdrafts and loans based upon cotton. They wanted overdrafts eliminated but were afraid that such a move would cost them business if the new rules were not clear and were not applied equally to all banks. The sweeping changes brought by the Federal Reserve Act disrupted the bank's business and inconvenienced the bank's officers and directors, but the disruption and inconvenience were not without profit to the bank. The end of large overdraft privileges for cotton traders at all banks meant increased profits for the banks.[40]

By the end of 1914, Houston banks were beginning to adapt to the changes required by the creation of the Federal Reserve. Some banks, most notably Union National, had problems with Federal Reserve regulators for several years, but most of the others quickly learned to live within the new banking system and indeed to profit from it. By that time the key features of the system were as follows. Both national and state banks were frequently examined by either the Office of the Comptroller or the state banking board. Noninterest-bearing deposits and unsecured deposits in state banks were guaranteed by the Guaranty Fund; national banks had no such protection. State banks also had an easier time lending money with cotton as security. They could also lend with real estate as security. National banking regulations were moving in that direction, however, and by the 1920s national banks operated under roughly the same rules as state banks. Both national and state banks had begun paying interest on small deposits. Just as they had in 1886, however, all banks still relied on large demand deposits to generate most of the funds for loans and other investments, and they made most of their profit on short-term loans to cotton dealers.

What was new about Houston's banks was their strength, stability, and growing capacity to compete with the banks of larger towns. The impact of the Guaranty Fund, the Panic of 1907, the mergers and acquisitions resulting from the panic and the need for size, and the creation of the Federal Reserve System had changed the face of Houston banking. By 1914 banks were larger and more closely regulated. They were increasingly integrated into a state and national banking system, and they were more stable, at least for the time being.

CHAPTER 4

Jazz Banking in Boomtown, 1914–29

From World War I to the beginning of the Great Depression, Houston and its banks enjoyed an era of remarkable expansion. With an improved channel linking Houston to the Gulf and a web of railroads connecting it to the interior, the city thrived on the increased demands for the raw materials produced in its region. Transportation advantages and the rise of large-scale firms allowed Houston to become the leading cotton exporting port in the world. Oil refineries and other manufacturing concerns spread along the ship channel. Each of these expanding industries spawned related economic activity, notably real estate construction, which added to the upward spiral of growth.[1]

Houston bankers were well positioned to assist in and profit from economic expansion. New federal and state regulations in place by 1914 gave the industry predictability and potential for growth. Well-developed ties to the cotton trade enabled Houston bankers to play a key role in its expansion. The city's banks had gained size through a series of mergers and were better able to help finance the growth of their major customers. As a result, from 1914 to 1929 bank profits soared to record levels. Numerous new banks entered the market and aggressively expanded services and the type and volume of loans. Bankers of the old school derisively referred to the new banking practices as "jazz banking," full of noise and flash but lacking in substance. Yet bankers who did not adapt to the changing nature of the Houston economy watched their share of the banking market decline. For the moment at least jazz banks fit the needs of a remarkably upbeat Houston economy.

Cotton was king in this era. From the end of World War I until the start of the Great Depression was cotton's golden age in Houston.

The number of bales exported from Houston in 1919 was just under 70,000. By 1930 that number had increased to more than two million. During the 1920s, Texans were growing more cotton, and the facilities to bring cotton from throughout the southwestern states to Houston improved. Those improvements paled alongside the strides made in handling cotton at the port of Houston. Huge new warehouses, cotton compresses, and channel side terminals were built in the 1920s, as Houston became the center of the world cotton trade.[2]

A brief history of Anderson, Clayton & Co., which moved its headquarters to Houston in 1916, suggests the importance of cotton to the city's economy and to Houston banks. The firm, founded by M. D. Anderson, Frank Anderson, and Will Clayton in Oklahoma City in 1904 and joined by Benjamin Clayton in 1905, took advantage of the opening of thousands of acres to cotton in West Texas, Oklahoma, and New Mexico and of the disruption of the old European-dominated cotton trade to become by the 1920s the world's largest supplier of ginned cotton. Along the way Anderson, Clayton established close working relationships with the large Houston banks, including the National Bank of Commerce, Union National, and South Texas Commercial National. The company depended upon the banks for credit and financial services, and Anderson, Clayton's business was an important source of profits for the banks.[3]

Westward expansion of cotton acreage played a key role in the rise of Anderson, Clayton and other Houston-based cotton firms. Western cotton farmers suffered far less from insect and disease problems because of the arid climate. Their fields had to be irrigated, but that could be a benefit because both drought and flood conditions could be avoided by properly timed applications of water. The flat terrain in the West also allowed the use of the largest and most modern machinery. All of these factors resulted in cotton of a higher quality grown in greater quantity at a lower cost to the farmer. East Texas suffered from some of the same problems that plagued cotton farmers throughout the South, including bollworms and the problems associated with tenant farming and sharecropping, but even there, cotton continued to be the most profitable crop. In 1880 cotton was grown on 2.5 million acres in Texas. By 1926 that figure reached 18 million acres, which is more cotton acreage than has been typically grown annually in the entire United States since 1960.[4]

Houston was the logical collection point for much of the state's cotton because the short-staple varieties grown in the western half of the state were better suited for foreign mills than for domestic mills. The ship channel and rail connections made Houston an ideal port for exporting cotton to Europe and Japan. Some Texas cotton went by rail by way of Dallas or Saint Louis to eastern mills, but in the 1920s the bulk of the crop moved by rail to Houston. There the bales were compressed if they had not already been so treated. The cotton was then loaded on oceangoing vessels from terminals on the ship channel. The rail lines ran directly to fireproof warehouses adjacent to the major terminals, including the Long Reach Terminal owned by Anderson, Clayton, where huge electric lifts transferred the cotton from railcar to storage and eventually into the holds of steamers. By handling and shipping large amounts of cotton as economically as possible, the major cotton firms made handsome profits despite a slight lowering of the price of cotton in the 1920s.[5]

Anderson, Clayton, Geo. H. McFadden & Bro.; Alexander Sprunt & Son, Inc.; and other large companies secured their positions by expanding into the growing, ginning, compressing, and milling of cotton, as well as the sale of cotton by-products. Before World War I most cotton dealers had purchased ginned cotton directly from the growers or local merchants. Anderson, Clayton had owned a few gins earlier, but after the war it bought numerous gins around the country and purchased unginned cotton directly from the farmer. In some cases Anderson, Clayton even raised its own cotton. One major advantage of gin ownership was easy access to cottonseed. As demand for cottonseed cake grew in the livestock feedlots of the Texas panhandle, and as uses for cottonseed oil expanded after 1915, seed-oil mills became an increasingly profitable sideline. Cotton compressing became equally profitable. Locating a compress at the company gin saved on railroad shipping costs and eliminated the costs of paying another group to compress its cotton. Anderson, Clayton even tried to mill its own cotton cloth near Houston but had only limited success. This vertical integration of the cotton business and the use of by-products took a great deal of money, some of it borrowed from Houston banks, but it ensured profitability in the cotton business until the massive disruptions of the 1930s.[6]

Ending the traditional control of the trade by European and New York financiers also increased the size and profitability of the major cotton firms. Before World War I, English firms centered in Liverpool had dominated the international cotton trade. These firms and others like them in Le Havre and Bremen on the Continent had either substantial lines of credit or the internal resources with which to carry vast stocks of cotton from the fall harvest until the mills needed cotton. These European firms also extended credit to the mills. Lacking these advantages, most American firms had difficulty breaking into the foreign market. Because Europeans bought and borrowed so much from Americans during World War I, however, the center of finance shifted from London to New York. The war also disrupted the flow of cotton from the American South to European warehouses. These circumstances presented Anderson, Clayton with access to credit and entry into a previously European-dominated market. It built large warehouses in Europe as well as the United States, and because of its control of cotton from the gin to the mills it was able to dominate the world cotton trade.

Until 1928, however, New York bankers and financiers continued to profit at the expense of southerners. To protect themselves from the rise and fall of cotton prices, the major cotton firms often sold cotton on the futures market and then rebought it as needed to ship to the mills. Merchants and investors in the New York futures market required delivery in New York and added a $3 to $5 a bale transportation charge when the cotton firms sought to repurchase cotton. By the 1920s no cotton was spun in New York or shipped from New York to European mills, yet the traditional transportation charge remained to burden southern cotton firms. In 1928, Anderson, Clayton had grown large enough and had enough surplus cotton to store 200,000 bales in New York to tender to the holders of futures contracts. Since those who owned futures contracts had no use for the cotton, they agreed to eliminate the New York delivery and the transportation charge. This incident reflected the weakening of the traditional dominance of New York financiers over the southern cotton trade.[7]

Anderson, Clayton had even greater leverage in its dealings with Houston banks. No one bank served as the company's lead bank in Houston. Second National perhaps did the most business with the company, but NBC, Union, and STCNB all lent money to Anderson, Clayton. These banks' growth was therefore to some degree dependent upon the growth of Anderson, Clayton and other large cotton firms. This linkage of the fortunes of cotton companies and banks was reinforced by family ties and by ties between boards of directors. In the case of Anderson, Clayton, Monroe D. Anderson served on the board of National Bank of Commerce. S. M. McAshan, Jr., whose father was president of South Texas Commercial National from 1928 to 1943, married the daughter of Will Clayton.

These close ties had always been typical of Houston banks and cotton firms. W. B. Chew, who was long prominent in the cotton business, was president of South Texas Commercial National when it was organized and later returned as a director in the 1920s. His son, J. H. Chew, who was also in the cotton business, served as a director of

National Bank of Commerce. J. M. Dorrance and J. K. Dorrance of Dorrance and Company, a cotton exporting firm, were directors and officers of South Texas Commercial National. Daniel Ripley and his wife, Edith, whose company managed the shipment of cotton, served as directors of South Texas Commercial National. J. M. Rockwell served on the board of Union National. E. K. and Charles Dillingham served on the board of South Texas Commercial National. All were cotton dealers. Of course, representatives of other businesses were also represented on the boards of directors of Houston's major banks. But as Table 4.1 suggests, at a bank like South Texas Commercial National, cotton dealers made up a sizable portion of the board. These directors' businesses needed extensive credit, and they were among the major customers of STCNB and other cotton banks.[8]

Cotton dealers were also major owners of several Houston banks. Of the 15,000 shares of stock in South Texas Commercial National in 1934, 5,051 were owned by those with a direct interest in the cotton trade. With 1,800 shares, Edith Ripley was the bank's largest individual shareholder. The ownership of Union National and National Bank of Commerce was not as closely associated with the cotton trade, but cotton dealers also owned significant blocks of stock in those banks. Such close ties between cotton firms and Houston's oldest and largest banks reflected the excellent profits that cotton financing long brought.[9]

Because of the importance of cotton to Houston's major banks, the large cotton firms could demand significant concessions in securing credit. For years they enjoyed overdraft privileges while maintaining large lines of credit. This credit was secured by unverified compress receipts. As Samuel Maurice McAshan, of South Texas Commercial National, put it in 1923, "In the height of the season, our cotton concerns being mostly large ones, require a great degree of freedom in handling their business and to handicap and harass them with unnecessary restrictions would probably accomplish nothing for us except a loss of the business." As long as Houston banks did not act in concert, and as long as federal regulation did not force changes, the large cotton firms could protect their traditional privileges with the effective threat to take their business elsewhere.[10]

Such privileges were tolerated by bankers—at least until the Great Depression—because of the profitability of cotton accounts. Even the largest Houston banks could not supply all the capital needed for the organization and operations of the major cotton-trading firms active in the region. Anderson, Clayton, for example, turned to a consortium of New York banks for credit soon after the company was organized in 1904. But major companies such as Anderson, Clayton

Table 4.1 Occupations of Directors of South Texas Commercial National Bank, 1916

Director	Occupation
James A. Baker	Attorney (Baker & Botts); banking (president)
Amos L. Beaty	Oilman (Texas Company)
R. Lee Blaffer	Oilman (Humble Oil Company)
Chester H. Bryan	Banking (retired)
Ennis Cargill	Office-supply distributor (Cargill and Company)
Charles Dillingham	Cotton; banking (chairman of the board)
Edwin Kirke Dillingham	Cotton (E. K. Dillingham and Company)
John Dorrance	Cotton (Dorrance and Company)
James D. Dawson	Cotton (Fidelity Cotton Oil and Fertilizer Company)
P. J. Evershade	Banking (cashier)
Thornwell Fay	Railroads (Southern Pacific)
Thomas J. Freeman	Attorney
F. A. Heitmann	Wholesale hardware (president, F. W. Heitmann and Company)
Robert Scott Lovett	Attorney; railroads (chairman of the board, Union Pacific)
James Everett McAshan	Banking (retired)
Samuel Maurice McAshan	Banking (second vice-president)
Henry F. MacGregor	Developer
J. V. Neuhaus	Grain dealer (South Texas Grain Company)
Edwin B. Parker	Attorney (Baker & Botts)
James A. Pondrom	Banking (first vice-president)
S. C. Red	Physician and surgeon
Daniel Ripley	Cotton; steamship lines (Daniel Ripley and Company)
J. J. Settegast, Jr.	Developer
Cleveland Sewall	Attorney; cotton (Gordon, Sewall and Company)

Source: STCNB, *Directors' Minutes.*

used the Houston banks for the transfer of funds to the country-side and for the collection of funds from buyers of their cotton. In peak season they borrowed money to purchase cotton. By the 1920s, Anderson, Clayton needed $400 million every October. At times, they also needed loans to expand their local warehouses. Houston banks supplied a portion of this needed credit, and in doing so flourished as the cotton business boomed from 1916 to 1930.[11]

Of the predecessors of Texas Commerce, South Texas Commercial National was the most intimately tied to the cotton trade. Commercial National and South Texas National had built up close ties to early-day cotton firms, and their major customers remained the major customers of South Texas Commercial National. After 1919, loans of up to 25 percent of a national bank's capital and surplus could be made to individual cotton-trading companies or to individual partners if the companies were copartnerships. These loans were secured by warehouse receipts on insured cotton equaling 115 percent of their value. Almost all the loans were further protected by futures contracts which ensured that a sudden drop in cotton prices would not erode the value of the cotton serving as collateral. The duration of such cotton loans was usually 90 days, but renewal was common. Some large firms, such as Anderson, Clayton, paid interests on their daily balance and had in effect a series of one-day loans. Interest rates ranged from 1 to 2 percent; however, because the sums involved were very large and the risk was low, profits were steady. For example, a list of some $50,000 in loans and overdrafts charged off to the undivided profits of South Texas Commercial National Bank in June, 1921, contains not a single cotton loan. Likewise, of some $400,000 in loans and doubtful paper criticized by the comptroller in 1923, none was cotton-related.[12]

That does not mean that cotton loans were without risk. Early in 1923 the large cotton firm W. M. Ward and Company went bankrupt and defaulted on loans to several Houston banks. South Texas Commercial National Bank responded by organizing a special committee to study cotton lending. The members of the committee were President James A. Baker, Vice-President Samuel M. McAshan, and directors Ennis Cargill, E. K. Dillingham, Cleveland Sewall, and S. C. Red. All were quite familiar with the cotton trade. Cleveland Sewall was president of Gordon, Sewall. Dillingham, whose father had been a pioneer in the cotton trade, was president of E. K. Dillingham and Company, a cottonseed-products brokerage firm. Cargill was a former bank officer and was experienced in a variety of businesses. McAshan's father and grandfather had been in the cotton business, and he himself had a lifetime of experience in making cotton loans. Baker was a lawyer; Red, a physician. Both had been with the bank since the 1890s and understood the workings of the cotton trade.[13] If anyone could take a long-term view of the cotton trade, it was this group. As the committee wrote: "We had the record of our own experience before us, this experience, as is well known to our Board, in most cases extending over a long period of time, the majority of the accounts having been for several years with the two old banks prior to our consolidation in 1912." [14]

In preparing its report to the bank's board of directors, the committee examined the financial statement of all but one of the major Houston cotton trading firms. Its five-page report, drafted by McAshan, listed potential trouble spots in cotton loans. Among these was the accepting of railroad agents' receipts in place of bills of lading before the arrival of cotton in Houston warehouses. Also cited were the taking of trust receipts from cotton men and the taking of receipts without information on the grade, weight, and condition of the cotton. Other practices discussed were futures contracts, forged bills of lading, and the reliability of compress receipts when the compresses were owned by the cotton men who were applying for loans. After discussing the possibility of hiring an inspector or having the Houston Clearing House hire an inspector to ensure the reliability of cotton receipts, the report recommended no basic changes in the bank's method of making cotton loans. Instead, it advised that the bank should continue to make loans based primarily upon how long a firm had been with the bank and upon a judgment of the honesty and reliability of the firm's cotton men. McAshan's committee summed up its advice by insisting that there should be no change in procedures for those who "have dealt with us through the varying conditions of business." [15] Procedures governing the mainstay of the bank's profitability, cotton lending, would not be hastily altered in response to problems with a single account.

In addition to loans to cotton merchants active in Houston, South Texas Commercial National also made more loans than any other Houston bank to rural banks in Texas and was the leading place of deposit for those banks (see Tables 3.1 and 3.2.) Many such loans to banks helped move the cotton from the field to the gin and then on to Houston. Before coming back to Houston in 1914, S. M. McAshan had been an officer in a bank in Waco, in the center of one of the state's most fertile cotton-growing regions. Because of the contacts he had developed in rural Texas, he was particularly adept at securing correspondent-bank business for STCNB. These correspondent banks even referred to STCNB customers applying for loans that were too large for them to handle. These loans were made only upon assurances of the integrity of the borrower by a correspondent banker well known to STCNB's officers. With the notable exception of trouble with loans to the First National Bank of Bastrop in 1921, STCNB had few problems with such loans, since McAshan made sure that the banks with which STCNB did business were exceptionally secure. Such loans to banks in the cotton-growing regions surrounding Houston contributed to the bank's growth and prosperity while facilitating the steady flow of cotton to markets.[16]

Because of the profits of the cotton trade and the personal ties to cotton traders, only federal regulators had the power to force STCNB and other Houston banks to change their methods of dealing with the cotton firms. Beginning in 1910 the comptroller of the currency curtailed the use of overdrafts by cotton firms. These overdrafts had been used as an automatic line of credit or instant bank loan. In the 1920s the Office of the Comptroller attempted to force Houston banks to secure better collateral for loans to cotton firms. Because M. D. Anderson was a director of the National Bank of Commerce, his company and that bank were particular targets of the comptroller. A letter of November 1, 1921, to the National Bank of Commerce from Deputy Comptroller T. P. Kane read in part:

> The report of an examination of your bank October 13, has been received, and shows an excessive loan to Anderson, Clayton & Company, consisting of non-negotiable demand drafts represented by memo receipts covering 6503 bales of cotton.
>
> Demand obligations, in order to come within the exception to Section 5200, U.S.R.S., as amended, must be secured by documents covering commodities in actual process of shipment. The acceptances in this case would not come within the exception to the section referred to, as amended, as they are not secured by documents covering cotton which is in actual process of shipment, the cotton being carried in stock until contracted for. The classification of this loan as excessive appears to be correct, and the loan should be reduced to the legal limit promptly.
>
> Anderson, Clayton & Company, a director's interest, also had an excess loan at the time of the previous examination. Furthermore, directors are subject to severe censure when found to be participating in violations of law. Care should be taken hereafter to see that the law with respect to the limit of loans is observed when extending accommodations.

The minute books reveal that at that time NBC had lent M. D. Anderson more than $700,000. His loan level never dipped much below that figure as long as he was a director, and there is no indication of a change in the collateral on these loans. Houston banks resisted every effort of the comptroller to limit the use of cotton as collateral to cotton that was in the process of shipment. In doing so, they expanded the amount of credit available and kept their major customers happy. The business of Anderson, Clayton was worth an occasional disapproving letter from the comptroller.[17]

As cotton increased in importance to the banks and the economy in the late teens and early twenties, lumber declined in importance. Lumber production plummeted from 1915 to 1930 in East Texas as the virgin stands of pine were depleted. Lumber had never been as directly important to Houston banks as cotton, because much of the expansion of the lumber companies had been financed by company profits and because many of the payrolls had been handled by banks in the small East Texas mill towns. Indirectly, however, lumber benefited banks by stimulating the regional economy and by creating fortunes which were often invested in bank stock. One such fortune belonged to Samuel Fain Carter, a director of South Texas National from 1902 until 1907, when he resigned to organize Lumbermans National Bank. Responding to the decline in importance of lumber, that bank changed its name to Second National Bank in 1923.[18]

Unlike lumber, oil and oil-related activities grew in significance after World War I. Advocates of industrialization had long been vocal in Texas, but their efforts brought only limited results until oil stimulated manufacturing along the Texas Gulf Coast and made possible the maximum utilization of the ship channel. Lumber, cotton, rice, and particularly railroad construction had caused a modest degree of industrialization. Fabricating shops for the railroads, large manufacturing shops which produced machines needed for the processing of rice and cotton, cottonseed mills, and mills which converted rough timber into more finished products developed between the 1880s and World War I. After the start of the war, however, the industrialization of the Houston region surged. Oil and related endeavors fed this increase.[19]

Oil demanded intricate tools and equipment for drilling and production. Oil transportation called for special railroad cars and extensive pipelines. Oil refining, which increasingly came to be concentrated on the Texas Gulf Coast, required a vast array of machines and many workers. Production of specialized products from the refined oil required more large factories and created more jobs. Coordination of these varied activities took a large administrative staff. Oil created many jobs in production, transportation, refining, sales and distribution, and in the manufacturing of more intricate items from the refined product. Many oil companies established headquarters in Houston, thus adding additional jobs.[20]

As in cotton and lumber, oil fortunes were often used to buy bank stock and representatives of major companies sat on bank boards. The career of R. Lee Blaffer, a long-term member of the board of South Texas Commercial National and a founder of Humble Oil Company, was a good example of the close connection between oil money and banks. Blaffer joined the board of South Texas National in 1911 and remained on the board of South Texas Commercial National after the merger. He retired in 1933 but returned in 1942 as chairman of the board. He owned a modest amount of stock and his place on the board helped cement the ties between the bank and an important depositor. Blaffer advised the bank on oil lending, but he seldom borrowed money from the bank. Instead, his oil business, like the lumber business of the Carter family, was financed by its profits and by the sale of Humble stock to Standard Oil of New Jersey in 1919.[21]

The limited borrowing by Blaffer and Humble typified the relationship between major oil companies active in Texas and Houston banks before 1930. Such companies seldom borrowed from Houston banks. Instead, they financed expansion with retained earnings, the sale of stock, or merger with larger companies. The major oil companies with administrative offices and large refineries in and around Houston kept substantial demand deposits in the city's banks to pay their employees and purchase goods, but they relied on money-center banks for major financing. One indication of the relative unimportance of oil loans to Texas banks was the focus of the most extensive study of Texas banking published in this era, Earl Bryan Schwulst's *Extension of Bank Credit*, which devoted 100 pages to cotton and only 10 to oil. Oil was a dynamic, profitable business in Texas in the 1920s, but the state's bankers remained dependent upon cotton.[22]

Yet, because of their stock ownership and the importance of their companies as depositors, in the 1920s more and more oilmen appeared on banks' board of directors. Indeed, Blaffer was not the only founder of Humble who was prominent in banking circles. Walter W. Fondren, one of Blaffer's partners at Humble, was on the board of National Bank of Commerce from 1918 to 1937. H. C. Weiss, another Humble partner, was on the board of South Texas Commercial National from 1923 to 1928. Stephen Power Farish, whose brother Will Stamps Farish was another founder of Humble and who was also briefly associated with the company was a director of Union National. Thus through the importance of their positions in the local community and through the purchase of stock, oilmen made their presence felt at Houston banks in the teens and twenties.[23]

Perhaps the most telling example of ties between banking and oil was the career of Ross S. Sterling, another founder of Humble. In 1925, Sterling sold his interests in Humble and turned to real estate, newspapers, and banking. He had long been a backer of the Houston Ship Channel and did much to develop the area along the channel. He owned the *Houston Post-Dispatch* and the Houston National Bank and was governor of Texas from 1931 to 1933. With the onslaught of the Great Depression, Governor Sterling experienced very serious financial difficulties. His bank almost failed, and he was forced to sell many of his interests, including the *Post-Dispatch*. Indeed, his bank was saved only through a cooperative effort by all the major banks in Houston. Undaunted by his defeat for reelection and his financial setback, Sterling went on to make a second fortune in oil in the 1930s. His impact on banking, however, was more negative than positive. He was what R. M. Farrar called a jazz banker who took excessive risks and bent the rules of banking. His story suggests that oilmen were not as adept at transferring their efforts to banking as the cotton dealers who preceded them as the kingpins of the Houston economy. Perhaps this was because oil was so profitable or perhaps because the skills needed to succeed in the oil business were not directly applicable to banking. At any rate, few oilmen followed Sterling's path from oil to banking.[24]

Another prominent Houstonian and backer of the ship channel was much more successful than Sterling at combining newspaper publishing, banking, and real estate speculation. By the 1920s, Jesse Jones had amassed a fortune in lumber and real estate and had begun to turn more of his efforts to newspaper publishing, banking, and government service. Jones became president of the National Bank of Commerce in 1922 and held that office until 1929, when he became chairman of the board. During that time he also increased his ownership of NBC stock,

Jesse Holman Jones
1874–1956

Jesse Holman Jones was born in Robertson County, Tennessee, but moved to Dallas, Texas in 1883, when his father, William Hasque Jones, joined his brother M. T. Jones in the lumber business. William Jones did not like the lumber business, and in 1886 he purchased a farm on the Kentucky-Tennessee border and the family returned with his family to the upper South. From then until his death in 1893, however, Jesse's father would temporarily move the family back to Dallas where the children went to school while he checked on his holdings in Texas. After the death of his father in 1894, Jesse returned to Texas for good and went to work for his uncle in the Dallas area.

When his uncle, M. T. Jones, died in 1898, Jones was appointed an

executor of his estate and moved to Houston, the headquarters of
M. T. Jones Lumber Company. Houston was to be his hometown for
the rest of his life. Jones prospered in the lumber business and enjoyed
the support of T. W. House, Jr., who was also an executor of M. T.
Jones's estate. Like others with access to capital and the good sense to
combine the cutting, milling, and marketing of East Texas timber in a
single concern, Jones made money. By 1902 he was in business for himself, but he, along with J. M. Rockwell, continued to operate M. T.
Jones Lumber Company.

When M. T. Jones Lumber Company was finally liquidated in 1905,
Jesse Jones had his own successful lumber business, and he also had
begun to build commercial and residential properties. He soon concentrated on commercial property and over the next twenty-five years
built a string of office buildings primarily in Houston, Fort Worth, and
New York. He also built and managed hotels, the most famous of
which was the Rice Hotel, in Houston. Jones was able to expand his
lumber and real estate holdings rapidly because he was a master at obtaining and using credit. His family background and his friendship
with prominent bankers like House helped him get his start, but it was
Jones's ability to obtain long-term notes from more than one bank that
served him best. He revealed his secret of success in 1949 when he
wrote to Cordell Hull: "As soon as I got a taw to play with, I began
buying real estate on long time, and building with no personal obligation on the notes." He had accounts in Dallas, Houston, and New
York for most of his life, and if one bank turned him down, he could
always go to another. Once he had established a record of success,
however, few banks turned down his requests for loans on the most
favorable terms.

As the trees were cut in East Texas and the lumber business declined,
Jones concentrated on banking, construction, newspaper publishing,
and government service. Jones was an original director and stockholder of Union Bank and Trust in 1905. He became one of its largest
stockholders when Union was converted into a national bank and acquired the Jones owned Merchants National Bank in 1910. Jones was
involved in several other banks and trust companies, but the bank with
which he had the longest association was National Bank of Commerce. He was a director of the bank from October, 1914, to October,
1916. By 1919, when he again became a director, he was the bank's
largest stockholder, and over the years he and his family came to own a
majority of the stock. He was president of the bank from 1922 to 1929
and again in 1934. He was chairman of the board from 1929 to his
death in 1956. Jones built one of his most beautiful structures to house
NBC in 1929, and for years that building, called the Gulf Building
after its major tenant, was the tallest building in Houston. In all he
built over thirty major downtown Houston buildings, and he seldom

sold a building once it was constructed. Along the way he acquired control of the *Houston Chronicle*, and as Houston grew so did the circulation of the *Chronicle*.

Government service and politics occupied many of the middle years of Jones's life. During World War I he assisted the Red Cross in Washington, D.C., and became an admirer of Woodrow Wilson. In 1924 he was the finance chairman of the National Democratic party, and in 1928 he arranged for the National Democratic Convention to be held in Houston. In 1932, President Herbert Hoover appointed him a member of the board of the Reconstruction Finance Corporation. In 1933, President Franklin D. Roosevelt named him the head of the RFC, a position he retained as long as he was in Washington. Jones was so successful and the RFC so needed to solve the problems of the Great Depression that by 1940 a writer for the *Saturday Evening Post* proclaimed his powers second only to the president's. During World War II, Jones was also secretary of commerce. After almost fourteen years in Washington he finally returned to Houston in 1945.

Back in Houston, Jones built a few more buildings during the postwar boom and watched over his many business interests. He had married Mary Gibbs in 1920, but the two never had children. In later years both took an active interest in philanthropy, and together they set up Houston Endowment. Jones died on June 1, 1956.

In the same letter to Cordell Hull in which he analyzed his financial success, Jones declared, "I have always regarded myself a liberal, and, except for voting for McKinley against Bryan, I have voted the Democratic ticket." He went on to reveal the reason for his one transgression against the Democratic faith: "While I was only 27 when Mr. Bryan first ran, and had no property of any kind, I could not understand what he meant by free silver, and voted accordingly." Some might question Jones's assessment of himself as a liberal but his insistence in the 1930s on cooperative action among businesses and his repeated calls for bankers to lend more money marked him as less conservative than most of his fellow business leaders. As the reason for his opposition to Bryan illustrates, however, Jones was more a pragmatist than an idealist. In the Houston bank crisis of 1931 and in his calls for the expansion of credit, Jones realized that what was good for Houston ultimately was good for business.

SOURCES: Jesse H. Jones to Cordell Hull, January 5, 1949, Jesse H. Jones Papers (Library of Congress). Also see Jesse H. Jones to Blanche Babcock, August 25, 1937, Jones Papers; Samuel Lubell, "New Deal's J. P. Morgan," *Saturday Evening Post* (November 30, 1940): 9; NBC, *Directors' Minutes* 8 (October 9, 1956): 24–25; Bascom N. Timmons, *Jesse H. Jones: The Man and the Statesman*; Shareholders' File, TCB Archives.

going from 1,574 shares, or 22 percent of the stock, in 1919 to 2,118 shares, or 45 percent, in 1929. Under Jones and his hand-picked successors NBC grew to be one of the leading banks in Houston.[25]

Jesse Jones and Ross Sterling were not the only prominent Houstonians to invest funds earned in lumber or oil in real estate. Indeed, the 1920s was one of the peak periods of real estate development in the history of Houston. The over 100 percent increase in the cities' population in the 1920s spurred residential construction. A writer for the *Houston Chronicle* summed up the beginning of the real estate boom when he wrote in 1920: "Real estate men are prosperous, now, simply because the people are prosperous, the city is expanding more rapidly than most people imagine, the demands for every description of improved property is way ahead of the supply." William C. Hogg, the son of former Texas governor James S. Hogg, whose family had also made a fortune in oil, helped meet this demand by developing the elite River Oaks subdivision. West University Place was another subdivision developed in the 1920s. Commercial construction in that decade remade downtown Houston. Before 1920 only eight buildings of more than 100,000 square feet had been constructed in the city. Between 1920 and 1929, as Table 4.2 illustrates, seven buildings of over 100,000 square feet opened their doors. Two of these, Jesse Jones's Gulf Building and the Humble Building, approached 500,000 square feet. Other major buildings erected in the 1920s included the Houston Cotton Exchange Building, the Warwick Hotel, the Neils Esperson Building, and the Petroleum Building. All of these ranged from nine to thirty-four stories and dominated the Houston skyline until the 1950s. Building permits offer one indication of the massive construction within the city limits. Permits totaling $10,398,000 were issued in 1921. This figure increased steadily throughout the decade until it reached a high of $35,320,000 in 1929. This boom in construction provided many jobs and helped speed the circulation of money.[26]

Real estate loans by Houston banks were necessarily small, however, because these banks did not have the capital to make loans for major construction projects. Except for cotton loans, banks were limited in loans to an individual borrower to 10 percent of their capital stock and surplus fund. In 1929, National Bank of Commerce had $1 million in capital stock and $2 million in the surplus fund. That meant that the most it could lend to an individual was $300,000. The cost of the bank's own building, which opened that year, was over $3 million, and it was kept that low by the efforts of Jesse Jones, who supervised the financing, construction, and development of the building. The bank had to turn to the New York Trust Company and the

Table 4.2 Major New Buildings in Houston's Central Business District, 1899–1930

Year Completed	Name	Square Footage	Floors
1899	Lomas & Nettleton	144,000	9
1908	Kress Building	165,000	8
1910	First National Life Building	195,000	24
1911	Southern Pacific	182,000	9
1912	Houston Bar Center	100,000	10
1912	West Building	107,000	6
1915	Texaco Building	178,000	13
1920	Pappas Building	109,000	8
1922	Main Building	507,947	15
1924	United Gas Building	98,000	10
1924	Houston Cotton Exchange	140,000	16
1926	609 Fannin	323,000	22
1926	Great Southwest Building	180,000	21
1927	Esperson Building	250,000	27
1929	Gulf Building	575,791	34
1930	Texas Professional Towers	100,000	20
1930	M&M Building	620,000	10

SOURCE: Property Research and Investment Consultants, Inc., "Houston's Office Space Market" (April 1975).

Note: Based on buildings in existence in 1975 and using the 1975 names of the buildings.

Metropolitan Life Insurance Company for the financing of its building. No regional concern could lend it enough money for its needs. What was true for the Gulf Building was also true for the other major downtown buildings constructed in the 1920s. Construction boomed, but the city's banks could handle only the smaller loans. Major downtown office buildings were inevitably financed by insurance companies, trust companies, and banks of the Northeast.[27]

While their lending limits were too low to finance major commercial construction, STCNB, Union, and NBC did play a role in the financing of homes and smaller commercial buildings. Typically the bank dealt through a lumberyard. Lumberyards were often actually building companies that advanced the materials and provided the labor and supervision for construction. They even arranged for loans for their customers. As in the case of cotton, banks built up close working relationships with certain lumberyards. They relied on the lumber-

The Gulf Building

Of all the buildings constructed by the Jesse Jones interests, the Gulf Building is perhaps the best known. Designed by Alfred C. Finn, Kenneth Franzheim, and J. E. R. Carpenter and executed in art deco moderne, or wedding-cake, style, the building was completed in 1929, just in time for a general decline in American business.

Like other buildings constructed by Jones, the building was named for its major tenant, the Gulf Oil Company. On the first floor, however, was the ornate lobby of National Bank of Commerce, and the bank's space in the building grew over the years as its business expanded. Twice expanded, the building has been extensively renovated and remains the site of Texas Commerce–Houston. It has been renamed the Texas Commerce Building.

Buildings have long been of significance to banks, and bankers have paid attention to even the smallest detail of construction and renovation. In 1921 and 1922, when South Texas Commercial National remodeled its bank building, its directors took special care to construct a sidewalk that "looked like a bank's." Such care was important because their banking quarters needed to bespeak solidity and security, wealth and prestige. Bank buildings were meant to be a form of signature or symbol of the bank.

SOURCES: Jesse H. Jones & Co.: *A Booklet Describing the Gulf Building* (Houston, 1929); *Houston Chronicle* (September 15, 1983); Robert J. Reid, *A History of the Gulf Building, 1926 to 1983* (Houston, 1983); STCNB, *Directors' Minutes* 2 (March 30, 1922): 261.

yards to screen their potential customers and often required a lumber-yard to guarantee a loan. These loans were usually short term but were frequently renewed for a period up to the legal limit of five years on real estate loans. Union National seemed to have made a few more such loans than did the other two banks. Perhaps this was because

R. M. Farrar and the Carter family were in the lumberyard business and knew the most secure companies. Perhaps it also was a holdover from the bank's days as a state bank, since state banks could more easily make loans with real estate as collateral. Use of real estate as collateral was long restricted by the comptroller of the currency. In 1925 the comptroller warned Union of excessive real estate loans held beyond "the statutory limit of five years." Union responded that it was giving the matter "constant and aggressive attention." While making fewer loans than most other banks, in this area at least Union National proved among the leaders. It continued to make real estate loans until the Great Depression, when the bank almost stopped making any kind of loan.[28]

As real estate and other aspects of the Houston economy grew, the need for lawyers also grew. Lawyers had long been an important part of the city's political and economic leadership. Every bank board and corporate board contained a requisite number of lawyers, many of whom often also served as mayors or city councilmen. O. T. Holt, for example, an attorney and mayor of Houston from 1902 to 1904, was on the original boards of directors of both South Texas National and National Bank of Commerce. Another attorney and original director of South Texas, Samuel Houston Brashear, served as mayor from 1898 to 1900. J. C. Hutcheson, Jr., was on the board of National Bank of Commerce and mayor in 1917–18. Besides serving as mayors, lawyers often held other important positions in the community. W. O. Huggins, an attorney and board member of National Bank of Commerce, was the editor of the *Houston Chronicle* in the 1920s. Probably the most important of the early-day lawyers was Robert Scott Lovett, a partner until 1904 in the firm Baker, Botts, Baker and Lovett. Lovett was a railroad lawyer who handled the business of Jay Gould's lines in Texas during the 1880s and 1890s. After 1904, when E. H. Harriman had consolidated his hold on the Southern Pacific and Union Pacific, Lovett worked for Harriman. From 1909 until 1924, except for a brief interruption during World War I, Lovett was president and chairman of the board of Union Pacific. He was also president and chairman of the board of Southern Pacific from 1909 until 1913. Along with other members of his firm Lovett was a member of the board of Commercial National Bank and after 1912 of its successor, South Texas Commercial National Bank.[29]

Lawyers served as a type of cement that bound banks, law firms, and major corporations in an alliance that fostered mutual prosperity. It was no accident that first Commercial National and then South Texas Commercial National were the major banks of the Southern Pacific and Union Pacific railroads. R. S. Lovett, chairman of both

James Addison Baker
1857–1941

James Addison Baker's career aptly demonstrates the interconnections between major Houston law firms and the city's other institutions. Known as Captain Baker, he moved to Houston from his native Huntsville, Texas, in 1872 with his father, Judge James A. Baker. By 1887, Captain Baker was a partner in his father's law firm. Baker, Botts and Baker specialized in representing railroad companies, the largest corporations in Texas at the time. Among its clients were the Missouri, Kansas and Texas; the International and Great Northern; the Texas and Pacific; the Galveston, Houston and Henderson; the Houston and Texas Central; and the Houston, East and West Texas. When many of these lines were consolidated in the 1890s into the Southern Pacific and Union Pacific systems, the firm also represented these lines.

As Captain Baker grew older, he spent more time managing and overseeing business and educational institutions than practicing law. Under his oversight and that of the managing partner, Edwin B. Parker, the firm grew from three lawyers in 1890 to twenty-five lawyers in 1926. Captain Baker became president of South Texas Commercial National in 1914, and the bank's deposits had more than tripled by 1927, when he ceased to take an active part in daily operations and became chairman of the board.

For much of his adult life Captain Baker was also chairman of the Rice Institute Board of Trustees. Baker's association with Rice began in 1891, when William Marsh Rice chartered Rice Institute and named the captain chairman of the trustees. The association ended at his death in 1941. He protected the endowment until the school opened in 1912 and after that supervised its steady expansion. He also helped select the school's original administrators and in numerous other ways ensured the survival of Rice in its infancy.

Serving with Baker on the Rice Board of Trustees in the early days were F. A. Rice, the brother of W. M. Rice, and James E. McAshan, of South Texas National Bank. Later Will Rice replaced his father on the board. After the merger of 1912, McAshan and Baker were major forces in South Texas Commercial National Bank. That bank always cooperated closely with Union National, of which Will Rice was a director and brother Joe was the president. Rice Institute was one of the major stockholders of South Texas Commercial National, trailing only the Ripley family and Captain Baker in shares held in the 1920s and 1930s. C. A. Dwyer, the business manager of Rice, was a director of

Union National from 1925 to its merger with South Texas in 1953. Thus Captain Baker sat in an exclusive club that controlled two major banks as well as the city's premier educational institution.

Baker was also an officer and director of many other Houston businesses. Among them were the Houston Abstract Company, Merchants and Planters Oil Company, the Houston Gas Company, Bankers Trust Company, and Guardian Trust Company. Through those companies he came into close contact with almost every other wealthy and influential Houstonian. Bankers Trust, for example, was organized in 1907 to lend mortgage money and to sell mortgages to investors. The president of that concern was Joe Rice. Later in 1912 it merged with Texas Trust, owned by Jesse Jones, and became Bankers Mortgage Company. That one company led Baker into close association with two of the major figures in Houston business in 1912.

Probably more than any other man of his day, Captain Baker was positioned to influence and observe all facets of Houston's business community. From that position he helped develop some of the city's major institutions. While Jesse Jones built buildings, James Baker built up his law firm, his bank, other major local businesses, and Rice Institute. Baker and Jones had unusual power. They were not the only citizens with influence, but, as the bailout of Houston banks in 1931 would prove, in the city of Houston, if these two were on the same side, others usually followed.

SOURCES: Officers and Directors Files, TCB Archives; Jesse Andrews, "A Texas Portrait: Capt. James A. Baker, 1857–1941," *Texas Bar Journal* (February 1961): 110–11, 187–89; T. M. Phillips, "James Addison Baker, 1857–1941," TCB Archives.

---

railroads, naturally kept his Houston business with banks on whose boards he sat and whose major officers included James A. Baker, a former law partner.[30]

One reason for the success that Jones and Baker enjoyed in the teens and twenties was the rapid expansion of credit and the increased circulation of money, as bank deposits in Houston grew from $370 per person in 1910 to $614 in 1920. With the rapid increase in population of the 1920s, that figure diminished to $573 per person in 1930, but for much of the 1920s, bank deposits per capita in Houston remained twice the national average. Not only were people able to deposit more money, but the federal government increased the availability of money through such institutions as the Federal Farm Loan Bank and the Federal Intermediate Credit Bank, both of which were established in Houston around 1920. Federal Reserve Board policy also expanded the money supply throughout most of the 1920s. All of this helped spur the Houston economy, which provided more jobs and allowed further increases in deposits. Savings and increased credit allowed by greater deposits bought homes, automobiles, and other consumer goods and helped capitalize further expansion of basic industries like cotton, lumber, and oil. Backers of speculative ventures also had greater access to credit. The age of materialism, the jazz age, was very much a part of the history of Houston and its banks in the 1920s.[31]

Banks, for example, financed the symbol of the jazz age: the automobile. In a manner similar to the home loan business, bankers relied on dealers to find the customers and bring them to them. STCNB made loans through Tension Motor Company and the Oldsmobile Sales Company as early as 1921. NBC dealt with the Meador Automobile Company. Union National seems to have been much less active in this business. In 1926 the directors of STCNB closely examined automobile financing and reached a similar conclusion to their 1923 analysis of the cotton industry: they should stick by their old established customers and examine any new business very carefully. As they put it, bank officers should "give consideration to each new proposition as presented, taking on, or rejecting, such accounts as in their discretion they might see fit."[32] By the mid-1920s, even conservative banks like STCNB and Union had begun to diversify away from their traditional reliance upon the cotton trade. Particularly noticeable was a slight move away from business lending toward consumer lending—at least indirect consumer lending. In this they were much like other Houston banks and banks across the nation.[33]

STCNB and Union National also followed some of the other trends of American banking in the 1920s. Both banks formed closely associated investment companies which purchased real estate and securities. In January, 1927, the stockholders of STCNB authorized the formation of the South Texas Commercial Company with a capital stock of $150,000. Stockholders of the bank received prorated shares of the company instead of cash dividends, and the dividend money was used to capitalize the company. Union National also formed such a company in March, 1926. Its original capital was $75,000, and its stock was distributed to the bank's shareholders in lieu of dividends. Both banks thus moved toward combining commercial banking and investment banking.[34]

Early in 1929, STCNB's directors decided that call loans to finance the purchase of stock on the New York Stock Exchange were "proper and desirable investments." Such loans were to be "reasonable amounts placed through our New York correspondents." The easy availability of such loans and the opportunity to buy stock by paying only a small percentage of the purchase price were later condemned as partial causes of the stock-market crash of October, 1929. This example indicates that STCNB was not averse to profiting from the speculative frenzy of the era, if they could do so in reasonable amounts and under the guidance of their well-established New York correspondents.[35]

The opportunity for profit quickened growth in the number of Houston's banks in the jazz age. The shakeout following the Panic of 1907 was forgotten as the number of banks increased steadily from 10 in 1919 to 21 in 1927, after which the number of banks again declined.

The causes of this decline were tightened regulation of state banks after the collapse of the Guaranty Fund and the preliminary tremors of the Great Depression. Because of the depressed price of cotton, state banks in rural Texas had an exceptionally high rate of failure in the 1920s. These failures drained the Guaranty Fund and led to increased assessments on solvent banks. The stronger banks often reacted as Union Bank and Trust had done in 1910 by converting to national banks. In the mid-1920s the state banking commission attempted to shore up the system with more stringent regulations. In Houston as in much of the rest of the state, forced liquidations or mergers arranged by the state banking commissioner followed. Three of the four banks that faded from the Houston banking industry between December, 1927, and December, 1929, were state banks. In desperation the Guaranty Fund Law was repealed in 1927 to prevent the further flight of healthy state banks. In all over 120 state banks—slightly less than 15 percent of the total number of state banks—converted to national banks during the 1920s.[36]

Economic problems also sped the demise of some Houston banks after 1927. Since they had made few loans to farmers, they were spared the plight of rural banks. Most problem loans of Houston's major banks were in real estate and consumer lending. Because larger, more established banks could in general operate more efficiently than could small new banks and had substantial demand deposits on which they paid little or no interest, they could afford to offer the most secure real estate and consumer borrowers a more attractive interest rate than could their smaller rivals. Small banks often accepted loans with more risk, thus earning R. M. Farrar's condemnation as "jazz banks." They lent money to individuals who never could have obtained credit before, and they financed projects that seemed speculative from the perspective of Houston's traditional bankers. Smaller banks had no choice if they hoped to grow. They had to make high-yield, high-risk loans.

These jazz banks fed the booming Houston economy of the 1920s.

Many individuals obtained credit and many projects were financed that would have been shunned by larger banks. As long as the economy experienced constantly accelerating growth, jazz banks experienced few problems. Starting in 1927, however, a slow decline in real estate construction reduced the demand for real estate loans, an area in which smaller state banks had specialized since they did not have the ties to established cotton firms or the resources to meet their needs. As economic growth slowed, few other lending opportunities were available. The weakest banks had little alternative but to liquidate or arrange to be acquired by a stronger bank.[37]

Slightly larger banks in turn saw the acquisition of these troubled banks as a way to gain the size needed for increased efficiency and profitability. Most of the state banks and the one national bank that disappeared between 1927 and 1929 merged with other banks. Unfortunately, as the economy continued to slow down, the loans brought to the now larger banks by the smaller partners often proved uncollectible. In trying to gain size, these banks only gained problems. Both Public National, which acquired Guaranty National in 1929, and Marine Bank and Trust, which acquired Labor Bank and Trust in 1928, found themselves in the unattractive position of being weakened instead of strengthened by their acquisitions. Both were soon part of National Bank of Commerce.[38]

For the most part Union National Bank, South Texas Commercial National Bank, and National Bank of Commerce avoided the problems of the state banks and the smaller, more aggressive national banks. Yet throughout most of the 1920s to compete for business with a growing number of aggressive banks, the predecessors of Texas Commerce expanded their lending. Union National, which had been severely criticized by the comptroller of the currency and whose directors had had to buy from the bank about $500,000 of bad loans in 1924, was particularly cautious, but as Table 4.3 demonstrates, even Union became more aggressive in the late 1920s.[39]

South Texas Commercial National Bank made more loans than did Union. By their own frequent admission bankers at STCNB lent primarily to cotton firms. These loans were exceptionally safe and were usually made to long-standing customers. But after all, stolid and secure STCNB also made call loans. They made other types of loans and attracted a variety of business customers, but perhaps not to the degree of NBC, First National, or Second National. By eschewing novel and slightly speculative loans, STCNB and especially Union National failed to grow as fast as the economy allowed. This missed op-

Table 4.3   Relationship of Loans to Deposits in
Houston Banks, 1925–31

End of Year	Union	STCNB	NBC	First National	Marine
1925					
Loans	$6,177,592	$15,695,109	$6,134,583	$21,683,800	$1,484,016
% Deposits	36.3	67.6	55.3	67.4	61.1
1926					
Loans	7,970,052	15,709,347	6,144,964	22,640,980	1,224,330
% Deposits	48.1	60.4	57.9	63.1	59.0
1927					
Loans	8,071,519	17,526,597	5,367,957	24,181,305	1,487,066
% Deposits	49.4	62.0	52.5	66.4	76.3
1928					
Loans	7,214,236	18,931,847	5,553,808	24,911,084	2,251,817
% Deposits	41.6	68.8	52.8	62.4	92.1
1929					
Loans	8,308,181	15,337,106	7,371,370	25,578,853	1,898,320
% Deposits	53.0	58.2	61.1	73.0	82.9
1930					
Loans	4,754,665	19,393,229	7,085,271	23,285,242	
% Deposits	31.9	63.2	51.9	60.6	
1931					
Loans	4,289,121	11,850,526	9,441,501	21,832,400	
% Deposits	32.1	46.3	46.6	61.6	

SOURCE: Statements of Condition, TCB Archives.

portunity is evident in the deposit figures shown in Table 4.4. Deposits were linked to loans, since a borrower was often required to keep compensating balances at the lending institution. As a customer grew in size, he generally kept his account at the bank which helped finance his expansion.

STCNB's lending policy and dependency on the cotton trade, which leveled off in the mid-1920s, caused slow growth of deposits. In 1922 for the last time in its history South Texas Commercial National outdistanced all other Houston banks in total deposits. By 1929 deposits at First National had increased by 36 percent. In that same seven-year period deposits at South Texas Commercial National increased by only 2 percent. It had sunk into second place among Houston banks with deposits only two-thirds as great as First National's. At Union deposits actually declined by 4 percent, and the

Table 4.4 Growth of Deposits in Houston Banks, 1912–29

End of Year	First National	STCNB	Union	Second National	NBC
1912	$11,905,119	$13,178,868	$10,628,483	$ 4,031,260	$ 2,209,772
1913	9,873,874	9,382,314	7,980,055	4,809,243	2,689,445
1914	8,490,256	7,277,105	6,257,823	3,329,381	1,295,291
1915	9,903,118	10,639,197	8,737,726	3,949,692	1,340,962
1916	18,340,137	15,318,460	15,171,703	7,953,799	2,491,311
1917	19,094,128	16,325,742	15,062,741	8,723,414	3,726,010
1918	16,843,496	11,758,886	13,650,060	6,201,342	3,373,722
1919	23,643,136	21,335,575	17,247,016	8,835,219	4,692,264
1920	22,537,560	16,325,142	15,536,412	7,664,556	4,521,468
1921	19,891,647	16,276,592	14,319,667	8,669,934	5,177,175
1922	25,804,569	25,923,025	16,281,520	10,866,225	5,899,598
1923	31,144,209	27,794,793	17,736,712	12,390,087	6,644,598
1924	33,059,196	25,993,560	16,661,159	14,918,978	8,862,215
1925	32,163,188	23,212,392	17,019,904	12,390,087	6,644,598
1926	35,882,465	25,993,560	16,577,467	16,421,410	10,609,418
1927	36,392,174	28,285,979	16,333,198	18,452,424	10,232,546
1928	39,896,444	27,523,143	17,327,076	18,516,629	10,527,580
1929	35,060,166	26,329,977	15,673,832	16,790,950	12,057,078

SOURCES: *Houston Post; Houston Chronicle;* Statements of Condition, TCB Archives.

bank fell from third place in deposits to fourth place among Houston banks.[40]

National Bank of Commerce, which had been a small bank in comparison to STCNB in 1922, increased its deposits by 104 percent between 1922 and 1929. In this period, Second National increased its deposits by 55 percent and passed Union to become the third largest bank. Both Second National and NBC had only about one-half the deposits of STCNB, but the phenomenal growth of these two relatively small banks paved the way for their emergence as major Houston banks in subsequent decades. Both banks avoided the extremes of Public National and Marine National while enjoying surprising growth. They seem to have been selective in lending money for speculative purposes while finding opportunities to lend in industries that were less mature than cotton. This meant that while their percentage of loans to deposits might be lower than STCNB, their interest earned on slightly more risky loans was greater and their chances of quickly improving their business were enhanced. Jesse Jones, for example, realized that Gus Wortham of American General Life Insurance Company had great talent. Because of favorable state laws and population growth Texas insurance companies also offered the chance for very rapid increases in profits. NBC lent capital to Wortham, and as his company grew, so did its deposits at the bank. Such insight into future areas of profitability was not entirely lacking at Union and STCNB, but neither proved as successful as NBC in pursuing new business opportunities. Jones was particularly adept at identifying able young businessmen and making them customers of NBC. Jones's willingness to take calculated risks in new fields produced many valuable customers for his bank.[41]

It is difficult to fault the managers of STCNB and Union National for their lending policies. Cotton lending and loans to well-established customers brought great wealth, and from 1914 to 1929, STCNB recorded annual profits as high as 25 percent of the bank's capital stock. At Union growth in deposits and lending was retarded by the problem loans purchased from the bank by a group of stockholders in 1924. The natural reaction was to be more conservative after that incident. It was also true that both banks were more like jazz banks than their managers would admit. Both had investment companies, and both made some types of consumer loans or loans for speculative purposes. NBC, on the other hand, did not have an investment company and throughout the 1920s usually had a lower percentage of its deposits as loans than STCNB's. To some degree, however, the habits of the 1920s led to problems in the 1930s for Union and STCNB. When the cotton trade and the correspondent banking business declined in the troubled 1930s, STCNB was left without any established lending alternatives. The same thing happened to Union National when home building declined. Lacking experience in other lending areas available in Houston, the banks simply reduced the number of loans. In the long run, failure to lend retarded the growth of deposits. When the economy began to grow again, Union National in particular found itself too small to fill the growing needs of its major customers.

CHAPTER 5

Avoiding Disaster, 1929–33

Before 1929 much of the history of the Texas banking industry was shaped by an effort to balance the need for larger, more stable banks with the desire to have a competitive banking system, free from the control of any small group. During periods of rapid economic expansion such as those from 1901 to 1907 and from 1919 to 1927, the number and competitiveness of Houston's banks increased without any noticeable decline in stability. With a slowing down of the economy, however, came instability, and in both 1907 and 1927 the number of banks declined rapidly. The decline after 1907 was relatively brief, and Houston banks entered a period of consolidation and slow growth in numbers. In part this was due to a round of mergers precipitated by the need to increase the size of banks to match the requirements of larger businesses. With the beginning of the Great Depression in 1929, however, the post-1927 decline turned into a near rout. By 1933 the number of banks had fallen from twenty-one in 1927 to thirteen where it remained for over a decade. By the same year the five largest Houston banks, First National, South Texas Commercial National, National Bank of Commerce, Second National, and Union National, controlled roughly 80 percent of all bank deposits in the city. For the moment concentration of banking services to ensure stability had won out over competitiveness.[1]

For a time even stability was in doubt as Houston banks faced the most severe crisis in their history. During 1930 and 1931, numerous economic weaknesses, including the overexpanded banking system of Houston, the decline of real estate values, problems in the oil and gas industries, and a gigantic surplus of cotton, made difficult the carrying out of normal bank operations and resulted in unusually high loan

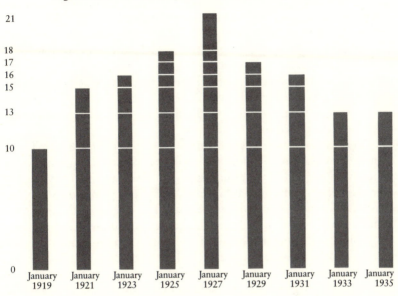

Figure 5.1. Number of banks in Houston, 1919–35.

SOURCES: *Houston Post; Houston Chronicle.*

losses.* Public confidence in banks, which had been eroded by news of banking disasters elsewhere, further declined with news of difficulties in local banks. In the days after the demise of the Texas Guaranty Fund and before federal deposit insurance, wary depositors stood ready to rush to get their money out of Houston banks. Since not even the most conservatively managed bank had enough cash on hand to pay off all its depositors, a run could have driven any Houston bank out of business. Faced with the threat of a run on their deposits, some banks chose to liquidate voluntarily. Others were acquired by larger and more secure banks. Figure 5.1 illustrates the resulting decline in the number of banks. The low point in this decline came in October, 1931, when two relatively large Houston banks were on the brink of failure.

* Banks consider deposits as liabilities and loans as assets because loans earn income. Out of income, a bank pays expenses and taxes and sets aside a reserve for possible loan losses. When a borrower cannot repay a loan or when the loan's collateral is reduced in value, federal and state regulations require that all or part of the loan be charged off. This charge is made against the reserve for possible loan losses.

Their failure was prevented by a cooperative bailout of the troubled banks arranged by the city's business leaders. The resolution of this crisis restored public confidence and prevented a disastrous run on other Houston banks. The worst was over by the close of 1931.

In much of the rest of the country banking conditions continued to worsen through 1933. Houston was spared more severe problems in part because its economy improved after 1931, but a good case can be made that the strong actions of Houston's bankers and business leaders in 1931 prevented trouble in later years. In contrast to the situation in many other areas, public confidence in business leaders and their institutions remained high in Houston.[2]

In December, 1929, at the start of this crisis period, South Texas Commercial National, Union National, and National Bank of Commerce were in good health, but two banks which were soon to be acquired by NBC—Marine Banking and Trust Company and Public National Bank—were decidedly unhealthy. The largest of these banks, South Texas Commercial National, had deposits of over $26 million, $1 million in capital stock, and a $1 million surplus fund. The net earnings for 1929 were an all-time high of $420,000. By 1929, South Texas Commercial National had a long and enviable record of successful and profitable lending. As the bank's auditors said in 1926: "In this connection we desire to say that, in our opinion, your loans are well distributed. The quality and character of these loans does not only reflect an infinite care and great conservatism in selection, but also bespeaks the high sense of responsibility which the bank feels toward its stockholders and depositors in the administration of its funds."[3]

Union National lagged behind STCNB in size. Its capital stock was $1 million and its surplus fund $1 million. Deposits totaled around $15.5 million in 1929, making Union the fourth-largest bank in the city, behind First National, South Texas Commercial National, and Second National. Union was noted for the conservatism of its lending policies. Much of this conservatism was due to R. M. Farrar, who upon becoming president of the bank in 1924 stated:

> My experience has resulted in one very positive conviction and that is that every contemplated bank loan should receive the most exacting scrutiny and no loan should ever be made where there is any apparent uncertainty whatsoever as to its being collected. Every element of doubt should be decided in behalf of safety. The cheapest commodity in this country is credit as evidenced by the appalling credit losses sustained by banks. It requires incessant alertness to keep a bank free from credit abuses. One man can quickly fill his bank with capital and undesirable

loans while it requires the vigilance of all concerned to keep a bank
liquid and free from credit abuse.

Although Farrar's conservative approach to lending retarded the
growth of Union in the 1920s, it assured that the bank would have no
problem weathering the storm of the early 1930s.[4]

Of the three banks National Bank of Commerce had grown the
fastest in the 1920s. By December, 1929, its deposits had increased
to slightly more than $12 million. During 1929 the bank doubled its
capital stock to $1 million and its surplus fund to $2 million. Under
the management of Jesse Jones, who was president from 1922 to 1929,
the bank pursued a policy of lending to reliable businessmen and displayed a willingness to take an occasional risk on their behalf. Aided
by Sam Taub, who was not a salaried officer of the bank but chaired
the loan committee, NBC attracted new and profitable loan customers
and their deposits throughout the 1920s.[5]

Deposits at National Bank of Commerce were further increased
in 1930 and 1931 by the acquisition of two struggling banks, Marine
Banking and Trust Company and Public National Bank. At the time
of acquisition neither bank gave promise of adding to the strength of
NBC, but over the long run both proved valuable additions. Marine's
roots ran back to People's State Bank, founded in 1919. That bank specialized in consumer loans and, like Planters and Mechanics Bank of
old, tried to be the little man's bank. Its history was even shorter than
that of Planters and Mechanics, and in February, 1925, its directors
declared the bank insolvent, turning over its assets to the state banking
commissioner. In the same month those assets were acquired by the
newly organized Marine Bank and Trust Company, which was also
chartered under the laws of the state of Texas.

It was not a good time to begin a state bank in Texas. Falling
cotton prices caused problems for the state's economy in 1926. That
year the largest cotton crop on record devastated cotton farmers by
causing prices to drop to 9.6 cents per pound as compared to 32.3
cents in early 1924. Those farmers were often rural banks' major customers, and, since most of the rural banks were state banks, the state
banking system was hurt by a subsequent round of failures in cotton-
growing areas. The bank failures strained the system of guaranteed deposits by requiring heavier contributions from the still-solvent banks
and by diminishing public confidence in state banks. Eventually, in
1927, Texas stopped guaranteeing deposits. By that year Marine Bank
was showing signs of weakness. In an attempt to grow larger and more
stable, the bank acquired Labor Bank and Trust in 1928, another state

bank, founded in 1925. By the end of 1929, Marine Banking and Trust Company, the new name of the organization, had deposits of only about $2.3 million and faced a bleak future.[6]

Marine Bank's activities offer a good case study of the source of Houston's banking difficulties in the late 1920s and early 1930s. Marine's problems had three sources. First, after the death in 1928 of its president, Denton Cooley, the bank suffered from a lack of experienced leadership. Second, the intense competition in Houston banking during the 1920s forced Marine to take excessive risks and incur heavy expenses in an attempt to become larger and more profitable. Third, as a state bank and one which had difficulty attracting new accounts, Marine accepted real estate as collateral for a very high percentage of its loans.

Cooley was an experienced banker with a good knowledge of Houston and the nature of state banks. He had worked as assistant cashier of Union Bank and Trust before it became a national bank in 1910 and continued with Union National until 1924, when he resigned as a vice-president and director after a dispute with other bank officers. In 1925 he took the lead in organizing Marine Bank and Trust. His decision to acquire the assets of People's State gave the bank deposits and customers from the very beginning, but it also brought loan losses. Still, Cooley managed to keep the bank solvent until 1928. By that time the Houston real estate boom had slowed. In an effort to achieve greater size and profitability, Cooley led the move to acquire Labor Bank. Like People's, Labor Bank added deposits and loan customers but brought still more loan losses when a further slowing of the economy impaired creditors' ability to repay their loans or diminished the value of real estate used as collateral. Before he could solve the problems of a shrinking market and the bad loans acquired with Labor Bank, Cooley was killed in an automobile accident. Those who followed him did not have his skill and standing in the business community. Fearful of being held liable for the losses of the bank, stockholders and directors began selling their stock at a reduced rate. Much of the stock was purchased by Jesse Jones and his associates, but even Jones could not revive the sagging fortunes of Marine Bank. Despite the reorganization of the bank as Marine Banking and Trust in late 1928, the damage was already done.[7]

Competition from other banks helps explain many of Cooley's decisions, as well as the inability of Marine to remain solvent after his death. Loans to established firms were usually the safest and most profitable in Houston, but to get these loans, a small bank like Marine had to increase its loan limit and demonstrate some degree of permanence. Increasing deposits and the surplus fund by acquiring another bank was a quick way of addressing such problems. But larger borrowers most often went to the established Houston banks, not the newcomers, leaving Marine with the smaller, riskier loans. Marine also had to advertise more and hire more people for the purpose of attracting customers instead of waiting for them to walk in the door. It also had to spend as much time and effort on small loans as did other banks on large loans. In August, 1925, the state bank examiner summed up the problems that its poor competitive position had brought to Marine. The bank had "too much slow paper." Loan losses were too high, and expenses were "too large for volume." The bank had "$12,000 to $15,000 in small unsecured loans, made largely to increase the popularity of the bank."[8]

Marine might have solved its management problems and built up its business even in the face of stiff competition, if real estate values and real estate construction had not dropped in the late 1920s. In a 1925 letter to the state banking commissioner the directors of Marine stated:

> As regards our carrying too large an amount of slow and undesirable paper through the financing of lumber yards, contractors and real estate, please be advised that we have time funds in excess of $300,000.00, a part of which we can rightfully use in investments ordinarily slow in liquidation. We believe loans of this character which we have, are unquestionably good and could be sold on today's market.

What was true of the 1925 market was not true of the 1929 market. As public confidence in real estate investments waned, Marine could not sell its loans to other financial institutions and could not convince investors and examiners that such loans were sound. As a result Marine's business foundered, and stockholders were only too willing to sell out to Jesse Jones and the National Bank of Commerce.[9]

Jones had demonstrated a penchant for saving banks on the verge of failure. In 1907 he had helped engineer the merger of Planters and Mechanics with Union Bank and Trust, and in 1910 he had arranged for his almost wholly owned Merchants National to be acquired by Union National. On both occasions Jones had purchased stock in the banks to keep them solvent and had managed to make a profit on his investment. In 1930, a time reminiscent of the Panic of 1907, Jones, a major stockholder and director of Marine, sought to profit again by shoring up the banking situation in Houston through mergers of smaller and weaker banks with larger banks. On March 15, 1930, National Bank of Commerce acquired all the assets of Marine.[10] Then in

October, 1931, National Bank of Commerce acquired Public National, a much bigger bank than Marine, having at the close of business in 1930 some $8 million in deposits.

Public National Bank also had begun as a state bank. In 1910, Guaranty State Bank, taking its name from the Guaranty Fund, was organized. When the Guaranty Fund began to show signs of weakness following the decline in cotton prices in 1920–21, Guaranty State changed to Guaranty National to avoid paying into the fund. In 1921, Public National Bank was also organized. The organization of these two banks was part of the general increase in the number of banks in Houston which followed the opening of the ship channel and the start of World War I. Subsequent events suggest that by the mid-1920s there were not enough competent bank managers and safe loans to ensure that all local banks would avoid excessive risk. At the end of 1925, Public had deposits of about $2.7 million, and Guaranty had deposits of about $1.9 million. Deposits increased through the close of 1927 but began to decline after that point. Like Marine, both banks needed to increase their size to increase stability and profitability, and in October, 1929, they consolidated under the charter of Public National. At the close of 1929, Public had deposits of about $8.5 million, but the increased size of the bank did not halt a further decline in deposits. Losses, many of them on loans gained with the acquisition of Guaranty National, also increased after 1929.[11]

Part of Public National's loan problems could be traced to a new phenomenon in the Houston economy, the boom-bust cycle in the petroleum industry. By 1930 the primary owners of Public National were W. L. Moody III and Odie R. Seagraves. Both had invested heavily in the development of natural-gas fields and the construction of pipelines. Moody and Seagraves, described by Gainer Jones, an officer at Public National, as "wheeler-dealers," were among those who seemed to believe that the prosperity of the twenties would never end. But when the price of gas and oil began to decline, their profits dropped, as did the value of the collateral on the many loans their own bank had made to them. When the news spread that Moody and Seagraves were in financial trouble and that the two had borrowed heavily from their own bank, depositors began withdrawing their funds from Public National. It was a quiet withdrawal and a gradual one because at first only the best informed of the Houston business community knew of the bank's problems. As one of the bank's employees saw it:

> Well, as the Depression got worse, all of us who knew the score at Public National knew that we were going down the drain. Our deposits had

gone down to $6-million, and withdrawals were steady. I remember our last day of business, Monday, October 26, 1931. We were almost out of cash. That day, I would often look down from the mezzanine to the main floor and watch the tellers paying out cash. They had barely enough to last until closing time.[12]

That Monday's problems had not been unanticipated by the banking and business elite of Houston. The previous evening Jesse Jones had organized a meeting to consider the problems at Public National and Houston National, the latter owned by Governor Ross Sterling. In a letter of October 29, Jones recounted to A. D. McDonald, of the Southern Pacific Railroad, the events of Sunday:

> Personally, I had been working on the proposition for more than a week and Sunday I called all of the bankers, the public service corporations, Mr. Lull, who was out of the City, and everyone that I thought could be helpful, to a meeting in my office on the 33rd floor of the Gulf Building. We were here all day Sunday, having cold lunches served by the Rice Hotel, and got away Monday morning at three o'clock without final success, but agreed to see the banks through Monday, and the Public National had considerable withdrawals Monday and Saturday.[13]

At the close of Monday's business day most of the group that had met in Jones's office the previous day reconvened to attempt once again to work out the details of a plan to save Public National and Houston National. Jones proposed that all the institutions represented at the meeting contribute to a guaranty fund for the two banks' problem loans and arrange the acquisition of the banks by healthier concerns. It was certainly not preordained that the plan would be accepted, but most of the group knew something would have to be done overnight if both banks were to be prevented from running out of cash and being forced to close the next day.[14]

In rescuing the Houston banks, Jones and the others were following the principles of voluntary cooperation and self-help touted by President Herbert Hoover as cures for the Depression. They even used the National Credit Corporation, created by leading financiers with the cooperation of the Hoover administration to elicit voluntary contributions to spur economic recovery, as a model for their actions. Voluntary action could succeed, however, only if everyone pulled his fair share—if, indeed, the fair share of each could be determined. Private rescue efforts also faced the opposition of traditionalists who held that weak banks or businesses deserved to fail and that in the long run the economy would be healthier after a little bloodletting.[15]

These problems thus were not easily resolved. It took the realization that there was a very serious crisis at hand which threatened all of

them before Houston's bankers would even meet. Jesse Jones fostered
this realization. Jones educated his peers about the acuteness of the difficulties at Public National and Houston National. He brought business leaders together to discuss possible solutions, and he took the
lead in hammering out a plan that required cooperative action.[16]

In order for his sales pitch for a bank rescue to succeed, Jones
required an audience that was willing to listen and to compromise.
S. M. McAshan, R. M. Farrar, and others were such an audience. They
became convinced of the need to do something. As McAshan put it in
a letter of October 27, 1931, to Captain James Baker:

> Both banks had stated they could go no further. It was made evident that
> the failure of the Public National would carry down with it the Washing-
> ton Avenue and Harrisburg Road banks in Houston, as well as one at
> Harlingen and some country banks which carry their reserves with the
> Public. The Houston National, it was estimated, would drag down about
> twenty interior banks which had their reserves deposited with the Hous-
> ton. Between the four Houston ones mentioned, they had about eight
> thousand others carrying different sorts of accounts with them. Dis-
> regarding the excitement, a black eye to Houston, and the loss of busi-
> ness the best banks here might have sustained due to the panicky feeling
> prevailing throughout the city generally, it was a really frightful thing to
> contemplate twenty-odd thousand of our fellow-citizens and countless
> thousands of others in the interior towns having their funds tied up by
> these failures.

The crisis required intervention because allowing events to pursue
their natural course would retard the economic growth of McAshan's
bank, city, and state.[17]

Coming to the conclusion that his bank must chip in to save weak
banks was not easy for S. M. McAshan. He was a hard-nosed, professional banker, not an entrepreneur involved in banks. For years he had
been appalled by banking practices at places like Public National and
Houston National because they violated his own deeply felt professional ethics. Now it galled him to dip into his bank's carefully nur-
tured coffers to rescue jazz banks. Yet McAshan was an intelligent
man. He realized the validity of the arguments in favor of a cooperative
rescue, particularly the argument that the image and reputation of all
banks and bankers would suffer if any bank failed in his city. His loyalty to his profession made him sensitive to the need to maintain a
good image in the public mind, but so too did the profit motive. He
realized that image and reputation were important in attracting customers. Bank buildings, bank officers, and bank directors all needed to
project the right image. It was this consciousness that prompted him

to write: "Also, of course, sound public policy forbade this bank, which is perhaps as able to take a cuffing as any, coolly standing aloof and refusing to help when others less able were stripping themselves to do so. To have done this would have resulted in our alienating many friends when the facts became known, as they would have in due time." [18]

R. M. Farrar, who shared McAshan's distaste for jazz bankers, had another reason for cooperating in the bailout of Houston National and Public National. He had long worked with Sterling to improve the ship channel and was loath to see the governor suffer the "personal and political consequences" of his bank's failure. The owners and managers of these banks were part of Houston's elite. While they often quarreled among themselves, they usually presented a united front to the outside world. Just as McAshan was reluctant to see the image of bankers besmirched, Farrar was reluctant to see the image of a city father damaged. [19]

Roy Montgomery Farrar
1870–1943

Roy Montgomery Farrar, remembered by his long-term employee Earl Dreyling as "a hardboiled professional banker," was president of Union National from 1924 until his death in 1943. Farrar was born in Saint Louis, Missouri and moved to Houston in 1885 to work in the lumber business. He became Jesse Jones's partner in that business in 1902. In 1912 he formed Farrar Lumber Company, which sold lumber at retail throughout Texas. He continued to manage Farrar Lumber until his death and is a good example of a lumberman who successfully converted to banking.

In 1915, at the urging of Jesse Jones, Farrar became president of the struggling National Bank of Commerce and remained in that office until 1921. He saw NBC through the boom-bust cycle of the World War I years and then left after a disagreement with Jones, the bank's principal stockholder.

Jones and Farrar were both independent, self-confident, and determined men. They gave a great deal of their time to the development of the ship channel and the port of Houston. One of the long-running controversies associated with the port was the location of the turning basin and the end of deep water. Jones was an advocate of dredging the channel to the foot of Main Street. Farrar considered that impractical and favored ending the channel downstream. In 1920 the two men disagreed in public over a bond issue which was intended to buy land for a downstream port terminal. The voters sided with Jones, but in the long run Farrar's views prevailed. Dredging all the way to Main Street proved prohibitively expensive, and as the city grew, it moved downstream toward the head of deep water. The short-run effects of the controversy were that Farrar and a few others resigned as directors and offices of NBC and sold their stock to Jones.

In 1924, Farrar became first a director and subsequently the president of Union National Bank, a bank whose major owners included the descendents of W. T. Carter, who had himself quarreled with Jesse Jones during World War I. Jones and Farrar retained a grudging respect for each other, but the distrust of Jones held by those at Union Bank made the bank bailout of 1931 more difficult.

In December, 1931, when Jones wrote Farrar about perhaps helping out still another local bank, Farrar responded:

> I would like to suggest that you get a pair of cheap cutters and cut that telephone wire.
>
> Do not constitute yourself a guardian or a Santa Claus for the community—none of us are in any way qualified to look after anything or anybody beyond our own affairs, and not so well for that, even.
>
> If you are unconvinced, I refer to the files of your own newspaper for conclusive evidence as to the one, and your own Note and Asset files as to the other.
>
> And the same observations apply to all the rest of us, bud, and put that in your pipe and smoke it.

Evidently Jones did not take offense at Farrar's bluntness and was not long troubled by their disagreements. At Farrar's death he wrote: "Few men have been more intimately and pleasantly associated for a longer period of time than Roy Farrar and myself." Jones noted, "I have never known a man to work harder and more hours, and who was more determined to make a success of his life." He went on to call Farrar his friend and a selfless public servant.

Of all those who worked with Farrar, James J. Clayton probably had the best insight into his character. In 1972 he recalled: "I worked for Mr. Farrar for almost twenty years. I won't be a Pollyanna and say these were happy years. Mr. Farrar was not that kind of man. He was stubborn, direct, blunt, candid, exacting, and demanding." Still, Clayton called Farrar "the professional banker without peer."

Farrar really came into his own in the 1930s. When he took over Union in 1924, the bank had some bad loans, and because of that experience and his own cautious nature Farrar failed to take full advantage of the healthy economy of the twenties. In the 1930s, however, the safety and reliability of Union attracted many new customers to the bank. Except for Farrar, none of the bank's employees suffered substantial salary cuts during the Depression, and depositors could get their money any time they wanted. In fact, Farrar even gave out money to his depositors during the bank holiday of 1933. He may have been unpleasant at times, but he certainly "made his depositors and his employees and his stockholders secure."

One reason his stockholders and fellow directors liked Farrar was that he applied the same bluntness and candor to himself that he did to others, and he sacrificed his personal gain for the good of the bank. When he was first hired as president, the board wanted to pay him $25,000 a year, but Farrar would accept only $20,000 a year because of the bank's problem loans. During the early years of the Depression he had his salary lowered to $13,500 a year. In 1935 the bank's executive committee met without Farrar and voted to raise his salary back up to $20,000. He refused to accept compensation in excess of $18,000 even though the bank was making record profits. It is no wonder that, when Farrar told the board in 1941 that he was getting old and that they should elect a younger man president, they ignored his advice.

This apostle of sound, conservative banking, a man who read history in his spare time, who chewed tobacco while closely examining the figures that told him how his bank was doing, earned the respect if not the goodwill of all those around him. As the writer of one of his obituaries put it, "There was no hypocrisy in his makeup."

Sources: R. M. Farrar to Jesse Jones, December 17, 1931, Jones Papers; NBC, *Directors' Minutes* 5 (October 19, 1943): 172; Interview with James J. Clayton by William Allison; Interview with Earl V. Dreyling by Allison, TCB Archives, UNB, *Directors' Minutes* 2 (January 8, 1935): 7; 3 (January 14, 1941): 5–6; 3 (August 23, 1943): 88–91; Sibley, *The Port of Houston*, 154–55; Timmons, *Jones*, 112–14.

Besides Farrar and McAshan those drawn to the meetings by the seriousness of the crisis and the entreaties of Jesse Jones included representatives of the major banks, trust companies, utility companies, and major corporations. Other individuals attending the meetings on Sunday and Monday were Frank Andrews, a director of Union National and a prominent lawyer and political power broker; W. L. Clayton of Anderson, Clayton; W. S. Farish of Humble Oil; H. C. Weiss of Humble Oil; J. T. Scott of First National; C. M. Malone of Guardian Trust; and B. D. Harris, who had returned to Houston to assume the active direction of Second National Bank. Various directors of the banks and the leading figures of the utility companies also wandered in and out of the meetings. It is probable that only Jones or Captain Baker could have assured the attendance of such a wide range of busi-

ness leaders. Captain Baker, however, was on the East Coast as the crisis mounted, and it fell to Jones to take the lead.

The burden of having his bank absorb Public National also fell on
Jones. He summed up his reasons for rescuing Public National and
Houston National when he told his board of directors at NBC:

> Contributing to the Public National guaranty fund and subscribing to
> the Sterling loan were patriotic acts, but good business as well. In all
> probability no greater crisis will ever exist in the social and economic life
> of Houston than existed at that time. Naturally, officers of the banks were
> reluctant and hesitant about doing the thing that meant a direct loss to
> their several institutions but it was the consensus of opinion arrived at
> after great deliberation, that whatever the cost to prevent disaster, it
> would be cheaper than not to prevent it.[20]

The details needed to implement Jones's general plan for a guaranty fund and the acquisition of the two weak banks by stronger
groups were the source of much of this "great deliberation." On Sunday the group called together by Jones discussed several alternatives
and determined the probable amount of loan losses in each bank was
determined. Governor Sterling had about $1.2 million in problem
loans at Houston National, and the Moody-Seagraves interests had
over $800,000 in problem loans at Public National. On Monday the
group concluded that Public National was too weak to reopen and
would have to be acquired by another, stronger bank. McAshan considered merging Houston National with South Texas Commercial
National, but eventually the Joseph Meyer family, which had long
owned an interest in Houston National, agreed to purchase the bank if
Sterling's loans were assumed by those represented at the meeting.[21]

Assuming the Sterling debt to Houston National presented another difficult problem, but eventually the Humble Oil Company, represented by Farish and Weiss, offered to purchase from Sterling the
Houston Oil Terminal Company for $405,000. Sterling then applied
that amount to his debt. The other $800,000 was taken out of Hous-
ton National with a fund accumulated as follows:

Union National Bank	$100,000
Union National Bank (trustee)	25,000
Guardian Trust Company	50,000
First National Bank	200,000
Second National Bank	100,000
South Texas Commercial National	100,000
State National Bank	30,000
Houston Land and Trust Co.	50,000
San Jacinto Trust Co.	10,000

City Bank and Trust Co.	8,000
Federal Trust Co.	7,000
National Bank of Commerce	100,000
Joseph F. Meyer, Jr.	20,000
Total	$800,000

Cooperation among all of these groups was aided by the interlocked nature of the boards of directors of the banks and trust companies. Guardian Trust was owned by the Baker family and others connected with STCNB, and Houston Land and Trust was owned by the Rice family and others connected with Union Bank or First National. San Jacinto Trust, City Bank and Trust, and Federal Trust were tied to Jesse Jones and the National Bank of Commerce. Humble's officers sat on the boards of most of the banks. The amount contributed was a roughly equal percentage of the total assets of the various banks. Each gave 7 to 10 percent.[22]

Taking care of Public National was more difficult. Part of the problem was that neither Farrar nor McAshan completely trusted Jones. When Jones offered to have his bank assume the burden of acquiring Public National, his rivals became suspicious. It took a telephone call from Jones to Captain Baker in Massachusetts at two o'clock in the morning and Baker's assurances to persuade McAshan to go along with Jones's wishes. In the end NBC was protected against loss by a fund of $1,175,000 and some $1,400,000 was deposited in NBC by the other banks to make sure that a run on the bank would not drain its cash. Contributors to the guaranty fund were as follows:

First National Bank	$ 150,000
STCNB	125,000
Union National Bank	125,000
Second National Bank	125,000
National Bank of Commerce	125,000
Guardian Trust Co.	50,000
Houston Land and Trust Co.	50,000
State National Bank	25,000
Houston Lighting and Power	125,000
United Gas Public Service	175,000
Anderson, Clayton and Co.	25,000
San Jacinto Trust, City Bank and Trust, and Federal Trust Co.	25,000
Anonymous	50,000
Total	$1,175,000

Those making deposits at NBC were:

First National Bank	$ 350,000
STCNB	300,000
Second National Bank	275,000
Union National Bank	275,000
State National Bank	100,000
Guardian Trust Co.	100,000
Total	$1,400,000

The group hoped in vain that Southern Pacific Railroad would give $200,000. In fact, at the last minute, Jones had to persuade McAshan, Farrar, and a few others to contribute $25,000 each in addition to their previous commitments to make up the $200,000 counted on from Southern Pacific. As McAshan put it later: "Malone and I both expected to raise a little at the last minute if we were compelled to do so in getting up the amount of guaranty necessary, both of us knowing Jones so well that we knew, when all thought the trade was closed, he would begin to ask for a little additional protection, just as he did." [23]

On Tuesday, October 27, 1931, the local newspapers announced the new management of Houston National and the acquisition of Public National by NBC. At Houston National and NBC the day was relatively calm. Customers seemed reassured of the safety of their deposits. Gradually word of the bank rescue spread in Houston, but few realized just how harrowing an experience it had been for those immediately involved in the crisis. [24]

As the banking crisis of 1931 receded in memory, Gainer Jones and the other officers of National Bank of Commerce busily tried to make a profit on Public National's old loans. When possible they carried the creditor over until the loan could be repaid, or they assumed all collateral if they judged that the creditor could not repay. When the creditor could not repay and the collateral was worthless, the bank wrote off the loan and charged it to the guaranty fund. Eventually all the loans were settled, and some of the guaranty fund was repaid to its contributors. This money was never repaid fast enough to suit R. M. Farrar, and the ink was hardly dry on the 1931 agreement before he was writing Jesse Jones asking for some of his money back. Eventually he got back the $25,000 extra that Jones had persuaded his bank to chip in at the last moment, but no more. As one of Farrar's employees put it:

> Afterward, it became Mr. Farrar's belief that in its rescue of the small bank the National Bank of Commerce actually made a profit. This very

well may have been true. But it was also true that Jesse Jones was gambling. He might have made a loss instead of a profit. The defect in Mr. Farrar's logic was that he could have had the deal himself, but turned it down. Just the same, for years afterward, Mr. Farrar would from time to time think about the $200,000 he put into the rescue fund in 1931 and then he would cuss and raise hell. I heard him on the subject many times.[25]

Memories of the Bank Salvage Effort

Gainer B. Jones came to the National Bank of Commerce from Public National and during the 1930s was in charge of collecting Public National's loans for the bank. He was born in Bryan, Texas, and was a lawyer and West Point graduate. He spent five years in the army during World War II. After the war he worked in the bank's trust and commercial-lending departments and as an organizer of suburban banks for NBC. In 1967 he retired from Texas Commerce as a senior vice-president.

Gainer B. Jones
1901–81

Perhaps the most eventful days of Gainer Jones's long career were Monday and Tuesday, October 26 and 27, 1931. During those two days, a plan was worked out to save Public National, and the bank merged with NBC. That Monday night as Gainer Jones waited at Public National, G. Norman Brown and other young employees of NBC waited in the lobby of the Gulf Building. They played cards, exchanged stories, and dozed. Finally, in Brown's words:

> At 3:00 A.M. the meeting broke up. Instantly awake I glanced out in the bank lobby where Mr. Robert Doherty, the bank's vice-president, stood beckoning to me with a slightly wiggled finger. To me this gesture was as emphatic as a drill sergeant's commands augmented by a bullhorn.
>
> "Tell 'em to report here at 8 o'clock," he snapped.
>
> "In the morning, Mr. Doherty?" I asked querulously, my voice resembling Alvin, the chipmunk.
>
> "Now! It *is* morning." And with that he left me standing there.
>
> Being too young for cardiac arrest, I was forced into taking a calculated risk. I took "em" to mean my counterparts at the Public. I charged out on silent deserted Main Street with my message of hope and rejuvenation. As expected, I found a groggy group of clerks and

bookkeepers in various stages of consciousness. My assignment completed, I hurried back to the scene of the historic event.

Along with bookkeepers and clerks, Gainer Jones also waited at Public National, and in a 1972 interview with William Allison, Jones left the following vivid recollection of the rescue and its aftermath:

> As the hours passed there we were—directors and staff—sitting in the Public National Bank and wondering if we would be rescued. At about 3 A.M. on Tuesday, October 27, a contract for Public National's merger into the National Bank of Commerce was brought in and was signed by the directors and officers. Then came a take-over crew from the Commerce Bank, and Public National's assets and cash and staff moved up Main Street two blocks or so to the Commerce Bank. Somebody up there suggested I go home and freshen up, because we had a busy day ahead of us.
>
> So I went home. As I approached the apartment where my wife and I lived, I saw the lights were on. I had been through so many disasters in recent days that these lights—it was 5 o'clock in the morning—looked to me like another alarm signal. To my relief I discovered that my father was up and shaving. I had forgotten that he was visiting us. As a life-long farmer, he always got up at 5 o'clock to start his day.
>
> It was my good fortune that I had some knowledge of the legal complexities in the Public National's bad loans. Collecting those loans became my job that day at the Commerce Bank and it continued as one of my responsibilities through the eight years that followed.

SOURCES: Officers' and Directors' Files, TCB Archives; Interview with Gainer B. Jones by William Allison, TCB Archives; *Houston Chronicle*, December 20, 1981; Recollections of G. Norman Brown, August 1985, TCB Archives.

While Gainer Jones and the other officers at NBC tried to recover as much as possible on Public National's loans, Jesse Jones busied himself reassuring the bank's major corporate customers and correspondent banks that his bank would withstand the strain of absorbing Public National. He wrote dozens of letters to acquaintances at Chase National Bank, National City Bank of New York, Mellon Bank, Continental Illinois, the Texas Company, Freeport Sulfur, and many smaller concerns. By doing so, he demonstrated that his role at National Bank of Commerce extended well beyond the city limits of Houston. Within the city his personal reputation and the bank's good record helped retain depositors' confidence. Outside the city he, much more than the institution, ensured corporate confidence in his bank.[26]

Jesse Jones's role in organizing collective action to prevent the failure of several Houston banks foreshadowed his subsequent actions as head of the Reconstruction Finance Corporation. His approach in Houston, which he characterized as "stopping the fire before it starts," was quite similar to the approach he took to broader problems in Washington. By identifying intrinsically strong concerns and then mobilizing resources to assist them, Jones shepherded vital economic institutions through temporary crises in the interest of the health of the entire economy. He did not envision permanent assistance to ailing companies, but rather short-term credit which would bolster those severely threatened by the unprecedented conditions caused by the Great Depression. His was a policy predicated on continued growth of private enterprise, not inevitable retrenchment or perpetual government intervention. The bank crisis in Houston illustrated several problems which would continue to hamper the efforts of Jones at the RFC. A severe crisis was required before most private businessmen would accept collective action. Even during a crisis, however, the calculation of costs and benefits of collective actions to a particular firm were inevitably part of the decision-making process. Calls to allow the economy to decline to its natural level and to abandon weak institutions were still heard. Jones sought to circumvent such problems by building a consensus that in the long run the self-interest of all involved would be served by actions which fostered the return of economic growth. In this endeavor, Jones's standing as one of the leaders of the Houston business community proved crucial in building support for the bank rescue, just as his standing as the businessman's representative in the New Deal proved crucial in building support for the RFC.[27]

With the close of 1931, Houston banks began to recover from the crisis of that year. While much of the rest of the country suffered banking problems during 1932 and 1933, Houstonians escaped serious difficulties. The city's economy rebounded from the Depression more quickly and the banking situation was shored up by the rapid departure of the weaker banks after 1929. Indeed, the number of Houston banks remained almost constant from 1932 to 1945. With competitive pressures diminished and the economy improving, as early as 1935 most Houston banks were making profits equal to those of 1929.[28]

Such a rapid return to profitability did not mean that the crisis of 1931 and the Great Depression were without impact upon Houston's banks. Three developments of enduring importance emerged from the 1929–33 era. First, the banking crisis and the Great Depression sent a shock wave through the local economy which changed its nature by helping displace cotton as the dominant force in the Houston economy. Second, this same shock wave encouraged the growth of large banks at the expense of smaller banks. Weaker banks either liquidated voluntarily or, like Marine Bank and Public National, were acquired by larger banks. The public, too, came to value safety and stability over easy credit and a broad range of financial services. Such safety and security were available only at large, long-established banks. Third, the Depression and the nationwide bank problems encouraged the federal government to broaden its role in banking. Federal regulation and federal agencies would also foster security over growth and innovation in banking. The banking crisis and the early years of the Depression acted as a midwife, easing the birth of what is now considered traditional Houston banking by facilitating the rise of oil, by enlarging the market share of the major banks, and by encouraging security-motivated regulation.

CHAPTER 6

King Cotton and Its Banks Dethroned, 1929–45

Between 1929 and 1945 oil and related industries replaced cotton as the driving force in the Houston economy and in Houston banks. Part of the reason for this reversal was the deterioration of the cotton trade. In the early 1930s the glut in the domestic cotton market, the increase in foreign growers of cotton, and the collapse of the export market sent shock waves through the cotton industry. These shock waves were eased for the major American growers of cotton by federal farm policy, which restricted the acreage planted to cotton and supported its price. Cotton traders, however, were hurt even further by federal regulations which cut down the volume of cotton grown domestically and made the American price of cotton uncompetitive on the world market. Houston banks and much of the Houston economy had long been geared to the cotton-trading business. The decline of the cotton traders, happening as it did at the same time as a halt in real estate construction, could have proved devastating to Houston, but it did not, in large part because oil was ready to take the place of cotton. The economic influence of oil in the region had grown steadily after 1901 with the expansion of oil production, the manufacture of oil-industry tools, and, finally, the construction of a large refining complex along the Houston Ship Channel in the 1920s. Thus by the 1930s, the regional oil industry had developed enough to cushion the economic impact of cotton's decline. This cushion and the development of a more varied industrial base left Houston in 1945 well positioned to benefit from the postwar boom.[1]

This transformation of the Houston economy created both problems and opportunities for Houston banks. Their continued growth demanded adjustment. Banks such as South Texas Commercial National with the strongest and oldest ties to the cotton trade faced particularly difficult transitions; those such as the National Bank of Commerce with stronger ties to the emerging oil-related industries and the ship channel manufacturers were in an excellent position to prosper in the years after 1929. The transition from a cotton-based to an oil- and manufacturing-based banking system thus shaped the competitive position of individual banks. It also brought broad changes in the lending procedures at the region's banks and created pressure to expand the size of the major banks.

Such changes did not become evident until after a period of discontinuity stemming from the Great Depression. For the local economy the period of severe disruption was relatively brief. As early as 1933, while most of the American economy continued to stagnate, the Houston economy began to rebound. As Table 6.1 shows, economic improvement increased deposits at the major banks to the levels of 1929.

Net profits also bounced back. In 1933, STCNB, for example, made $421,000 in net earnings, which was a slight improvement over its previous record earnings of 1929. By the end of 1933, Houston had returned to its long historical pattern of sustained economic growth. Indeed, as Table 6.1 shows, the years after 1933 witnessed a steady growth in bank deposits, reflecting the return to health of the economy.[2]

Although deposits in the major Houston banks had returned to normal, the operations of these banks and the overall market structure of Houston's banking industry had been altered by the changes brought by the bank crisis of the early 1930s. Some of the jazz banks which had thrived in the heated economy of the 1920s failed to survive the difficulties of the Great Depression. Federal banking regulation coupled with the psychological effects of the Great Depression encouraged the expansion of national banks over state banks and large banks over small banks, reversing the trend of the 1920s toward greater competition among a growing number of banks.[3]

It is important to realize, then, that the combined effects of changing regulation and the trauma of the Depression disrupted traditional banking practices in Houston. By 1935 the period of sharp discontinuity in the growth of the economy and in banking practice was over. But the stage was set for a more long-lasting change: the decline of the cotton trade and its importance to Houston banks. Bankers had already made what many probably considered a temporary move out of the cotton business. Concern for stability had increased their desire for safe loans. Cotton companies, which had been the backbone of the loan business at South Texas Commercial National, were no longer as safe as they once were, and because of the climate of the times, banks were unwilling to take risks to revive the cotton trade. Instead, in the mid-1930s they waited for the cotton merchants to revive themselves.

Table 6.1 Growth of Deposits in Houston Banks, 1929–46

End of Year	First National	STCNB	Union	Second National	NBC
1929	$ 35,060,166	$ 26,329,977	$15,673,832	$ 16,790,950	$ 12,057,078
1930	38,436,798	30,664,452	14,894,142	17,380,967	13,659,049 [a]
1931	35,426,514	25,548,446	13,332,730	17,338,343	20,252,646 [b]
1932	33,771,044	25,160,250	14,725,598	20,776,964	19,308,998
1933	33,133,146	32,445,745	19,377,123	22,024,301	21,342,102
1934	42,572,158	38,874,995	22,090,051	24,807,899	27,874,932
1935	46,053,641	42,106,361	23,412,668	25,156,541	30,144,392
1936	50,270,111	47,135,492	25,707,698	30,248,844	38,026,742
1937	49,558,110	41,694,710	27,433,524	26,750,290	27,499,689
1938	52,893,582	46,935,385	31,789,623	30,524,734	45,110,641
1939	60,348,516	50,292,893	34,227,048	32,738,925	55,795,156
1940	67,733,841	57,178,536	36,158,743	35,867,129	61,425,738
1941	76,827,338	54,845,991	39,206,605	42,553,181	77,620,960
1942	92,948,145	85,674,503	46,188,078	56,424,951	110,157,942
1943	115,717,826	85,138,712	54,491,390	68,552,667	131,602,912
1944	138,536,797	99,266,840	61,440,404	104,263,090 [c]	156,111,731
1945	178,755,474	122,586,937	76,572,019	164,797,525 [d]	179,071,670
1946	177,967,520 [e]	100,926,967	61,592,758	144,054,702	162,706,359

SOURCE: Statements of Condition, TCB Archives.
[a] Merged with Marine National Bank.
[b] Merged with Public National Bank.
[c] Merged with San Jacinto National Bank.
[d] Merged with Guardian Trust Co.
[e] Merged with State National Bank.

Before the Great Depression, Houston's banks had long thrived by financing the region's growing cotton trade. The development of railroads; a deepened and widened ship channel; large, efficient cotton trading companies; improved warehousing and compressing techniques; and the rise of new patterns of trade between Houston and foreign cotton mills had made the city the number-one cotton exporter in the United States by 1930. While even the largest Houston banks could not supply enough capital for major cotton-trading firms active in the region, they profited by providing banking services, holding deposits, and lending for the purchase of cotton.

The Great Depression jolted Houston's cotton trade out of traditional patterns. Starting in 1929 and continuing at a quickened pace after 1933, the export of American cotton to Europe went into a steep

**Table 6.2   Number of Cotton Bales
Exported from Houston, 1919–48**

Year	Bales	Year	Bales
1919	69,839	1934	1,386,611
1920	466,185	1935	1,607,657
1921	478,141	1936	953,943
1922	719,942	1937	1,195,606
1923	1,065,612	1938	939,966
1924	1,821,828	1939	1,716,483
1925	1,796,671	1940	333,211
1926	2,551,439	1941	48,765
1927	1,968,969	1942	0
1928	2,299,513	1943	0
1929	1,876,413	1944	475,838
1930	2,183,028	1945	850,872
1931	2,655,094	1946	834,401
1932	2,854,506	1947	678,111
1933	2,340,630	1948	756,969

SOURCES: S. Deane Wasson, *Fifty Years a Cotton Market: Houston Cotton Exchange and Board of Trade Brochure,* 1924, 50; Jacobs and Golding, *Houston and Cotton: Commemorating Seventy-five Years of Leadership and Progress as a Cotton Market,* 75.

decline, and foreign production of cotton surged. According to Lamar Fleming, of Anderson, Clayton: "Foreign production increased from 9,602,000 bales in 1931/32 to 18,354,000 bales in 1936/37." As the world consumed more foreign cotton, "Exports of American cotton declined from 8,754,000 bales in 1931/32 to 4,816,000 bales in 1934/35 and 3,353,000 bales in 1938/39." In 1929 the Smoot-Hawley Tariff raised duties on imports into the United States, thereby cutting imports and reducing the ability of European countries to pay for American cotton. At the same time, the world price of most other crops began to drop much more sharply than cotton. Farmers in Brazil, Argentina, and other countries began switching to cotton. They were able to undercut the American price because between 1929 and 1934 federal policies and agencies forced up the price of American cotton and reduced the acreage planted. As a result, much less cotton moved out of the port of Houston to foreign markets. Table 6.2 gives dramatic evidence of this reduction in the cotton trade.[4]

Tables 6.2 and 6.3 also suggest the reason for the government farm policy that led to acreage reduction and price supports. In the

1920s and early 1930s, in an attempt to combat falling prices, Texas cotton farmers planted more cotton. The resulting glut was disastrous for cotton farmers, but less damaging to the cotton dealers and their Houston bankers. The planting of more cotton depressed the price of cotton even further and increased the amount to be shipped. Lower prices and higher volume helped the American cotton merchants keep their competitive advantage. Higher volume meant that, while the cotton dealers were paying less per pound, they were buying enough extra pounds to retain a near constant demand for loans at Houston banks. Through 1931 the lending level at Houston's major banks remained near the average figure for the late 1920s. After that, however, lending declined slowly until 1934, at which point it declined precipitously and remained low for a decade. This sharp decline around

Table 6.3   Bales of Cotton and Tons of Cottonseed Produced in Texas, 1920–40

Year	Number of Bales	Tons of Cottonseed
1920	4,345,000	1,934,000
1921	2,198,000	1,978,000
1922	3,222,000	1,433,000
1923	4,340,000	1,931,000
1924	4,949,000	2,201,000
1925	4,163,000	1,851,000
1926	5,628,000	2,505,000
1927	4,352,000	1,938,000
1928	5,105,000	2,274,000
1929	3,940,000	1,755,000
1930	4,037,000	1,798,000
1931	5,300,000	2,370,000
1932	4,500,000	2,006,000
1933	4,428,000	1,973,000
1934	2,401,000	1,069,000
1935	2,956,000	1,316,000
1936	2,933,000	1,306,000
1937	5,154,000	2,294,000
1938	3,086,000	1,373,000
1939	2,846,000	1,183,000
1940	3,234,000	1,318,000

SOURCE: Michael T. Kingston (ed.), *The Texas Almanac and State Industrial Guide, 1984–1985*, 467.

1934 was linked to New Deal farm programs, including the plowing up of already planted cotton in 1933 and commodity credit corporation loans. The Commodity Credit Corporation, which was overseen by Jesse Jones and the RFC, lent to farmers with cotton or other major commodities held in storage as collateral. These commodities were consistently valued above the market price. To be eligible farmers were also required to take a portion of their land out of production. Begun in October, 1933, CCC loans by 1934 significantly reduced cotton acreage and slightly increased the price of cotton by removing some of the commodity from the market. Also in 1934 Congress passed the Bankhead Cotton Control Act, which made crop reduction compulsory. Crop reduction and CCC loans forced the price of cotton up from a low point of around 5 cents a pound, but, as Lamar Fleming pointed out, it cost the American cotton trader high volume and a competitive price. The loss of that advantage together with increases in foreign production explain the waning of cotton exporting and cotton lending.[5]

The decline of cotton most hurt those Houston bankers which traditionally had lent large sums of money with limited risk to move the crop through the city. Banks like South Texas Commercial National had a few problems with cotton loans in the early 1920s, but by and large cotton brought exceptional profits and few losses.[6] These few isolated troubles in the 1920s could not have prepared STCNB for the far more serious problems brought by the decline in the region's cotton trade in the early 1930s. Table 6.3 depicts the long-term decline in cotton production in Texas that underlay the problems facing many Houston banks in the 1930s. With the exception of 1937, production of ginned cotton and cottonseed from 1932 to 1940 was far below the average of 1920 to 1931. Not until the period 1949 to 1965, when new hybrid seed and improved techniques increased the yield per acre, would the 1920s average production levels be equaled. Cotton was clearly in decline in Texas in the 1930s.[7]

In response to the serious problems brought by the withering of the cotton trade, South Texas Commercial National reprinted in 1933 the report drafted by its committee on the cotton trade in 1923 and renewed its previous pledge to stay with established customers among the major cotton traders. But by 1935 the bank had begun to reduce its cotton lending. Most cotton loans were of 90 day duration or less. Some of these were customarily rolled over for as long as the borrower desired. This short-term duration allowed South Texas Commercial National, most of whose loans were in cotton, to reduce total loans by $8 million, or almost 40 percent, from December, 1930, to December,

1931. From the end of 1934 to the end of 1935 the bank again reduced loans by 40 percent. Other banks followed a similar strategy, shifting from cotton to other investments.

Houston bankers had several options for the money that once went to finance the cotton trade. One of their options, however, was not real estate, which in the 1920s had added significant diversity to their loan portfolios. Houston was overbuilt by 1929, and real estate construction would not return to the 1920s level until after 1945. Indeed, during the decade of the 1930s, only one building of over 100,000 square feet was erected in Houston's central business district (see Table 8.1). Construction of homes and businesses outside the central business district also declined dramatically. Thus Houston banks were unable to expand or even retain their old level of lending in real estate when faced with the decline of the cotton lending.

Instead of seeking a new area to lend funds, STCNB and Union invested heavily in government securities. Since the cost of their money diminished as interest rates declined, their profit margin remained relatively high with such investments. In the first six months of 1935 more than 80 percent of STCNB's $812,000 in undivided profits came from the sale of U.S. Treasury Bonds and Treasury Notes. Previously, most of the bank's profit had come from payments on loans. President S. M. McAshan described this change at South Texas Commercial National in a letter of September 16, 1936, to Chairman James A. Baker. McAshan wrote:

> We formerly did a large loan business, among other things upon cotton and other commodities and real estate. We had our little company, which is now no more. In those days our deposit and loan business went hand in hand; now our business is largely one of obtaining free and low-cost deposits, charging for services where balances do not compensate, and investment and trading in securities, principally of the United States Government.

What was true at South Texas Commercial National was also true at other Houston banks, including Union National Bank. Instead of cotton loans or real estate loans, government securities became the major source of investment and profit at these banks.[8]

Since U.S. securities could easily be converted to cash, they had the added advantage of making the bank impervious to depositors' rapid withdrawal of their money. For most years in the 1930s, STCNB was near 100 percent liquid. That is, it had enough cash and government securities to cover the withdrawal of almost all its depositors. Knowing this, few depositors ever asked for their money. In this way

End of Year	Union	STCNB	NBC	First National	City National*
1930					
Loans	4,754,665	19,393,229	7,085,271	23,285,242	2,917,546
% deposits	31.9	63.2	51.9	60.6	82.1
1931					
Loans	4,289,121	11,850,526	9,441,501	21,832,400	2,128,383
% deposits	32.1	46.3	46.6	61.6	73.8
1932					
Loans	4,526,946	8,503,997	8,993,676	17,117,449	1,875,758
% deposits	30.1	33.8	46.3	50.7	63.1
1933					
Loans	3,160,318	7,320,083	7,940,852	12,452,960	1,589,622
% deposits	16.3	22.3	37.2	37.6	53.8
1934					
Loans	2,766,473	8,963,899	8,456,340	12,543,957	1,796,630
% deposits	12.5	23.1	30.3	29.5	34.8
1935					
Loans	2,744,496	5,490,838	6,257,003	10,996,767	2,580,272
% deposits	11.7	13.0	20.3	23.9	29.9
1936					
Loans	3,461,881	4,563,413	9,558,478	13,536,897	2,726,669
% deposits	13.5	9.7	25.1	26.9	24.1
1937					
Loans	3,420,901	5,274,539	9,724,677	13,204,221	3,053,318
% deposits	12.5	12.7	25.9	26.6	25.2
1938					
Loans	3,081,312	5,041,099	9,296,557	13,491,302	3,488,458
% deposits	9.7	10.7	20.6	25.5	25.9
1939					
Loans	2,980,732	6,387,088	10,501,910	17,663,948	3,845,270
% deposits	8.7	12.7	18.8	29.3	20.3
1940					
Loans	2,940,132	5,427,784	9,958,989	19,357,030	4,051,129
% deposits	8.1	9.5	16.2	28.6	15.9
1941					
Loans	3,710,535	7,349,609	13,325,151	24,557,832	5,299,796
% deposits	9.5	13.4	17.1	32.0	17.5
1942					
Loans	3,066,668	5,478,261	11,265,909	15,964,573	5,584,580
% deposits	6.6	6.4	10.2	17.0	13.5

Table 6.4   Relationship of Loans to Deposits in Houston Banks, 1930–45

End of Year	Union	STCNB	NBC	First National	City National*
Table 6.4			*(continued)*		
1943					
Loans	2,549,193	6,668,195	9,696,315	13,922,797	6,116,541
% deposits	4.7	7.8	7.4	12.0	10.0
1944					
Loans	3,242,606	6,274,008	13,515,205	17,223,398	9,565,659
% deposits	5.3	6.3	8.7	12.4	11.4
1945					
Loans	3,943,681	13,012,763	19,955,767	30,579,079	18,227,925
% deposits	5.2	10.6	11.1	17.2	16.2

SOURCE: Statements of Condition, TCB Archives.
* City Bank and Trust until 1934.

the trauma of the Great Depression and the cotton problems worked together to move STCNB out of the business of making loans. Table 6.4 indicates the magnitude of this shift. Loans dipped below 10 percent of deposits at the close of 1936. That compares with figures of around 60 percent of deposits in the 1920s (see Table 4.3). Although most of the loans that STCNB still made in the mid-1930s were probably cotton loans, in comparison to the previous decade, the cotton business at STCNB had almost vanished.[9]

After the mid-1930s, cotton lending never again approached the dominance it had enjoyed at banks such as South Texas Commercial. Some of the largest cotton firms active in Houston, such as Dorrance and Company, experienced severe financial difficulties and never returned to prominence. Others, notably Anderson, Clayton, moved outside the domestic cotton business, becoming an international cotton company and eventually a diversified food-products company. The second level of involvement by the major Houston banks in cotton, the financing of the cotton trade through loans to banks in the cotton-growing regions, also diminished after the mid-1930s as cotton production steadily moved westward, away from the regions in central Texas with close traditional correspondent ties to Houston banks. Government lending programs for farmers also reduced this business. The cotton trade in Texas rebounded after 1945, but it never again regained its previous position of dominance in the major Houston banks or in the regional economy of Houston.[10]

Like Union National and South Texas Commercial National, most other Houston banks reduced lending and purchased government securities in increased amounts during the mid-1930s and then again during World War II. They continued to make only a limited number of blue-chip cotton loans and almost no real estate loans. The fact that National Bank of Commerce, First National Bank, and a few other large Houston banks, however, also began making loans for oil production and for oil-related manufacturing, partly explains their higher lending level shown in Table 6.4.[11]

By the time the cotton trade declined, the petroleum industry was ready to move to center stage. Before 1930, oil development on the coastal plain of Texas and Louisiana created great wealth, fostered the construction of an extensive pipeline system, and hastened the construction of giant oil refineries which grew into the largest manufacturing establishments in the region. Yet before the 1930s, oil was of surprisingly limited importance in the business of regional banks. To understand why this was so requires a brief examination of the changing financial situations of two quite different segments of the oil industry: the major, vertically integrated companies with operations on the Gulf Coast and the smaller, independent producers who remained vitally important in the discovery of oil reserves. From the perspective of Houston banks, the majors generally were too big; the independents, too risky.

Size, not familiarity with Houston bankers, was clearly the reason major oil companies seldom borrowed from the city's banks. The companies which became Texaco and Gulf Oil both emerged from the Spindletop field ninety miles east of Houston, and from the first decade of the century forward, both relied heavily on administrative offices in Houston to coordinate their southwestern operations. Yet from the beginning, these two local companies had capital needs far exceeding the capacities of the largest Houston banks. Gulf's predecessor company was incorporated in 1901 with a capitalization of $15 million, at a time when the deposits of the largest bank in Houston were around $3 million. Their limited size left Houston banks more observers than participants in the growth of vertically integrated oil companies capable of surviving in competition with the industry's giant, Standard Oil of New Jersey. When, for example, both Gulf and Texaco made decisions in 1906 and 1907 to build multimillion-dollar pipelines from their major Gulf Coast refineries at Port Arthur, Texas, to the rich new oil fields of eastern Oklahoma, both went out of the region for financing. The high cost of major pipelines, tanker fleets, modern petroleum refineries, and similar investments pointed the "Texas" Company to New York City and "Gulf" Oil toward its financial roots in Pittsburgh.[12]

Of course, the major oil companies had numerous smaller local needs which flowed naturally to banks in the region. In refinery towns such as Port Arthur, Beaumont, Baytown, and Pasadena, local banks supplied services ranging from handling payrolls and clearing checks to making personal loans to local executives. In Houston, such services were performed for the large regional administrative offices of Texaco, Gulf, Humble, and other majors. Before the founding of the National Bank of Commerce, Jesse Jones helped persuade Texaco to locate an impressive new headquarters building in downtown Houston in 1908. Later, Jones was instrumental in negotiating the deal which made Gulf Oil the lead tenant in the building completed in 1929 to house the National Bank of Commerce. The two companies shared this landlord-tenant relationship for almost half a century. Texaco and Humble Oil and Refining Company had equally long-lasting and multifaceted ties with STCNB. Both the Houston banks and the major oil companies benefited from close working ties as well as from close personal ties cemented by representation on boards of directors. These ties facilitated the business of each but did not extend to the provision of credit by the local banks for the extensive capital needs of the oil companies.[13]

Independent petroleum producers, the backbone of the oil drilling and production business in the Southwest, needed capital more in line with the resources of Houston banks, but these companies generally lacked the security of operations necessary to gain financing from local banks. Indeed, before the late 1920s few banks anywhere in the nation could justify risking money in one of the least predictable of America's industries. When the price of oil rose high enough, intense drilling activity began. When a find was made, newly discovered oil was produced as rapidly as possible, since under existing law everyone with a lease above a field had an incentive to recover as much oil as possible before others drained the field. As a result prices fluctuated wildly with each major strike. This presented a bankers' nightmare of uncertainty, a situation which was captured in the reminiscences of one of the nation's pioneer energy lenders, Hugo A. Anderson, of the First National Bank of Chicago. In a speech delivered in 1954, Anderson recalled:

> My introduction in the field of oil financing began in a moderate manner with a small independent oil company, but it did not take long to build up a larger loan account with the opening of the prolific Oklahoma City field in 1929, with wells costing $150,000. Oil was bringing a price of around $1.00 a barrel at the time and I felt that even if it dropped to fifty cents, I still would be safe with my loans. I need not tell my fellow bank-

ers in this room how I felt when crude oil dropped to ten cents a barrel,
following the discovery of our nation's largest field, the East Texas Field,
in September, 1930.[14]

Whereas independent oilmen might learn to live with the romance of
the booms and busts of their industry, Anderson and his fellow bankers
could not. The Houston banks were no exception. Despite the importance of oil exploration and production to the region's economy, they
seldom lent money to independent oil companies before the 1930s.

Although local banks provided little of the financing for oil drilling, they shared indirectly in the profits from oil fields developed
around Houston. Successful drillers, landowners, and leaseholders
often invested part of their earnings in less speculative pursuits, notably bank stock and real estate. Dan A. Japhet's investment strategy
exemplified how oil money flowed to Houston's banks. A cotton merchant and wholesaler, Japhet owned land near Houston upon which a
major oil strike was made in 1921. In 1921 and 1922 he purchased
over five hundred shares in National Bank of Commerce and in 1921
became a director of the bank. As part owner and director of a local
bank, Japhet, and others like him, achieved a position of prestige in the
community. More practically, participation in the affairs of a bank
facilitated the wise management and diversification of oil profits by providing access to information on the most attractive investment opportunities within the region.[15]

Not until the late 1920s did banks become more directly involved
in financing oil production. By then Hugo Anderson and First National of Chicago had begun to establish lending procedures which
would insulate the bank from the extraordinary risks often involved in
oil exploration. Several of the major New York banks, led by Chase
National, also began to venture into this as yet uncrowded lending
area. Hedging against price changes and against the cutthroat competition among producers in the same field remained the key concern of
bankers.

Several Texas banks entered oil lending in direct response to the
opening of the giant East Texas field in 1930. This field stretched for
more than forty miles, and its output flooded an already glutted market for oil in the United States. The major companies did not control
most of the leases in this field, and hundreds of independents scrambled
to drill in the area. Fred Florence, of the Republic National Bank
of Dallas, found the opportunities presented by the opening of the
world's largest oil field too enticing to ignore. He recognized correctly
that the obvious risks of oil lending were far outweighed by the wealth

to be created from this giant pool of oil. He and other Dallas bankers began making short-term loans payable from flush production. Such loans generally were made on the basis of the carefully evaluated productive capacities of properties undisputedly owned by the borrower. By the late 1930s, Republic National and First National of Dallas had joined First National of Chicago, Chase National of New York, and several smaller banks, notably First National of Tulsa and National Bank of Commerce of Tulsa, as the most significant energy lending specialists active in the southwestern oil fields.[16]

Houston banks were slow to join the competition, in part because they were not well located to participate in the development of the East Texas oil field. Yet as oil production increased in Texas, the major Houston banks could not long ignore the most dynamic segment of the regional economy. As befitted their conservative management, several large Houston banks followed the lead of Dallas banks in seeking ways to lend money for oil production with an acceptable margin of safety.[17]

National Bank of Commerce was one of the leaders of early oil lending in Houston. As a commercial lender which prided itself on the security of its loans, NBC sought to extend its reputation into the new field of energy lending by concentrating heavily on making loans to the most successful of the Houston-based independent oilmen. Its list of oil loans in the 1930s was short and repetitious. R. E. (Bob) Smith, Claude Hamill, Pat R. Rutherford, J. S. Abercrombie, Paul Kayser, and William Keck headed the list, which would serve as a good start for a hall of fame of Texas oilmen active in this era. These individuals or their companies received the bulk of the bank's oil loans. Most of the loans were short term, ranging from 5 days to 90 days, but these commitments were routinely rolled over and expanded. Collateral generally included claims to oil from producing properties, stock in established petroleum companies, and chattel mortgages on drilling rigs or other equipment.

Almost all notes were also endorsed by one of the oil men from the above list, emphasizing an important distinction stressed by the bank. National Bank of Commerce was not in the business of lending for oil production; it was in the business of lending to individuals with sterling credit records and growing personal and business connections to the bank. That these individuals planned to use their loans in oil-related activities was indicated by the relatively high interest rate and short term of the loans, but NBC made these loans on the reputations and business sense of its gold-star list of borrowers, not on conditions in the oil industry. Thus in its earliest involvement in oil loans, the bank established a pattern which proved durable. Loans to blue-chip companies and individuals seldom involved significant long-term risks. As STCNB previously had done in the cotton trade, NBC found the best performers in the oil industry, tied them to the bank, and lent to them again and again.

In many cases, NBC originally established contact with the leading independent oilmen of the 1930s through the varied business, civic, political, and personal connections of Jesse Jones. Men like Pat Rutherford and Paul Kayser established early, strong ties to Jones, who served as a lightning rod, attracting young capitalists of promise, ambition, and energy. In addition to such personal attributes, these men succeeded in part because of the support and advice of mentors such as Jones and in part because of their ready access to credit at substantial regional financial institutions such as NBC. Once anointed as an acceptable risk by Jones and by his bank's demanding loan and discount committee, an independent oil operator could count on the bank to lend its support and expertise through times of rapid expansion or temporary crisis. Such support from a major Houston bank greatly improved an oilman's chances of long-term success. In the years after the discovery of the East Texas field, such circles of cooperation grew steadily between NBC and a growing number of oilmen of substance.[18]

By the late 1930s, the bank regularly lent Rutherford, Abercrombie, Hamill, Smith, and Kayser money on predictable terms for whatever purposes these men made their requests. But other, less familiar oilmen faced close scrutiny before obtaining oil loans from those charged with protecting the integrity of NBC. The history of a loan ultimately made in February, 1934, to a smaller drilling concern illustrates the steps the loan and discount committee deemed necessary to justify approval of a 20 day loan of $4,000. The application was accompanied by a financial statement showing "adequate and substantial balances," and it offered security for the loan in the form of a chattel mortgage on "one unencumbered complete drilling rig," as well as the assignment of a drilling contract for $18,000 payable to the drillers from an established Oklahoma-based oil company. Such security was not, however, considered sufficient protection for a $4,000 loan. Instead, the bank sent an officer to ask officials of the Gulf Refining Company about "the moral responsibility of these individuals." In addition, the officer was required to supply "a written appraisal to substantiate the value of the rig, verify the drilling contract and ascertain the status of the rig." Almost two months later, after the officer's report revealed that the equipment in question was currently working and valued at approximately $20,000, the loan was approved and even increased all the way up to $4,500. After this drilling concern stood with its feet in the door for two months, the bank's officers finally authorized its loan. Subsequently, increasingly large loans were routinely approved, and a substantial banking relationship steadily developed.[19]

Until more predictability and order could be imposed on the chaotic oil industry of the early 1930s, careful, cautious banks had little choice except to avoid all oil loans or insulate themselves from the risks of the industry by procedures similar to NBC's. A change in government regulation, however, imposed more orderly production patterns and allowed commercial banks to increase the volume and change the procedures of oil lending. At the heart of the change in the 1930s was the Texas Railroad Commission, a state regulatory agency based in Austin which played a critically important role in limiting the production of oil each month to a level roughly equal to the predicted demand for petroleum at a target price. In a joint quest for conservation of natural resources and for price stability and profitability in the oil industry, commissions in the major oil-producing states asserted the authority to dictate the acceptable level of production from oil properties within their respective states. Interstate compacts among the state commissions assured that market demand for the nation as a whole— as estimated monthly by the U.S. Bureau of Mines in the Department of the Interior—would be apportioned to each state according to historical patterns of production. A federal law forbidding the sale across state lines of oil produced in violation of state laws was the final component of the system of production control which ultimately emerged from the overproduction crisis of the 1930s. Because Texas was the nation's largest producing state, the operations of its prorationing system, which was built around the Texas Railroad Commission's monthly allowable production figures for wells throughout Texas, were central to the workings of the system as a whole. The production controls which evolved in response to conditions specific to the 1930s proved durable and effective in fostering a stable and profitable domestic oil industry in the post–World War II era.[20]

The Texas Railroad Commission provided several previously missing prerequisites for the development of more aggressive approaches to oil lending. The first was the promise of price stability based on an effective regulatory authority with coercive powers generally accepted by all segments of the petroleum industry. This meant that banks could begin to view oil in the ground as a predictable type of collateral which could be recovered systematically and efficiently over many years, a far

cry from the situation which had prevailed with unrestricted flush production. In the bargain, prorationing based on sound engineering
practices which promoted conservation also resulted in increased oil
recovery—or, from the bankers' point of view, increased collateral. Finally, the regulation of oil production on the basis of maximum efficient recoverable production fostered the growth of the professional engineering expertise needed to estimate the amount of oil recoverable
from a specific field. The largest banks in New York, Chicago, Dallas,
and Tulsa moved steadily toward a new age of oil lending in the 1930s,
as they hired professional petroleum engineers to evaluate reserves.[21]

Houston banks were somewhat slow to move into the modern era
of oil lending, perhaps because they were making profits with other
types of loans and investments or were content with the lending methods developed before the coming of effective prorationing. Union National and South Texas Commercial National continued to make a reduced amount of blue-chip cotton loans but most of their deposits
remained invested in U.S. government securities through 1945. At
NBC, throughout the 1930s, both the volume and the individual size
of oil loans steadily increased, but the loans followed the design of the
personal loans for oilmen established in the early 1930s, not the pattern of loans on oil production being established by the leading oil
lending banks of the era. The elite of regionally active producers continued to gain relatively easy access to credit at NBC. The list of eligible borrowers gradually expanded as newcomers gained acceptance,
usually with the personal and at times financial endorsement of successful oilmen with accounts at the bank. By World War II, NBC had
participated in multimillion-dollar loans with Chase National Bank of
New York and National City Bank of New York. It had built a solid
portfolio of oil loans to the most trustworthy Houston-based producers. It had even ventured to lend a small sum of money to a Texas
company for operations in Mexico. In short, in the decade before
World War II, NBC carefully found its way in the evolving field of oil
lending, while less aggressive banks such as Union and STCNB clung
to cotton and the safety of government securities.[22]

The outbreak of war brought an extraordinary demand for oil
which helped ease the overproduction crisis of the 1930s. NBC maintained its prewar oil lending patterns during the mobilization, thereby
helping assure the flow of funds for drilling into the hands of large independent oilmen. After mobilization, production, not exploration,
became the order of the day. Texas fields—which had been the national
symbol of the oversupply of oil in the 1930s—were depleted rapidly to
supply the war effort.[23]

World War II also hastened industrial expansion and thereby added to the economic diversity of the region. Often obscured by the spectacular profits from the cotton trade or oil production, an industrial base for the region's economy had slowly developed along the Houston Ship Channel. Armour opened a fertilizer plant in 1914. Texas Portland Cement Company took advantage of the abundance of shell in Galveston Bay and opened its channelside plant in 1916. Other manufacturing concerns followed. Oil refineries and cotton compress companies dominated the channel through the 1920s. Other manufacturers were integrated into these two primary industries. Fertilizer companies, for example, used by-products from the processing of cottonseed oil and petroleum. Chemical companies also used by-products from refining, and they supplied the sulfuric acid needed in the refining process. The abundance of sulfur along the Gulf Coast, however, allowed chemical companies and fertilizer companies to move away from a strict dependence upon cotton and oil. The production of chemical-based fertilizer and of chemicals for export increased in the 1930s. Wheat and rice mills established in the 1920s added another measure of independence from cotton and oil. Still, during the 1930s oil refining became the dominant channelside industry. By 1940, the fourteen refineries along the channel accounted for 10 percent of the nation's refining capacity and were the major industrial employers of the region. While this heavy concentration in refining made the Houston economy susceptible to declines in the price of petroleum products, the creation of numerous new jobs in the refineries and the measure of diversity added by cereal mills, cement plants, and chemical plants helped convert Houston from simply an exporting center to a center of trade and manufacturing.[24]

The demands of World War II spurred the growth of petroleum refining and petrochemical and chemical production along the channel. The war created needs for explosives and high-octane fuels. With access to Southeast Asia cut off by the Japanese, America lost its supply of natural rubber. That meant that synthetic rubber had to be produced, and much of it was made in large industrial plants on the upper Texas Gulf Coast. During the war, some $600 million was invested in the production of chemicals and petrochemicals. Continued high investments in these growth industries in the years after the war created a permanent industrial complex along the Gulf Coast.

Companies producing chemicals and petrochemicals were usually national in scope, and the move of national and even international companies into Houston was another significant part of the transition of the Houston economy from 1935 to 1945. Monsanto Chemical

Company, Dow Chemical Company, General Tire and Rubber Company, Goodyear, DuPont, Armco, and Union Carbide all moved into the ship channel region in these years. Humble Oil and Refining, Shell Oil, Texaco, Phillips Petroleum, and Sinclair Oil extended their interests along the ship channel to include chemicals.[25]

Away from the ship channel, oil had also fostered the development of the oil-tool industry prior to 1940. Hughes Tool Company and Reed Roller Bit Company were manufacturing oil field equipment in Houston before 1920. Both companies were famous for their drill bits. They were soon joined by Cameron Iron Works, which made a name for itself by manufacturing blowout preventers. In 1925, Hughes Tool, the largest of these concerns, was valued at $2 million. The three companies grew in the 1930s as oil production increased.

World War II attracted major steel companies to the ship channel and led to the expansion of the fabricated-metals industry already in place in other areas of the city. Steel was needed for new construction along the ship channel as well as for the upswing in shipbuilding that accompanied the war. Cameron Iron Works went to work manufacturing depth charges for the U.S. Navy and constructed a new plant outside of Houston. Hughes Tool and Reed Roller Bit also manufactured war-related items.[26]

With supplies of traditional fuel scarce, the war also accelerated the growth in demand for natural gas. By the start of the war, most Gulf Coast refineries and sulfur plants were using natural gas as a fuel, and its ready availability had been one inducement for manufacturers with extensive need for energy to locate near Houston. When the war increased demands for all types of energy, natural gas was soon being transported nationwide. In 1944, Tennessee Gas Transmission Company was formed and in a short time was operating over a thousand miles of pipeline reaching eastward from Texas. All in all, World War II accelerated a process of industrial growth begun earlier, and Houston's economy became increasingly industrialized around a rapidly expanding core of oil-related industries.[27]

Restraint is necessary, however, in comments regarding the degree of industrialization by 1945. The mining and shipping of raw materials such as petroleum and sulfur remained vital to the local economy. The shipping of agricultural commodities, primarily wheat, rice, and to some degree cotton, remained important. The manufacture of finished products remained limited. General Tire and Goodyear, for example, made synthetic rubber in Houston, but they made tires in Ohio. By 1945 only in oil refining and oil-related manufacturing had the regional economy moved forward into the large-scale manufacture of high-value finished products. The oil refining complex along the Houston Ship Channel and the remainder of the Gulf Coast produced almost one-third of the nation's refined petroleum products. Companies such as Reed Roller Bit, Cameron Iron Works, and Hughes Tool manufactured an increasing array of sophisticated oil-related equipment. But, overall, Houston's economy in 1945 had a limited, narrowly specialized manufacturing sector.

The involvement of Houston banks with the growing manufacturing sector was also limited, but here too National Bank of Commerce moved more quickly to adjust to the changing economy than did Union National or South Texas Commercial National. NBC, for example, lent Goodyear $1 million in 1944 as part of a $100 million loan arranged by a New York bank.[28] Most of the large national companies that migrated to Houston from 1930 to 1945, however, did not need credit from Houston's banks. Goodyear could have obtained credit elsewhere. Instead, the major manufacturing concerns needed a place to house deposits, handle their payrolls, and provide other banking services. Jesse Jones's visibility in national politics and his close ties to the nation's businessmen gave his bank access to the executives of the newly arrived major corporations.

As a prominent government official from 1931 to 1945, Jones was the best-known Houston businessman of his era. Had he been secretary of agriculture for fourteen years, he no doubt would have possessed a certain celebrity and name recognition that would have been of use to his bank after World War II. But to many businessmen, Jones was not simply another face in the news. In the 1920s he played a prominent role in the Democratic party and was one of their chief fund raisers. As head of the Reconstruction Finance Corporation, Jones was personally involved with businessmen throughout the nation, often offering assistance to companies with serious financial troubles. As secretary of commerce, he was involved in many phases of the economic life of the nation. Finally, in his work on war procurement, Jones brought together businessmen to mobilize their efforts to meet a national emergency. In sum, from the 1920s to 1945, Jones was one of the most visible representatives of business in the country, and in his work he established contacts with businessmen throughout the nation.

Jones also took pains to introduce his friend A. D. Simpson, who became president of the bank in December, 1934, to valuable contacts across the country. For example, according to a February, 1934, report to the board of directors on his visit with Jesse Jones in Washington:

Mr. Simpson mentioned that while with Mr. Jones in his suite at the hotel, Mr. Jones was, as usual, primarily inquisitive for news and information pertaining to the affairs of the bank and with the bank foremost in his mind took occasion to contact by telephone a high executive of a prominent oil company to convince that official of the need of a bank account for his company with the National Bank of Commerce of Houston, Texas.

Such contacts, initially made through Jesse Jones, proved invaluable to Simpson and his bank. For years Simpson brought one or two large loans from national companies to the bank each month. Invariably, he presented loans like the $1 million Goodyear loan to the Executive and Discount Committee, and with the loans came deposits and other business.[29]

Albert Dee Simpson
1881–1960

One of the chief reasons National Bank of Commerce grew rapidly after 1935 was its president, Albert Dee Simpson. Houston banks commonly had a chairman or principal owner who took little interest in the day-to-day management of the bank. W. B. Chew, Charles Dillingham, Jesse Jones, and James Baker never worked in their banks day after day. They were out in the city and the nation serving as visible symbols of the banks and establishing valuable business contacts. Certainly these men played essential roles in the strategic decisions made at their banks, but they left the tactical decisions of running them to others. Simpson, who became president of the bank in 1934, excelled at this type of management.

Simpson enjoyed the confidence and friendship of scores of businessmen around the country. Of course, he was aided in this by Jesse Jones, but it was Simpson who, after Jones helped open the door, firmed up the bank's relationship with new corporate customers. He was, as Gus Wortham, of American General Insurance Company, said, "a great business getter."

Simpson, who had started with the bank as a director and officer in 1918, was more than simply a good public relations man. He was a good banker who understood what customers wanted in their bank. He once said of his bank: "We give market service, credit information, data on buying power, labor, religious, educational, cultural, recreational, and civic conditions." Making sure the bank did all these things was a difficult and time-consuming job. At his death his son said of him, "Daddy's whole life, his friends, his civic work and everything he did centered on the National Bank of Commerce." It is easy to understand then why as late as the 1950s he was the man at NBC that competitors feared. They knew that he was the person most likely to take business from them.

In 1948 Simpson became vice chairman of the board. After retiring from active duties in 1958, he served as honorary chairman of the board until his death in 1960.

SOURCES: Noah Dietrich to Jesse Jones, August 8, 1938, Jones Papers; Ben F. Love, "People and Profits: A Bank Case Study" (Master's thesis, Southwest School of Banking, Dallas, 1967), 14, 22–23; Interview with J. W. McLean by Joseph A. Pratt; *Houston Chronicle* (December 26, 1960); *Houston Post* (December 26, 1960); Interview with Gus Wortham by William Allison, TCB Archives.

Jones and his hand-picked lieutenants also provided stability of leadership for NBC in an era of rapid economic change after 1929. Except for the long illness and death of President N. E. Meador in the early 1930s, NBC's leadership remained healthy and unchanged from 1929 to 1945. Despite his duties in Washington, Jesse Jones continued to write his bank regularly, set yearly salaries and policy goals, and attend meetings when possible. Several of NBC's competitors were not blessed with management continuity as they sought to adjust to the ongoing changes in the regional economy. Captain James A. Baker, chairman of the board of STCNB, died in 1941. The bank's long-term president, S. M. McAshan, died in the same year. In 1943, Union National Bank lost its president, R. M. Farrar. Management succession poses serious problems for most organizations in even the best of times. But losing strong leaders and searching for replacements in a time of rapid change can have a lasting effect on an organization's performance. The move of the Houston-area economy away from cotton and toward oil and manufacturing in the 1930s and 1940s presented difficult challenges for even the most experienced managers. In adjusting to this transformation of the regional economy, continuity as well as the skill and visibility of management at the National Bank of Commerce provided an advantage over several of the bank's rivals.[30]

By the early 1940s continuity of leadership, willingness to pursue a more aggressive lending policy, and the visibility of Jesse Jones on the national scene had made National Bank of Commerce much larger than Union National or South Texas Commercial National. The increased size of NBC was crucial in maintaining the long-term relationship it enjoyed with home-grown firms like Hughes Tool and in attracting new customers. NBC could not lend Hughes Tool all the money it needed, but it continued to make modest loans and to provide needed services. By the end of the war, for example, it was on the verge of moving into international banking. For firms like Hughes Tool or Cameron Iron Works, who did more overseas business after the war, that was an important service. Smaller Union and South Texas Commercial National could not easily afford to expand their range of services, and they had a more difficult time keeping up with even the limited loan demands of their major customers. Major corporations migrating to Houston after the early 1940s usually preferred both the services NBC could offer and the prestige of association with a larger, more nationally recognized bank.[31]

Size and the preeminence associated with size could be gained the fastest by arranging mergers. Between 1944 and 1946 two of the major downtown Houston banks grew by merging with smaller competitors. In 1944, Second National merged with San Jacinto National. In 1945 it merged with Guardian Trust Company. These mergers helped increase deposits at Second National from $68,552,677 at the end of 1943 to $164,797,525 at the end of 1945. In 1946, First National merged with State National, thereby regaining the lead in total deposits from National Bank of Commerce (see Table 6.1). Perhaps because their leadership was in a period of transition, the directors of Union and STCNB discussed but did not finalize a merger. These mergers climaxed a period of rapid growth by First National and Second National

Table 6.5   Percentage Increase in Deposits of the
Five Largest Houston Banks, 1935–45

Bank	1935	1945	Percent Increase
Second National Bank	$ 25,106,361	$ 164,797,525	555.1
National Bank of Commerce	30,144,392	179,071,670	494.0
First National Bank	46,053,641	178,755,474	288.1
Union National Bank	23,412,668	76,572,019	227.1
South Texas Commercial National Bank	42,106,361	122,685,937	191.1
All Houston Banks	214,680,190	1,007,370,120	369.2

SOURCE: Statements of Condition, TCB Archives.

in the decade from 1935 to 1945. In the same period, the National
Bank of Commerce and City National Bank kept pace with the growth
of their rivals without resorting to mergers. Union and STCNB did
not; in fact, as Table 6.5 illustrates, both lagged behind the average for
all Houston banks.[32]

The relatively slow growth of South Texas Commercial National
and Union National in comparison to other major Houston banks reflected in part their difficulties in adjusting to changes in the regional
economy after 1935. Local banks which first evolved successful oil
lending strategies and attracted the business of new manufacturing
firms far surpassed the two banks. NBC had close ties to independent
oilmen and to a growing number of national companies with operations in Houston. By contrast, STCNB had long-standing ties to the
traditional cotton firms of Houston. The loss of cotton business at
STCNB could be only partly offset by its handling of the local business
of major oil companies such as Humble and Texaco, since the bank
was far too small to fill the major credit needs of such companies. By
1945, NBC was tied to the region's future; South Texas Commercial
National, to its past.

CHAPTER 7

Creating Stability

*Bank failures and near failures in the early 1930s jolted the confi-*dence of bankers and depositors alike, producing a strong and lasting sentiment for conservative banking practices. This sentiment found expression in the creation of a security-based bank regulatory system whose primary goal was safety of deposits. In the wake of the banking crisis after the great crash, security won out over competitiveness; size and stability, over easy entry and fear of concentration of power. The banking reforms of the 1930s fundamentally altered the rules governing the operation of commercial banks and introduced a long era of stability in the industry during which bank managers conducted their business within clearly defined, strictly enforced regulatory boundaries.

Although the bank crisis of the early 1930s shaped the emergence of a security-conscious banking system, the New Deal banking reforms also reflected the impact of broader historical trends. In the decades before the Great Depression, the often competing goals of innovation and security had alternately shaped the evolution of commercial banking. From the 1880s to 1907 banking was fluid, with both management custom and banking law taking on new forms. Between 1907 and about 1915 state and federal regulations and the shock waves of the Panic of 1907 tightened the regulatory rules and lessened competition. From 1916 to 1929 this trend reversed. Rules were relaxed. Competition increased, and once again banking entered a more innovative stage. It was probably inevitable that the pendulum would swing back toward stability, but that it swung so far and stayed so long was the result of the mentality created by the banking crisis of the early 1930s.[1]

For the predecessors of Texas Commerce and the other Houston banks, the arrival of this more stable order had several implications.

First, the drive for stability accelerated the movement, begun in the late 1920s, toward concentration of deposits and banking functions in fewer hands. Second, the guarantee of deposits and other uniformly enforced safety measures reduced competition and eliminated the competitive advantage of a conservative bank like Union National, which from 1929 to 1933 attracted customers by its record of security. Third, the sale of preferred stock to the RFC and other measures designed to bolster credit offered opportunities for NBC and other more aggressive banks to seize a larger share of the Houston banking market. Fourth, in the long run the new rules and managers' reactions to them did much to change the hierarchy of Houston banks. But before these changes can be made clear, the laws behind them, which stayed in place into the 1970s, need explanation.

A wave of some 9,000 bank failures between 1929 and 1933 convinced Congress that drastic steps were needed to salvage the financial system and restore public confidence in banks. After newly inaugurated President Franklin D. Roosevelt declared a national bank holiday in the spring of 1933, Congress passed the Banking Act of 1933, generally known as the Glass-Steagall Act. Two years later, the Banking Act of 1935 produced another series of bank reforms. As these two acts were being implemented, the federal government also used the Reconstruction Finance Corporation to strengthen banks hard hit by the Depression. In addition, far-reaching reforms of the closely related securities industry climaxed in the creation of the Securities Exchange Act of 1934.

The overall impact of these reforms was to create a much more secure and stable commercial banking industry and to segregate it from other financial services industries such as investment banking, savings and loans, and insurance. The impulse toward security was embodied in numerous reforms governing many aspects of banking, and an understanding of its impact on banking requires an overview of several different types of regulation contained in the reforms of the 1930s.

The linchpin of security-based regulation was federal deposit insurance under the direction of the newly created Federal Deposit Insurance Corporation. The FDIC began on January 1, 1934, as a temporary fund contributed by banks to insure individual deposits up to $2,500. A permanent corporation was soon set up with contributions from the United States Treasury, the Federal Reserve Banks, and participating banks. Larger individual accounts were insured and over the years the guaranteed amount has grown steadily to the present level of $100,000. Participating banks continue to pay a percentage of their deposits to the corporation. Whereas in the past many banks had chosen to establish reputations as institutions capable of assuring the safety of customers' deposits, beginning in 1934 the FDIC guaranteed security of deposits for all member banks.

Once the federal government entered the deposit insurance business, it had a strong interest in regulating more closely the competitive practices of banks. A second major component of the 1930s banking reforms was thus the regulation of interest rates charged by banks. By prohibiting banks from paying interest on demand deposits and allowing the Federal Reserve to limit the level of interest paid by banks on time deposits, the government removed the option for bankers to compete aggressively for deposits. In the years after 1935, the ready access of bankers to an ample supply of interest-free demand deposits became the pillar of stability for the commercial banking industry. Only after other financial intermediaries began to compete successfully with commercial banks for these demand deposits in the 1960s and 1970s did bankers join the call for deregulation of their industry.

A third significant element of 1930s banking reform was the segregation of commercial banking from other related activities. Much-publicized abuses by commercial banks deeply involved in investment banking and securities trading in the 1920s paved the way for the separation of commercial and investment banking in 1933. This measure most directly affected the largest New York banks, but even the much smaller Houston banks had been involved in various aspects of securities underwriting. Banks throughout the nation were forced to choose whether they would become commercial or investment banks. It was hoped that segregation would increase accountability to regulators while also diminishing competitive pressures.

Geographical restrictions on competition were also strengthened during the 1930s. The traditional prohibition against interstate banking was confirmed, as was the power of the states to regulate branch banking within their boundaries. Entry into banking was made more difficult through the stipulation that new banking charters would be issued only where the need for a new bank in a community had been established. Overall, such legislation created an additional regulatory hurdle for those seeking a new bank charter while maintaining unit banking in Texas.

A final important banking reform of the 1930s was the strengthening of the powers of the Federal Reserve over various aspects of bank operations. Although the Federal Reserve was created in 1913, not until 1935 was it given the powers to become a strong central bank capable of monitoring the banking system and disciplining its behavior.[2]

Once in place, the new bank regulations reinforced the trend toward fewer but larger, more secure banks. This trend began with the banking crisis and near collapse of the economy between 1929 and 1933, which caused several Houston banks to liquidate voluntarily or to merge. The widespread bank failures of this era changed public attitudes toward banks. Instead of seeking out the aggressive and innovative banks as they had in the 1920s, people sought the safe and secure bank. Usually that meant a large, conservatively managed bank. Changes in the economy also increased the concentration of deposits and banking services in fewer but larger banks. With real estate construction and consumer spending in decline, and with only the largest, most stable firms surviving the chaotic changes in the cotton industry, smaller banks found their loan limits were too low for the needs of the remaining cotton firms and the demand for automobile and home loans much diminished. Figure 7.1 illustrates the increased concentration of deposits from 1929 to 1933.

After 1933 bank deposits were not quite so heavily concentrated, but the percentage in the top five banks remained higher than the

Figure 7.1. Percentage of bank deposits in Houston held by the top five banks, 1924–46.

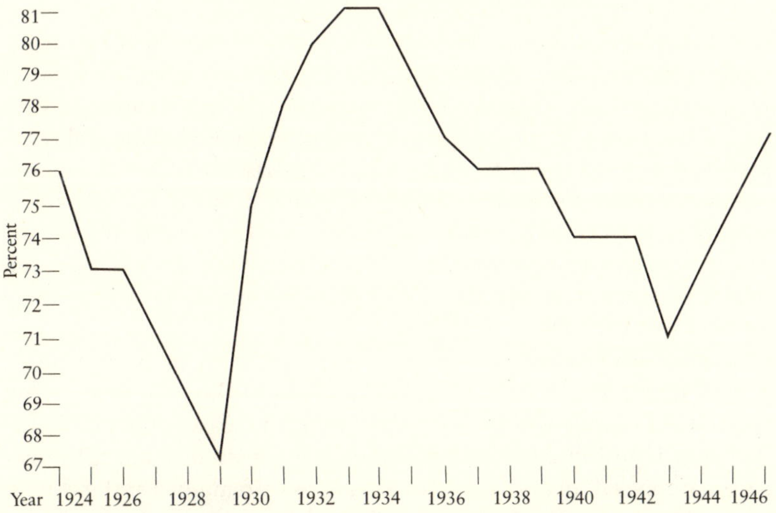

SOURCES: December Statements of Condition, TCB Archives.

1920s average until World War II. The new federal regulations and the policy of federal agencies help explain this continued concentration after 1933. The influx of capital by the RFC tended to favor the major banks, since the RFC purchased the largest blocks of stock in the large banks most able to repay the agency. Restrictions on entry and on interest rates constrained either the creation of new banks or their taking customers away from established banks by offering higher interest rates. Deposit insurance also helped prevent new competitors from entering the banking industry and reduced the number of banks. A requirement for deposit insurance was a close inspection of both state and national banks by the state banking commission, the FDIC, the Office of the Comptroller, and the Board of Governors of the Federal Reserve System. Managerial practices were closely watched. Weak banks were forced to close or were restructured with help from the Reconstruction Finance Corporation. Applications for the organization of new banks were closely scrutinized and a clear case of need had to be proven.

The results are evident in aggregate statistics. In Texas in 1925 there had been 834 state banks and 656 national banks, a total of 1,490 banks. In 1940 there were 393 state banks and 446 national banks, a total of 839 banks. Total deposits, however, increased from $1,101,011 in 1925 to $1,923,528 in 1940. In that period, the deposits of state banks actually went down, but the increase of the national banks' deposits more than offset the decline.[3]

As was true for the state as a whole, this increasing concentration of deposits was accompanied by substantial growth at Houston's larger national banks. National Bank of Commerce grew particularly fast, in part because it successfully merged with Marine Bank and Public National Bank while losing very little on defaulted loans. Table 7.1 reveals just how rapidly NBC grew in comparison to other banks, but it also demonstrates how fast the major banks grew in comparison with their smaller competitors. In the mid-1930s, the return to health of the Houston economy spurred the growth of the city's large, stable banks. In contrast, troubled Houston National and some smaller banks actually lost deposits.[4]

This faster rate of growth by a handful of large banks was only a part of the dramatic changes in the Houston banking industry. While the control of deposits by the major banks increased, the number of banks in Houston decreased and then remained constant. Of Houston's 21 banks doing business in 1927, only 13 remained at the close of 1932. Those same banks functioned without additional competition until 1942. During World War II, banks once again began to enter and

Table 7.1   Percentage Growth of Deposits in Houston Banks,
1929–35

Bank	December, 1929	December, 1935	Percent Increase
First National	$ 35,060,166	$ 46,053,641	31
STCNB	26,329,977	42,106,361	60
Second National	16,790,950	25,156,541	50
Union National	15,673,832	23,412,668	50
NBC	12,057,078	30,144,392	150
All other Houston banks	159,693,311	214,680,190	34

SOURCE: Statements of Condition, TCB Archives.

exit the industry, and at the close of the war there were 16 banks in Houston. The decline in banks between 1927 and 1933 was unusual in the history of Houston, as was the long period without a change in the number of banks. After 1900 the number of banks had changed every two or three years, and except for the years just after 1907, the general trend had been an increase in numbers. The long period of stable numbers from 1932 to 1942 reflected the slowdown of economic growth and the cautiousness encouraged by the banking crisis of the early 1930s. But it also reflected the success of federal laws which limited entry into the banking industry.[5]

While federal law and federal regulators encouraged stability and security, conservative bank managers did the same. The fact that regulators and bankers shared similar goals did not, however, mean that bankers welcomed expanding regulatory involvement in their industry. Indeed, the more traditional Houston bankers often resisted the implementation of new regulations designed to enhance security; these men of the old school greatly valued autonomy and strongly believed that their banks could return to health without the intervention of government. Besides, the creation of the Federal Deposit Insurance Corporation and other measures which forced all banks to be equally secure robbed the most cautious banks of a traditional strength. They could no longer claim to be the safest places for depositors' money.

A closer examination of the response to change by Union National Bank, one of the more conservative Houston banks, is instructive here. The actions of Union National Bank epitomized the "we can take care of ourselves" approach to banking. When President Roosevelt declared the national bank holiday, President R. M. Farrar, of

Union National, chose to ignore him. An employee of Union National recalled later: "We pretended we were closed. But we had customers who needed cash for their payrolls. And I suppose it was as illegal as hell, but Mr. Farrar gave those companies all the cash they needed. He said his bank didn't need any 'bank holiday excuse' for refusing depositors their money."[6] Union had a reputation for security of deposits, and it was committed to protecting this reputation regardless of government demands that it cooperate in a collective effort to revive the banking system as a whole.

Union's commitment to its personal brand of security was well summarized in 1935, when Frank Andrews nominated Farrar for another term as the bank's president:

> During the last five years of extraordinary strains and pressures he has met all the requirements of sound and conservative banking and has courageously carried this institution to a haven of safety and success, as demonstrated by the report of the year's work which the Directors have just considered. Mr. Farrar, we think you have done all that any man could have done during these rapidly changing and colorful years; that your success is marked, distinct and satisfactory.

Farrar and Andrews realized that a reputation as a "haven of safety" would bring success with the public in the 1930s.[7]

Although most major Houston banks shared this attitude toward the benefits of security, few sought security with quite the single-mindedness of Union. In the days before federal deposit insurance was fully implemented and accepted by the public, the reputation of Union as an entirely safe bank attracted depositors. Table 7.2 shows that the bank's reputation was well deserved; it maintained sufficient funds readily available to pay off depositors. Union was the extreme example of a bank which strove for security of deposits without regard for the impact of this strategy on the long-term expansion of lending.

Yet even security-conscious banks faced significant adjustments in operating procedures during the 1930s. The experience of South Texas Commercial National Bank offers a good case study of the impact of regulatory changes on a cautious but not excessively conservative bank. Letters from the comptroller of the currency increased sharply in 1933 at STCNB. The bank was instructed not to have its trust department arrange the sale of stocks that would benefit its securities department. Indeed, trust was increasingly set apart from the rest of the bank after 1933. The bank was also warned that loans by the bank to executive officers were no longer permitted. In September, acting under the prodding of the comptroller, the bank liquidated its investment subsidiary,

Table 7.2   Comparison of Liquidity in Houston Banks, 1929–45

End of Year	Union, Percent	STCNB, Percent	NBC, Percent
1929	47.5	42.2	50.5
1930	70.0	45.0	50.3
1931	63.9	45.6	46.6
1932	68.8	64.0	55.8
1933	88.2	78.7	62.2
1934	95.8	90.4	80.3
1935	92.7	78.7	79.8
1936	90.9	92.0	77.3
1937	92.1	89.6	78.3
1938	93.8	90.7	83.3
1939	94.9	88.0	83.6
1940	95.0	90.4	83.7
1941	93.1	86.1	83.0
1942	95.6	93.0	90.2
1943	97.1	91.7	93.1
1944	96.5	94.1	91.0
1945	96.6	90.0	88.0

SOURCE: Statements of Condition, TCB Archives.
NOTE: Liquidity equals cash and U.S. securities as a percentage of deposits.

the South Texas Commercial Company. On January 1, 1934, STCNB, like all other members of the Federal Reserve System, became part of the FDIC.[8] In general, the new federal banking regulations forced the bank's officers to exceed even their long tradition of security-conscious banking.

By forcing all banks, even those which had pursued a cautious path like South Texas Commercial National, to adopt uniform and more secure policies, new federal regulations reduced competition. Laws governing interest rates on deposits were the best example of this change. Interest rates on various types of deposits also had been the target of regulatory changes before 1935. Commercial banks commonly paid no interest for personal deposits before the 1890s, but they often paid interest on deposits by other banks. After the 1890s changes in federal regulations and increased competition from state banks led to the widespread paying of interest for both time and demand deposits in Houston banks. Average interest on time deposits was usually set at around 4 percent and was consistent from bank to bank in Houston. The Houston Clearing House helped enforce the paying of uniform rates of interest, but from time to time banks seeking to increase business would raise their interest rates. In the late 1920s the payment of high interest on deposits was often cited as a cause of deteriorating profitability and eventual bank failure. With the onslaught of the banking crisis and the Depression, Houston banks began to lower interest rates. The lower rates became enshrined by regulations aimed at restoring profitability and preventing bank failure. The regulations ended the payment of interest on demand deposits and set a historically low ceiling on rates which could be paid on time deposits. Union National began reducing interest paid in 1931, well before the implementation of such regulations. At that time it reduced interest paid on time deposits from 4 percent to 2½ percent on amounts up to $5,000 and reduced the rate on amounts over $5,000 to 1½ percent. The bank reduced its interest rate on checking accounts from 2 percent to 1½ percent minus the amount required to receive interest. In the mid-1930s the Federal Reserve forced all banks to end the payment of interest on checking accounts and established interest rates for time deposits at about Union's 1931 level. As established by the Federal Reserve, interest rates on time deposits stayed low through World War II and into the 1950s. The prohibition on interest on demand deposits and uniformly low rates on time deposits meant that Union and all other banks had the same secure source of low-cost funds on time deposits.[9]

Federal deposit insurance also reduced potential competition and increased security. The FDIC worked much like the old Texas Guaranty Fund. One major difference, however, was that all national banks were required to join and most state banks were strongly encouraged to join. When deposit insurance took effect in 1934, 815 Texas banks, including the 464 national banks in the state and 351 state-chartered banks, were members. Another 138 state banks were not members. Gradually, however, most state banks joined the FDIC. While reluctant to see the implementation of deposit insurance because of their unhappy experience with the Texas Guaranty Fund, Texas bankers soon came to appreciate the FDIC. Most credited it with ending the hoarding of money outside banks and with increasing the public's confidence in banks and reassuring depositors that they need not rush to a troubled bank and withdraw their funds before it failed. In comparison to earlier periods, the rate of bank failure in Texas remained very low from the 1930s into the 1970s.[10]

Deposit insurance, however, took away a significant competitive advantage from banks such as Union National or South Texas Commercial National. Despite lowering their interest rates between 1930 and 1935, they attracted new depositors because of their reputations as secure and conservatively managed banks. Depositors realized that their money would be safe in these two banks. In turn Union and South Texas Commercial National could maintain their profit margins and still achieve safety by investing in government bonds. These bonds paid a lower return than the traditional loan business of banks, but since the cost of money went down and the amount of deposits went up, the banks' profits actually increased. By 1935, individual deposits up to $5,000 were protected by the FDIC and were as safe at any other bank as they were at Union or South Texas Commercial National. Customers selected their bank on the basis of location, interest rates, or service. Union and South Texas Commercial National no longer had a significant advantage over their rivals.[11]

In fact, the creation of the FDIC and other measures aimed at security probably did Union National Bank, in particular, a disservice by encouraging its managers to be excessively cautious. In 1933, for example, the acting comptroller wrote Union:

> It is believed that in the interest of conservatism and sound banking, every reasonable effort should be put forth during this period to build up and strengthen the capital structure of our banking institutions. If you have not already done so, it is therefore requested that you give special consideration at this time not only to the net earnings but also to the capital and surplus accounts of your institution, salaries, expenses of operation and to the advisability of reducing or deferring dividend payments to your stockholders for the time being, all in the interest of further strengthening the surplus or reserve accounts of your institutions.

F. M. Farrar replied for his bank: "Our dividends in 1930–31 were reduced from 10% to 6%; salaries reduced from 10% to 35%; interest paid on savings from 4% to 2½% up to $5,000.00 and 1½% above $5,000.00. Interest paid on checking accounts has been restricted in number, and in rate reduced from 2% to 1½% less reserve requirements." In short, the comptroller did not need to advise Union to be more conservative; Union was already too conservative for its own long-term good.[12]

Both Union and STCNB had a chance to move away from this government-encouraged conservatism by taking advantage of the RFC's offer to purchase preferred stock in their banks. In late 1933, STCNB and Union considered the question of increasing their capital by selling preferred stock to the RFC. The Roosevelt administration hoped to pump money into circulation and thereby revive the economy by increasing the amount banks could loan. Since loan limits were determined by capitalization, a purchase of stock by the RFC increased the amount a bank could lend an individual customer and added to the total available for lending. Both made credit more available for businesses. Many bankers, however, were reluctant to have their stock purchased by the RFC. They feared that the public would consider this a sign that their banks were near insolvency, and they also resented increased government control of their industry. Many also believed that credit should be further deflated instead of inflated. Jesse Jones acknowledged these attitudes in a radio address in August, 1932: "There has been too much reluctance on the part of banks, trust companies, insurance companies, etc., to borrow for the purpose of relending, not alone from the RFC but also from any source. Most banks have been endeavoring to get as liquid as possible, some of them too much so for the public good." [13]

Not surprisingly, neither South Texas Commercial National nor Union asked the RFC to purchase preferred stock in their banks. Their presidents S. M. McAshan and R. M. Farrar, respectively, believed that credit should be tightened instead of loosened. They both took pride in the stability and independence of their banks. Despite the personal urgings of Jesse Jones, they never agreed to a stock purchase by the RFC. Perhaps the association of Jones with the RFC even hurt the effort to get Union and South Texas Commercial National to sell preferred stock, since Farrar, in particular, remained bitter about the resolution of the bank crisis of 1931. [14]

Other Houston banks, however, took advantage of the offer of the RFC to increase their capital by purchasing preferred stock. Second National Bank sold $1 million in preferred stock to the RFC, and First National greatly aided its reorganization in 1934 by selling $2 million in preferred stock. First National of Houston was the oldest and traditionally the largest bank in the city, but in 1934 bad loans and poor management decisions forced the bank's officers and directors to get a new charter and reorganize as the First National Bank in Houston. Almost immediately the bank's management asked the RFC to purchase preferred stock. The sale of $2 million in stock allowed the bank to double the amount it could lend, and by 1935 First National was once again a healthy bank. [15] National Bank of Commerce also sold $2 million in preferred stock to the RFC in 1934. This infusion of capital allowed NBC to increase its liquidity while maintaining its lending level. As Tables 7.2 and 6.4 demonstrate, NBC stayed around 80 to 90 percent liquid from 1934 to 1945 yet also kept loans at about 20 percent of deposits. Since its increased loan limit enabled NBC to make loans to the most stable large companies, it was probably as secure as the slightly more liquid Union and STCNB. The purchase of preferred stock maintained security, increased the loan limit, and allowed the opportunity to attract major new customers. While Union and South Texas Commercial National were content to pursue a cautious policy that favored their established customers, National Bank of Commerce retained its old customers and gained more. Some long-term customers of NBC, such as Hughes Tool, had grown quite large by the end of the 1930s. As such companies grew, so did NBC, and its deposits and loans increased faster than those of other major Houston banks.[16]

By the late 1930s, the rules of banking which would dominate until the 1970s had become clear. Competition and risk would be reduced by restricting entry into the industry, by enforcing standardized low interest rates, by eliminating interest rates on checking accounts, and by guaranteeing deposits. Bank practices, notably the limitation of loans to a relatively low percentage of assets, reinforced such security-based regulations. Frequent inspections enforced these rules and put a premium on doing things by the book to avoid exchanges with regulators. States retained authority over branch banking within their boundaries. Stricter enforcement of the rules against directors serving on more than one bank board were more strenuously enforced. The double liability of directors—who before the mid-1930s could lose both the value of their stock and an additional penalty up to the value of their stock—was also ended. Minor modifications in this system of regulation would be required by the increased need for credit in World War II. In the 1950s, bank managers would begin to probe gently for possible loopholes in these laws, as, for example, when they began to expand the system of chain banks made up of minority interests in smaller banks. But by and large, the rules of 1940 were the rules of 1960.[17]

Some bankers learned more quickly than others that room remained within this security-based system for maneuvering and limited risk taking. Mastery of these lessons helped their banks grow larger than their more cautious competitors. Under the direction of Jesse Jones, the National Bank of Commerce cautiously expanded the availability of credit in the mid-1930s. NBC took advantage of the purchase of preferred stock by the RFC to expand its loan capacity. It moved more directly into oil lending than did its more conservative competitors. During the war, the bank showed no reluctance to lend to defense-related industries. NBC also aggressively pursued national corporations. Its deposits had surpassed Union's in 1931, when it merged with Public National, but South Texas Commercial National remained well ahead of NBC in deposits until 1938. That year NBC closed the gap to within $1 million in deposits. The next year NBC passed STCNB and never trailed that bank again. Certainly the decline of the cotton trade hurt South Texas Commercial National. In the long run, its investment in government bonds instead of loans also hurt. Changes in regulation, such as the implementation of the FDIC, robbed safe and secure STCNB and Union of some competitive advantages. But the managers of these two banks also proved timid in exploring the limits of regulatory constraints on their banks' operations. Regulations alone did not keep the security-based system in effect for several decades. Conservative habits hardened to convictions by the trauma of the early 1930s meant that many bankers had little inclination to take risks and to confront the uncertainty of competition.[18]

Even during World War II, South Texas Commercial National and Union National took a more conservative course than National Bank of Commerce. The impact of the war was very similar to the impact of earlier New Deal programs and agencies. First, the war was very expensive and was financed in large part by bond sales. As they had at the start of the New Deal, Union and South Texas Commercial National purchased large amounts of these bonds. The war also increased wages while decreasing consumption of many goods through rationing. More money moved into savings accounts without any appreciable increase in interest rates. NBC also invested in bonds and reaped the benefits of increased savings. By 1943 all three banks had about 55 percent of their deposits invested in U.S. securities. NBC, however, still had more capital stock and a larger surplus fund, and through the efforts of A. D. Simpson and Jesse Jones, the bank extended credit to major firms vital to the nation's defense. Because of Simpson and Jones, the bank had the will and the contacts to move more aggressively into the business of making loans to large borrowers.

At least one large regional manufacturing firm, Cameron Iron Works, permanently moved its account to the National Bank of Commerce as a result of Jones's willingness to move aggressively and without paperwork on war-related projects. First National Bank of Houston had handled much of Cameron's banking before World War II. When the company won a substantial contract to manufacture antisubmarine weapons early in the war, its president, James S. Abercrombie, approached First National for a loan to carry out this defense-related project. To his surprise, his loan application was rejected. Jesse Jones, who was involved in procurement for the war effort through the Defense Plant Corporation, a subsidiary of the RFC, quickly arranged for a loan through NBC for Cameron's financing. Abercrombie responded by changing banks, a decision which proved quite profitable for NBC when Cameron grew rapidly after the war.[19]

At Union National Bank the story was quite different. As its major local customers grew in size, they found their bank too small to fill their needs. Brown & Root, a Houston-based construction company, did business with Union National Bank in the 1920s and 1930s. During World War II, when the company vastly expanded, Union proved too small to lend the sums needed by Brown & Root. In 1945, the company switched to First National Bank.[20]

The adjustments in banking during World War II and the Great Depression were part of a broad historical pattern of change. Houston's largest banks traditionally had served primarily the needs of the largest businesses in their region. Before 1900 Houston's banks had been slow to extend credit and service to most people. In the 1920s several bankers left the employment of the major banks and opened their own banks, providing increased service and credit. But banks grew too numerous for the pool of competent bank managers and took excessive risks which were compounded by the financial trauma of the Great Depression. One result was the near collapse of the Houston banking system in 1931. Bankers reacted sharply to this crisis, cutting back the flow of credit that was sorely needed to foster recovery. In the defense of bank managers, it should be noted that Houston had no bank failures, and the city was spared the worst rigors of the Depression. For those banks, however, which after 1931 pushed to expand credit and obtain new business, increased deposits and expanded loan portfolios were the rewards. In this sense, those who forgot the worst horrors of the Depression, obtained the largest possible loan limit, and pushed the security-based rules toward their limits profited over more cautious rivals. They gained the business of aggressive entrepreneurs and the major companies that would dominate the postwar era.

The ability of Houston's major banks to grow hinged on management decisions and management philosophy. Those bank managers who first adapted to the new security-based regulations by exploring the limits to competition and innovation in a system designed to protect depositors from both often fundamentally and permanently improved their market position. The divergence in management between the more aggressive NBC on the one hand and the more conservative STCNB and Union on the other illustrates this point. All three banks continued to grow after World War II, but NBC expanded more rapidly by capitalizing on the base of deposits, business ties, and attitudes toward regulation developed in the pre-1945 era.

CHAPTER 8

Responding to a World of Opportunities, 1945–56

Building on the economic recovery of the late 1930s and the frenzy of war-related investment along the Texas-Louisiana Gulf Coast, the Houston area enjoyed an era of rapid development after World War II. Population in Harris County increased at more than double the national average from 1940 to 1960, growing by almost 30 percent in the 1940s and almost 40 percent in the 1950s. As a result, Houston, the nation's twenty-first-largest city in 1940, had climbed into the number-seven spot by 1960. In the process, it passed such established cities as Cleveland, Washington, Saint Louis, Milwaukee, San Francisco, and Boston. In this same period, value added by manufacturing in the Houston region expanded by a factor of ten. Such statistics marked the performance of the regional economy as extraordinary, even in the context of a rapidly growing national economy.[1]

Several sectors of the economy fed the postwar boom. Most obvious was the burgeoning complex of petroleum-related industries. The production and transportation of oil and natural gas generated intense activity throughout the Southwest. In response, the manufacture of the tools and equipment used in these businesses increased, particularly in the Houston area. Oil refineries continued to expand steadily on the Gulf Coast, where they were joined by a new generation of manufacturing plants for the petrochemical industry, which was one of the fastest-growing industries in the nation from the late 1930s through the early 1960s. A variety of factors, including the availability of raw materials and close operational and ownership ties between petrochemical production and oil refining, made the Gulf Coast the favored location for the construction of the capital-intensive plants of this dynamic industry. A growing array of petroleum-related activities propelled the postwar expansion of the Houston economy.

The regional economy, however, was by no means one-dimensional in this era. Construction of a new generation of high-rise office buildings downtown and of housing and commercial developments in the suburbs supplied numerous jobs. The growing population of Houston fostered the continued expansion of local manufacturers and retailers while also helping to persuade numerous companies based in other parts of the nation to migrate to the city, a development best symbolized by the opening of major primary-metals manufacturing plants in the region during and after World War II. Amid all of this activity, traditional commodity processing and shipping industries such as cotton and rice continued to contribute to Houston's economic health and diversity.

After the war, Houston's bankers thus faced a new world of opportunities. As befitted traditional bankers made even more conservative by the trauma of the Great Depression, they responded gradually, each with one eye focused on security while the other scanned the economic horizon in search of new competitive opportunities. In two particularly attractive areas, oil and real estate lending, the major Houston banks hired specialists who understood new trends and could develop new methods of lending to minimize risks. Attracting and retaining such specialists required higher salaries and more liberal benefits. To fill the banks' growing needs for professionally trained staffs, several of the local banks instituted management development programs modeled after those employed by the much larger money-center banks. These more highly trained employees then took advantage of ongoing improvements in transportation and communication to expand the reach of the Houston banks more widely into the region surrounding the city, into previously untapped markets in Texas, and into neighboring states. This aggressive expansion of lending activities was matched by a marked increase in the use of banks by broad segments of the population; total bank deposits in Houston increased from less than $350 million in 1940 to approximately $2,265 million in 1959.[2]

Nowhere were the changes in Texas banking more visible or more important than in oil lending. As the war ended, many in the oil industry wondered about the adequacy of oil supplies for postwar demands. The United States and the world seemed on the brink of an era of sustained expansion in the use of energy, and oilmen and their bankers wondered what adjustments would be required from the traditional practices of the industry. One overriding fact, however, quickly became clear. The demand for oil grew markedly after the war, and oil drilling picked up in response. The average number of drilling rigs active in the United States rose steadily in the decade before 1955, when drilling

Figure 8.1. Rotary-rig count in Texas, the Southwest (Texas, Oklahoma, Louisiana), and the United States, 1949–56.

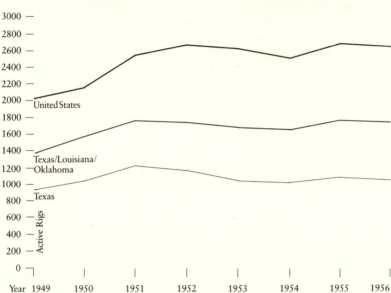

SOURCE: Hughes Tool Company, Rotary Rigs Running—by States, Annual Averages.

activity reached a peak not matched again until the late 1970s. All regions of Texas reflected this trend, with West Texas leading the way (see Figure 8.1). Oil production, transportation, refining, and marketing expanded along with drilling activity, as the national oil industry took advantage of a growing demand for oil and regulatory-induced stability to enjoy an exceptionally prosperous decade.

From a banking perspective, this surge in drilling translated into a large potential market for capital. According to E. O. Buck, the founder of the National Bank of Commerce's oil lending department in 1947, "56,000 wells were being drilled creating a money demand of some $150 million a week." Most banks had yet to become comfortable lending in this long unpredictable industry. Buck recalls that about 1947, "four banks in the United States were providing most of the demand. The problem was certainly not the opportunity to lend the money, but rather the lack of expertise involved with making that type of loan."[3] In a city which was a traditional center of activity for the southwestern oil industry, any bank which aspired to leadership in

Emergence of Modern Oil Lending

E. O. Buck

A pivotal figure in the development of oil lending at National Bank of Commerce was E. O. Buck, whose career well illustrates the close connection between the coming of professional reservoir engineering to the oil industry and the movement of major banks in Texas and the money centers into lending to oil producers. Born in 1904, Buck graduated from Texas A&M with a degree in industrial engineering before going to work for the Texas Railroad Commission (TRRC) in the 1930s. As one of the commission's first petroleum engineers, Buck worked with others in the oil industry and state and federal government to establish prorationing of oil production as a means of bringing a semblance of order to a traditionally chaotic industry. His tenure at the TRRC put him in contact with oil producers throughout the state.

In the late 1930s, Buck put his engineering knowledge and his connections in the oil industry to work as an independent consultant who appraised the value of oil properties for banks such as National Bank of Commerce in Tulsa, which—along with a handful of other banks at this time—sought to develop more scientific oil lending procedures. As an independent broker in the emerging field of oil lending, Buck brought together banks interested in making loans in this area with independent producers in need of capital. During World War II, Buck continued to work with independent producers in the Southwest as a representative of the Petroleum Administration for War, which coordinated the mobilization of the oil industry.

When he came to the National Bank of Commerce in Houston as the head of the oil department in 1947, Buck thus had varied experiences which prepared him well to understand ongoing changes in oil production and to evaluate the numerous opportunities in oil lending. As the volume of oil lending grew, Buck gradually expanded his staff by adding petroleum engineers with applied experience gained working for major oil companies. One of his early additions was John Townley, another graduate of Texas A&M, who worked for Texaco before coming to NBC, where he became the head of oil lending after Buck's retirement.

SOURCES: Interview with John Townley by Joseph A. Pratt, June 24, 1983; Interviews with E. O. Buck by Joseph A. Pratt, August 8, 1982, June 8, 1983, TCB Archives.

the years after World War II inevitably became deeply involved in the oil industry.

In the decade after 1945, all the largest Houston banks became more active in oil lending. By building oil lending departments around the expertise of professionally trained petroleum engineers with experience in the oil industry, these banks turned to specialists to create secure lending procedures and to evaluate the potential worth of oil-producing properties. Men like Buck, of the National Bank of Commerce, and Joseph Nalle, of the Texas National Bank, came to their jobs with professional training, experience in petroleum engineering, and a wealth of personal contacts in the oil business. As they set about applying their knowledge to the banking business, such men displayed an aggressiveness somewhat at odds with the tone of traditional banking. Any doubts that the risk and romance inherent in the oil business were incompatible with the traditional conservatism of banking were quieted, however, by the performance of the petroleum-engineers-turned-bankers. They proved capable of evaluating opportunities in oil with the cold eye of the economist and the sharp eye of the engineer, not the gambler's eye of the old-fashioned wildcatter.

In these boom years of early oil lending, even "cold economics" yielded excellent results. When Buck joined the National Bank of Commerce in 1947, he promised that he would leave after a year if he did not bring in $10 million in loans. His first year figure approached $18 million, a total which quickly grew to a range of $30 to $40 million a year by the mid-1950s. At that time, oil-related loans accounted for approximately one-third of the bank's total loans and provided a ready, profitable, and relatively safe new outlet for the use of the increasing deposits generated by postwar prosperity. At NBC in this period, oil lending consistently and profitably absorbed all the funds the bank's managers were willing to commit. Indeed, available deposits proved insufficient to fund the growing opportunities in oil lending, a situation which engendered intense competition for available funds between oil and other growing lending areas such as real estate.[4]

Oil loans spread the reputation and the presence of NBC into broad areas of the state and ultimately the Southwest, where the bank previously had conducted little business. This was an important step for NBC and the other large Houston banks, which traditionally had stayed closer to home, concentrating on the region immediately surrounding Houston or tied to it through the cotton trade. Loans from Houston banks to oil producers throughout the Southwest reinforced existing economic ties between the Gulf Coast and the producing regions in the interior. Once banks developed safe procedures for making loans secured by oil production, the flow of much of this business toward Houston was as predictable as the flow of oil through pipelines from throughout the Southwest to the Gulf Coast refineries.

The evolution of oil-related lending after World War II went forward in the obscurity of the deliberations of loan committees in banks of various sizes, philosophies, and locations. The re-creation of the history of the evolution of oil lending in this critical period is made difficult by the lack of information about the lending patterns of individual banks. The absence of systematic records from South Texas Commercial National and Union National prevents the compilation of a comprehensive history of oil lending at all of the predecessors of Texas Commerce—Houston, but detailed records from National Bank of Commerce provide an instructive case study of the evolution of oil lending practices at one of the major Houston banks.

Modern oil lending began in earnest at NBC with the arrival of E. O. Buck. The bank previously had sought to expand its oil lending by hiring a petroleum specialist who reported to a vice-president and thus did not personally make presentations to the loan and discount committee. Buck recognized that the traditional bankers who ran the discount committee would feel uncomfortable with loans secured by oil production instead of personal loans to individual oilmen. To enable him to educate his superiors on the safety and the profitability of such loans, he asked for and received the right to present his loans directly to the loan and discount committee. Recognizing the potential profitability of oil lending, the bank's top managers agreed. By acknowledging their own limitations in this important new area, finding and hiring an expert, and granting him a degree of autonomy unusual in the bank's past, they made possible the rapid expansion of the bank's involvement in a vital, fast-changing sector of the regional economy.

Buck quickly transformed NBC's traditional oil lending procedures, bringing the bank in line with the practices evolving at the major oil lending banks in the nation. In the process, he added NBC's name to that list. Several clear differences distinguished the bank's traditional loans to prominent local oilmen from its growing volume of oil-production loans. Greater confidence in the predictive power of petroleum engineering allowed Buck and other professional oil lenders to extend the term of ordinary oil loans. Whereas bankers once had demanded repayment from flush production over 30 to 90 days, they now could safely lend money for three to five years, secure that repayment would proceed regularly and predictably from the regulated flow of oil sustained over years by the best practicable recovery techniques. Traditional bankers might not understand the internal logic of the Texas Railroad Commission or the finer points of petroleum engineering, but they understood quite well the internal logic of lending, and they showed little reluctance to commit funds to an area characterized by high levels of security and excellent rates of return.

As oil-production loans grew, what constituted acceptable security became increasingly standardized. In addition to traditional financial statements, NBC and its competitors in this field required would-be borrowers to submit reports on the probable productive capacities of oil properties used as collateral. Such reports, which were routinely prepared by professional engineering consulting firms and were verifiable by the bank's own petroleum engineers, became the centerpiece of the oil lending process. Since engineering reports on reserves could only estimate how much oil ultimately would be recovered from a particular property, the banks built in extra measures of security by basing loans on the low rather than the high range of reserve estimates and by then leaving a cushion between the predicted value of recoverable reserves and the amount of the loan. Good engineering knowledge combined with conservative banking practices thus removed much of the risk inherent in lending against collateral which could not be precisely valued. During this formative era of modern oil lending, relatively low and constant interest rates, a stable price for oil assured by an effective prorationing system, and a rising demand for oil combined to remove other uncertainties which might have affected the repayment of loans. Under such conditions, oil production loans proved quite safe and consistently profitable.

All oil loans were by no means the same, since every field had special characteristics, and every producer had special needs. But one overall trend was clear, at least in the reports of the oil lenders at National Bank of Commerce. Scientific evaluation of reservoirs allowed the banks to move away from making loans based primarily on personal evaluations of an oilman's "moral responsibility." Personal reputations would, of course, never be completely removed from lending decisions. But oil-production loans could now be approved more by the numbers presented in engineering reports than by the grapevine's impression of an operator's reputation. This allowed NBC to extend its efforts in oil lending from its previously limited list of producers deeper into the ranks of independents, enabling the bank to spread its risks and expand its business much more rapidly.

The standard lending arrangement between small independent producers and NBC in the 1950s read as follows:

> $ __x__ to __[name of borrower]__ increasing total indebtedness to $ __y__ to be repaid $ __z__ monthly (or 65% of the runs, whichever is greater) together with interest at the rate of __a__ % per annum, and to be secured by a Deed of Trust on properties in __[one or more names]__ Counties, Texas, and an assignment of oil runs therefrom.

The amounts ranged from a few thousand dollars up to NBC's legal lending limit, which exceeded $1 million in these years. The interest rate stayed relatively constant in the 4 to 5 percent range. The names of independent oilmen active throughout the Southwest appeared, the vast majority of the counties being in Texas, although late in the decade Louisiana parishes showed up with more regularity. Variations of this agreement crowded the minutes of the bank's executive and discount committee in the 1950s.[5]

In pursuing the business of small independent producers, NBC by no means abandoned its previous commitments to the larger ones who had taken the bulk of the bank's oil loans before World War II. Indeed, prominent oil-and-gas producers such as R. E. (Bob) Smith, Pat Rutherford, Paul Kayser, J. S. Abercrombie, and Gardiner Symonds continued to make frequent use of the bank for both individual and corporate financial needs, and they were joined after the war by other major independent producers, notably John Mecom. The working ties between the bank and these oil-and-gas men were solidified in the postwar years by their inclusion on the board of directors of NBC, where all six served in the 1940s and 1950s.[6] Seats on the board were concrete evidence of the importance of these men to the bank.* As directors, they continued to provide expert advice and business connections valuable to the bank's expanding oil department. According to E. O. Buck: "Pat Rutherford and Jim Abercrombie were the unofficial oil-related advisory board before the [oil] department was created. The officers at N.B.C. relied heavily on these men for information about individuals, companies, etc. Since the bank didn't have any experts on the staff, we used our directors." Buck's oil division built directly on the previous efforts of such oilmen-directors, and their personal knowledge of conditions in the oil industry remained important to the bank even after the development of a specialized oil lending operation with a permanent staff.[7]

Lending on oil-producing properties to these directors, to numerous smaller producers throughout Texas, and even to the large, vertically integrated companies was the mainstay of the oil division in its formative years of rapid expansion, and these loans provided a strong impetus for the overall growth of the National Bank of Com-

---

* The dates of service on the board of NBC and its successors of these prominent oilmen were as follows: J. S. Abercrombie (JSA Company and Cameron Iron Works), 1946–73; Paul Kayser (El Paso Natural Gas and Gulf States Oil Company), 1946–74; John Mecom (South Oil Company), 1951–68; Pat Rutherford (independent oil companies), 1951–83; R. E. Smith (independent oil companies), 1954–73; and Gardiner Symonds (Tennessee Gas Transmission Company), 1947–63. At the deaths or retirements of these men, representatives of their respective companies generally replaced them on the board.

merce in the decade after World War II. During this period, bank loans secured by pledges of future income from producing properties which had been appraised by professional petroleum engineers helped finance an impressive oil boom in the Southwest.[8] Such loans were especially important in hastening the orderly development of oil deposits in the rich Permian Basin in West Texas and southeastern New Mexico. They helped independent producers secure their niche in the industry by fostering the flow of development capital into their hands.

Because of their early involvement in oil, their close personal connections to many of the most active producers, and their proximity to the major fields of the Southwest, the largest banks in Dallas and Houston emerged among the national leaders in oil lending in the 1950s. In this one important, fast-growing area, the Texas banks had professional expertise, experience, and records of innovation and success on a par with those of their much larger competitors in New York and Chicago. They still trailed far behind the money-center banks in their legal lending capacities for individual companies, but they did not trail in their professional capacities to find, evaluate, and design loans to these companies. Oil lending was the first area in which the major Texas banks emerged as serious competitors of the larger, more established money-center banks.

Because NBC lacked the resources to fund its growing volume of loans secured by oil production, it began selling participations in such loans originated in Texas to money-center banks. By the early 1950s, NBC's ability to generate profitable oil loans far exceeded its capacity to fund them. In search of money to lend, it struck a bargain with Bankers Trust of New York calling for that bank's regular purchase of participations in oil loans originated by NBC. For a fee of ¼ percent of interest, NBC agreed to sell an 80 percent participation in packages of oil-production loans to Bankers Trust. A fee of a quarter of a point on multimillion-dollar loan packages generated substantial revenues, making the oil department of NBC largely self-financing and facilitating its rapid expansion through the addition of new petroleum engineers to its staff. Bankers Trust also benefited from this arrangement. It had been chosen as a potential partner by NBC's management because of its lack of experience in oil lending relative to several of its New York competitors and its desire to establish a presence in this area. Bankers Trust hoped to minimize some of the risks in a highly competitive new field by utilizing the proved expertise and the established connections of NBC. Significantly, the junior partner in terms of size was the senior partner in terms of professional expertise. Because the banks needed each other, this arrangement proved both profitable and durable.[9]

Participations flowed downstream—from New York to Texas—as well as upstream—from Texas to New York. Throughout the 1950s, NBC regularly funded small portions of large loans made by money-center banks to major oil and natural-gas companies. A small percentage of a major loan to a large oil company was a substantial account for NBC in an era when its legal lending limit stayed in the range of one to two million dollars. A 5 percent participation in a multimillion-dollar loan to a major oil company headed by Bank of America or Chase National also had a strong underlying message: NBC was recognized as a player—albeit still a small one—in the big leagues of oil lending.

While developing a thriving business in oil-production lending to majors and independents, NBC also continued to help finance other aspects of the local operations of major national oil companies such as Gulf Oil, Texaco, Humble, Stanolind, and Richfield. For example, two major oil companies turned to NBC in the 1950s for loans totaling several million dollars to construct new service stations throughout Texas. Shell Pipeline Company was also an active borrower as it and other pipeline companies approached commercial banks for a portion of the vast capital needed to build extensive lines to gather oil and gas from fields throughout the Southwest and transport it to markets both in the region and on the East Coast.

Lending to major oil-and-gas companies was not, however, the central function of the Houston-based banks in this formative era of modern oil lending. The majors' access to credit from outside the region assured their continued expansion with or without loans from Texas banks. More important to the development of the oil industry as a whole was the role of Texas banks in identifying promising ventures by innovative regional oilmen and supplying the credit needed to integrate the maturing southwestern oil industry into the national market. In the booming postwar oil industry, opportunities abounded for relatively small oil operators to prosper and grow by recognizing and responding creatively to changing conditions in the oil industry. Local banks often were best situated to identify such men and to finance their endeavors.

A brief history of the company built by one such man, E. C. (Eddy) Scurlock, helps illustrate this process. After gaining experience selling oil products for others, Scurlock created his own oil-marketing company in Houston in 1936. Scurlock Oil Company prospered initially by bringing together small sellers of oil products with small buyers, and Scurlock turned to National Bank of Commerce to help him coordinate the flow of funds in both directions. After World

War II, Scurlock recognized gaps in the existing oil transportation system and responded by developing the means to bring oil produced in isolated locations into the pipeline systems of the major oil companies. He used a growing fleet of trucks to pick up crude in isolated locations and deliver it to the nearest pipeline. He then built small gathering pipelines to replace the trucks if production from a field grew to justify the investment. By the late 1950s, Scurlock had built a system of transportation which included water terminals along the Mississippi River and Intercoastal Canal, more than 2,000 miles of gathering lines, and a fleet of transport trucks numbering almost 200. His operations, along with competing systems, helped integrate previously isolated oil producers into the national oil economy. Although Scurlock's privately held company was largely self-financing, NBC provided investment capital at several critical junctures in the company's history, financial services which facilitated the growth of this high-volume business, and personal advice about varied aspects of the business. Scurlock remained loyal to the bank which had provided assistance early in the life of his business, and he became an advisory director of NBC in 1961 before taking a seat on the board in 1964. This seat later went to Scurlock's successor, Jack Blanton, who remained on the board of Texas Commerce after Scurlock Oil was acquired by Ashland Oil in 1982.[10]

The other major predecessor of Texas Commerce, Texas National Bank, played a similarly significant role in helping finance the early development of Zapata Off-Shore Company, another oil-related firm which grew to national prominence beginning in the mid-1950s. George Bush, who later became vice-president of the United States, and J. Hugh Liedtke, subsequently the head of Pennzoil, formed Zapata Petroleum Corporation with headquarters in Houston in 1953, the same year Texas National Bank (TNB) was created through the merger of South Texas National and Union National Bank. TNB quickly established mutually profitable working ties with Zapata Off-Shore Company, an 80 percent–owned subsidiary of Zapata Petroleum organized in 1954 to explore offshore, initially in the Gulf of Mexico off the coast of Louisiana. Zapata thus joined the ranks of a relatively new branch of the oil industry, offshore drilling, which had begun in earnest in the decade after World War II. Because most of the early offshore activity was concentrated off the coast of Louisiana and Texas, Houston quickly became the administrative center for many offshore drilling companies. Companies such as Zapata needed substantial financing early in their histories, since even the first generation of offshore drilling rigs often required several million dollars in initial investments plus funds to cover high operating costs. As Zapata sought to establish it-self in a highly competitive and risky industry, it turned to Texas National Bank for Houston-based banking services. Loans from Texas National to Zapata for drilling rigs and vessels to tend the rigs established the growing company as one of the bank's most significant oil-related accounts in the late 1950s. Numerous other Houston-based offshore drilling contractors—including Rowan Drilling Company, Prince Marine Drilling and Exploration Company, Falcon Seaboard, and Standard Oil Company of Texas—appear regularly in the loan minutes of National Bank of Commerce and the surviving records of Texas National Bank.[11] As with numerous other companies serving the specialized needs of the oil industry, the Houston banks found excellent opportunities for business in financing the early development of local concerns which often expanded rapidly into national and international companies.

Two natural-gas companies which ultimately grew into prominent national firms were also among those who came early to National Bank of Commerce. El Paso Natural Gas Company was the creation of Paul Kayser, who had been a lawyer in the Houston firm which became Liddell, Sapp, Zivley & LaBoon before entering the natural-gas industry in 1928. Kayser recognized a promising business opportunity in supplying natural gas to the growing West Texas city of El Paso. With capital originally supplied by both Jesse Jones and Judge James A. Elkins, he organized a company which steadily grew to become a major producer and transporter of natural gas and related products throughout the Southwest. From these early years, NBC and El Paso Natural Gas maintained close business and personal ties, the bank supplying investment capital for the company and for the exploration activities of Kayser and other officers in the company in the developing West Texas oil-and-gas fields. El Paso Natural Gas maintained offices in Houston, and its ties to NBC were reinforced by the service of Kayser and subsequently of other officers on the board of NBC.

Tennessee Gas Transmission Company, which evolved into the diversified conglomerate Tenneco, had similar early ties to NBC. Tennessee Gas became a major interstate shipper of natural gas early in its history, and the high capital requirements of this endeavor quickly catapulted the company's needs far beyond the lending capacity of NBC. The bank nonetheless retained account relationships with both the company and its head, Gardiner Symonds, who served on the bank's board. In a sense, NBC grew with companies such as El Paso Natural Gas and Tenneco, for relationships with these dynamic companies enhanced both the reputation and the technical expertise of the bank. At times, NBC also used its ties to such once local concerns to complete transactions which generated notice within the national oil industry, helping solidify the bank's standing as a major participant in this field of lending. Such was the case in 1955 and 1956, when NBC's oil department helped put together a $76 million financial package used by Tenneco in its successful bid to acquire a large refinery and producing properties near Denver. Because its major New York bank was backing a competing bidder for the property, Tenneco turned to its Houston bank for assistance. This early successful foray into what was to become an increasingly competitive lending area, the financing of acquisitions by oil-and-gas companies, provided one more highly visible indication of the bank's steady progress toward parity with its larger competitors in oil lending.[12]

Several Houston-based manufacturers of equipment used in the oil industry also were significant parts of National Bank of Commerce's oil-related business. Indeed, one of the bank's largest and most important ongoing account relationships throughout much of its history has been that of the Hughes Tool Company. Born in the Gulf Coast oil fields in the first decades of the century, this company prospered initially through the efforts of two pioneers of the Texas oil industry, Howard Hughes and Walter Sharp. Crucial to its growth was its development of a revolutionary rotary rock-drilling bit, which was widely adopted by oil-and-gas drillers. To produce a growing inventory of bits and other oil tools, Hughes Tool steadily expanded its Houston manufacturing plant, which quickly became one of the largest manufacturing establishments in the city. National Bank of Commerce handled the company's substantial local payroll while supplying a variety of financial services to the company. In return, Hughes Tool maintained large deposits at NBC. After the 1930s, Hughes Tool entered the national spotlight as an umbrella organization holding the diversified parts of the business empire of Howard Hughes, Jr., the son of one of the founders. The Oil Tool Division of Hughes Tool—which included the company's traditional, Houston-based oil-tool business—remained the most significant ongoing link between the bank and Hughes Tool. Howard Hughes's empire expanded to include holdings in a large regional brewery on the site of Hughes Tool's manufacturing plant in Houston, Trans-World Airlines (TWA), several Las Vegas casinos, and Paramount Pictures, but National Bank of Commerce had little connection with Hughes's nonoil-related ventures, although it frequently participated in large loans headed by New York banks to finance the growth of TWA. Instead, NBC continued to serve as the lead bank in Houston for the hub of this far-flung empire, the Oil Tool Division of

Hughes Tool. This historically close working relationship continued after 1972, when Howard Hughes sold the Oil Tool Division, which then became a publicly owned company under its traditional name, Hughes Tool Company.[13]

Looking back at the formative years of the oil department at National Bank of Commerce, E. O. Buck recalled that "Out our window each morning were more opportunities than we could handle."[14] In responding to these opportunities, NBC and other Texas banks played significant roles in financing the maturing of the southwestern oil industry. Well before this era, the large, vertically integrated oil companies had established highly organized systems to coordinate the production, transportation, refining, and marketing of petroleum. But not until the coming of prorationing and the establishing of new channels of credit did segments of the oil industry underneath the vertically integrated majors move toward the same sort of overall coordination. In the decades after the 1930s, independent oil producers in the Southwest took advantage of stable prices and expanding production to establish systematic access to both credit and markets. The Texas banks became important suppliers of credit to oil producers in developing oil fields in the Southwest; they also helped finance improvements in the oil-related industries which grew to supply and service the independent oil industry. Credit and financial services could be crucial to the success of the endeavors of companies such as Scurlock Oil and the numerous other regional concerns which helped create a prosperous, smoothly operating independent oil industry well integrated into national markets. As such enterprises grew, so did the oil-related business of the region's banks. Thus in this vital sector of the regional economy, these banks and many locally based companies matured together.

Oil was not, of course, the only expansive portion of the regional economy in the postwar years, and National Bank of Commerce, Texas National, and other major Houston banks moved into several other newly significant lending areas while also increasing their involvement in traditionally important areas, notably real estate lending. The regional boom after 1945 included the rapid expansion of expenditures on various types of construction. The growth of real estate lending by Houston's banks to a level rivaling that of oil lending was a natural response to the surge in regional construction in this era.

As with oil lending, the existence of detailed historical sources from which to reconstruct the real estate lending activities of National Bank of Commerce makes it an instructive example of the involvement of one major Houston bank in this important area.[15] The record of loans made by NBC suggests several general conclusions concerning

Table 8.1   Major New Buildings in Houston's
Central Business District, 1931–56

Year Completed	Name	Square Footage	Floors
1935	Chamber of Commerce Building	530,550	22
1947	Southern National Bank	388,892	22
1948	1114 Texas Avenue	91,440	16
1951	Gulf Building Annex	200,000	12
1952	First Continental Life	125,000	5
1952	3100 Travis	325,000	12
1953	Melrose Building	181,000	21
1953	Texas Commerce Bank	276,400	15
1955	Houston Club Building	351,328	18
1955	Capitol National Bank	560,000	21
1956	Century Building	1,000,000	12
1956	Bank of the Southwest Building	835,245	24

SOURCE: Property Research and Investment Consultants, Inc., "Houston's Office Space Market" (April 1975).

NOTE: Based on buildings in existence in 1975 and using the 1975 names of the buildings.

its real estate lending. Although the most visible results of postwar construction in Houston were the numerous new office buildings (see Table 8.1) which redefined the city's skyline, NBC had little direct involvement in this type of construction, which demanded sums of capital far beyond the lending limit of any of Houston's banks. In the suburban growth ringing the downtown business district, NBC was deeply involved on a wholesale level through substantial loans to the major mortgage companies active in the region. In addition, the bank took its first steps into the financing of large-scale commercial developments such as suburban shopping centers, an area dominated in the 1950s by out-of-state financial institutions with much greater resources than those of the Houston banks. Taken as a whole, NBC's varied involvement in real estate and construction lending in the decade after World War II broke new ground in an area which has remained a significant part of the bank's portfolio of loans.[16]

John E. Whitmore fostered the growth of real estate lending at NBC after World War II. When he arrived at the bank in 1945, Whitmore found the same basic situation which faced E. O. Buck several years later. Both were specialists in lending areas which the bank hoped to expand, but both had to build from the ground up in organizing lending procedures and staff support in their respective areas. The lack of a real estate department at NBC in 1945 might seem curious; after all, the majority stockholder and chairman of the board had made much of his fortune in real estate transactions. But Jesse Jones generally segregated his real estate transactions from the business of the bank, and Whitmore found no tradition of intensive involvement in this area when he arrived. Recognizing an excellent opportunity, he began appraising properties, recommending loans, and bringing in new business. The results were impressive and immediate. By 1954 real estate lending had expanded enough to justify the creation of a real estate lending department and the hiring of additional real estate lending specialists. Whitmore turned to T. J. Bettes, one of the largest mortgage companies in the region, in search of new assistants, and there he found first Max Schutte and later Lloyd Bolton. These two men subsequently guided the evolution of real estate lending as Whitmore moved into the bank's top management.[17]

The Formative Years of Real Estate Lending at NBC

John Edwin Whitmore

John E. Whitmore arrived at the right place at the right time when he joined the National Bank of Commerce in November, 1945. Born in 1907, the son of an insurance agent, he was raised in Tucumcari, New Mexico. After attending the University of New Mexico, he went to work in 1929 for a real estate insurance firm in Albuquerque, where he learned the fundamentals of appraising and financing real estate. After the onset of the Depression, Whitmore took a job in 1934 with the Home Owners Loan Corporation (HOLC), a federal government agency established to refinance home loans in danger of being foreclosed. Whitmore spent the rest of the decade in the Dallas office of the HOLC, where he examined properties and established their selling prices in preparation for lending decisions. While rising to the position of deputy to the regional manager of the Dallas office of the HOLC, he earned a law degree in night school. Service in the navy brought him to Houston, and when he decided to stay on after the war, he found employment at National Bank of Commerce.

He began with an office in the basement of the Gulf Building making FHA loans, but he steadily became more deeply involved in real estate lending as others in the bank found out about his background and sought his advice. His close ties to mortgage companies were reflected in his election as president of the Houston Mortgage Bankers Association, a post seldom held by a commercial banker.

Whitmore's sixteen years of involvement in various phases of real estate before he joined NBC helped him respond effectively to the changing real estate market of the post–World War II era. His early entry into mortgage warehousing placed NBC at the forefront of this lucrative business. His recollections of the initial comments of a mortgage loan broker who was to become a long-term customer of the bank suggest the attraction of warehousing to those in the industry:

> I understand you have a system developed to lend money to mortgage companies on mortgages in transit to the final investor. I've been doing business with another bank and every time I have to fund a mortgage I must put up some stock my wife and I own as collateral. Now that limits my lending ability to the value of the stock we own. Your way—there'd be no limit to the business I could do as long as I have the mortgages sold.

The development of mortgage warehousing and other real estate lending arrangements by NBC and other Houston banks facilitated the residential construction which remade the face of Houston during the postwar suburban boom.

Whitmore's success in building a real estate lending department staffed by specialists with experience in mortgage companies helped establish this area as one of the largest activities of the bank, while also establishing the bank as the leader in mortgage warehousing in the city. Thus Whitmore left a lasting legacy in this lending area before becoming the bank's president from 1965 to 1969. Then as chairman from 1969 to 1971 and senior board chairman from 1972 to 1973, he guided the organization through a challenging era of transition from a unit bank to a multi-bank holding company.

SOURCES: Interview with John E. Whitmore by Joseph A. Pratt, June 15, 1983. Also see Interviews with John E. Whitmore by Walter L. Buenger, August 17, 1982, September 17, 1982; Interview with John E. Whitmore by Walter L. Buenger and Joseph A. Pratt, December 16, 1985.

Whitmore's development of a substantial business for the bank in mortgage warehousing allowed NBC to keep pace with changes in real estate construction and financing amid the construction boom in Houston after World War II. The introduction of long-term mortgages and the involvement of the Federal Housing Administration (FHA) in the home loan business encouraged home ownership among segments of the society that had not owned homes before the 1930s. If they were to keep pace with the resulting boom in housing, builders and mortgage companies required credit arrangements far different from the short-term mortgages to a relatively limited number of purchasers common in earlier days. Whitmore's understanding of these needs helped him recognize in mortgage warehousing an opportunity for NBC to profit while facilitating local development.

As a mortgage warehouse, NBC provided a mutually profitable location for local developers to store mortgages as they accumulated large packages for ultimate conveyance to long-term investors, usually the nation's largest insurance companies. One prominent mortgage warehouser at NBC, for example, was American General Investment Company, the mortgage subsidiary of American General Insurance Company. During the postwar construction boom around Houston, American General had a close working relationship with one of the nation's largest real estate underwriters, the Metropolitan Life Insurance Company. American General quite naturally turned to its primary bank, NBC, for assistance in financing short-term loans to local developers and in storing for short periods packages of mortgages awaiting shipment to long-term investors.

For a relatively low interest charge, locally active mortgage companies thus gained access to a convenient warehousing service. For its part, NBC received excellent new accounts characterized by large demand deposits and secure loans. As the early leader in mortgage warehousing among its Houston competitors, NBC seized and retained much of this business. Indeed, a standard entry in its loan books throughout the decades after 1945 reads as follows:

> __$ x__ to [name of a large Houston-based mortgage company], a line of credit to be made available on the company's short-term notes, to bear interest at the rate of __y%__ per annum and to be secured by assignments of FHA and conventional type real estate loans with commitments from insurance companies to purchase. Presented by Mr. Whitmore.

Such loans ranged all the way up to $1.5 million in this era, and the borrowers included most of the major mortgage companies active in the region. The Gulf Building was no doubt the most elegant warehouse in the city, and the storage of mortgages awaiting shipment to insurance companies proved a quite profitable business for the bank.[18]

NBC also provided loans directly to a few prominent builders active in Houston and surrounding areas. Construction lending was somewhat riskier and more competitive than mortgage warehousing, and NBC followed its traditional, conservative instincts in financing construction. After taking great care to design loans so as to minimize potential losses in this area, the bank participated in substantial loans for the construction of apartment complexes in outlying areas of Houston, in growing suburban towns such as Lake Jackson, south of Houston; and in Port Arthur and Beaumont, two cities about one hundred miles east of Houston. The design of such construction loans embodied considerable security for the bank. NBC's share in the loans tended to be for a relatively small portion of the total loan, with major mortgage companies, other local banks, and, at times, large money-center banks taking most of the remainder. These early construction loans generally extended for thirty- to thirty-five years, and they usually were secured by deeds to the property underlying the project. The notes were endorsed for FHA Mortgage Insurance and came with the personal guarantee of the builders that all bills would be paid and the project would be completed. Finally, the loan agreements generally stipulated that the borrower obtain a "takeout" commitment from an institutional investor to purchase the entire loan after completion of the project. Even with such security designed into these loans, NBC made fewer construction loans than did several of its competitors, notably Texas National Bank. Indeed, as in early oil lending, NBC generally stayed away from construction lending unless the builder had established a track record of success and was a known customer of the bank.

In Houston's burgeoning suburbs, its downtown banks found an expanding outlet for construction financing. The building of the first generation of shopping malls around Houston in the 1950s required resources beyond the capacities of the local banks, since $10 to $15 million was needed to complete one of the early shopping centers. NBC participated in the financing of such developments through involvement in loan packages headed by money-center banks and large insurance companies. Such was the case, for example, in the construction of the Gulfgate Shopping Center, south of downtown Houston, in the mid-1950s. NBC took a 10 percent participation in a multimillion dollar loan headed by First National of Boston and Chemical Corn Exchange Bank of New York. The loan was secured by a deed on the property and by assignments of the loan commitment to two large insurance companies. It was also guaranteed by the principal owners of Gulfgate. The involvement of Houston banks in such large-scale construction projects generated good profits while also helping introduce them to the intricacies of financing large construction projects.[19]

The spread of the suburbs reflected the growing affluence of the era, and those segments of society which used newly available mortgages to buy homes also sought credit for consumer goods. NBC helped provide such consumer credit in the same way it funded mortgages, at the wholesale level, through loans to companies which provided credit to consumers. Perhaps the largest such loans were to the major automobile companies, which regularly borrowed substantial sums from NBC to use in funding their automobile credit programs in the region. General Motors Acceptance Corporation (GMAC) had pioneered in financing automobile purchases in the 1920s, and its major competitors established similar plans in the 1950s. In a region where the ownership of a car was almost essential, the funding of a portion of the needs of automobile credit programs generated steady business for NBC. The bank also provided regular loans to other large retailers with credit programs, notably farm-machinery companies and department-store chains. NBC also participated at the wholesale level in the business of general consumer credit through loans to various chains of finance companies. Amid the expansion of consumer spending in the prosperous postwar years, many banks moved directly into consumer lending, but NBC chose instead to remain primarily a wholesale bank not heavily involved in direct lending to consumers. It sought to profit indirectly from the growth of consumer credit while avoiding both the risks in this area and the large commitment of resources and personnel needed to evaluate and administer masses of small loans. This choice reflected the bank's unwillingness to move too far from its traditional strength, lending to major businesses, but it also meant that NBC's competitors moved ahead of the bank in an area which would grow in significance in the postwar decades.[20]

The wholesale consumer credit business developed by NBC was part of a broad and significant trend evident in the 1950s, the regular lending of large sums to companies entering Houston from other parts of the country. As one of the nation's fastest-growing urban markets, Houston naturally attracted the attention of many nationally active firms looking for opportunities to expand. When such companies made the decision to extend their businesses into Houston, they often needed a local bank to smooth the way. NBC was the bank of choice for many of these companies. In the 1940s and 1950s, the bank developed an impressive list of national accounts which included several major airlines, chemical companies entering the region, nationally active meat-packers, primary-metals manufacturers who established plants along the ship channel, farm-implement and heavy-equipment companies, and an array of other concerns. NBC was particularly successful among local banks in attracting the business of established firms which moved into the Houston market. Its involvement with these national companies often took the form of participations in large loan packages headed by their lead banks in the money centers. But even small participations provided a beachhead from which the bank could attempt to capture more of the business of these blue-chip firms.[21]

NBC's early success in this highly competitive market must be attributed primarily to the efforts of two men: Jesse Jones and A. D. Simpson. Simpson traveled extensively after the war in search of new business, and his work involved far more than simply greeting prospective customers and mentioning the name of Jesse Jones. Because of their large size and established credit records, the national companies on which Simpson called had ready access to credit from a variety of other sources. Simpson might open discussions on the basis of a company's previous recognition of Jesse Jones, but he did not capture an account unless he could offer an attractive package of services. On this point, the recollections of one of Simpson's colleagues are instructive: "I remember once he brought back from New York a big account that made us unusually happy. In a loan committee meeting, we were talking about it and Simpson said: 'This was just a pushover. I worked on this company's financial man for only ten years.'" The nation was coming to Houston in the 1940s and 1950s, and before his retirement in 1958, Dee Simpson pointed the way to Jesse Jones's bank.[22]

Houston's dynamism attracted people as well as business in the late 1940s, and one of those who migrated to the city played a crucial role in establishing the National Bank of Commerce in international lending, another new lending area which was to grow steadily in significance. George Ebanks was a Canadian with varied experience in international banking when he moved to Houston because "you could walk down the streets and feel things happening—growth." He also recognized that international banking was not yet well-developed in the city and that he would have an excellent opportunity to build such business as the trade through the port of Houston expanded. In choosing a job, Ebanks was swayed by the idea of working for Jesse Jones's bank, and he joined NBC in 1948.[23]

After spending several years learning about the bank's operations and about the local economy, Ebanks received approval to establish a foreign department, a name later changed to the international department. In the early 1950s, Houston banks had limited experience in this area. Before the disruption of the traditional patterns of cotton trading by the Great Depression, several of the city's oldest banks had been introduced to international finance through their involvement with cotton trading firms, but the post-World War II era presented a series of new challenges. At NBC Ebanks faced the task of building an international department from the bottom up in a bank with no traditional foreign connections, no cable address for conducting such trade, and considerable skepticism among top managers about the advisability of entering an area so far outside their experience and involving relatively large sums of money.

Ebanks did, however, possess several advantages which aided his efforts. First, he had the strong support of Jesse Jones, who had become interested in various aspects of international finance during his tenure in Washington, and good access to Jones when he needed approval for ideas resisted by the bank's top managers. In addition, he had the Houston economy, whose expanding trade presented excellent opportunities for increasing the bank's international activities. As trade through the port grew and as numerous Houston-based companies began to expand into international markets, the bank steadily followed the movement of goods and companies into the world economy.

One avenue to foreign expansion for the bank was fuller participation in the flow of cotton through Houston, which revived briefly in the decade after World War II. As cotton moved from Houston to Japan and other parts of Asia, NBC supplied letters of credit for buyers for the major Texas-based cotton shippers, who traditionally had obtained credit from Houston banks to help finance their cotton trade within the United States. A similar pattern developed in the region's rapidly growing rice industry. The marshlands along the Texas-Louisiana Gulf Coast spawned several major rice-milling companies which purchased rice for their mills in part with credit provided by Houston banks, including NBC. When these companies became major exporters of rice to Cuba, Puerto Rico, and other foreign markets, their Houston banks smoothed the way by providing letters of credit and other services. In the early 1950s, Ebanks arranged large loans for use in the development of the rice trade to Cuba, but the bank's loan committee turned down the loans as too large and too risky given the bank's unfamiliarity with Cuba. After entreaties by Ebanks, Jones reversed this decision, thereby enabling the bank's international department to enter competition with both the money-center banks and its major Houston competitors for this potentially lucrative business. Subsequent events in Cuba ratified both the loan committee's skepticism and Jones's confidence in Ebanks. The Cuban revolution resulted in the forfeiture or the renegotiation of many of the loans of United States banks in Cuba for the rice trade, but NBC managed to recover its loans. Thus in one of its earliest ventures in international lending, the bank witnessed the benefits of being both careful and lucky in lending in nations with unstable political systems.[24]

Other aspects of international banking were less volatile. Indeed, much of the bank's business in this area consisted of assistance to established customers as they expanded into other industrialized nations. Perhaps the best example of such business was the bank's close cooperation with Hughes Tool as that company expanded into international markets after World War II. To a company with limited international experience, the strategic choice to move into other nations raised a variety of questions. Whom should the company see in London to explore the prospect of establishing a manufacturing plant in Great Britain? Ebanks had the answers, and he visited London with representatives of Hughes Tool in an expedition which ultimately resulted in the company's construction of a major new manufacturing complex near Belfast. Could the company transport explosives across the border into Canada? Again, Ebanks had the contacts needed to resolve this question. As Hughes Tool and other Houston-based companies expanded their operations in international markets, the services of a local bank with an effective international department proved quite useful. The bank's knowledge and contacts facilitated such expansion, while at the same time solidifying the account relationships between the bank and several of its most important customers.

This was all part of a larger process, the growth of Houston as an international trading center. Commodities trading, particularly in cotton and rice, led the way but was quickly reinforced by the activities of the oil-related companies based in Houston but active throughout the world. The evolving international departments of NBC and other large Houston banks played a significant role in encouraging the growth in volume and variety of Houston trade. Bankers such as George Ebanks served as unofficial goodwill ambassadors for Houston as they traveled through the world. They also assisted city officials in organizing various international trade conferences. Finally, the banks encouraged other nations with growing trade ties to Houston to establish foreign consulates in the city, facilitating the flow of people, goods, and information. All in all, the banking community helped accelerate the emergence of the city as an important center of international trade.[25]

International lending was a significant departure in NBC's postwar evolution, but it did not rival other categories of loans in size. After oil and real estate, most of the rest of the bank's business came from loans to local businesses based in the Houston metropolitan area. One of the largest metropolitan accounts was Houston Lighting and Power, the utility company which served a broad area around Houston. The major banks in the city traditionally shared this account. The participation of each bank was based on its size, and NBC generally organized and managed these loans. But the rest of the region's banking business was both diverse and highly competitive, as banks sought to attract and hold accounts through a combination of personal ties and good services.

Unlike oil and real estate lending in the postwar era, the remainder of the bank's local business does not lend itself to simple generalizations. Instead, the local activities of banks such as NBC and Texas National Bank touched every phase of Houston's development. In the years immediately after World War II, for example, major regional retailers required substantial financing as they responded to the growing consumer demands of the region. In this era, NBC also expanded its traditional business with the region's largest insurance company, American General. Underneath such prominent concerns were numerous smaller, less visible companies which provided a variety of goods and services for a rapidly growing region. NBC's important metropolitan accounts included Houston's largest chain of parking lots, a major scrap-metals producer, and the producers of metal products required by the region's booming construction industry. The growing economic diversity in the Houston metropolitan area presented an increasing array of business for the city's banks.

One broad pattern stands out in National Bank of Commerce's diverse lending activities in the years from 1945 to 1956: the diversification of the bank's loan portfolio as petroleum-related activities and a steady maturing of the regional economy presented a variety of opportunities. Traditional stalwarts of the bank, loans to prominent businessmen in the Houston metropolitan area, came to share the spotlight with relatively new types of lending. Oil and real estate loans surged to the forefront, and national and international accounts also became more significant. Accompanying this new diversity in lending was the geographical expansion of the bank's influence, as the regional economy grew to encompass surrounding areas and as the bank became increasingly involved in the state and national economies.

Although the Houston economy expanded after World War II, the position of its banks within the national banking industry nonetheless remained largely unchanged. In an era of low rates of inflation and cheap, abundant energy, the pattern for commercial banks throughout the nation was orderly expansion. During this extended period of security-based banking, government regulations assured banks of interest-free demand deposits, insured deposits, and limited competition from other financial service industries. Within this regulatory framework, the major concerns of most commercial banks in this era were to secure adequate deposits to finance the postwar boom while protecting or expanding market share against competition from other local banks.

In an era when Texas grew significantly faster than the nation as a whole, it was not surprising that its banks also grew faster than the national average. The major banks in Dallas and Houston were doubly blessed, since within Texas the large urban centers were far outgrowing the rest of the state. Amid such extremely favorable market conditions, the major Texas banks expanded steadily. The National Bank of Commerce, for example, more than doubled its deposits in the decade after 1946. Yet while growing rapidly, Houston's banks proved unable to close significantly the gap in size between themselves and the much larger money-center banks. This gap posed a significant problem, since the resources of a bank determine the amount it can legally lend to its customers.

A Journey to the East

During the postwar boom in the regional economy, the limited lending capacities of the largest Texas banks relative to those of the much larger money-center banks was not simply a concern of local banks eager for greater profits. The lack of sufficient local sources of developmental capital also affected the operations of major Houston-based firms. This was particularly true of business enterprises which began as regional concerns and grew into nationally and internationally active companies. Perhaps the best example of such a company was Hughes Tool Company, which grew from the Gulf Coast oil fields to become the major manufacturer of drilling bits in the world. Hughes Tool and its principal owners, Howard Hughes and Howard Hughes, Jr., had strong historical ties to the National Bank of Commerce. But as the company grew, it required funds far beyond the bank's capacities. Thus in the boom years after World War II, representatives of Hughes Tool regularly made the trek, hats in hand, to the money-center banks in New York. The company's long-term chief financial officer, Calvin Collier, remembers these trips as far from pleasant. Air travel in the 1950s was neither as comfortable nor as dependable as it subsequently has become. Trips to arrange loans could easily absorb much of a work week, with a full day of bouncing around in a prop plane on each end. Though large in terms of the Houston economy, Hughes Tool was simply one of many national accounts of the New York banks. As such, it did not command the special attention of the New York banks that it

Figure 8.2. Comparison of deposits of National Bank of Commerce (Houston) and First National City Bank (New York), 1930–63.

SOURCES: Ben F. Love, *People and Profits*, 43–45; Harold van B. Cleveland and Thomas Huertas, *Citibank, 1812–1970*, 319–23.

did of NBC. Indeed, Collier recalled one particularly frustrating bargaining tactic of the New York banks, the introduction of new conditions for loans late in the week when the weary borrower might be persuaded to compromise to go home. The potential borrower could accept these conditions or face the prospect of staying in New York over the weekend to complete negotiations on Monday. Collier recalled that "there were many Thursday afternoons that I would cancel my flight back for Friday afternoon because I knew I wasn't going to make it, and I never did forget that."

Bouncing up to New York for a week or more away from family, while routine work and various other obligations accumulated in Houston, was not exactly a vacation. Those who made such trips regularly in the years before the bank holding company movement in Texas no doubt took a measure of satisfaction from the growing competition in the Houston banking market during the 1970s and 1980s, when the money-center banks began calling aggressively on Houston businesses rather than waiting for them to come to New York. Although there is no hard evidence that Hughes Tool was denied access to needed capital in these years, it is clear that frequent journeys to the East were costly, time-consuming, and personally draining for those involved.

SOURCE: Interview with Calvin Collier by Joseph A. Pratt, November 27, 1984.

Most banks in Texas towns and cities had little practical reason to compare their size with that of the largest banks in the nation, but the major Houston and Dallas banks did have reason for concern. As Texas prospered, many of the state's most important businesses became increasingly active in national and international markets. Constrained by the state's unit banking laws, the major Texas banks could not grow rapidly enough to serve the financial needs of such companies. New York and Chicago banks continued to supply the bulk of the financing needed for their expansion, and the major banks in Texas generally had to settle for relatively limited participations in such loans.

Conservative lending policies fostered by the experience of the Great Depression further limited the amount of money available for loans. After the early 1930s the rule of thumb followed at NBC under Jesse Jones was that total loans should not exceed 40 percent of deposits. Tables 8.2 and 6.4 (p. 116) show that from 1933 until the mid-1950s the city's major banks seldom exceeded Jones's guideline for NBC. From 1945 forward, however, these banks gradually expanded their lending activity, in part by shifting funds from government securities into lending. By the early 1960s lending levels once again

Table 8.2 Relationship of Loans to Deposits in Houston Banks, 1945–63

End of Year	Union	STCNB*	NBC	First National	City National	Bank of the Southwest†
1945						
Loans	3,943,681	13,012,763	19,955,767	30,579,079	18,227,925	31,701,341
% Deposits	5.2	10.6	11.1	17.2	16.2	19.2
1950						
Loans	4,912,847	46,564,639	73,113,519	95,516,715	61,930,256	95,099,208
% Deposits	6.5	35.3	29.4	38.0	30.8	43.7
1955						
Loans		84,602,004‡	134,127,353	127,940,868	121,803,662	157,272,069
% Deposits		39.4	36.5	42.0	34.5	51.7
1960						
Loans	114,848,675		169,442,233	247,736,158§		205,195,198
% Deposits	44.0		41.8	35.0		48.4
1963						
Loans	174,105,434		261,107,502	320,686,146		275,193,946
% Deposits	60.5		51.0	40.8		53.9

SOURCE: Statements of Condition, TCB Archives.
* South Texas National Bank after 1949.
† Second National Bank until 1956.
‡ Merged to form Texas National Bank in 1953.
§ Merged to form First City National Bank in 1956.

equaled those of the 1920s (see Table 4.3, p. 87). The most aggressive lenders—notably Bank of the Southwest—established a clear competitive advantage in attractive new accounts in the postwar economic boom.

In their efforts to expand the resources available for lending, Houston's bankers made use of several traditional paths toward greater size. They expanded their legal lending limits by plowing profits back into their capital stock; they solicited demand deposits to increase the funds available for lending. Houston banks also helped satisfy the demand for credit by regional concerns in a way much in keeping with their history. Through their ties to money-center banks, they arranged large loans and participated in these loans up to the limit allowed them by law. The Houston banks also helped mobilize credit for their booming urban-industrial region by offering their correspondent banks in less dynamic outlying regions of the state the opportunity to participate in loans to Houston-area businesses. This was an important source of deposit growth for big-city banks in Texas, as witnessed by the fact that interbank deposits within Texas more than doubled from 1946 to 1956, while such deposits increased only 40 percent throughout the nation.[26] Because of its fast growth relative to the established industrial centers on the East Coast as well as to the smaller towns in Texas, Houston thus attracted funds from both the money centers and the outlying countryside. The large Houston banks with well-established correspondent ties in both directions served as conduits for the flow of investment capital into the region.

In their quest for greater size, the fastest path available to the Houston banks was the merger route. This approach had been used repeatedly by the banks in the past, and a new wave of mergers in the 1940s and 1950s enabled several prominent downtown banks to grow rapidly while redefining the market structure of Houston banking. Second National Bank of Houston (later renamed Bank of the Southwest before being merged into MCorp in 1983) introduced this wave of mergers during the war years, when it acquired the San Jacinto National Bank of Houston in 1944 and the Guardian Trust Company in 1945, producing a bank whose size was on a par with the largest banks in the city. Then in 1953 the merger of Union National Bank (then the sixth-largest bank in Houston) and South Texas National Bank (the fifth-largest) again altered the downtown banking industry. The most significant merger of this era came three years later, when City National Bank merged with First National Bank. This union of two of the four largest banks in Houston combined the traditional strengths of the oldest bank in the city, First National, with the energy and innovativeness of one of its fastest-growing banks, City National. The result was a single new concern, the First City National Bank of Houston, with almost double the deposits of National Bank of Commerce and Bank of the Southwest, its major competitors in the region. Even this new leader among Houston banks, it should be noted, was only the thirty-seventh-largest commercial bank in the nation in terms of assets. Taken as a whole, the mergers of the 1940s and 1950s pushed the major Houston banks to a new level as measured by both aggregate deposits and the amount each bank could lend to an individual customer.

Yet despite their obvious attraction, mergers had several limitations as strategic responses to the need for greater size. Under Texas unit banking laws, mergers required the physical combination of the facilities and personnel of the two banks into a single location. This meant that the newly created bank had to give up the site previously occupied by one of the merger partners. Location was an important determinant in the choice of a bank by an individual or business, and there was no guarantee that the accounts of the bank forced to move to complete a merger would follow the bank down the street to a new location. The act of moving proved costly and taxing, as banks generally minimized the disruption of business by completing the entire move in one long weekend of carting records and equipment from one building to the other. Finally, the process of sorting out the duties of two sets of employees trained to perform the same basic functions often caused confusion and uncertainty. Beyond such practical problems was a broader limitation on the reliance on mergers for growth: the limited pool of potential merger partners became smaller with each succeeding merger. As the largest banks paired off in the 1950s, a final constraint—the possibility of anticompetitive implications under the antitrust laws—also loomed in the background.

The state's unit banking law was not the only constraint on the growth of Houston's banks after World War II. Bank managers could have moved a step toward greater lending capacities simply by accepting more risks. The relatively low percentage of total deposits used to fund loans in the 1950s, for example, was a choice made by the management, not imposed by law. Such choices serve as reminders of the lasting impact of the Great Depression on bankers, who quite understandably valued security of deposits over profitability at a time when memories of widespread bank failures remained vivid.

Yet within the boundaries set by managerial concern about security of deposits and the barrier to expansion posed by antibranching restrictions, in the decade after 1945 the predecessors of Texas Com-

merce responded creatively to the opportunities in their rapidly growing region. Their banks grew steadily, in part by organizing specialized
lending departments and lending procedures designed to meet the
credit needs of fast-growing sectors of the regional economy such as oil
production, in which the major Houston banks emerged among the
nation's lending leaders. Although their assets remained far smaller
than those of the nation's largest banks in the mid-1950s, the era of
sustained expansion in the postwar years pushed Houston's leading
banks to a new scale which would require far-reaching adjustments in
their operations and management.

CHAPTER 9

Merging for Size and Management Succession

 ═══════════════════════════════════════

In the early 1950s, the National Bank of Commerce was in many ways a picture of success. It was among the largest banks in one of the fastest-growing regions in the nation, and its list of blue-chip accounts included many of the most prominent firms and individuals in Houston. On the bank's letterhead as chairman of the board was the name of Jesse Jones, Houston's best-known businessman and civic leader. Although smaller than NBC, Texas National Bank also prospered in this boom period in the region. Looming before both banks, however, were difficult questions of how to obtain greater size and management succession. They needed to grow rapidly to protect their market position among Houston banks and to become more competitive with the much larger money-center banks which had strong working ties with many of the major businesses in their region. As they grew beyond the scale of traditional Houston banks, they needed to create management systems suited to a growing, changing industry. Finally, NBC in particular needed to find a new generation of leaders to replace its aging managers and its guiding spirit, Jesse Jones, who died in 1956.

NBC did not begin abruptly searching for new management when Jones died. Several years earlier, responding to the opportunities presented by post–World War II expansion, those in control of the bank sought to find younger managers capable of carrying on the traditions which had made NBC one of the most profitable, secure, and largest banks in Houston. In short, they sought younger versions of themselves. This choice was understandable; the top management of NBC had ample reason to be proud of its organization and to be loyal to the approach to banking employed by its primary owner, Jesse Jones.[1]

Yet in the long run, the effort to maintain the traditions of Jesse Jones's bank after he and his generation had passed from the scene presented problems for the bank. One such problem was obvious. Where could the bank hope to find a new Jesse Jones with the capacity to fill the key roles performed by him? Moreover, how would the authority of such a Jones-like figure be altered as the increasing dispersal of stock gradually separated ownership and management? Less obvious were problems caused by the bank's success in growing larger. How could the highly personal approach to management traditionally practiced at NBC be adapted to the bank's increasingly large and complex operations? What sort of manager would be required to make such adjustments? Finally, how would management traditions established in a tightly regulated banking environment have to be adjusted when the breakdown of regulatory boundaries brought increased competition? In the early 1950s, the managers of NBC simply wanted to find their next generation of managers. But as they conducted their search during the next decade, these concerns confronted them at every turn. For in the 1950s and 1960s, a far-reaching transition in the scale, speed, and competitiveness of banking fostered a managerial revolution in the industry as traditional methods of bank management gave way to modern techniques adopted from other industries and taught by business schools. Thus as National Bank of Commerce looked for a new generation of managers capable of maintaining traditions established in its past, a new and very different future beckoned for the banking industry.

Management succession is, of course, a perennial concern of top business leaders, whose final obligation is to prepare their organization to function effectively without them. But for NBC during the 1950s, management succession presented special difficulties. The first was obvious from even a glance at a photograph of the bank's top officers; most were either nearing or past normal retirement age. For a time, the bank's top management seemed determined to rewrite the city's actuarial charts; but, inevitably, death and retirement struck swiftly in the mid-1950s, removing three of the four men who had been instrumental in guiding the bank's fortunes for decades. Jesse Jones died in June, 1956, at the age of eighty-three; Sam Taub, who had contributed mightily to the success of the bank as the chairman of the executive committee from 1940 to 1956, had died earlier that year at the age of seventy-nine. Long-term vice-chairman A. D. Simpson withdrew from active participation in the bank's affairs in 1958 at the age of seventy-eight. Suddenly only Robert P. Doherty, who had been president of the bank since 1948 and who was sixty-seven years old in 1958, remained from a top management team which had functioned smoothly for decades.[2]

An Epidemic of Management-Succession Problems

This 1958 photograph of an aged A. D. Simpson and Robert P. Doherty standing in front of a portrait of the recently deceased Jesse Jones aptly summarizes the management-succession problems common to many Houston banks in the 1940s and 1950s. The top managers were growing old, yet they remained in the shadows of the giants of the previous era. These problems meant that the merger wave among downtown Houston banks in the post–World War II decades was driven by more than the quest for greater size. Management succession was an equal incentive.

Every major bank merger in Houston in this era was motivated in part by the search for new management. Both Union National Bank and South Texas Commercial National Bank suffered from the deaths of several prominent managers in the 1940s and early 1950s, preparing their management to agree to a friendly consolidation in 1953, which created the Texas National Bank. At the same time, leaders of the First National Bank—the city's oldest and long its largest bank—explored numerous merger options aimed in part at infusing new blood capable of shaking the organization from its lethargy. In the 1940s, death took both J. T. Scott and F. M. Law, who had been the bank's top managers since before World War I. Many vice-presidents of the bank in the 1940s either left to manage other banks or were major stockholders and descendants of B. A. Shepard, who owned virtually all of the bank's stock at his death in 1891. The Shepard family members were often interested in many things other than bank management. So the bank was driven to find new managers or a merger partner with good management. The quest ultimately led to the most significant merger of this era, the combination of First National and City National. Finally, National Bank of Commerce sought to catch up with First City while acquiring a new generation of management by merging with Texas National in 1964.

The reasons for the management-succession problems of this era included general factors as well as factors specific to banking in Houston. In common with many American businesses in this era, the local banks had no mandatory retirement age, and many aging bank managers proved reluctant to step aside to make room for successors. In an industry characterized by tight, centralized control, the grooming of successors was often neglected, in part out of fear of creating a challenge to top management authority. Aggressive younger managers tended to avoid banking in this era, since the industry traditionally paid salaries low by the standards of other industries while also generally requiring young officers to serve long and at times tedious apprenticeships. By setting strict boundaries on both the activities and the operating procedures of banks, the security-based regulations of the 1930s no doubt further discouraged many creative young managers from entering banking. Such conditions made it difficult for banks to recruit new management talent, assuring a shallow pool of potential successors when top management positions had to be filled.

Several more specific factors heightened the leadership problem after World War II. The first was simply a matter of timing. The generation of Houston bankers who entered the industry during the flush years after World War I proved a hearty lot. As they grew older, the pool of potential replacements within their organizations was diminished by the absence of normal hiring during the Great Depression and World War II. Thus by the 1950s, several banks had aging top managers and a cluster of young, relatively inexperienced officers but few seasoned managers poised to assume top spots. In the decade after World War II, most banks needed a new generation of middle managers to keep pace with the industry's growth as well as a new cluster of top managers capable of responding to fundamental changes in the market such as the decline of cotton lending and the rise of oil lending. All major Houston banks confronted this dual management-succession problem as they adjusted to postwar prosperity. Most addressed it with a combination of more active recruitment, more formal management training programs, and mergers.

SOURCES: Interviews with John Whitmore by Walter L. Buenger, August 17, 1982, September 17, 1982; Interview with W. A. Kirkland by Walter L. Buenger, July 3, 1985, TCB Archives; William A. Kirkland, *Old Bank–New Bank: The First National Bank, Houston, 1866–1956.*

The key to the success of this team had been a clear division of labor among men well suited for their specific roles. In addition to putting the team together and overseeing its performance, Jesse Jones had provided the strategic overview essential to the emergence of NBC as one of the leading banks in Houston. Although National Bank of Commerce was only one part of Jones' business empire, he understood how the various parts fit together and how the empire as a whole fit into the broader financial, political, and civic patterns of Houston. He had the mind-set of a strategist interested in long-run trends, and even after he withdrew somewhat from the bank's management because of his advancing age, he remained the source of the broad vision which guided the bank's progress.[3]

In filling in the details, Jones relied heavily on officers of the bank. Dee Simpson, a close friend of Jones, took various titles after coming to work at the bank in 1918, but his primary responsibilities remained constant. He took the role of "Mr. Outside" in meeting and servicing major customers and potential customers of the bank. The bank's internal operation, however, was the domain of "Mr. Inside," Robert Doherty, who was a conservative banker cast from the same mold which had produced two of the leaders of the previous generation of Houston bankers, R. M. Farrar and S. M. McAshan. Within the bank, Doherty was known as a stern, often aloof boss who demanded from subordinates the dedication and attention to detail which he demanded of himself. He was equally demanding of those who would borrow money from his bank, and he ruled the loan committee as surely as he ruled the bank. It was said that he could "feel a bad loan as if by osmosis," and under his control National Bank of Commerce maintained its reputation as a bank which avoided risky loans by dealing primarily with proven companies and well-established individuals.[4]

The last member of the management team, Sam Taub, further protected the quality of the bank's loans by bringing to its operations an extensive knowledge of the Houston economy and of the individual companies in the region. Taub and his brother Ben managed J. N. Taub and Sons, a wholesale tobacco firm which they had founded with their father and built into one of the largest concerns of its kind in the Southwest. Taub was a close associate of Jesse Jones, and he had become a director of NBC in 1915 at the first board meeting following Jones's acquisition of a controlling interest in the bank. Although Taub was never paid to manage the bank, he nonetheless took an active role in its management as a one-man credit department appraising values and risks. His council and leadership as chairman of the executive committee proved valuable on a wide range of issues affecting the bank's finances and loans.[5]

The complementary skills of Jones, Simpson, Doherty, and Taub assured that the bank rested in capable hands until the mid-1950s. Given the division of labor within this management team, however, difficult adjustments inevitably accompanied the departure of one of its members. Such problems were compounded in the brief span from 1956 to 1958, when three of the four top managers departed, leaving Bob Doherty alone at the top. There he encountered competitive conditions which forced "Mr. Inside" to respond to changes in the bank's external environment while also challenging banking practices ingrained by almost forty years of experience.

An able crew of vice-presidents stood ready to assist Doherty, but none seemed to Doherty to be ready to assume a leadership role in the bank. Long-term employees such as P. C. (Pete) Rehrauer, Gainer Jones, J. H. Garrett, and A. F. Fisher had entered National Bank of Commerce before World War II, and they had been joined there after the war by other officers such as John Whitmore and E. O. Buck. This cluster of managers had matured together as they built the bank's business under the guidance of Simpson and Doherty. Age, however, was not the primary obstacle standing between these experienced bankers and the presidency of the bank to which they had devoted much of their lives. Instead, their most debilitating liability was a lack of exposure to the overall operations of the bank. Doherty's responsibilities on Jones's team of top managers was dictated by a clear division of labor, and Doherty applied this same approach in his assignment of duties to vice-presidents. Whitmore became the real estate specialist; Buck was the energy lender. Other officers had similar specialized areas of experience. Doherty orchestrated the efforts of these specialists, exercising authority over the overall operations of the bank and showing little inclination to groom these middle managers to prepare them to replace him in the future.

Robert Pace Doherty
1891–1967

Robert P. Doherty was the man most responsible for the conservative approach to new borrowers at the National Bank of Commerce. Doherty was born in Fort Worth and began his banking career at the First State Bank in Kingsville, Texas, in 1914. He joined NBC in 1917, and by 1925 he was the assistant cashier. When A. D. Simpson became president in 1933, Doherty was named vice-president and then executive vice-president. While Simpson made calls throughout the country and the city, Doherty ran the bank.

Doherty had a reputation as being the archtype of the traditional banker. Even those who liked him often admitted that he was a silent man who lacked skill in dealing with subordinates. Others saw a different side of Doherty. One of these was Gainer Jones, who left this remembrance of him:

A few years after I had joined the National Bank of Commerce—those years when, for the most part, I was collecting on those bad loans we brought over from Public National Bank—I was worrying about my status. Nobody ever told me that I could consider myself a permanent member of the staff. I felt nervous about my situation. Anybody would.

So I asked Bob Doherty if, after I straightened out the Public National loan portfolio, I could consider myself permanent. He said to me: "Mr. Jones will be in town tomorrow. Go upstairs and talk to him." So the next day I went to the top of the Gulf Building and saw the famous Jesse Jones and, hiding my anxiety as best I could, I asked him about my future. Mr. Jones asked me a question and before I could answer he answered it himself. Then another question and he answered that himself. And so on. Maybe five or six questions and I didn't get the chance to answer a single one. Then Mr. Jones said: "Forget about going any place else. We have a place for you here." I didn't press the matter.

In retrospect, I saw several things in this incident. First, if Bob Doherty had thought badly of me he never would have sent me to see Jesse Jones. And, so, without a doubt, Bob had phoned Jesse Jones and told him about me and so on. Certainly Mr. Jones didn't know anything about me. Second, Bob was giving me the opportunity to get better acquainted with the "big boss," the man who virtually owned the bank. And, finally, Bob knew that my self-confidence would be built up when Mr. Jones himself told me that I had his confidence and that I would go home and tell my wife what Mr. Jones had said.

If you ask me, Bob Doherty was a pretty adept man in human relations.

Indeed, Doherty proved adept at managing the day-to-day operations of National Bank of Commerce in a highly centralized managerial structure which gave him considerable authority over most aspects of the bank's operations. As long as Jesse Jones lent his image and prestige to the bank, as long as Sam Taub gave of his knowledge of the region's business, and as long as A. D. Simpson handled public relations, Doherty proved a remarkably successful banker. He deserves much of the credit for the almost 500 percent increase in NBC's deposits from 1935 to 1945 and for the continued success of the bank in the postwar years.

Doherty became president of the bank in 1948 and chairman of the board and chief executive officer in 1958. He continued in that position after Texas National and NBC merged to form Texas National Bank of Commerce. He did not retire from active management of the bank until 1966, forty-nine years after he began work as a teller at NBC.

During his last decade at the bank, however, death removed Jones,

Simpson, and Taub, forcing an aging Doherty to shoulder more and more of the burden of managing and representing the bank. For example, like other bankers before him, he served as a member of the Rice University Board of Governors. He was also almost solely responsible for most strategic decisions. He kept the bank out of the credit-card business and retained the focus on commercial accounts. In the late 1950s and early 1960s, he also attempted to find and promote younger managerial talent in the bank. As was the case with many traditional bankers accustomed to exercising control over their organizations, Doherty had difficulties in grooming others to share authority in the bank's management, setting the stage for a serious problem of management succession.

SOURCES: Love, "People and Profits," 22–23; Interview with Gainer B. Jones by William Allison, TCB Archives; Interview with Robert A. Doherty, Jr., by Walter L. Buenger, September 30, 1983, TCB Archives; Interview with J. W. McLean, by Joseph A. Pratt, August 13, 1984, TCB Archives; *Houston Chronicle* (June 25, 1967); R. P. Doherty, Jr., to Mike Quinn, June 30, 1982, TCB Archives.

A more fundamental problem loomed with the passage of time after Jones's death. Doherty was determined to run the bank as he felt Jesse Jones meant it to be run. This made him quite resistant to change. He had succeeded as a banker by systematically and diligently carrying out the details of business within a strategy and structure established and periodically adjusted by Jones. The death of Jones meant that adjustments would no longer be forthcoming from the top, and Doherty was as inexperienced as a strategist as his subordinates were in running the loan committee.

This had not been a problem before the late 1950s, in part because Jones was still alive and in part because few basic adjustments had been required in the relatively stable, predictable banking industry from the mid-1930s through the 1950s. In this earlier era, ownership rested squarely in the hands of Jesse Jones. Top managers were hand-picked by Jones and served at his pleasure. These managers owned little stock and received relatively low salaries in comparison to top managers in other industries and to bank officers in more recent times. Their authority and autonomy were commensurate with their compensation, since the owner and the board retained considerable power over most fundamental decisions. In the operations of the bank, Doherty's relationship with his officers was much the same as Jones's relationship with him: the superior exercised clear and unequivocal authority. Policy came down to Doherty, who then pushed it down into the organization. When matters requiring decisions arose in the bank, Doherty had the final say. This sort of centralized decision making filled the needs of a small organization competing in a relatively homogeneous market.

The primary goals of the bank were security of deposits, asset quality, and asset growth. Profitability was, of course, desirable, but short-run profits were seldom the primary objective of the bank in the Jones era. Indeed, Jones even coordinated his varied business concerns through other institutions—the Bankers Mortgage Company (a consolidation of two trust companies) and Jesse Jones and Company, which held his lumber, farming, and collateral interests. By segregating such potentially risky personal business ventures from the affairs of the National Bank of Commerce, Jones sought to safeguard the bank's reputation while deflecting possible questions about his financial ties to the bank. Loan quality was protected by a conservative lending policy. Financial information about potential borrowers was, of course, critical in the loan committee's deliberations, and Sam Taub and Robert Doherty served as the principal interpreters of such information. Doherty exercised final authority over most credit decisions, and his personal judgment of a loan applicant's credit worthiness and character could outweigh statistical analysis of financial data in his decisions.

Although the bank's officers made calls on current and prospective customers, their general attitude was that sufficient good loans would seek out a quality bank; if they looked too hard for business, they feared, they would find only bad loans. The same sentiment argued against aggressive advertising campaigns to expand the market for the bank's services. This attitude was embodied in an often-repeated company legend regarding the time two young officers approached Robert Doherty about erecting a sign on the Gulf Building to indicate that it was the headquarters of National Bank of Commerce. His reply: "What the hell do we need a sign for? Gus Wortham and Ben Taub know where the bank is."[6] The bank's innovative approaches to oil and real estate lending suggest that the managers were willing to respond creatively to new opportunities. But, all in all, they proceeded cautiously and deliberately in seeking new business. Their conservative approach to banking reflected prevailing attitudes in the industry during the stable era of security-based regulations after World War II.

All this is not to suggest that traditional bankers such as those in charge of NBC before the 1960s were somehow inferior to their mod-

ern counterparts. Rather, they simply worked in a different environment. In the context of their own times, these men were excellent
bankers, and their bank compiled a remarkable record of growth over
more than four decades. This can be attributed in part to an intangible
aspect of the bank's management philosophy, the extraordinary commitment of the bank's officers to Jesse Jones. Most of the top managers
had been associated with Jones in some capacity before coming to
work for NBC. They took a special pride in the ongoing achievements
of their leader, and this pride translated into loyalty and dedication to
Jones's bank. The public image of Jones as a business, political, and
civic leader gave his bank a special identity within the Houston business community. This image and personal loyalties to the man behind
it provided the organizational glue which bound the bank together
into an effective and proud organization.

Despite its past success with this traditional, conservative approach to banking, however, in the 1950s National Bank of Commerce
began losing ground to its largest local competitors. During World
War II, Second National, which changed its name to Bank of the
Southwest in 1956, grew rapidly by arranging a series of acquisitions
and mergers. The creation of Texas National in 1953 elevated another
competitor to near-equal status. Then in 1956, First National Bank of
Houston and City National Bank merged to create First City National,
which far outdistanced the size of its nearest rival. NBC had held
first place in size among Houston banks in 1955, but the union of the
second- and third-largest banks formed a combination with almost
double the deposits of NBC. Call reports on bank deposits at the end
of 1957 produced further disquieting news, as second place among
Houston's banks was claimed by Bank of the Southwest (see Table 9.1).
Of course, size alone does not measure a bank's performance, but
NBC's declining market share nonetheless challenged its management
to reassess the bank's situation.

The problem of management succession as well as the broader
problem of the impending transition between two very different eras of
bank management thus loomed large at National Bank of Commerce
in the 1950s. During that decade and the early 1960s, the bank's top
management repeatedly stumbled in its efforts to find the next generation of bank leadership. The quest for management succession in an
age of transition and rapid growth involved the bank in several contro-
versial and much-publicized episodes, including a major merger which
came unraveled in 1964. Indecision and lack of direction by the bank's
leadership on this crucial issue for a time threatened to stall the considerable momentum which the bank had built over decades of
growth.

Table 9.1 Growth of Deposits in Houston Banks, 1946–64

End of Year	First National	City National	STCNB	Union	NBC	Bank of the Southwest
1946	$177,957,520	$114,275,436	$100,926,967	$ 61,592,758	$162,706,359	$144,054,702
1947	205,230,937	137,780,081	112,712,229	66,815,571	184,847,184	166,085,294
1948	221,815,205	160,564,430	115,729,792	66,000,026	201,352,567	185,964,450
1949	228,258,231	171,740,920	123,756,994	70,086,742	214,775,421	194,656,763
1950	251,362,986	201,370,065	131,980,575	75,062,595	248,865,121	218,041,198
1951	251,260,582	220,459,820	136,115,770	80,701,512	259,172,100	231,931,007
1952	263,402,832	258,471,043	139,221,472	76,722,098	283,573,366	250,504,512
1953	283,821,771	301,980,336	212,642,723*		322,011,063	270,144,036
1954	301,783,400	322,207,202	217,367,639		331,000,733	272,087,290
1955	305,162,651	351,615,039	214,574,170		367,759,219	304,169,518†
1956	642,304,380*		235,330,667		361,691,437	338,784,886
1957	642,737,637		228,054,236		345,301,949	351,253,091
1958	708,031,011		236,205,553		370,883,068	356,958,213
1959	660,404,719		249,452,097		373,226,865	378,508,957
1960	708,197,062		261,025,443		405,836,990	424,035,678
1961	751,615,914		282,541,112		484,860,463	467,628,033
1962	816,979,834		278,371,486		495,051,283	479,436,378
1963	785,755,036		272,867,361		472,513,408	468,712,938
1964	900,319,456				778,722,638*	535,384,405

SOURCE: Statements of Condition, TCB Archives.
* Merged.

Given the significance of the interrelated problems of management success and growth, it is not surprising that Jesse Jones sought solutions in the decade before his death. Upon his return to Houston from Washington, Jones began to survey the field for potential merger partners for National Bank of Commerce. Such a merger would solidify the standing of NBC as one of the largest banks in Houston while also infusing new personnel and resources into the organization. In 1946, Jones proposed a consolidation with the South Texas Commercial National Bank, the fifth-largest bank in Houston. Unfortunately for Jones, STCNB had little interest in merging with its once-smaller competitor and coming under the control of archrival Jesse Jones. A verbal offer of merger by Jones was followed by a letter summarizing the proposal to the officers of South Texas Commercial National. Their board passed a unanimous resolution to the effect that "Mr. Jones be advised that we are not interested in considering the consolidation proposal." Eighteen years were to pass before STCNB, under new leadership as a part of the Texas National Bank, merged with the National Bank of Commerce to form Texas National Bank of Commerce.[7]

In the years immediately after he was spurned by South Texas Commercial National, Jones continued to explore the possibility of a major merger. In the early 1950s, one obvious target for acquisition was First National Bank, the oldest bank in the city. First National, traditionally one of the two largest banks in Houston, also faced management-succession problems as it sought to defend its market position against the challenge of two rapidly growing newcomers, NBC and City National Bank. Both of these relatively young rivals were looking for ways to expand quickly, and one solution to the problems of First National was a merger with one of them.

Representatives of First National first approached Jesse Jones about the prospects of merger. Details of the subsequent negotiations are sketchy at best, but several accounts suggest a fascinating case of missed opportunity for National Bank of Commerce. All of the accounts agree that Jones had a difficult time negotiating with top managers at First National, who were uncertain of their prospective roles within a Jones-dominated organization and who had problems arriving at a consensus in discussing the proposed merger with Jones. Beyond such generalizations, however, there is little concrete information about the actual course of the talks between the two banks.[8]

A convincing version of the events which unfolded has been supplied by one of the principal actors for First National, George Brown of the Houston-based Brown & Root Construction Company. Years after the failure of the merger negotiations, Brown sought out Ben Love, who had assumed control of Texas Commerce Bank, to recount his version of the breakdown of discussions with Jesse Jones. Brown, who was a major customer and stockholder of First National in the early 1950s, recalled that he approached Jones with the idea to merge the troubled bank into National Bank of Commerce. Brown believed that such a merger made sense for both organizations; in addition, he would have an opportunity to repay Jones for support provided to Brown & Root during its early years, when Jones had shown confidence in the future of the developing firm. By arranging a merger which would make Jones's bank far and away the largest bank in Houston, Brown felt that he could make a sensible business deal while also helping to create an organization which would be the final jewel in Jones's business empire. The two men set to work on the details of the proposed merger, Brown shouldering much of the responsibility for sorting out the bargain. After spending long hours settling various issues, the two men finally completed their work late one night. According to Brown's retrospective account, they shook hands on a mutually acceptable agreement to merge the two banks, and Brown went home to a good night's sleep with a sense of a hard job well done.

The next morning, his sense of satisfaction was shattered by a phone call from Jesse Jones, who observed that he had been thinking over their talks from the previous night and that the two needed to meet again and reconsider several details of their previous negotiations. Brown proved less than enthusiastic. He hesitated to reopen discussions on a deal which he considered completed. He ended the phone conversation, and with it the merger negotiations. He then turned to Judge J. A. Elkins at City National Bank and began negotiations which ultimately led to the 1956 merger between that bank and First National. The trader's proclivity in Jones to wrest one final concession thus apparently cost him one of the deals of his lifetime, a merger which would have firmly established his institution as the predominant bank in Houston. As the primary owner and the managers of National Bank of Commerce contemplated the road not taken, they could not help but observe far up the path in terms of size a new rival, First City National Bank, which they would pursue for two decades before finally gaining parity in the 1970s.[9]

After a series of potential mergers had failed to come to fruition, the management succession problem at NBC remained in the mid-1950s. Jesse Jones made one more strong bid to solve the problem before his death by recruiting a man somewhat similar to himself in temperament and experience to become the president of the bank. Allan Shivers had come to know Jones through a variety of business and political connections. As Shivers prepared to run for his third term as governor of Texas in 1954, he began serious discussions with Jones regarding the prospect that, if defeated, he would come to Houston to become president of National Bank of Commerce. Such plans were put on hold when Shivers won the election, and subsequent efforts to bring Shivers into the management of the bank after the completion of his term fell just short of success. Perhaps Jones saw a bit of his younger self in Shivers, who had a record of leadership in both the public and the private sectors. Indeed, subsequent events validated Jones's judgment of Shivers, who was an active and influential director of National Bank of Commerce from 1957 through 1977, while also gaining recognition as one of the leading bankers in Texas for his work at Austin National Bank. As with the unsuccessful merger proposals in the late 1940s and early 1950s, events seemed to conspire against National Bank of Commerce in its search for new management. A new Jesse Jones had been identified but not quite harnessed to the bank's management team.[10]

Jones's death in 1956 brought a sense of urgency to the ongoing quest for management successors. The first response of the bank's leaders was a bold stroke, but one which ultimately proved unsuccessful. In 1958 the search for a young president capable of assuming control of the bank after a brief training period led to Marvin Collie in an unlikely location, the law firm of Vinson, Elkins, Weems and Searls. The Elkins of the partnership was Judge J. A. Elkins, a long-term friend and business rival of Jesse Jones. Elkins was the guiding force in the rise of First City National Bank, and the selection of a partner in his law firm for the presidency of NBC provided an interesting twist to the increasingly heated competition between the two largest banks in Houston. Collie had no experience in bank management, but he was a nationally respected specialist in tax law and was well suited to represent the bank in the community. The demonstrated abilities of Collie seemed to meet the demonstrated need of the bank for new leadership. The directors of NBC judged the potential benefits of his appointment to far outweigh the dual risks of hiring an outsider without banking experience and of being perceived as having to go to "First City's law firm" for leadership.

Two prominent members of the board, former Governor Allan Shivers and oilman Pat Rutherford, took the lead in recruiting Collie, who was then introduced to Robert Doherty on a hunting trip. Doherty's approval of Collie cleared the path for a realignment in the bank's management, with Doherty becoming chairman of the board and chief executive officer and former vice-chairman Simpson becoming honorary chairman in preparation for his impending withdrawal from active management. Just below the new president on the organization chart, if not necessarily in their own minds, was a group of seven long-term officers of the bank who took the new title senior vice-president. Symbolic of the bank's problems in entering its post-Jones era was that Doherty did not assume the title of chairman until 1958. Jones's name continued to appear on all bank statements and reports for eighteen months after his death.

For his part, Marvin Collie saw great opportunities in his admittedly risky new situation. He accepted the job as president with the understanding that Doherty, now aged sixty-seven, would step down in approximately two years, leaving the top position in the bank to Collie. Thus the young lawyer would have the opportunity to learn the business from a man regarded as one of the most experienced and knowledgeable bankers in Houston. Collie believed that Houston was on the verge of a period of prolonged growth which would require far-sighted and aggressive business and civic leadership. He saw the bank presidency as an excellent position from which to exert such leadership. Indeed, as a former partner at Vinson & Elkins and president of National Bank of Commerce, Collie would have the opportunity to bridge two of the most significant circles of influence in Houston, those traditionally centered around Judge Elkins and Jesse Jones.

Collie's initial outlook proved much too optimistic. He did not anticipate the skepticism which inevitably greeted an outsider in a close-knit organization traditionally held together by deeply felt loyalty to a strong personality. To long-term officers bypassed by an outsider who had not paid his dues within the organization, the new title senior vice-president offered little solace. Indeed, the whole idea that the bank was forced to go outside for new leadership must have rankled men who had been afforded little realistic opportunity to develop the sort of broad exposure to the bank's operations now promised to Marvin Collie. Thus the new president faced the unenviable task of quelling the skepticism of his older, more experienced subordinates.

Yet even this was to prove less demanding than his efforts to satisfy his superior, Robert Doherty, who demonstrated little inclination to loosen his grip on the reins of power. By 1958, Doherty had devoted more than four decades to the development of the bank; he spent his remaining decade attempting to protect it from decline and to safeguard its traditional methods of operations from changes which he considered ill-advised. His ways had worked; it is hardly surprising that he did not embrace change as he approached his seventieth birthday. Nor is it surprising that he did not eagerly embrace his young potential rival, Marvin Collie.

Instead, Doherty seemed intent on encouraging the new president to take on a role somewhat similar in some respects to that recently relinquished by A. D. Simpson, who had long served as the public spokesman for the bank and the unofficial head of customer relations. Collie soon found himself making regular appearances at social functions while being largely excluded from real input into such matters as loan-committee decisions. When Collie supervised the remodeling of the bank's facilities, Doherty disapproved; when he helped upgrade the trust services of the bank, Doherty offered scant encouragement or praise; when he suggested a more aggressive calling program to build the bank's accounts and expand its declining market share, the old hands made it clear that National Bank of Commerce did not have to seek out business.

Collie's situation at the bank steadily deteriorated as Doherty and the older officers became increasingly certain that this previously untested lawyer was simply not cut out to be a banker. Feeling that he had not been given the fair chance to prepare which he had been promised, Collie resigned the presidency and returned to his law practice in January, 1961, after less than two years at the bank. In that short time, Collie of course had not completely mastered the intricacies of banking; nor had the bank's management been fully supportive of his difficult endeavor.

The personal recriminations which inevitably accompanied the breakup of this strained marriage masked a mounting tension underlying the bank's awkward handling of the affair. When the bank's senior officers explained that Collie simply had not worked out as a banker, they meant that he did not mirror their attitude and approach to banking. Collie did not become a banker in this inherited image; he was not allowed to break the mold with innovations designed to respond to an increasingly competitive environment in which NBC was not keeping pace with other more aggressive rivals. As Collie went back to the practice of law, the bank's top management again took up the search for management succession without directly confronting an uncomfortable dilemma; to be effective, new leaders might have to push the bank out of traditional patterns established in an earlier era.[11]

In the wake of the Collie episode, National Bank of Commerce confronted the 1960s with a combination of pride in its past and concern for its future. The brief decline which had followed the death of Jones in 1956 had been reversed in the late 1950s, and the growth in deposits from 1958 through 1963 allowed the bank to expand slightly its share of the deposits held by the four largest banks in Houston. Yet despite such growth, there was reason for concern. No longer was NBC engaged in a battle for the title of the largest bank in Houston; instead, as Table 9.1 shows, it was struggling to avoid slipping permanently into third place behind the expanding Bank of the Southwest. Alone at the top stood First City National Bank, which was controlled by the managers of the old City National who had begun the postwar era managing a bank less than 60 percent as large as NBC before vaulting past several once-larger banks through a combination of internal growth and a major merger in 1956. As NBC attempted to defend its market position against the intense competition of these two rivals in the early 1960s, Doherty, now past seventy and increasingly hampered by serious illnesses, assumed the dual responsibilities of chairman and president. He realized that the quest for greater size and for management succession now demanded decisive action if the bank was to avoid slipping back into the pack among the major Houston banks.[12]

A major merger made sense. By returning to the strategy originally explored by Jones after World War II and then successfully employed by First City to redefine the market structure of Houston banking in 1956, the bank could address the related problems of growth and management succession in one dramatic stroke. In the process, NBC's leaders might put to rest any lingering doubts about its management in the post–Jesse Jones era. If the proper merger partner could be found, both additional size and a new generation of management might be acquired quickly, allowing NBC to close the distance separating it from First City. Risks were involved in opting for instant growth through merger; indeed, the process of putting together two organizations with separate histories, management philosophies, and leadership presented numerous pitfalls. But as management and several prominent directors of NBC looked for a suitable merger partner, such risks seemed necessary.

One logical merger candidate was Texas National Bank, which seemed intent on breaking away from its conservative traditions. Texas National had been created in 1953 through the consolidation of South Texas National Bank and Union National Bank. Before the merger, the two concerns had shared conservative management philosophies, ties to the Houston economy which stretched back to the turn of the century, and a common skepticism about Jesse Jones while occupying buildings across the street from each other. Their merger had gone forward with no serious problems, but the resulting bank had never quite succeeded in expanding its share of the Houston banking market. It remained the fourth-largest bank in the city.

Tunneling Under the Unit Banking Law:
The Merger of South Texas National Bank and Union National Bank

The Texas National Bank Building (now renamed simply 1200 Main), was the home of Texas National Bank from 1955 until 1964, when TNB merged with National Bank of Commerce. This new building was, however briefly, a symbol of the determination of TNB to become one of the dominant banks in Houston. The difficulties experienced by TNB with the state's unit banking in the years before the completion of the Texas National Bank Building suggests how the law constrained bank mergers in that era.

Little else stood in the way of the consolidation of South Texas National Bank and Union National, which had a long history of close relations when they merged in 1953. Directors of Commercial National and the early-day South Texas National were among the original organizers of Union Bank and Trust. By the time those two banks merged in 1912 to form South Texas Commercial National, Union had become a national bank. The two institutions were friendly competitors. S. M. McAshan and R. M. Farrar, the two long-term presidents of the banks, were neighbors who took long walks together in the evenings. The two men and their banks shared a cautious and conservative approach and a reliance on the cotton trade and traditional corporate customers like Southern Pacific Railroad. The glory days for both banks came before the mid-1930s, when they began to grow less competitive and to slip down in the ranks of Houston banks. Expansion at both banks was slowed by the deaths of long-term leaders in the early 1940s. South Texas Commercial National lost its chairman of the board, James A. Baker, in 1941, and President McAshan died the same year. R. M. Farrar, of Union National, died in 1943. .

South Texas Commercial National seemed particularly hurt by the early death of S. M. McAshan and did not take full advantage of the prosperity brought by World War II. In an effort to restore its competitiveness and upgrade its image, the bank brought in McAshan's son

Harris as president in 1948 and shortened its name to South Texas National Bank in 1949. That was not enough to catch up with the leading Houston banks, and in 1953 South Texas sought out a merger with its neighbor across the street, Union National.

Union National's president, George Hamman, had been with the bank since 1907 and was in poor health (he died before the year was out). The bank's managers also realized they were slipping further behind in the race for deposits and quality loans. A comfortable merger with the bank across the street seemed a perfect way to recapture some of the momentum and prestige of the pre–World War II days.

Given the common bonds and identity of interests between the two banks, they reached a tentative agreement to merge with little difficulty. Before the announcement of an intent to merge, the larger bank of the two, South Texas National, had begun planning for the construction of a new office building to house its expanding operations. Upon completion of the merger, the newly created Texas National Bank looked forward to a time in the near future when it could move into its modern new building, which it would share with Continental Oil. But a short-term problem remained. The unit banking law was being strictly enforced in the 1950s, and regulatory approval of the prospective merger was contingent on the movement of the two banks into a single location as stipulated by the law.

The banks and regulatory authorities finessed this problem through a creative compromise. The lawyers for South Texas National noted a decision by the Texas attorney general in 1950 which allowed a bank to open a drive-in window in a garage across the street from its main building. At that time the attorney general ruled that such an arrangement would not violate the state's antibranching restriction if the main building and the drive-in window were connected by a permanent tunnel. The opinion concluded that an opposite interpretation of the law would "sacrifice the real spirit of the law to pure literalism." To gain approval to merge, the two banks tested the limits of "pure literalism." At an expense estimated at $50,000 and at the cost of obstructing the flow of traffic on one of the city's major downtown streets, a small tunnel was completed under the street to connect the buildings occupied by the two applicants to merge. Once a single message traveled through the tunnel, the two buildings were officially proclaimed to be a single site for regulatory purposes. The tunnel never again was used. Texas National carried on its business in both buildings until the opening of its new facility. And society was again protected from the dangers of branch banking.

SOURCES: Texas National Files, TCB Archives; Interview with Earl V. Dreyling by William Allison, TCB Archives; Interview with James J. Clayton by William Allison, TCB Archives; *Houston Chronicle* (February 15, 1983); *Houston Post* (May 11, 1953); Interview with Jean Dupree by Walter L. Buenger, August 5, 1983, TCB Archives.

In the late 1950s, Texas National Bank experienced a brief management-succession problem of its own. Since 1953 the president had been Harris McAshan, a fourth-generation professional banker whose family had long guided the operations of South Texas Commercial National Bank. But in 1959 illness forced McAshan to retire prematurely at the age of fifty-three, and the bank faced the task of quickly replacing a top manager well before he had been expected to step down. McAshan had helped prepare the way for his own departure, however, by instituting an executive training program to recruit, train, and advance young managers in the bank. Thus the crisis which might have accompanied McAshan's early retirement was cushioned by the depth of middle management previously developed by the bank.

Stepping up as president in 1959 was J. W. (Bill) McLean, an experienced banker, though only thirty-seven years old. McLean had been recruited by Texas National Bank in 1958 from a position as vice-president at the First National Bank and Trust Company of Tulsa, Oklahoma. During a decade of employment there, he had been involved broadly in lending and in the overall management of the bank. He entered Texas National Bank as senior vice-president and advisory director with the expectation that he would ultimately become president. The resignation of McAshan less than a year later elevated McLean into the presidency.

McLean could count on the assistance of a strong chairman, Dillon Anderson, who had been a director of the Union National Bank before assuming the same responsibilities at Texas National after the merger. Anderson was married to a granddaughter of W. T. Carter, at his death in 1921 the largest stockholder in Union National, and he was a partner in the major Houston law firm of Baker, Botts, Shepherd and Coates. This firm traditionally supplied both officers and directors for STCNB, including fellow law partner James A. Baker, Jr., whose family had been active in the bank and its predecessors since the 1890s. Before becoming chairman of Texas National, Anderson was a national security adviser to President Dwight Eisenhower, and his years in Washington gave him a visibility in the Houston business community akin to that previously enjoyed by Jesse Jones. Dillon Anderson's national reputation as a political figure and a popular writer gave the bank a presence in the regional and national financial community that contributed to its new image as an organization on the move.[13]

Texas National Bank faced an uphill battle in the 1950s as it sought to increase its share of the Houston banking market. One of its first moves was to build a modern new banking facility. South Texas National began planning for the building before the merger with Union, and its completion in 1955 provided a modern new home within which the formerly separate banks could grow easily into a single, unified organization. The executive training program begun earlier by South Texas National helped fill the new building with professional and ambitious young bankers. An innovative public relations campaign sought to build a public perception that Texas National Bank was a growing force in the Houston financial arena while publicizing the variety of customer services offered by the bank. Efforts to differentiate itself from its larger rivals in Houston and to take the lead in tapping a new market for banking services included the launching of the first bank credit-card program in the city. Texas National also sought to expand its already significant presence in the so-called middle market for commercial loans, hoping to establish a specialized appeal to small and middle-sized area businesses which might feel lost in the crowd among the larger accounts attracted by National Bank of Commerce and First City National Bank.[14]

Despite such initiatives, Texas National failed to expand significantly its share of the Houston banking market during the late 1950s and early 1960s. It stayed a distant fourth in the race for deposits, remaining roughly 60 percent of the size of NBC and 40 percent of First City. During this time McLean learned sobering lessons which in 1963 he summarized for his executive committee in a detailed memorandum outlining the reasons why he favored a merger with NBC: "The cost of really competing to a smaller bank is so great, percentagewise, that its ultimate percentage earning power can never compare favorably [with larger competitors] over the long term." He reminded the committee that "after 'running as fast as we can' these past few years, we have not even 'stood still,' but rather have slowly slipped further behind" in the contest among Houston's four largest banks for market share. McLean believed strongly that "we must consider *deposit growth* a primary objective," and "to the extent that we can achieve deposit growth through consolidation, we are tremendously better off, in addition to having gained precious time." The conclusion of McLean's memorandum made a persuasive case for the merger by examining the alternative available to Texas National Bank: "I have had a long time to consider the painful problems of consolidating these two very old institutions. But, I am convinced that these problems will not be nearly so painful, or expensive as the only alternative available to us. That, of course, is to continue to do battle with *three* larger competitors, with each becoming relatively larger." He added, "We might never have this same opportunity again."[15]

In the premerger planning at Texas National Bank, the potential for painful problems during consolidation was diminished by the presumption that the top management of Texas National soon would control the management of the consolidated bank. Both Anderson and McLean believed that the merger offered the most direct route to their ultimate destination, the control of a much larger Houston bank capable of more fully serving the booming regional economy. The risks obviously were real; merger lore is littered with the disappointed careers and ambitions of officers from the smaller of the two consolidating organizations. Yet in this case, history seemed to be on the side of Texas National Bank. The leadership of National Bank of Commerce appeared ready to surrender power after a long, frustrating search for a new generation of managers. Anderson and McLean had few doubts about their abilities to control events.

From the perspective of both banks, the merger made sense. If events worked out as expected, former members of both organizations would become part of a dominant new Houston bank while fulfilling strategic goals previously established by the consolidating organizations. NBC would finally solve its management-succession dilemma. Texas National Bank would move into the top echelon of Houston banks. And above all, the two banks together would be in a much improved position to keep pace with Houston's growth. The consolidated resources of the two banks would create a new institution with a higher lending limit and greater resources for financing the development of a region which was outstripping the capacities of a banking system constrained by the state's unit banking law.

Negotiations leading to the merger announcement involved only a small group from each bank and went forward without publicity. Taking leading roles were Doherty and directors John T. Jones and Gus Wortham representing National Bank of Commerce and Anderson and McLean from Texas National Bank. Much of their negotiation focused on the exchange value of the two banks: What would be the value placed on each bank for the purpose of determining the distribution of stock in the consolidated organization? Initially, NBC favored a $1:2$ exchange in which Texas National would receive $33\frac{1}{3}$ percent of the consolidated bank's stock. TNB sought a $3:5$ ratio, which translated into a $37\frac{1}{2}$ percent share for the smaller bank. Robert Doherty argued for the use of the market value of the banks' stocks as the most important criterion for determining their relative values, and on such a basis, he advocated a $1:2$ exchange. Texas National's negotiators countered that the stocks of the two banks were not widely enough traded to generate stock prices sufficiently precise to serve as the sole measure of exchange value. They favored instead greater reliance on the core deposits of each bank, a comparison which suggested a 35 to 40 percent share for their bank. After numerous meetings to exchange and reconcile statistics on market value, adjusted book value, earnings, value of real estates, deposits, trusts, and other factors, a compromise emerged. Texas National Bank received the 37½ percent share it had sought after agreeing to allow the National Bank of Commerce to pay a stock dividend which increased its shares outstanding by approximately 18 percent.[16]

The top positions in the new organization were more easily determined. Heading the new Texas National Bank of Commerce would be Robert Doherty, whose title would be chairman of the board and chief executive officer. John T. Jones and Dillon Anderson would serve as vice-chairmen of the board, giving each of the merger partners a strong voice near the top. The president would be J. W. McLean. Texas National would also supply the chairman of the executive committee, James Baker, Jr., and the vice-chairman, R. D. Randolph. The board of directors would consist of fifteen men selected from the board of NBC and ten from the board of TNB. Such arrangements reflected the relative size of the two organizations, and the choice of individuals to fill the various slots posed few difficulties.

One last detail of critical importance, however, was the question of management succession. Age seventy-two and seriously ill, Doherty was clearly in need of a successor; at the age of forty-one with more than fifteen years' banking experience, including four years as president of the fourth-largest bank in Houston, McLean was the obvious choice. Indeed, the acquisition of McLean and the cadre of young middle managers who had come up through Texas National Bank's management training program was a primary motivation for the merger from the perspective of the National Bank of Commerce. The representatives of Texas National Bank agreed to merge only after what they considered a firm commitment that within one year Doherty would retire and his spot would go to McLean. This commitment was not, however, spelled out in the merger proposal submitted to either government regulators or the shareholders for approval.[17]

The first hurdle in the merger process was approval by government regulators. The merger proposal came at a particular sensitive time in the history of bank mergers. On June 17, 1963, the U.S. Supreme Court blocked a proposed merger between the Philadelphia National Bank and the Girard Trust Corn Exchange Bank, declaring it illegal under Section 7 of the Clayton Act. In explaining the significance of this case, William Orrick, Jr., assistant attorney general in charge of the Antitrust Division of the U.S. Department of Justice, called the *Philadelphia Bank* case "the most important antitrust case of the year and, perhaps, the decade." He explained that "the most obvious impact of the case is, of course, that it brought the entire bank merger field under the Clayton Act." The banking community had been placed on notice that henceforth bank mergers would be subject to intense scrutiny, the Antitrust Division of the Justice Department using criteria long applied to industrial mergers.[18]

One month after the *Philadelphia Bank* decision, the boards of directors of National Bank of Commerce and Texas National Bank approved the basic terms of the plan of consolidation previously worked out in negotiations among the two banks' leaders. Final approval of the comptroller of the currency would come only after consideration by both the Antitrust Division and the Board of Governors of the Federal Reserve of any potential anticompetitive consequences of the proposed merger. In their submittals to these regulatory authorities, the banks' lawyers went to great lengths to show that this proposed merger differed greatly from the one recently rejected in the *Philadelphia Bank* case. They offered detailed statistics showing a decline in market concentration in the banking industry in the eleven counties surrounding Houston during the years after 1953 (see Figure 9.1). As the popu-

Figure 9.1. Decline in market concentration, 1953–63.

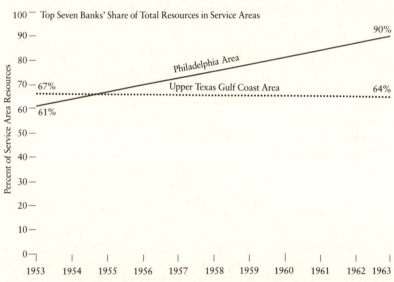

SOURCE: "NBC Consolidation with TNB—Antitrust Considerations," File 4691B, Liddell, Sapp Records.

lation of the Houston area had spread into the suburbs, the large downtown banks had been blocked by the state's unit banking law from opening offices in the suburbs. Numerous new banks had arisen to serve this expanding market, in direct contrast to the situation in Philadelphia, where the long-run trend had been toward increased concentration and fewer banks. The submissions in support of the merger proposal argued further that the consolidated bank would have less than 20 percent of its relevant market, a figure which the *Philadelphia Bank* decision had suggested as an upper limit for allowable mergers. The submissions also reminded the regulators that the three largest banks in Texas, Republic and First National of Dallas and First City of Houston, had all previously grown through mergers and concluded that the proposed merger would create one additional organization capable of competing with these large banks in Texas while also attempting to capture more of the business of growing Houston-based firms which had taken their business to money center-banks large enough to handle their credit needs. The new bank would be larger than National Bank of Commerce, but it would remain—like NBC— the second-largest bank in Houston and the fourth-largest in Texas.

The initial reaction of both the Antitrust Division and the Board of Governors of the Federal Reserve was concern for the potential anticompetitive effects of the proposed merger. Citing evidence in the banks' application of substantial competition between the two banks, the Federal Reserve's advisory opinion to the comptroller of the currency concluded as follows: "A consolidation of the Texas National Bank . . . and the National Bank of Commerce . . . would eliminate a substantial amount of competition and significantly increase the size of the area's second largest bank. This proposal would have a strongly adverse effect on competition." The Antitrust Division delayed its decision for six months as it wrestled with the array of questions left unanswered in the *Philadelphia* decision. Finally, the comptroller agreed that Houston was not Philadelphia and that the merger would not significantly decrease competition in the highly fragmented and relatively unconcentrated Houston area banking market.[19]

Having disposed of the basic legal objection blocking the merger, the comptroller of the currency could then consider the arguments of the banks concerning its benefits. According to the banks' application to the comptroller for approval to consolidate, "The fundamental reason for the consolidation is the compelling need in the Upper Texas Gulf Coast for additional banking services of a breadth and character which neither participating bank alone is in a position to render." The two banks offered telling statistics to support their assertion that their small size relative to the financial needs of the region's major businesses hampered efforts to compete effectively for the accounts of the largest Houston-based firms. Legally restricted from lending more than $3.2 million to a single account, NBC was forced to share many of its largest loans with money-center banks. In 1962, for example, its ledgers showed a total of more than $150 million in loans originated by NBC but placed elsewhere because of the bank's low lending limit. Indeed, many big businesses in the region bypassed the local banks completely, taking their accounts directly to the much larger banks in New York and Chicago. Of course, National Bank of Commerce could not present statistics on the loans it might have made to such concerns, but it did remind regulators of a previously published Federal Reserve study which had revealed that in 1955 New York banks had lent to businesses headquartered in Houston approximately $360 million, a larger amount than these banks had lent in any other city outside New York. A merger between the second- and fourth-largest banks in Houston would not create a bank capable of competing on anything approaching equal terms with the money center banks. But by creating a new bank with a lending limit of approximately $6 million and the resources to expand the specialized services available to its largest customers, the merger would enable Texas National Bank of Commerce to compete more effectively with banks outside the region for the business of large Houston-based companies and of the increasing number of businesses migrating from other parts of the nation to the growing Houston area.[20]

Such arguments proved persuasive, and after the comptroller of the currency granted approval for the merger in January, 1964, a joint stockholders meeting was called to ratify the proposal. By this time the consolidation had the separate approval of the boards and the shareholders of each bank. Little public opposition had been voiced by officers or prominent shareholders of either bank. The strong backing of the top officers who had negotiated the agreement removed most doubts, and the merger gained overwhelming support. With projected deposits of between $750 and $800 million; a solid foundation of profitable, well-secured loans to blue-chip Houston businesses and prominent individuals inherited from both National Bank of Commerce and Texas National Bank; and a stable full of ambitious and able young managers provided by TNB, the new Texas National Bank of Commerce seemed capable of mounting an immediate challenge to First City's reign as Houston's dominant bank. If the two organizations could be molded into one, the merger had the earmarks of success for all involved.

The physical consolidation of two banks into one building, which was necessitated by Texas's unit banking law, was the first obstacle to successful consolidation. The movement of equipment was well planned and efficiently executed, but there was little planning to ensure the smooth integration of the personnel from the two banks into a unified organization. To avoid the disruption of business, much of the move took place over a long weekend, with former employees of Texas National Bank moving uptown from their relatively new quarters in the Texas National Bank Building to the Gulf Building. There they found an excellent facility, though one suddenly strained by the extraordinary new demands being placed on it. They also found a confusing and potentially stultifying doubling up of people and job responsibilities. Many jobs now had two claimants, a situation guaranteed to induce considerable uncertainty in all employees concerning their exact responsibilities, the proper lines of authority, and, ultimately, their career prospects. The officers from the smaller bank were also generally younger than their counterparts from NBC, a combination of liabilities which could only dampen the enthusiasm which had fueled Texas National Bank's growth in the years immediately before the merger.

At the Gulf Building, the arrivals from down the street also encountered an essentially alien working environment. The top officers from NBC maintained a cool distance from their subordinates and even from each other. In sharp contrast to the more relaxed and informal atmosphere formerly enjoyed by employees of Texas National Bank, the consolidated bank retained both the building and the formal tone of the staid National Bank of Commerce. Indeed, the highly centralized and hierarchical style of decision making at NBC differed markedly from the system in which most of the middle managers from Texas National had been trained.

Differences in the ages and the self-images of the officers from each bank heightened the resulting tensions. The older officers from NBC had heard more than once in the merger negotiations that their bank was exploring this merger primarily as a way to acquire new managers. Resentment was inevitable, as was skepticism concerning the abilities of their young and relatively inexperienced new colleagues. And lurking just beneath the surface was an attitude of "us"—the proven bankers with a proud tradition of running a profitable, secure bank—against "them"—the upstarts from a smaller bank who seemed intent on taking control of Jesse Jones's bank.[21]

Much of what might be described as a conflict of corporate cultures became focused on the critical issue of lending philosophy. As the two banks struggled to become one and as the partisans of each of the former banks struggled to assert control over the new organization, a growing controversy over lending practices came to symbolize the widening split between the two camps. Former officers from NBC were quick to criticize in public and in private the previous lending practices of Texas National Bank. From the perspective of Robert Doherty, whose banking philosophy had been shaped by the experience of the Great Depression and patterned after traditions established by an earlier generation of Houston bankers, McLean and his subordinates had been unreasonably aggressive in pursuing new business in the years before the merger. Jesse Jones's bank had built its business by supplying loans secured by deposits or by the personal reputation of the borrower, and Doherty and his colleagues were not about to see this long tradition of security and profitability sabotaged by what they considered a modern variant of jazz banking.

McLean was most sensitive to such charges, for he knew that the label "liberal banker" was "just about the most destructive kind of criticism one can receive." Recognizing that such criticism could be used to undermine his position in the bank, McLean sought to dispel it by citing his experience in bank management as well as his work on the American Bankers Association's Credit Policy Committee. He faced a serious handicap, however, in that the criticism did not require substantiation to retain its impact. When auditors from NBC reported back informally to their friends that the books of Texas National Bank were strewed with "bad loans," their comments could not be easily refuted by appeal to hard facts. McLean could point out—as he did in a letter to the board after his resignation—that under his tenure Texas National Bank had reduced the bank's classified loans from about 5 percent to less than 2 1/2 percent; that the bank's average net loss on commercial loans over that five-year stretch had been 0.13 percent of the average loans outstanding; and that over the same years, Texas National's yield on average loans was 5.02 percent, compared to a yield of 4.82 percent for the National Bank of Commerce during the same period.[22] But such numbers were pebbles tossed against the side of a mountain of tradition.

The management practices developed over forty years by NBC had not included most of the methods used by the management of Texas National Bank in trying to build business before the merger. Aggressive advertising, systematic call programs in which officers devoted considerable time and energy to the "marketing" of bank services, an emphasis on lending to an expanding "middle market" of small and medium-sized companies, and the issuance of bank credit cards were all outside the experience of National Bank of Commerce. "Bad loans" became an all-encompassing symbol for the basic differences between "us" and "them," between the traditional banking practices which had been so successful in the age of Jesse Jones and the new approach to bank management which loomed on the horizon in the early 1960s.

Robert Doherty and J. W. McLean embodied these two different approaches to banking, and it was hardly surprising that their personal relations crackled with the tensions within Texas National Bank of Commerce. Unlike Marvin Collie before him, McLean was no novice dependent on Doherty for his banking education. He was an experienced banker with a track record of success and an eagerness to apply well-developed ideas about management in a challenging new situation. Secure in the assumption that he would succeed Doherty within a year, McLean went about the difficult task of helping mold the organization which he would soon head. For his part, Doherty—old and ill but as strong-willed as ever—was determined to safeguard the future of his bank. Given his commitment to the traditional banking practices which he had implemented for decades, first at Jesse Jones's request and then in honor of his memory, it was almost inevitable that Doherty would decide that McLean lacked the ability to run the bank. Given Doherty's personality and temperament, it was then certain that he would do whatever he thought had to be done to remove McLean and save the bank.

Before a year had passed after the merger, Doherty had decided to push McLean out of the line of succession by removing him from the presidency and making him a vice-chairman of the board, where, in Doherty's words, he would "assume duties to which he is well fitted, namely, customer relations and public relations." But McLean had no intention of becoming the new "Mr. Outside" while others ran the bank. Not only would his removal from the presidency call into question his abilities as a banker, but it would also raise fundamental questions about the integrity of the entire merger, since Texas National Bank representatives had agreed to the merger only after assurances that McLean would succeed Doherty.[23]

With the battle lines drawn, the first major skirmish took place when Doherty sought the support of the bank's executive committee for his plan to move McLean out of the presidency and thus out of immediate consideration for the position of chairman. Although the executive committee had a majority of former NBC officials, it surprised Doherty by rejecting his plan. This left Doherty no option except to take the matter before the board as a whole. There a 15-to-10 NBC majority might be expected to back him in a showdown with McLean. Yet even that vote was suddenly less than secure after the experience with the executive committee, and the Doherty forces thus took steps to increase their support on the board.[24]

The climax to this dispute came at a dramatic shareholders' meeting on January 19, 1965. In preparation for a proxy battle, Doherty and his supporters lined up the support of large shareholders. Several individuals who owned substantial blocks of stock were in Washington celebrating the inauguration of President Lyndon Johnson, and this group flew back to Houston for the shareholders' meeting aboard director John Mecom's personal plane. Once the meeting began, events moved quickly and inexorably. First came a demand for cumulative voting in the election of directors. Then three new nominees for director were submitted. After several indignant speeches by representatives of the Texas National Bank faction, the election was held using cumulative voting. NBC's majority—which was anchored by the approximately 30 percent of the bank's shares owned by the Houston Endowment—held firm. When the votes had been counted, a 15-to-10 NBC majority had been expanded to 17 to 8. What had begun as a friendly merger had become in effect a hostile take-over.[25]

The take-over was completed by the flight of former Texas National Bank officials from the bank. J. W. McLean and Dillon Anderson had been reelected to the board, but both resigned immediately in protest over the realignment of the board. In the aftermath of the proxy fight, most of the young managers who had come from Texas National Bank followed McLean out of Texas National Bank of Commerce. The migration also included former directors and accounts of the Texas National Bank. Thus concluded what came to be called the "bloody merger," and the outcome of this conflict had significant short- and long-term impacts on the evolution of Texas Commerce Bank.

The short-term costs were visible and disturbing to the bank's stockholder and managers. The quest for growth and management succession had fueled the impulse to merge, and now the attainment of either of the objectives was in doubt. Once again, an effort to find a successor for the ailing Doherty had failed; in addition, most of the well-trained young middle managers from Texas National Bank who had seemed ready to inject energy into an aging institution were gone. The impact of a good merger gone bad also was felt on the bottom line. The pair of directors removed from the board as a result of cumulative voting represented two old-line Texas National Bank accounts of real substance, the Southern Pacific Company and Southwestern Bell Telephone Company. These accounts and others acquired in the merger migrated to competing banks. By the end of 1965, deposits at the TNBC had slipped by $66 million, a drop of more than 8 percent during a year when most major Houston banks recorded substantial increases. The bank's stock price temporarily reflected investor response

Table 9.2 Selected Statistics on Texas Commerce Stock

Year	Average Shares Outstanding (thousands)	Number of Shareholders	Price High	Price Low	Net Income Per Share	Annual Dividend Rate at Year-End
1965	16,000	n.a.	n.a.	n.a.	$0.41	n.a.
1966	16,000	n.a.	n.a.	n.a.	.43	n.a.
1967	15,172	n.a.	$7.50	$5.50	.52	$0.25
1968	15,172	n.a.	7.50	7.00	.58	.27
1969	15,172	n.a.	7.50	6.00	.64	.28
1970	15,172	n.a.	7.50	5.50	.78	.31
1971	15,172	n.a.	11.00	7.50	.89	.34
1972	16,585	n.a.	16.50	10.50	.96	.36
1973	17,921	n.a.	24.25	14.50	1.14	.40
1974	20,726	4,336	25.38	11.00	1.36	.45
1975	22,365	4,809	20.00	14.13	1.54	.50
1976	23,730	5,193	21.75	17.25	1.67	.55
1977	25,984	16,057	19.63	15.82	1.93	.61
1978	27,225	19,696	20.86	17.13	2.36	.70
1979	28,861	21,290	22.88	17.75	2.85	.80
1980	29,138	19,164	33.75	20.38	3.48	.92
1981	30,609	19,940	45.00	31.50	4.49	1.10
1982	31,771	19,942	43.75	27.00	5.35	1.28
1983	32,223	19,472	46.63	32.00	5.50	1.42
1984	32,503	19,416	48.25	36.75	5.64	1.56
1985	32,677	18,190	44.00	25.88	1.62	1.56

SOURCE: Annual Reports of Texas Commerce Bank and Texas Commerce Bancshares.
NOTE: Results have been adjusted to take into account stock dividends of 9.127% in 1968, 5.455% in 1969, and 10.35% in 1971. They have also been restated to take into account a 2-for-1 stock split on December 16, 1980.

to the take-over before it steadily increased (see Table 9.2). Such developments created public relations problems which caught the bank's management by surprise. Long accustomed to avoiding the limelight of publicity, the bank now faced a wave of local and national media coverage which generally portrayed the bank and its top managers in an unflattering light. Taken together, these short-run results of the failed merger left the bank much less strong than it had hoped to be by the end of 1965.

Although the short-term results of the merger were discouraging, its long-term impact on the bank proved more positive. Despite the drop in deposits during 1965, at year's end the consolidated bank nonetheless held more than $200 million more in deposits than had been claimed by National Bank of Commerce on the eve of the merger. TNBC had vaulted toward the size of First City National Bank and in the process had distanced itself from the remainder of the pack. The merger also produced a stronger capital base, allowing a higher lending limit with which to pursue new business in the future.

The combination of the stockholdings of the two banks had another important impact on the future management of the bank which was little noted at the time. The merger of 1964 pointed the way toward the subsequent control of the bank's affairs by professional managers less constrained by dominant stockholders than those of the past. Although numerous large stockholders from both banks retained substantial blocks of stock in the consolidated institution, none now had the potential power to control bank policy, at least not without building a coalition of stockholders. The growing separation of management from ownership was greatly accelerated by the merger of 1964, which hastened the move toward control of the bank by professional managers.

As long as National Bank of Commerce had been tightly controlled by Jesse Jones or by individuals and groups loyal to his memory, fundamental managerial changes were unlikely. Thus despite far-reaching changes in the bank's size and in its competitive and regulatory environments, its top management clung to traditions and attitudes which had proved successful in an earlier time. Those who did not conduct bank business in the Jones mold were deemed unfit for leadership. Yet the highly personalized banking world of Jones's era was passing, as a combination of factors, including the growing scale of operations, intensifying competitive pressures, and the loosening of regulatory constraints pushed Texas Commerce into a new era. The inability of those in control of the bank to confront these broad underlying changes in banking in the decade after the death of Jesse Jones muddled the search for management succession. They defined their task narrowly (find a replacement for Doherty) instead of broadly (try to understand the ongoing transition in banking and then find managers well suited to the changing times). Given the understandable loyalty of these men to the traditions of Jesse Jones's bank, it was probably inevitable that they would have difficulties accepting successors. The Collie episode and the bloody merger of 1964 helped clear the way for a new era of management by forcing the old guard to confront the cost of continued resistance to change.

When the dust cleared after the highly charged confrontation of

1965, a crucial figure in the transition from Jones's era to a new era of bank management emerged, providing an ironic solution to NBC's long-standing management-succession problem. Those in charge of the bank had cast about outside their organization for almost a decade in search of a replacement for Doherty. In the effort to prevent McLean from becoming the head of the organization, Robert Doherty took a harder look for possible successors among the former high-level officers of National Bank of Commerce. There an obvious choice finally emerged: John E. Whitmore, who was fifty-six years old and had eighteen years' experience at NBC at the time of the merger. Whitmore had spent most of his career as a real estate lending specialist. His contributions had been acknowledged by promotions up the ranks to the position of senior vice-president; but, in keeping with Doherty's general treatment of his officers, Whitmore had not been groomed for top-management responsibilities. After the consolidation, however, Whitmore served as chief lending officer while also supervising the development of administrative policies and practices to govern the bank's lending functions. After McLean's resignation, Whitmore became president. As if to prove that the solution to the much proclaimed succession problem had always been at hand, Whitmore guided the bank through a most difficult transition era by working to salvage as much benefit as possible from the merger, overseeing the creation of a more flexible holding-company structure, and helping bring a new generation of management into the bank.

CHAPTER 10

Financing a Maturing Region, 1956–71

While the events surrounding the 1964 merger unfolded within Texas Commerce, the region outside its doors continued to move toward economic maturity. Houston's population more than doubled between 1950 and 1970, and its expanding work force found employment in an increasingly diversified economy. Oil drilling and production had been the region's glamour industry in the decade after World War II, but in the mid-1950s a sharp, sustained decline in oil drilling in Texas and throughout the Southwest shifted the focus of attention to other sectors of the regional economy. The most visible growth industry of this period was real estate construction, which produced a new generation of downtown office buildings as well as the suburban developments which spread farther and farther out from the central business district. Houston's newly constructed big-city skyline was a fitting symbol of its ranking as the nation's sixth largest city in 1970. More than a century of expansion had pushed Houston to a new level of size and maturity, with an increasingly diverse economy no longer easily categorized as cotton- or oil-based.[1]

The expansion of a variety of economic activities in and around Houston encouraged the diversification of the business of the city's largest banks. Table 10.1 summarizes the relative size of the major lending groups in the Texas Commerce Bank from 1967 through 1971. It reveals a lack of growth in oil-related lending but shows clearly that this did not translate into an overall stagnation of the bank's business. Instead, the pause in the expansion of oil drilling and production loans allowed the bank to use more of its resources to fund other growing areas of the regional economy. Within the bank, all lending areas except oil prospered. The statistics on loans by the specialized lending groups within the bank emphasize the diversity of opportunities avail-

Table 10.1　Loans by Lending Groups at Texas Commerce, 1967–71

Year	Real Estate	Energy	Metropolitan	International	National
1967	123,020,094	93,855,068	200,248,583	27,031,327	45,885,791
1968	145,682,904	83,715,518	229,874,590	13,407,476	66,180,476
1969	126,732,337	66,210,382	257,738,584	10,448,515	81,112,501
1970	147,941,885	60,327,661	255,183,221	15,153,420	103,538,022
1971	161,200,509	71,949,658	285,369,606	48,381,394	85,503,926

SOURCE: End-of-year Balance Sheets, Financial Accounting, TCB Archives.
NOTE: "Real estate" and "energy" are organized by industry: the rest, by geography. "Metropolitan" includes businesses based in or around Houston; "International" consists of accounts outside the United States; "National" is made up of U.S. companies with headquarters outside the Houston area.

able to TCB. The oil-related core of industries remained a potent engine of growth in this era, but the continued expansion of other types of economic activity reflected the growing maturity of the regional economy.

Conditions in the southwestern oil industry after 1956 limited the bank's opportunities for growth in oil lending. As shown in Figure 10.1, drilling activity in Texas and throughout the United States plunged from the heights of early 1955, and by late 1957 the oil industry was reeling from a sharp downturn in domestic drilling. Drilling had always been cyclical and highly sensitive to changes in the price of oil, since the economic viability of projects hinged on a price for oil high enough to cover the costs of exploration and drilling. But the prolonged and largely unpredicted decline in drilling which began in the mid-1950s severely affected all regional concerns directly or indirectly involved in the industry, including those banks which had been pioneers in creating modern oil loans. By the late 1950s, it had become clear that this downturn was not temporary, and those conducting business in this sector of the regional economy had to adjust to a steady decline in drilling.[2]

The underlying causes of this decline were beyond the control of oil bankers and, indeed, of domestic oil companies. The southwestern United States had been the center of oil production in the non-Communist world for much of the twentieth century, but this changed in the 1950s as oil deposits in the Middle East proved larger and less expensive to produce than those in the United States. Oil produced in the Middle East initially found markets primarily in Europe and Japan,

Figure 10.1. Rotary-rig count in Texas, the Southwest (Texas, Oklahoma, Louisiana), and the United States, 1955–73.

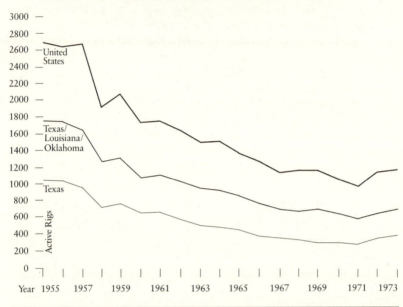

SOURCE: Hughes Tool Company, Rotary Rigs Running—by States, Annual Averages.

but its presence in the world oil market prevented a rise in the price of oil, which might have revitalized the domestic petroleum industry. As a result, the price of oil adjusted for inflation actually declined slightly in the decades before 1973, assuring that drilling prospects in the United States would steadily diminish as companies completed more and more of the projects which were economically feasible at the prevailing price of oil.[3]

The pattern of oil loans and the lending procedures established at Texas Commerce after World War II changed little in the years from 1956 to 1971. Loans on oil production from proved reserves remained central to the bank's energy business. Predictable oil prices throughout this era removed much of the guesswork from the lending process, as did the growing knowledge of reservoir engineering available to the bank's petroleum engineers for use in projecting future production from oil properties. It should be noted that oil lending by TCB did not dip as dramatically as did the drilling-rig count, since the bank's loans were generally on the production of oil already discovered, not on ex-

ploration for new fields. Commercial loans to oil-related manufacturers—notably Hughes Tool Company—and to oil equipment-supply
companies remained another important part of the bank's portfolio of
energy loans, as did loans for the transportation of oil and natural gas.
Although the oil department did not greatly expand its lending in this
era, it nonetheless helped attract and hold substantial deposits from oil
companies.[4]

As the leading oil lending banks adjusted to new realities in the
domestic oil industry in the 1950s, they became increasingly sophisticated in developing special loans to meet the needs of oil producers. In
the 1950s and 1960s, loans secured by oil production proved to be
flexible, durable financial arrangements used by all sectors of the industry to manage income from oil properties. In helping oil producers
maximize their profits while taking full advantage of available tax
benefits, these loans channeled funds into the hands of those most
likely to use them to find and produce new oil reserves.[5] Loans secured
by future oil production were of special significance to banks serving
major oil producing regions, and the large Houston- and Dallas-based
banks were leaders in this specialized type of loan.

Throughout the 1950s and 1960s, oil lenders at Texas Commerce
and other major energy lenders in and beyond Texas developed a dependable, profitable business in production-payment loans. The bank
originated and participated in such loans to producers of all sizes, in-

---

The ABCs of Oil Production Payments

One particularly significant type of oil-production-payment loan
came to be known as an "ABC loan" in reference to the three participating parties. The first two parties were the oil company and the
bank or insurance company involved. The third party was usually a
nominally capitalized corporation organized specifically to purchase
the production payments. Two specific types of production payments
were used by the industry. The so-called carved out production payment was used to maximize tax benefits of the depletion allowance or
recovery of intangible drilling costs. The so-called reserved production
payment was used in acquiring producing properties with a degree of
pre-tax income.

In the carved out production payment, "A" (the company) would
designate a dollar amount to be repaid from the proceeds of future oil
production. The legal instrument creating the production payment
would also stipulate an interest rate to be paid from production. The
production payment was then sold to "C" (the nominally capitalized

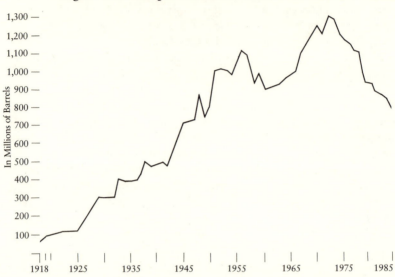

Figure 10.2. Oil production in Texas, 1945–85.

corporation), who borrowed the money from "B" (the bank or insurance company). The loan from the financial institution carried a lower interest than the production payment, creating a profit for "C" which was usually donated to a nonprofit entity such as a church or university.

In the reserved production payment, a fourth entity was involved in the transaction, since there would be a change of ownership of the producing property. "A" (the seller of the property) would reserve a dollar designated production payment at a specified interest rate. In addition, he would assign any remaining interest after payout of the reserved production to the "Purchaser" for a cash consideration. Simultaneously with the sale to the purchaser, "A" would sell to "C" the reserved production payment; "C" in turn would borrow the money from the financial institution "B." After payout of the production payment, the purchaser would be entitled to all proceeds from sale of production from the property.

Each participant benefited from a well-designed ABC transaction. The bank received excellent, large, relatively risk-free loans secured by the predictable flow of proved reserves. In converting future reserves into present income, oil companies gained flexibility in planning their financial affairs. The nonprofit institution which served as a go-between received a fee for its services. Just as petroleum engineering backed by the intervention of the Railroad Commission allowed producers to plan the orderly flow of oil reserves from the grounds, production-payment loans allowed them to plan the financial flows generated by oil production.

The exact origins of the ABC transaction have been lost to history—or at least clouded by several differing recollections of who introduced this arrangement. Most oil lenders active in the 1950s credit their counterparts at Republic National Bank of Dallas with perfecting the ABC loan in the form which prevailed in the 1950s and 1960s. This conclusion seems warranted by that bank's early and increasing involvement with such loans in the decade after World War II. As in any other such innovation, numerous bankers, lawyers, and oil men contributed to the growing sophistication and widespread application of ABC loans. By the early 1950s, National Bank of Commerce and other major Houston banks began responding to the growing demand for ABC loans as oil companies recognized their considerable advantages. The money-center banks did not, of course, sit idly by and watch this lucrative new business flow into the upstart Texas banks. Instead, they learned from smaller competitors in the Southwest and quickly used the ABC concept to make loans beyond the capacities of banks such as NBC. Throughout this era, the Texas banks participated in large production-payment loans led by money-center banks. They also regularly "overlined" loans larger than their legal lending limit to their larger correspondents in New York and Chicago. These patterns of ABC lending remained consistent from the early 1950s through 1969, when changes in the tax code reduced the usefulness of ABC loans in the tax planning of oil companies.

ABC loans inevitably attracted the attention of critics of the oil industry who opposed the oil depletion allowance as an unwarranted tax break for the big oil companies. These loans and the tax codes which made them attractive were hardly symbols of the fairness of American tax laws. Yet the banks and their lawyers did not write the tax codes; they merely looked for ways to use them in the interests of their clients. Separated from the broader political question of equity among classes of taxpayers and evaluated as an economic policy designed to encourage the production of oil, the combination of tax breaks for oil producers and ABC loans appears almost elegant; it was certainly effective in channeling funds into the hands of oil producers. Indeed, ABC transactions became a vital part of the financing of the domestic petroleum industry in the post–World War II decades.

SOURCES: Interview with E. O. Buck by Joseph A. Pratt, June 8, 1983; Interview with John Townley by Joseph A. Pratt, June 24, 1983; Interview with John Sears by Joseph A. Pratt, August 8, 1983, TCB Archives; see also Alvena Pitts, "Oil and Gas Banking: A Challenging Job," *Woman Banker* (January–February 1968): 14, 27–28.

cluding the vertically integrated major oil companies as well as independent producers. A $119 million production-payment loan in 1956 to Standard Oil of New Jersey originated by National Bank of Commerce, with participation by numerous other banks, was widely cited in the bank's institutional advertising as the largest loan in the history of the bank and as a symbol of NBC's growing maturity. Until the changes in the tax code in 1969, production-payment loans remained the most significant type of oil loan for Texas Commerce and its predecessors.[6]

With little opportunity for substantial growth in oil lending, TCB's oil department looked for other opportunities. One likely source of business was the expanding chemical industry, whose accounts traditionally had been handled in part by lending officers who were also active in oil. The petrochemical and chemical industries were significant sources of industrial growth along the upper Texas Gulf Coast in the years after World War II, as this region became one of the largest petrochemical centers in the world, producing an estimated 40 percent of all of the nation's petrochemicals by the 1960s. Texas Commerce thus had the good fortune of being in the geographical center of one of the nation's fastest-growing industries in the decades after World War II. Yet by the mid-1960s, the bank still had not established a strong presence in this dynamic sector of the regional economy.[7]

After a survey indicated that the chemical industry would lead all Houston-area industries in value added by manufacturing in 1970, John Whitmore, TCB's president, moved to establish a more aggressive calling program in this area. In 1967 he turned to W. N. (Bill) Davis, an engineer with job experience at several major chemical companies. Davis formed a chemical division around several accounts previously served by the oil division and the national division. At the time, only a few money-center banks—notably First National City Bank, Chase Manhattan, Bank of New York, and First Chicago—had separately organized chemical lending groups. With the help of a marketing survey to identify potential new accounts, Davis spearheaded a more aggressive calling campaign which gradually expanded the bank's lending to chemical companies. Then in 1970, Davis was named to head a new division which contained both chemical and oil-and-gas accounts and reported to a newly named vice chairman of the bank, Jack Horner, a recently retired Shell Oil executive. This new organizational structure was subsequently adjusted in 1975, when oil and chemical loans were again placed in separate divisions, the former under experienced oil lender John Townley and the latter under Davis. As would be expected in any realignment of a company's structure, Texas Commerce at times used trial and error in search of the right combination of structure and personnel to foster the growth of its new venture into chemicals while at the same time protecting its traditional strength in oil lending.[8]

Although lending to domestic oil producers was not an expansive part of TCB's business from 1956 to 1971, oil-related accounts contributed significantly to the growth of the bank's international lending. Loans to finance the trade of cotton and rice had made up the bulk of the bank's previous international activity, but after the mid-1950s the mix of business in this area changed as oil replaced cotton as the primary impetus for expansion. In this period, the bank's international loans to finance cotton exports declined as new sources of credit emerged while Memphis grew as an important center for the cotton trade. At the same time, numerous oil and oil equipment manufacturing companies based in Houston were responding to the lack of growth in the domestic industry by aggressively expanding their international activities. As these traditional customers of Texas Commerce moved into the European, Latin American, and Middle Eastern markets, the bank followed. The desire to meet the specialized needs of valued Houston-area accounts increasingly active in foreign trade thus fed the expansion of the international division of Texas Commerce Bank after the mid-1950s.[9]

The most important categories of international loans can be summarized as follows: (1) medium-sized Texas-based oil companies active abroad; (2) oil-equipment manufacturers, led by Hughes Tool and Cameron Iron Works, with growing sales abroad; (3) the national oil companies of several Latin American nations—notably Pemex of Mexico and Petrobras of Brazil—which borrowed money primarily to finance the purchase of oil equipment from Houston-based firms; and (4) foreign banks. As each type of account grew, so did the pressures on the international division at Texas Commerce. What had begun as a one-man operation in 1949 was becoming an increasingly significant aspect of the bank's operations, one which integrated Texas Commerce's Houston headquarters into a network of financial activities throughout the world.[10]

By the late 1960s, the international division had reached a crossroads. If it hoped to become more active in international finance, it needed to establish a permanent presence in London and New York. For several decades, the bank had followed its major customers outside the United States by extending services from Houston through individual officers who traveled extensively. But as the international activities of major customers increased, this traditional approach was no longer sufficient to fulfill their diverse needs. To better service such accounts, the bank made a series of decisions between the late 1960s and early 1970s which firmly positioned it as an organization committed to a more aggressive posture in international finance.

The earliest and perhaps the most significant of these commitments came in August, 1968, when TCB announced the purchase of a 35 percent share of Burston, Howard deWalden and Company, Ltd., an established London merchant bank, for a price in excess of $1 million. A merchant bank was not the same as a commercial bank in the United States, in that it did not take deposits or process checks. Instead, it concentrated on bringing together potential lenders with potential borrowers for a fee. Unlike a commercial bank in the United States, a merchant bank could also underwrite securities. The newly named Burston and Texas Commerce Bank, Ltd. thus gave Texas Commerce a flexible presence in the traditional capital of international finance. Further, the purchase gave TCB a stake in a going concern, thereby avoiding the lengthy process of creating a new institution. In becoming the first bank from the southwestern United States with an affiliate in London, TCB proclaimed its intentions to become a serious competitor in European markets. A permanent presence in London facilitated the bank's efforts to meet the needs of customers active in international markets while also giving it more direct access to Eurodollars, a source of funding which began to increase in importance in the 1960s.

The growth of the Eurodollar market reflected the increasing interdependence of the world's economies and the influence of U.S. regulations. American corporations active in Europe in the 1950s began depositing large dollar sums in London banks, including London branches of U.S. banks, for convenience and because these depositors could receive higher interest rates than U.S. regulations permitted domestic banks to pay. As the amount of dollars held in Europe grew, in the 1960s the United States enacted a series of regulations which sought to stem the flow of dollars to Europe by limiting the amount of dollars U.S. banks and corporations could transfer from domestic operations to foreign transactions. Such regulations gave the nation's major financial institutions strong incentives to establish foreign offices not subject to domestic restrictions and therefore capable of participating more freely in the expanding market for dollars held outside the United States. By the 1960s the Eurodollar market had become important in establishing prevailing rates on numerous international financial transactions. It was also becoming a vital source of liquidity for many U.S. banks. Burston and Texas Commerce was not subject to U.S. government regulations, and it was well situated to monitor and participate in the Eurodollar market and to help arrange loans in European currencies.[11]

The purchase of a share of a London merchant bank was followed quickly by several other decisions which enhanced the capabilities of Texas Commerce in the field of international finance. First, in 1969, TCB joined a parade of major banks into offshore branches which could take part in international currency trading and take deposits and make loans in Eurodollars. By establishing a branch in Nassau, Bahamas, Texas Commerce took advantage of that nation's liberal laws governing financial institutions while avoiding the restrictions imposed on domestic banks by U.S. regulations. Although little more than a post-office box managed by a trust company, this branch office enabled Texas Commerce to carry out various important international transactions which were constrained by U.S. law. All currency trading, negotiations for loans, and documentation of transactions for the Nassau branch took place in Houston. Such offshore operations were becoming an integral part of the operations of all major U.S. banks active in international financial markets; TCB's Nassau branch further established its credentials in this fraternity by assuring unrestricted access to Eurodollar markets on equal terms with the money-center banks.[12]

The staffing of permanent offices in areas of the world economy important to TCB's major customers further strengthened the bank's international activities in the 1960s and early 1970s. One important location for a variety of reasons was New York City, traditionally the center of international finance in the United States. The Edge Act of 1919 allowed U.S. banks to own indirectly foreign subsidiaries while also granting the right to establish offices throughout the United States to service international customers, accept deposits related to foreign transactions, and refer potential new customers to the parent bank. In February, 1969, Texas Commerce established an Edge Act office in New York City. According to the first manager of this office, "TCB–Wall Street" initially served primarily as a clearinghouse for securities. Instead of continuing to rely on New York correspondent banks to handle the delivery, receipt, and transfer of securities traded on behalf of the bank and its customers, TCB now found it profitable to maintain an office in New York for this and other purposes. This decision reflected the growing volume of securities transactions carried out by the bank on its own behalf as well as for its customers, which included Houston securities dealers, mutual funds, insurance companies, correspondent banks throughout Texas and the Southwest, and trust customers. In addition to such practical considerations, the symbolic appeal of establishing a presence on Wall Street no doubt contributed to the creation of a permanent New York office.[13]

Soon after, Texas Commerce opened a series of representative offices in important markets around the world. The first came in Mexico City in 1971, and it improved the bank's handling of the accounts of numerous long-term customers from the Houston region which had become increasingly active in Mexico. In the small world of international banking and politics, one factor which smoothed negotiations for the authorization of the Mexico City office were the bonds of friendship forged by prominent Mexicans who had been receiving medical treatment at the Texas Medical Center in Houston. Other Latin American ports were almost as near to the thriving port of Houston as was Mexico, and the strong trading ties between Houston-area concerns and Latin American interests encouraged the spread of TCB's business south of Mexico. Representative offices grew with this trade in Caracas and São Paulo. The bank's working relationship with one important group of international customers—the national oil companies of numerous Latin American nations—was further strengthened by their establishment of permanent purchasing offices in Houston, near the oil tool and service companies which had expanded from their original bases of operations in Houston to supply worldwide markets.[14]

A separate important source of international activity by Texas Commerce was the financing of trade between Japan and the United States. Houston had become an important port of entry for Japanese exports to the United States, and Texas Commerce steadily built its involvement in such trade. Early ties to Japan had been made by National Bank of Commerce under the leadership of Jesse Jones and the direction of the founder of that bank's international division, George Ebanks. Throughout the 1950s and 1960s, these early ties grew with Japanese trade with Houston. Japanese banks and trading companies became important accounts for the international division, and as their trade with Houston-area concerns expanded, many of these companies established Houston offices. Texas Commerce responded by opening a representative office in Tokyo in 1972. In subsequent years, the bank staffed offices in Bahrain and Hong Kong in an ongoing effort to provide personal, accessible services in regions of special interest to its customers. An additional step of considerable importance was the establishment of a full-service commercial branch in London in 1973 to supplement the investment and wholesale banking activities of Burston and Texas Commerce.[15]

Taken as a whole, these various moves into international markets represented a clear departure in the history of Texas Commerce. The expanding international division contributed geographical diversity to the bank's traditional operations in Texas. Permanent offices in foreign nations gave TCB's officers direct, continuous exposure to international financial markets, challenging the traditional provincialism of the Texas bank while proclaiming to customer and competitor alike a commitment to participate fully in the broad world of finance beyond the comfortable boundaries of its home state. Thus a series of forceful moves overseas after 1968 had given TCB the necessary ingredients for future growth: established foreign offices, a group of experienced personnel, and an image as an emerging new competitor in international finance.

Texas Commerce found another opportunity to become more competitive with money-center banks much closer to home. Situated in one of the best real estate construction markets in the nation in the 1950s and 1960s, Texas Commerce sought ways to participate more fully in Houston's building boom. Real estate construction was by no means a new enterprise in post–World War II Houston, but the pattern of construction after the 1950s was more conducive to the broader involvement of regional banks than had been the case in earlier eras, when larger financial institutions from outside the region had dominated the financing of major construction projects in Houston. In the 1950s, Texas National Bank became an innovator in financing real estate construction, albeit on a small scale. Then in the 1960s Texas Commerce gradually developed expertise and experience in this area. By 1971, despite the severe constraint of a legal lending limit far below the sums needed to finance major projects, Texas Commerce was capable for the first time in its history of taking a significant role in the financing of large-scale construction in its own region.

Throughout the twentieth century, the construction of office buildings had almost continuously remade the city's skyline, but two intense bursts of building in the 1950s and 1960s were of special significance to real estate lenders. The first came in the decade after 1952, when more than 7 million square feet of office space were added to downtown Houston, approximately doubling the city's existing downtown office space and pumping several hundred million dollars into Houston's economy through construction expenditures. After a brief pause to allow for the absorption of this new space, a new cycle of building began in the late 1960s, and the completion of three large buildings from 1967 to 1970 added almost 2.7 million more feet of downtown

Table 10.2   Major New Buildings in Houston's Central Business District, 1957–71

Year Completed	Name	Square Footage	Floors
1957	Gibraltar Savings Building	100,000	5
1957	Houston's Citizens Bank	225,000	14
1958	Central National Bank	267,000	14
1960	Texaco Annex	248,000	16
1960	First City Bank	780,000	33
1961	American Building	225,000	10
1961	Lincoln Liberty Building	120,000	8
1962	Exxon Building	1,429,800	46
1962	500 Jefferson	420,000	21
1962	Tenneco Building	1,152,724	32
1963	Houston First Savings	182,000	12
1963	Southwest Tower	262,891	20
1965	Southwestern Bell	520,000	13
1967	Houston Natural Gas	541,000	28
1968	Houston Lighting & Power	508,000	27
1970	One Shell Plaza	1,600,000	50
1970	Gordon Jewelry	100,000	10
1971	Entex Building	880,000	35
1971	Marathon Manufacturing	484,000	21
1971	Two Shell Plaza	533,000	25
1971	First City East	460,000	13

SOURCE: Property Research and Investment Consultants, Inc., "Houston's Office Space Market" (April 1975)

NOTE: Based on buildings on existence in 1975 and using the 1975 names of the buildings.

office space (see Table 10.2). The 1960s also witnessed an important departure in the development of Houston, the construction of numerous large office buildings in multiuse developments outside the central business district.[16]

Texas Commerce was well positioned to take advantage of the excellent market for construction lending in the 1960s. In the 1950s, National Bank of Commerce under the leadership of John Whitmore had established a large and profitable business in mortgage warehousing, and this special form of real estate lending continued to expand in subsequent decades. NBC remained the leader in this type of lending in its region, and the merger of 1964 strengthened its already strong position by adding a smaller but well-developed mortgage warehousing operation from the Texas National Bank. This activity remained a pillar of strength for Texas Commerce in the decades following the merger, supplying a reliable business which generated substantial loans and deposits.

Texas National Bank's primary contribution to real estate lending after the merger was not, however, in mortgage warehousing, but rather in real estate construction loans. In the years before 1964, those in charge of Texas National's "Warehouse, Real Estate & Construction Loan Department" developed a more flexible approach to real estate construction lending than had their counterparts at NBC or other large Houston banks. Under the direction of T. O. Taylor and with the technical expertise of Lawrence Lee, Texas National became an innovator in lending for real estate construction in the Houston area in the post–World War II era.

These two men serve as fitting symbols of the longevity of employment in the traditional world of banking. Lee entered banking at fourteen, finished high school while on the job, and remained at his post for fifty-one years before retiring. As he responded to changes in construction during the post–World War II building boom, Lee thus could draw on a lifetime of experience in real estate lending in the Houston market. While at Texas National, Lee specialized in designing real estate construction loans to suit the needs of borrowers, most of whom were brought into the bank through the efforts of T. O. Taylor, whose banking career at Texas Commerce and its predecessors spanned forty-eight years. Financing of commercial developers was one area in which Texas National proved capable of competing effectively with larger rivals in Houston in the years before the 1964 merger.[17]

After the merger, Taylor and Lee brought their experience and knowledge to Texas Commerce, where they hastened important changes in the bank's real estate construction lending. National Bank of Commerce traditionally had avoided most construction lending, limiting its activities in this area primarily to loans to well-established developers who were long-term customers of the bank. Taylor and Lee brought a more aggressive attitude and a keener technical understanding of the intricacies of real estate lending to Texas Commerce. Under their direction after 1964, the bank's real estate department gradually expanded its construction lending while seeking to retain its traditional strength in mortgage warehousing. This expansion accelerated in the 1970s, as the bank became more aggressive in this area.

The growing maturity of Texas Commerce as a real estate construction lender is illustrated by a brief history of one of its most significant accounts, Gerald D. Hines Interests. This Houston-based concern entered the construction business in the 1950s, building warehouses and other small structures. By the 1980s, it had grown into a nationally prominent concern, with skyscrapers and other large projects throughout the nation to its credit. Texas Commerce came of age in real estate lending by helping finance the projects of Hines and other similar Houston-based firms. The bank learned as it progressed with its major accounts from relatively small-scale projects to major buildings, or, as real estate lenders at Texas Commerce preferred to say, "from gas stations to Gallerias."

Hines came to Houston in 1948 with a degree in mechanical engineering from Purdue University. In search of good investment opportunities in the early 1950s, he began constructing small buildings and warehouses. Financing from local banks proved sufficient for these early projects, but Hines encountered difficulties in 1957 in negotiating financing for his first office building in Houston, a small office for General Electric. At that time, the dominant Houston banks, including First City National Bank and National Bank of Commerce, lent money for real estate construction primarily on the signature of the builder. That is, these banks hesitated to take deeds of trust against the loan liability, preferring instead to require the builder to assume personal liability. This was in the conservative tradition of personal banking, in which the major banks preferred to extend credit on the basis of an individual's personal worth rather than on the merits of the project in question.

Hines found a different attitude at Texas National Bank, where Taylor and Lee were developing new approaches to real estate lending as a way to gain ground on their larger competitors in Houston. Indeed, their loans to Hines and others in the late 1950s broke new ground in the city's construction lending by moving away from the sole reliance on personal liability. Instead, they structured loans around deeds of trust and mortgages, thereby encouraging local builders to undertake larger projects. In a steadily growing city, Texas National profited as the builders prospered. For Hines, this meant steadily progressing to more significant projects in the 1960s. As the square footage and height of his buildings rose from five stories to sixteen stories in the early 1960s, his need for financing grew proportionately.

Hines Interests reached a new scale of activity when it undertook the construction of One Shell Plaza, which at fifty stories and 1.6 million feet in gross area was both the tallest and the largest building in Houston upon its completion in 1970. Yet as the firm steadily expanded, it also threatened to outgrow its local sources of financing. Hines initially looked out-of-state for the $30 million needed for the construction of One Shell Plaza. He was offered financing which required, among other things, full personal liability for the loan for Hines and each of his partners. Finding this stipulation unacceptable, Hines returned to Houston, where he put together a consortium of lenders led by First City National Bank and including all of the major Houston banks. Texas Commerce was a significant participant in this loan, which was at the time the largest construction loan totally funded by Houston banks. The successful completion of the One Shell Plaza project established Hines as a major builder in Houston while also involving the city's banks in financing real estate development on an unprecedented scale.

Before this project and others like it in the 1960s and 1970s, the largest buildings in downtown Houston generally had been built by oil companies with financing supplied by their East Coast banks. Such banks as First National Bank of Boston had long been leaders in the financing of large office buildings, and they brought to their work financial resources, a wealth of experience, and invaluable contacts with long-term financers which Houston banks could not yet match. Despite their collective efforts in constructing One Shell Plaza, Houston's major banks were still too small and lacking in experience to challenge the larger, established banks in New York and Boston in real estate construction lending for giant projects. Yet as Houston's skyline continued to grow and as Houston-based builders such as Gerald Hines expanded their activities, local banks sought to increase their participation in this growth sector of their banking market.

For Texas Commerce, this meant going to school to master the details of large-scale construction financing. Gerald D. Hines Interests provided many of the lessons to be studied; leading real estate lenders from First National of Boston served as tutors. By the late 1960s, Texas Commerce had emerged as Hines's lead bank in Houston, and when Hines put together plans for the Galleria, an ambitious, multiuse development southwest of downtown Houston, Texas Commerce joined as a participant in a loan package headed by First National of Boston. The Galleria project included a major hotel, a large shopping area, and an office-building complex. Acquiring land leases and air rights leases and putting together the different parcels of land involved to the satisfaction of the many various tenants proved anything but easy. In fact, according to Gerald Hines, the Galleria project required one of the most complex construction loans ever made. Guiding the principles through the maze of difficulties was King Upton of First Boston, one of the deans of construction lending in the nation. Handling much of the work for Texas Commerce was Lloyd Bolton, who had trained for his responsibilities as head of real estate lending under John Whitmore, T. O. Taylor, and Lawrence Lee.

Texas Commerce profited in several ways from its participation in the construction of the Galleria. It gained invaluable exposure to the techniques of modern real estate lending as practiced by one of the leaders in conservative financing of large-scale projects. In addition, it solidified its relationship with Hines, who emerged from this era as one of the dominant Houston builders, while also beginning to move onto the national stage. The best evidence of the growing maturity of Texas Commerce in real estate lending came several years after the completion of the first phase of construction of the Galleria. On phase two of the project, Texas Commerce served as the lead bank for the loan, with First Boston as a participant. Fuller participation in a major regional industry from which Texas Commerce traditionally had been excluded was clearly at hand.[18]

The bank's growing size also allowed it to expand its participation in the financing of the numerous local concerns which had always provided the bulk of the business of Texas Commerce and its predecessor. In the post-World War II era, records on real estate and oil lending were kept separate from those on the bank's other business, which was lumped together under the undescriptive label "metropolitan" lending. Yet despite the special status accorded to real estate and oil lending in the bank's organization of lending groups, the catch-all metropolitan division remained a major contributor to the bank's growth. As shown in Table 10.1, this was especially true in the 1960s. This expansion of lending to area concerns engaged in a wide variety of economic pursuits was the clearest evidence of the growing maturity of the region. The sharp fluctuations in the oil industry after 1973 tended to divert attention from the growing variety of economic activities in the bank's major markets. But before and after 1971, Texas Commerce carried on a substantial, prosperous business financing the development of the numerous and varied types of commerce, industry, and services generated by the growth of a major city.

One particularly important such account was American General Insurance, whose diversified operations grew with Houston and the Southwest from its founding in the 1920s. From these early days, TCB and American General maintained a multifaceted business relationship which consistently ranked as one of the bank's largest accounts. TCB made loans to American General for a variety of purposes, ranging from working capital to acquisitions to support for its mortgage

Producing Dollars from Concrete

An example of the diversity of metropolitan lending was the account of D. M. Carothers. Houston's twentieth-century growth relied heavily on an expanding highway system. It is not surprising, then, that parking lots became big business in Houston and that a businessman's bank, such as National Bank of Commerce, would count among its valued, long-term accounts the historical leader in this industry, Allright Auto Parks, Inc. Allright grew from its founding in 1926 by D. M. Carothers as a downtown Houston parking lot into a nationally active concern with several thousand lots in more than seventy cities.

Carothers understood early that in a dynamic city such as Houston parking lots could be profitable on several levels. Most obviously, substantial fees could be charged for parking in prime locations convenient to the city's business center. Aside from land-acquisitions costs, little investment or operating expense was required. Yet over the long run, the potential for even greater profit consisted in choosing locations wisely, holding them as they appreciated in value, and then "turning properties for higher and better use." Carothers thus became a special sort of real estate developer, and he inevitably came into contact with another man active in downtown Houston real estate, Jesse Jones. The two men established what might best be described as a banking and trading relationship, which blossomed in the late 1940s after Jones acquired a piece of property from Carothers for the construction of a parking garage for Jones's Rice Hotel. Both men owned real estate in the northern part of Houston's business district, and on several occasions they traded leases or otherwise rearranged their holdings. Meanwhile, National Bank of Commerce built a substantial banking relationship with Allright Parking, which grew so rapidly throughout the postwar era that it laid claim to the title "the world's largest parking company."

In the late 1970s, Allright was involved in one last real estate transaction with Jesse Jones's old bank. As Texas Commerce sought to put together a block of downtown property for the construction of a new skyscraper, its focus came to rest on a block of land which Allright had acquired bit by bit over several decades. As in the days of Jones, a trade was struck among friends which included the transfer of several nearby pieces of property owned by Texas Commerce to Allright in exchange for the block of property needed to construct what became the Texas Commerce Tower. Finally, the old personal ties which had long cemented the business relationship between the two concerns weakened in the 1980s with the retirement of Carothers and the purchase of his company by foreign investors.

SOURCES: Elizabeth Ashton, "Houston's Doctor of Urban Decay," *Texas Business* (March 1982): 51−53.

company. In addition, the bank handled the personal accounts of many of American General's top executives, while also providing cash-management services such as securities clearances and trust services. American General solidified this working relationship by providing the bank with substantial deposits, handling the various insurance needs of the bank, and, perhaps most significantly, supplying several valued directors for the bank. Benefits flowed in both directions through the long-standing business and personal ties between these two growing Houston area concerns that were active in different portions of the financial-services industry.[19]

Despite the importance of such large accounts as American General Insurance, metropolitan lending included much more than simply a few very large accounts. The sustained growth of the metropolitan division reflected the bank's success in attracting a broad range of accounts of businesses of all sizes. It also reflected several important changes within the bank. One impetus for change was the merger of 1964, which altered the mix of metropolitan accounts by adding numerous new accounts from Texas National Bank to NBC's traditional relationships with a select list of the largest companies in the region. Texas National had established account relationships with numerous small businesses in the 1950s and early 1960s as it sought growth in a banking market in which most of the larger accounts were considered taken. While combining these two diverse collections of Houston area accounts after 1964, the new bank expanded in both areas.

More aggressive expansion of the metropolitan division began in the late 1960s, with the implementation of a systematic calling program which greatly expanded Texas Commerce's presence throughout Houston-area banking markets.[20] The bank's metropolitan division gradually reached into every corner of the region's economy, from retailers who sold goods ranging from groceries to diamonds, to scrap-metal producers, to stock brokers. The surge in metropolitan lending in the 1960s was at once the bank's response to the growing array of opportunities in its region and the primary impetus for the growth and diversification of the bank.

As reorganized in this era, the metropolitan division also encompassed a "Southwest" section, which included all Texas customers outside the Houston metropolitan area as well as those in Louisiana, Arkansas, Oklahoma, and New Mexico. This organizational structure reflected the judgment of TCB's management that the Southwest was best treated as a natural extension of the Houston market, since many of the same industries, companies, and individuals served by the bank's specialists in the metropolitan division were also active in other parts of the Southwest. This "energy belt" of states presented excellent prospects for the broader application of the expertise and experience built up by the expansion of metropolitan lending. In the early 1970s, the bank began canvassing the major markets of the Southwest in the same organized manner which was proving successful in the Houston area. In these years, the growing number of companies headquartered outside the Southwest but with operations in the Houston area also began receiving more systematic attention lending officers at Texas Commerce.

A final tie connecting the bank to the section of the nation surrounding Houston was the correspondent-banking division, which served the banks in smaller towns throughout the Southwest in much the same way that the specialized lending groups served other customers. In its role as a bankers' bank, Texas Commerce provided to smaller banks generally located outside large cities numerous important services, notably clearing of checks, data processing, trust services, and expert assistance on investments, and advice on a variety of issues from problem loans to advertising. In return, these banks left large compensating balances at TCB. By 1970, more than 500 correspondent banks had $100 million in deposits at Texas Commerce, providing much-needed funds with which to keep up with the demand for loans. Correspondent-banking ties facilitated the flow of potential investment funds from smaller cities and towns in Texas and the Southwest with moderate loan demand to the more dynamic economies of the big cities such as Houston. In this sense, dollars in search of profitable opportunities followed the same path to the big city taken by several generations of people from small towns in the decades after World War II.

Because of the relatively low inflation in the 1950s to mid-1960s, country bankers generally were content to leave large compensating balances with the big-city banks without much concern for other, potentially more profitable uses of their money. Without computers to assist them in analyzing the differences in the short-term yields from alternative uses of their money, most made a predictable choice: they maintained the tradition of exchanging interest on their funds for services from the big-city banks. In a world of banking at once more personal and less concerned with short-run profitability than banks subsequently became, the big-city banks competed for correspondent banking business with enticements ranging from good, efficient services to ample quantities of refreshments at annual get-togethers for the country bankers in Houston.

The involvement of each bank in the correspondent banking business in the 1950s and 1960s was much influenced by its history. Texas National Bank, for example, benefited from the strong historical ties of its largest predecessor, South Texas Commercial National, to the outlying regions which previously had been major cotton-growing areas. As Tables 3.1 and 3.2 illustrate, STCNB had long had the most highly developed correspondent banking business in Houston, and TNB continued this tradition in the 1950s. Conversely, National Bank of Commerce had never been a leader in correspondent banking, and it struggled to develop a broader network of correspondent relationships in the years before its 1964 merger with TNB.

The major Houston banks took this business quite seriously, since large deposits were involved. Each had staffs of correspondent-banking specialists who spent much of their time traveling through the state calling on existing accounts, as well as potential new ones. The fraternity of correspondent bankers resembled traveling salesmen more than traditional bankers. Before the widespread adoption of computers and the coming of the bank holding company to Texas, the correspondent banking business serviced by these men generated valuable deposits for their banks while helping bind together the financial system of Texas and surrounding states. The expansion of correspondent banking made an important contribution to the geographical diversification of Texas Commerce and its predecessors before the advent of the holding company.[21]

TCB's growth in all areas except oil lending in the years from 1956 to 1971 pushed the bank to a new level of activity. In these years Texas Commerce made great strides in developing more systematic approaches to marketing and more sophisticated types of loans to meet the needs of an increasingly diverse regional economy. The bank's growth in the years after the 1964 merger pushed its deposits over the long-contemplated billion-dollar barrier for the first time in 1970, in the process significantly closing the gap in size between Texas Commerce and its primary rival in Houston, First City National Bank. Yet despite this growth in deposits and the impressive records of the lending departments in responding to changes in their specialized areas of the economy, the bank as a whole faced a fundamental constraint as it sought to adjust its operations to ongoing changes in the market for banking services. The state's unit banking law blocked changes essential to the bank's future growth.

One serious concern for the major Houston and Dallas banks was their inability to grow large enough to service the banking needs of their most coveted potential customers, the largest businesses in their regions. While Texas Commerce sought to keep pace with First City National Bank of Houston for primacy among Houston's banks, money-center banks continued to capture a substantial share of the banking business of the region's largest concerns. A survey published in the early 1970s by the Federal Reserve Bank of Dallas after interviews with 42 of the 100 largest businesses in Texas found strong working ties between many of these companies and large banks in New York, Chicago, and California. The survey concluded that "The main reason for this outflow of banking business is clearly the size of Texas banks. Banks in the state are simply too small to compete effectively with large out-of-state banks."[22] The implication was equally clear: if Texas banks were to halt the traditional pilgrimage of large Texas companies to money-center banks, they would have to grow substantially larger. This would require some modification of the state's unit banking law.

This imperative to grow large enough to capture the banking business of large Texas businesses was not felt uniformly by all banks throughout the state. Indeed, only a handful of large banks in Houston and Dallas could realistically aspire to such growth. Nor was this imperative felt by the mass of bank customers in Texas. Most average Texans worried about whether they could obtain a car loan from their local bank, not about whether Texaco or Hughes Tool had to go to New York to conduct banking business. One reason the unit banking law remained strictly interpreted was that most small-town banks and most average bank customers felt no great urgency on this issue. Those who did feel such urgency—that is, the top management of the largest banks in Texas—thus could not expect broad political support for their efforts to alter the law. They faced a choice between two difficult approaches to loosening the constraints imposed by unit banking. They could lobby to change the law, provoking an inevitable wave of protest that the big-city banks wanted to "gobble up" their smaller country cousins, or they could try to find a backroad around the existing law, seeking to avoid open political confrontation with defenders of unit banking by discovering or creating loopholes in the law.[23]

Pending the success of either of these two approaches, Texas Commerce and its major competitors in Texas could only continue to seek the growth necessary to service the needs of the dominant businesses in Texas through mergers between unit banks. As they had done throughout their histories, they could consolidate with other large downtown banks, thereby quickly boosting their legal lending limit and accumulating the personnel and resources needed to serve the needs of large corporate customers. Of course, Texas Commerce had learned all too well the possible pitfalls of such mergers in 1964. But even if the bank had been willing to forget its recent past and try again, no logical downtown merger partners large enough to make much difference remained by the early 1970s. Under the existing law, the largest Houston banks had no realistic strategy for maturing with their region and its major industries into banks capable of competing more equally with the larger banks in the traditional money centers.

While seeking to make up ground on these larger concerns, Texas Commerce and other downtown Houston banks also faced a different sort of competitive pressure from smaller banks in suburban Houston. Despite several significant mergers between major banks in the 1950s and 1960s, these decades witnessed the steady decline of the market share of downtown banks such as Texas Commerce in the banking industry in and around Houston. The antibranch law blocked the downtown banks from pursuing the flight of people and businesses to the rapidly growing suburbs. Tunnels could be used to finesse the unit banking law when the bank to be acquired was across the street, but tunnels could not reach from downtown to the beltway and beyond. As new banks sprang up to serve the booming Houston suburban market in the 1950s and 1960s, Texas Commerce Bank, First City National Bank, and Bank of the Southwest—the three largest downtown banks produced by the wave of mergers in this era—searched for ways to protect their traditional dominance of the banking market in the Houston metropolitan area.

Since direct ownership of other banks was forbidden, the downtown banks found ways to benefit indirectly from suburban expansion. The most prevalent arrangement was chain banking, a phrase used to describe one bank's ownership of a minority interest in another. Through the purchase of stock, a bank or individual investors involved in the affairs of a bank could establish a measure of control in another bank. The Bank Holding Company Act of 1956 gave tacit approval to such arrangements when it required any company owning 25 percent or more of the outstanding stock of two or more banks to register with the Federal Reserve Board as a bank holding company.[24] By remaining silent on cases which involved less than a 25 percent interest, this law prepared the way for the spread of "24.9 percent banks." The owner of the large minority interest in a smaller bank could wield considerable influence; indeed, when reinforced by substantial holdings of individual investors friendly toward the management of the larger bank, a 24.9 percent interest could often be parlayed into effective control. Many large banks purchased less than 25 percent of numerous smaller banks, thereby establishing a loosely coordinated system of banks. This type of chain banking was particularly popular in Texas since it was the best available avenue for the creation of working ties between banks operating under the state's unit banking law.

Thus on the eve of the holding-company movement in 1971, the Federal Reserve Bank of Dallas estimated that almost half of the total bank deposits in Texas were held by the more than 430 banks in the state affiliated with chains. With more than 70 percent of its total deposits in chain banks, the Dallas standard metropolitan area was the center of chain banking activities in the state. But although banks in the Houston area were much less involved in chains than their counterparts in Dallas, the Federal Reserve's study nonetheless estimated that more than 40 percent of Houston's bank deposits were in chain banks.[25]

Clearly, chain banking had grown into a significant part of the banking business in Texas. For Texas Commerce and other large banks in the state, chain banking offered a roundabout and imperfect means for following the spread of the cities into surrounding suburbs. In the years from 1950 to 1971, Texas Commerce built a close working relationship with six Houston-area banks outside the central business district. These ties were cemented by ownership of up to 24.9 percent of the stock of the outlying banks, by personal ties between the management of Texas Commerce and the suburban banks, and by very strong correspondent banking relationships. Map 10.1 shows the location of the banks in the Texas Commerce chain, along with the year TCB first purchased its minority interest in each bank.

The involvement of Texas Commerce in chain banking began in the last decade of Jesse Jones's tenure as chairman of the board of the National Bank of Commerce. In 1950 a group of investors headed by Jones organized Reagan State Bank, which subsequently remained the largest link in the downtown bank's chain. As the first-established and largest suburban affiliate of Texas Commerce, Reagan State provides an instructive case study of chain banking. A brief history of this bank suggests how chains operated while also revealing the close working ties which developed between banks as they sought to coordinate their operations without violating the unit banking law.

Jones initially purchased more than 50 percent ownership in the newly organized Reagan State Bank through the Commerce Company, one of his wholly owned operating companies, which at the time also owned more than 50 percent of the capital stock of the National Bank

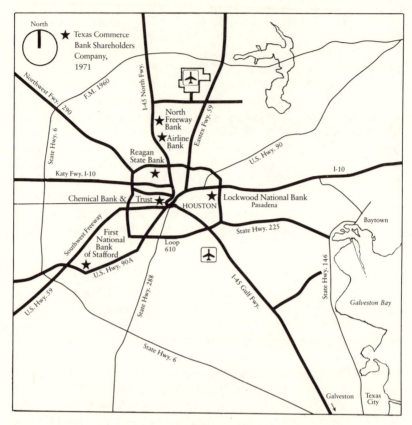

Map 10.1. Texas Commerce Bank's Chain-Banking System.

of Commerce. The original board of directors included J. H. Creek-more, counsel for many of Jesse Jones's corporations and later president of the Houston Endowment; W. L. Doherty, the son of the long-term president of the National Bank of Commerce, Robert P. Doherty; Milton Farthing, a nephew of Jesse Jones and an officer in the Commerce Company; John T. Jones, another nephew of Jones, who was president of the *Houston Chronicle* Publishing Company; and Gainer Jones, a prominent officer of the National Bank of Commerce. In subsequent years, numerous officers of NBC, including John Whitmore, continued to serve on Reagan's board as representatives of the Jones interests. In addition to holding a seat on the board, Creekmore served as a vice-president of the bank from 1950 to 1968, during which time he sat on the loan and discount committee at Reagan. Thus from the day the new bank opened its doors, individuals closely connected to Jesse Jones and his varied enterprises held positions which assured that Reagan State would work closely with National Bank of Commerce.[26]

Common ownership and shared directors and officers did not mean that the downtown bank directly controlled the operation of its suburban affiliate. Instead, this chain-banking arrangement simply facilitated cooperation between the two banks while encouraging the adoption of similar management philosophies at the two concerns. Reagan State enjoyed what amounted to an especially favorable correspondent relationship with its larger part owner. NBC served as Reagan's primary depository for funds, handled its clearings with the Houston Clearing House Association, sold loan participations to it to strengthen the smaller bank's loan portfolio, purchased loan participations from Reagan to enable the smaller bank to handle loans beyond its legal limit, acted as trustee of its retirement plan, furnished investment advice, assisted its customers in exchanges of securities, referred customers to Reagan, helped find and evaluate new personnel, and provided regular advice on many phases of banking. In addition, NBC performed Reagan's data processing. Affiliation with a much larger, established downtown bank thus gave Reagan State and NBC's other affiliates access to expert advice and specialized services not easily available to unaffiliated suburban banks.[27]

Benefits from this arrangement flowed in both directions. Through chain banking, NBC profited indirectly from postwar suburban growth far from its downtown location. With its traditional emphasis on serving the commercial banking needs of Houston's major businesses, NBC had little experience in lending to consumers and small businesses, and chain banking permitted NBC to participate in such markets through the activities of its affiliates. Close ties to suburban banks also allowed NBC to refer its downtown customers to friendly banks in residential areas for a variety of banking needs, particularly automobile financing and home mortgages. Chain banks also maintained substantial correspondence balances with NBC to offset the expense of the services performed by the larger bank.[28] The best available evidence that such chains were profitable to Texas Commerce's predecessor was that it sought them out and maintained them. The same was true of NBC's major competitor in Houston, First City, and the large downtown Dallas banks.

From the early investments of Jesse Jones and friends until the advent of the bank holding company movement in the early 1970s, the ownership of the chain banks shifted several times. Jones's holdings in suburban affiliates had been administered through the Commerce Company before his death in 1956. These holdings subsequently went to Houston Endowment, the charitable foundation established by Jones to manage much of his business empire. After the 1964 merger, however, Houston Endowment began selling its interests in these banks to individuals who had helped forge the links in the chain-banking system through ownership of stock in both Texas Commerce and the various affiliates. Such transfers of ownership posed no immediate threat to the working relationships between TCB and its suburban chain banks. Any uncertainties over the long-run implications of such sales was quieted in 1968, when the newly created Texas Commerce Shareholders Company strengthened the chain by acquiring minority interests in Airline, Reagan State, First National of Stafford, Lockwood National, and Chemical Bank and Trust.[29]

These purchases gave a strong minority ownership in each of the five banks to a company directly affiliated with TCB. The Texas Commerce Shareholders Company made its acquisitions with funds generated by special stock dividends paid by Texas Commerce. The acquired stock was then placed in trust for the account of the bank's shareholders. In choosing to create a subsidiary to hold the stock of its chain banks, TCB followed the example of Republic National Bank of Dallas, which earlier had established the Howard Corporation to administer investments in the interests of its shareholders.[30] Through this new arrangement the management of Texas Commerce could more easily coordinate its involvement in the affiliated banks. The Shareholders Company also promised to be more flexible and more easily expandable than had been the previous cooperation among individual investors friendly to TCB. The Texas Commerce Shareholders Company thus represented a step toward the holding-company concept which finally emerged in the 1970s.

Yet no matter how well organized, a chain of 24.9 percent banks had several distinct limits as a means of coordinating the activities of numerous banks. A minority interest, even if bolstered by additional holdings of friendly investors, might not always translate into effective control. This was particularly so in the early 1970s, when government regulators began to look more closely for evidence of undue influence by large banks in the operations of their affiliates. Thus directors and officers identified as representatives of the minority interest walked a fine line as they sought to avoid the appearance of coercion while building coalitions capable of producing desired managerial policies. A more fundamental limitation to chain banking was that each bank in the chain was considered a separate organization in the calculation of its legal lending limit. No matter how closely the affiliated banks cooperated in referring business and in participating in each others' loans, they could not make loans based on their combined lending limit. This was not a significant problem from the point of view of suburban banks primarily involved in consumer lending; it was, however, a serious drawback from the perspective of a downtown Houston bank seeking to grow rapidly in order to compete more effectively with much larger money-center banks. These weaknesses of chain banking from the perspective of the largest banks in Texas assured that they would continue to search for alternative routes around the unit banking law.

The excursion of Texas Commerce into chain banking provides a fitting symbol of the bank's overall pattern of growth in the years before 1971. As the regional economy surged ahead during the long era of postwar prosperity, the bank's management gradually altered traditional attitudes toward marketing, becoming ever more aggressive by the 1960s in building new business. Yet no changes in management attitudes could loosen a more fundamental constraint on the bank's expansion, the existing regulations governing unit banking in Texas. Without a greatly expanded lending limit, Texas Commerce could not respond fully to the opportunities presented by the growing maturity of Houston. As the bank's influence spread throughout a larger section of the Southwest and into international markets, it regularly encountered limitations because of its small size relative to its competitors and to the needs of its major customers. Diversity of operations would have to be accompanied by substantial new growth if Texas Commerce was to mature with its region into an institution capable of competing on more equal footing with money-center banks.

To step up into the ranks of the nation's major banks would have required difficult adjustments by the bank's management even in the absence of changes in the bank's economic or regulatory environments. The size and aggressiveness required to become more than a relatively small regional bank inevitably would call forth basic changes in the operation of the bank. But such managerial adjustments did not take place in an era of stability of markets and regulation. Instead, the transition from the traditional management practices to the quite different approach to banking required to run a growing bank in an increasingly competitive industry went forward in the 1960s and 1970s amid epoch-making changes in both the regional economy and the regulatory framework governing financial institutions.

The next three chapters examine three major challenges which confronted those in charge of Texas Commerce after the 1960s: the development of a new system of management; the creation of a state-wide holding company; and the response to sharp and largely unpredictable fluctuations in the mainstay of the region's economy, the petroleum industry. These three challenges to bank managers in the 1970s and 1980s were not, of course, isolated issues which were addressed separately. Rather, they were closely related concerns which demanded the attention of bank managers during a long era of extensive changes in banking.

CHAPTER 11

Industrial Management Comes to Texas Commerce

The sustained growth and diversification of the regional economy called into question the traditional approach to bank management. In the decade after the 1964 merger, Texas Commerce underwent a fundamental managerial transition, as management techniques and attitudes inherited from a slower-paced, less competitive era of banking were replaced by an approach to management adapted from modern industrial corporations. Until 1964, the management-succession problems had focused on the search for a new top manager; after 1964, the focus gradually shifted to the search for a new type of management. The traditional approach to banking employed by Jesse Jones and his counterparts in other Houston banks was replaced by a quite different approach closely identified with the man who emerged in control of the bank's management in the early 1970s, Ben Love.

Traditional bank-management practices long suited the needs of even the largest Houston banks. For much of the twentieth century, these banks were tightly held by owners who took a direct role in strategic decisions while entrusting day-to-day affairs to hand-picked operating officers. Since Texas banks were limited by the unit banking law to a single location, their managers were primarily concerned with local market conditions. They provided a narrow range of services under the close supervision of regulatory authorities who maintained strict competitive boundaries between commercial banking and other financial services industries. Aggressive marketing or even detailed market research was not required by these traditional banks, since they generally had ample opportunities for lending in a booming regional economy. Highly centralized management was the norm in a banking industry characterized by geographically restricted markets, the use of rudimentary data processing techniques to keep track of transactions, and strictly enforced regulatory constraints on competition. At National Bank of Commerce, South Texas Commercial National Bank, and Union National Bank, the chief operating officer personally approved most important decisions, often with the guidance of the bank's principal owner.

In the decades after World War II, this traditional approach to bank management was undermined by several related processes of change. The most obvious was the growing scale of the bank's operations and the size and diversity of the markets in which it operated. Further increasing the demands on management was the acceleration of the speed of bank transactions through the introduction of ever more powerful computers. Finally, in the 1960s and 1970s the basic regulatory boundaries within which banks had operated for decades began to shift, unleashing intense competitive pressures which threatened to overwhelm existing centralized management systems. The response of Texas Commerce was the adoption of a more market-oriented approach to management patterned after decentralized systems long utilized by modern business enterprises in industry.[1] This included the creation of more formal financial controls, which produced sophisticated measures of profitability not traditionally required by bank managers. It also included the creation of a decentralized management structure with more clearly defined lines of authority and responsibility, more systematic marketing, and increased concern for long-run planning.

Such changes in the recent past were the culmination of broad historical trends affecting Texas Commerce. From the late nineteenth century forward, the steady growth of the bank's business encouraged the professionalization of management. The three generations of the McAshan family who guided the affairs of Texas National Bank and its predecessors embodied this record of growing professionalism in bank managers.[2] Each generation faced new and more complicated demands; each responded by instituting changes aimed at expanding the organization's capacities to manage an increasingly large and diverse business. As the regional economy surged forward after World War II, the long-run trend toward greater professionalization of bank management manifested itself in several important ways, notably the growing specialization of lending officers, the evolution of separate departments responsible for specific lending areas, the creation of more formal programs for training newly recruited managers, and the adoption of more systematic methods for evaluating credit risks.

The most obvious of these adjustments was a movement away from reliance on the small group of general-purpose lending officers who traditionally had handled most of the banks' accounts. Officers with more specific expertise were needed to build accounts in the specialized lending areas which played such a central role in the bank's expansion after 1945. E. O. Buck in oil, John Whitmore in real estate, and George Ebanks in international lending brought to the National Bank of Commerce training and experience in areas not previously mastered by the bank's lending officers. Their counterparts at Texas National Bank included Joseph Nalle in oil lending and Lawrence Lee in real estate. Recognizing the need for innovations to take advantage of the development of specific growth industries in the Houston economy, the top management of these banks hired specialists from the industries in question, exposed them briefly to the overall operations of the bank, and then granted them considerable autonomy in devising new lending procedures suited to the needs of the industries they served. The deliberations of the loan and discount committee remained the ultimate safeguard against ill-advised actions by the specialized lending officers, and the top managers who dominated the committee were most demanding when the younger specialists introduced new types of loans not previously offered by the bank. In several instances at NBC—notably the introduction of long-term loans to oil producers based on reserves in the ground and the relatively large commitments of funds for the development of the rice trade between Texas companies and foreign nations—the lending officer involved had to overcome considerable resistance from the loan and discount committee before obtaining its approval to proceed. Although this temporarily slowed the bank's expansion, it also provided a measure of insurance against departures from traditional lending practices which exposed the bank to unacceptable risks.[3]

After such specialized lending areas gained acceptance, the next stage in their evolution was the organization of permanent departments to expand the efforts of the individuals who had guided the bank's entry into the specialized lending areas. By the early 1950s, the major predecessors of Texas Commerce had distinct oil, real estate, and international departments which slowly but steadily added new lending officers. By adding staff support and new specialists, the bank freed the founders of the new departments from some of the routine work which had grown with the growth in loans. In oil lending, the retention of fees from the sale of loans to larger banks provided the oil department with a modest source of revenue, separate from the bank's general budget, with which to build up its staff.[4] The new specialists, who generally were hired from major companies in the industry to which they would make loans, also brought both new ideas and new enthusiasm to their departments. In turn, these departments increasingly became the focal point of the bank's efforts to respond effectively to changes in the numerous specialized markets which made up the bulk of its business.

As their operations grew rapidly, the large Houston banks faced a common set of problems: Where could they find the new managers required by growth; how could the wave of new employees required be efficiently integrated into the banks' ongoing operations? How could new officers, once trained, be retained in light of the low salaries and minimal benefits traditionally offered by banks? Most of the banks hired specialized lending officers in the oil and real estate fields from the engineering staffs of major oil companies and the technical staffs of large mortgage companies. For certain other specialists, they turned to the leaders in the banking industry, the large New York banks. The dynamism of Houston and the opportunity for advancement in growing organizations proved sufficient to attract capable employees.

Although National Bank of Commerce succeeded in attracting able specialists in this period of rapid growth, it fell behind several local competitors in training the growing number of middle managers needed to administer its mounting volume of increasingly diverse business. The bank established no formal training program for its new employees, relying instead on an informal approach to executive training which had proved sufficient in an earlier time of fewer employees and simpler operations. In general, this entailed exposure of a new employee to the details of the job he was hired to perform, with little effort to introduce him to the overall operations of the bank. This segmentation was reinforced by the traditional procedures of the loan and discount committee. Lending officers scheduled to present loan applications to the committee awaited their turns outside the meeting room before entering individually to address the committee. As a result, they remained unexposed to the lending practices and relationships evolving in areas outside of their own specialties. By harnessing lending officers quickly into their special areas, the bank reaped short-term benefits in the form of immediate expansion of these crucial areas. The long-run cost of this approach, however, was the lack of development of a future generation of top managers with varied administrative experience and exposure to the overall operations of the bank.

This contrasted markedly with the innovative approach to executive development used at South Texas Commercial National Bank. The bank shortened its name to South Texas National Bank in 1949 and began a decade-long quest to become more competitive with NBC and the other, larger Houston banks. In this drive for competitiveness,

South Texas faced many of the staffing pressures experienced by NBC, but its young president, Harris McAshan, recognized the need for a more systematic method of selecting and training new managers. In exploring his options on this matter, he looked for ideas to National City Bank of New York (now Citibank), one of his bank's major New York correspondents. National City had a highly developed and much publicized executive training program which McAshan adapted to the more limited needs of South Texas National. The executive training program he established in the early 1950s recruited employees from universities with good reputations in the region and then rotated them through all general phases of the bank's operations for eighteen to twenty-four months. Systematic exposure to varied aspects of the bank's operations helped identify the areas within the bank best suited to the talents of new employees while also giving them a sense of the overall functioning of the organization. The effect of this program was most evident in the long-term success of its alumni in banks throughout the region and the state.[5]

The idea of adapting the most highly developed management programs of money-center banks came quite naturally to the large Houston banks, which were growing along paths traveled decades earlier by the largest banks in the nation. As the Houston banks became too large to continue to manage various functions in the highly personalized traditional manner, they looked to New York for possible models of more modern bank management. One instructive example of such borrowing was the creation of a credit department by National Bank of Commerce during and after the 1930s. The man chosen to build this department, William Tandy, had spent several years earlier in his career in the credit department of the National Bank of Commerce of New York, one of the nation's largest banks in the 1920s. Tandy's recollections of his hiring are suggestive:

> Mr. Doherty said he saw the need for a credit department, because every loan officer was doing his own credit investigations. This was inefficient and, for a big bank, unsatisfactory. Now setting up a credit department where none had existed before called for many innovations. I built files on every Houston businessman of substance and on every company and bank in Texas that I might be asked about. I set up for Mr. Doherty the same kind of credit information system that I had seen at the National Bank of Commerce in New York.[6]

As this file of information grew, it augmented the considerable credit information available to the bank's officers through the bank's one-man credit department, Sam Taub. By the time of Taub's death in 1956, the bank had the beginnings of a systematic source of data for use in the critically important functions of calling on accounts and evaluating credit worthiness. In Jesse Jones's era of banking, most of the credit work of NBC could be safely entrusted to the personal knowledge of active directors and officers on the loan committee. But as the bank grew, even someone as knowledgeable as Sam Taub could not be expected to keep track of all of the financial information required in its daily operations.

The processing of financial information of all kinds was at the heart of the business of banking, and long-run improvements in the technology used to store and analyze such data had an indirect, but nonetheless significant, impact on the evolution of bank management. Data processing as traditionally performed by individual employees with simple calculating machines limited the number and the speed of transactions, placing a basic technical constraint on the size of banks. Computers revolutionized the business of banking by speeding the flow of money through the financial system while allowing individual banks to process transactions in ways and at speeds never before possible. Computers greatly enhanced the capacities of managers to accumulate and analyze information about their banks. At the same time, computers posed new challenges to traditional bank managers by accelerating the pace of banking and by allowing consumers of financial services more easily to calculate potential returns from various available uses of their funds. By fundamentally altering the processing of information about financial transactions, computers made possible a revolution in the financial-services industries. As modern computers enhanced competitive pressures, commercial banks had to adopt more sophisticated management systems to defend or expand their traditional market positions.[7]

In the decades after World War II, technical advances in information processing went hand-in-hand with the growing professionalism and specialization of middle managers to undermine the traditional approach to bank management. Yet as the largest Houston banks gradually adopted some of the attitudes and practices long associated with industrial management, a decided difference between these organizations and most modern industrial concerns remained: ownership was not yet separated from control. As had been the case in the early twentieth century with a variety of industrial companies, the dispersal of ownership of Texas Commerce in the 1950s and 1960s prepared the way for the creation of a more modern management system in which professional managers controlled both operations and long-run planning.

Table 11.1   Percentage of Texas Commerce Controlled by the
Largest Single Shareholder Group, 1952–73

End of Year	Bank	Shareholder	Percent
1952	NBC	Jesse Jones Interests	58
	STNB	Baker Family	9
	UNB	Carter Family	34
1963	NBC	Jesse Jones Heirs	49
	TNB	Carter Family	11
1968	TNBC	American General Insurance Company	35
1973	TCBK	American General Insurance Company *	22

SOURCES: Stockholders' Files, TCB Archives; *Directors' Minutes; Stockholders' Minutes,* TCB Archives.
* Percentage of Common and Class B Common Stock.

While the professionalization of management at Texas Commerce proceeded gradually over decades, Table 11.1 shows that the dispersal of the bank's stock after the early 1950s was more abrupt. Mergers were important in reducing the concentration of ownership. The merger of Union and South Texas National in 1953 brought together two banks with large blocks of stock held by several dominant owners, in the process reducing the control of the major owners of both organizations in the newly created Texas National Bank. Similarly, the 1964 merger between TNB and National Bank of Commerce diminished the strength of the most important stockholders of each in the Texas National Bank of Commerce. This merger was particularly significant in its impact on the substantial block of NBC stock originally accumulated by Jesse Jones and subsequently held by the Houston Endowment. The 1964 merger reduced this Jones block from a majority interest in NBC to a controlling interest in TNBC. This controlling interest was subsequently dispersed in 1968, when the Houston Endowment sold its holdings in the bank. Another impetus for the broader dispersal of ownership was the bank holding company movement in Texas. After 1971, Texas Commerce acquired member banks throughout the state through exchanges of stock, thereby dispersing ownership of the organization far beyond Houston. Finally, the listing of Texas Commerce Bancshares on the New York Stock Exchange in 1974 assured that it would be traded more widely throughout the nation.

The largest block of stock in Texas Commerce throughout these

years was that amassed by Jesse Jones before his death in 1956, and the
Houston Endowment faced difficult choices in managing Jones's former holdings in the bank. Initially, those in charge of Houston Endowment were not eager to dispose of their holdings in "Jesse Jones's
bank"; after all, these were Jones loyalists who shared their late men-
tor's pride in the standing of the National Bank of Commerce. Yet as a
charitable foundation, the endowment faced a variety of pressures to
get out of the banking business. Growing political concern regarding
the possibility of abuses of power by foundations which controlled
major economic institutions focused on just such issues as the control
of a major bank by a charitable foundation. In addition, public concern over the operations of foundations yielded new regulations that
required them to pay out a minimum percentage of their endowment
annually. If investments such as bank stocks did not yield this targeted
percentage, then foundations would face the distasteful necessity of
reaching into their endowment to make up the difference. By the mid-
1960s, Houston Endowment found its bank stock a source of considerable controversy and began looking around for possible buyers.[8]

The prominent role played by Houston Endowment's block of
stock in the proxy battle which climaxed the bloody merger of 1964
further strengthened the foundation's incentive to get out of the banking business. The endowment's stock had been the unshakable foundation of Robert Doherty's continued control of the National Bank
of Commerce. As negotiations for the 1964 merger proceeded, leaders
of the smaller Texas National Bank were understandably concerned
about the possibility that the endowment's substantial holdings would
be used to ensure the dominance of NBC in the merged concern. The
crucial role ultimately played by representatives of the Houston Endowment in the proxy contest of January, 1965, justified their earlier
concern while again pointing up the potential significance of this block
of stock in future disputes which might arise regarding management
practices at the bank. For its part, the Houston Endowment did not
relish the publicity generated by such episodes, which fed an already
mounting political movement to place restrictions on the involvement
of foundations in the affairs of operating industries. The most obvious strategy for reducing political uncertainties was for the endowment to sell its holdings in businesses such as Texas National Bank of
Commerce.[9]

A logical candidate to purchase Houston Endowment's stock in
the bank emerged in 1965. John Mecom, an independent oilman who
had been a director of the bank since 1954, originally approached the
endowment in 1965 about the possible purchase of a piece of land he

needed to expand a hotel owned by Mecom. In response, representatives of the endowment suggested that Mecom might be interested in buying more substantial parts of Jesse Jones's former empire. Negotiations produced a spectacular deal in which Mecom agreed to purchase for a reported sum of $85 million a package of properties including the *Houston Chronicle*, the largest daily newspaper in Houston; the Rice Hotel, a large downtown hotel; assorted properties associated with the hotel; and the endowment's stock in the Texas National Bank of Commerce. With the preliminary announcement of the proposed deal, Mecom seemed poised to become a Jesse Jones-like figure on the Houston scene, with varied business holdings and broad involvement in the civic life of the city.

The implications of such a deal for the bank were far-reaching. In 1966, Mecom replaced Robert Doherty as chairman of the board of the bank in anticipation that he would acquire a controlling interest of its stock upon the completion of the larger transaction with the Houston Endowment. Yet even his friends and long-term associates within the bank were somewhat skeptical that oilman Mecom would come to exert the sort of guiding influence over the bank long exercised by Jesse Jones. The two men differed markedly. Mecom lacked Jones's experience as a banker. An independent oil producer who was a plunger by nature, Mecom lacked the mind-set of the strategic planner, the role that Jones had played so successfully during his years at the bank. But

---

The Brief Reign of Chairman Mecom

John W. Mecom
1911–1981

When Houston Endowment sought to sell off properties from the business empire of its founder, Jesse Jones, John Mecom seemed a logical purchaser. By 1966 the fifty-four-year-old Mecom had parlayed a fortune originally made as an independent oilman into diversified business holdings whose value was variously estimated at between $200 million and $500 million. In addition to extensive oil-producing properties on the Gulf Coast and the Middle East, Mecom held a controlling interest in other ventures as varied as the Warwick Hotel, which he refurbished and transformed into one of Houston's finest hotels, and Reed Roller Bit, a growing oil-tool company based in Houston. Even before his attempt to purchase the package of Jones's properties held by the Houston Endowment, Mecom was a highly visible figure in Houston. On occasion business writers referred to him as "the world's largest independent oilman," a claim not easily verified in a sector of the economy in which most holdings, like Mecom's, remained privately held. Thus when Mecom and J. Howard Creekmore, the president of Houston Endowment, began negotiating Mecom's acquisition of various properties previously owned by Jesse Jones, there was no reason to doubt Mecom's capacity to raise the purchase price. The package deal ultimately agreed upon included Mecom's purchase of the *Houston Chronicle,* the largest newspaper in Texas; the Rice Hotel, long one of the major downtown Houston hotels; and a controlling interest in Texas National Bank of Commerce, for a total price of approximately $85 million. In December, 1965, Mecom gave Creekmore a $1 million check for earnest money and promised to complete payment in six months.

Everyone involved initially seemed quite happy with the proposed transaction. Creekmore cited the "long and pleasant association between the Jones and Mecom families" in announcing the sale. He recalled that more than fifty years earlier Jesse Jones had lent money to Mecom's father, John, a rancher and rice planter with mules as security for the loan. He concluded, "We feel that the sale of these properties to John Mecom is good for Houston and for Texas." For his part, Mecom seemed genuinely excited by the prospect of taking an even larger role in the economic and civic life of Houston, and he quickly showed that he was interested in being more than an absentee owner of his new properties.

Immediately after the announcement of the purchase agreement, Mecom's name appeared on the *Chronicle*'s masthead as the newspaper's new publisher. In January, 1966, Mecom was elected chief executive officer and chairman of Texas National Bank of Commerce, replacing the seriously ill Robert Doherty. In addition, he named his long-time friend in the bank's energy lending department, E. O. Buck, to the board and promoted him to the newly created post of vice-chairman of the board. Mecom then oversaw the operations of the newspaper and bank for the next five months.

Although the inside details of what happened next remain subject to much conjecture, the outcome does not. Because most of his vast fortune was tied up in long-term investments which he was unwilling or unable to alter, Mecom could not raise the cash needed to complete the purchase by the agreed-upon date. As the deadline neared in June, 1966, Mecom visited Creekmore's offices to ask for the Houston Endowment's assistance in obtaining long-term financing for the deal. One can only imagine the scene which followed. Creekmore's office in Jones's old Bankers Mortgage Building had been preserved as it had appeared when Jones held sway there in the 1920s and 1930s, complete with a green hue from old-fashioned window shades. Mecom's journey to negotiate with Jones's loyal lieutenant proved futile. There was to be little negotiation. Creekmore held to the original agreement, refusing to help Mecom arrange the financing. A dispute quickly arose. Mecom walked out. His one-million-dollar check became a contribution to the charitable funds of the endowment. The next day, J. Howard Creekmore's name replaced that of Mecom as publisher of the *Chronicle,* a change explained only by a terse statement that "you can say that the Houston Endowment always has owned the *Chronicle,* and still does." On June 22, 1966, TCB released the announcement of Mecom's resignation as chairman and chief executive officer, with Ben Taub becoming chairman and John Whitmore moving up to become chief executive officer. The brief reign of Chairman Mecom had come to an abrupt end.

SOURCES: "A Deal Done In," *Time* (June 17, 1966): 62; "John Mecom Heads Texas Commerce," *Houston Chronicle* (January 18, 1966): 1, 10; "John Mecom, Oilman, Buys Largest Block of Stock in Texas/Commerce," *Bank News* (January 15, 1966); Stanley Brown, "The Big Deal That Got Away," *Fortune* (October 1968): 164–66, 180–92.

---

even if Mecom had been a replica of Jesse Jones, he would have encountered difficulties as the head of Texas Commerce Bank in the late 1960s. Mecom's situation at the bank was complicated by the fact that he could not be an owner-manager in the mold of Jones; instead, he faced the more difficult situation of attempting to exert leadership while building coalitions to ensure that his large minority stockholdings would constitute working control. In addition, the banking industry was rapidly becoming more complex and more competitive. In the emerging new era of banking, the personal touch which traditionally had been sufficient to build a successful bank would have to be augmented by the application of modern management techniques adapted from other industries and from professional management schools. The days of Jesse Jones—or of John Mecom—had passed in banking.[10]

After the collapse of its deal with Mecom, the Houston Endowment still desired to sell its bank stock, but the pool of potential buyers was somewhat restricted. In the spring of 1968, persistent rumors in the Houston business community suggested that the Houston Endowment was considering the sale of its TCB holdings to a group of out-of-state investors. One Texan who took strong objection to the prospect of the control of this major Houston bank by out-of-state investors was Gus Wortham, a long-term friend and business partner of Jesse Jones.

Wortham had founded American General Insurance Company in 1926 with funds supplied in part by Jones before becoming a director of National Bank of Commerce the following year. In a long association with the bank in which he ultimately progressed from the youngest to oldest member of the bank's board, Wortham took an active interest in the evolution of the bank. Indeed, American General invested in NBC from the early history of both organizations into the 1960s, at which time American General held approximately 5 percent of the stock of TNBC. Wortham and American General also had traditionally been among the bank's largest accounts. Thus Wortham's decision to attempt to buy the Houston Endowment's interest in 1968 was a natural outgrowth of his long-term involvement with the bank.[11]

All in the Family

The close business ties between American General and Texas Commerce Bank and the strong personal ties between individuals active in each company made a family affair of American General's purchase of Jesse Jones's old block of stock in the bank from the Houston Endowment. Gus Wortham summed up the historical ties between these organizations in a speech to TCB's employees after the purchase: "I'm an early depositor—and the oldest borrower this bank has. Had it not been for Jesse Jones, there would be no American General." Given these strong bonds, once negotiations began in earnest in the spring of 1968, it was not surprising that the transfer of ownership went smoothly.

Benjamin Woodson, the second-in-command at American General, took part in arranging and carrying out the purchase, and his account suggests the comfortable tone of the transaction. Once the top management of American General decided to make a serious overture for the stock, they quickly reached a tentative agreement with J. Howard Creekmore, the head of the Houston Endowment. On March 19, 1968, Woodson and E. R. Barrow, of American General—who was an old friend of Creekmore—went to Creekmore's office to sign a contract for the purchase of more than 800,000 shares of TCB's stock, which represented most of Houston Endowment's outstanding holdings in the bank, for a total price of approximately $44.5 million, or $55 per share. In a scene reminiscent of that played out by John Mecom two years before, the representatives of American General signed a contract expressing an intent to purchase by May 17, 1968 and tendered a check for $1 million in earnest money. The news of the intended purchase was then publicized in a joint news bulletin.

All similarities to the Mecom episode ended, however, when Wood-

Benjamin Woodson,
J. Howard Creekmore, and
E.R. Barrow

son and Barrow returned to Creekmore's office in May to complete the purchase. On the way, Woodson stopped by to secure from his banker—John Whitmore, then president of TCB—a cashier's check for the remainder of the purchase price. He then walked out of the bank, went several steps down the sidewalk to the entrance of the Bankers Mortgage Building, and carried the check into Creekmore's office. There the two men from American General found Creekmore and Everett Collier, the business editor of the *Houston Chronicle*. Creekmore called over to TCB and asked for the delivery of the Houston Endowment's stock certificates from its safe-deposit box in the bank's vault. When the certificates arrived, Creekmore stacked them in front of him and read the vital information off each as Woodson made a list of the registration number and the number of shares represented by each certificate. After each certificate had been checked by both parties, it was transferred from Creekmore's diminishing stack to a growing stack of certificates in front of Woodson. Upon completion of the list, Woodson added up the total number of shares by hand, multiplied this number—807,375—by the agreed-upon price per share—$55—made several calculations to include other considerations such as the earnest money, and came up with a figure of $43,558,252.05. He then produced the cashier's check for that amount. The men shook hands all around as a photographer from American General recorded the exchange of the check and the stock certificates for the scrapbooks of the two parties. Woodson recalls that "there was wonderfully good feeling all around" as Creekmore displayed a copy of the front-page story on the transaction which was to run in the evening edition of the *Chronicle*. The men from American General then took their newly acquired stock certificates next door to their long-term stock registry agent, Texas Commerce Bank. Once the stock had been reissued in American General's name, it was then taken to the bank's vault and placed in that company's safe-deposit box, which was just across from the Houston Endowment's box, where working control of Texas Commerce previously had rested. The deal was done.

SOURCE: Interview with Benjamin Woodson by Joseph A. Pratt, June 18, 1985.

The announcement of American General's intent to purchase Texas National Bank of Commerce on March 20, 1968, was greeted with enthusiasm within the bank's family, since it put to rest some of the uncertainty about the changes which might have accompanied transfer of working control into the hands of outsiders.[12] Wortham and Ben Woodson, his designated successor at American General, quickly held a series of meetings with all levels of the bank's management to drive home a simple message: American General would take an active interest in the bank, but it would not institute far-reaching changes in strategy or management. It would treat the bank as a major investment, not as a potential subsidiary. Unlike John Mecom before him, Wortham expressed no interest in assuming the powers of the chairmanship. Indeed, Wortham went to great lengths to assert his complete confidence in the bank's current management, which had been headed by John Whitmore since the proxy battle of January 1965: "I've known John Whitmore since he's been with the bank. He was in real estate, then. It's been interesting to watch this man grow. I've found that when people of ability are elevated to positions of great responsibility, you can see them grow."[13] While thus asserting his full support of Whitmore, Wortham left open the possibility that he or Ben Woodson might someday head the bank after Whitmore's retirement. A new era of stable ownership and leadership seemed at hand.

Yet just when the question of the control of the bank's largest block of stock appeared to be resolved, changes in the law governing bank holding companies suddenly reopened it. The Bank Holding Company Act of 1956 allowed "one-bank holding companies," an arrangement which made it possible for a company such as American General to own a single bank along with its other nonbanking businesses. Under this law, a bank owned by a one bank holding company was subject to supervision by the existing array of bank regulatory agencies, but the holding company itself was not. Amid a wave of one bank holding company growth in the late 1960s, however, Congress began to reevaluate the 1956 law. In December, 1970, the Bank Holding Company Act was amended to bring one-bank holding companies under stricter government controls. Under the amended law, any company owning 25 percent or more of the voting stock of a bank was subject to the same regulations as a bank. American General's ownership of approximately 35 percent of Texas Commerce Bank suddenly posed a problem.[14]

Given the obvious fact that banking was not the primary business of the insurance company, American General looked for a way to sell its TCB stock without unduly disrupting either the market for shares in Texas Commerce or its own financial planning. The Federal Reserve Board proved hard to please, but after extended haggling, a plan for divestiture was finally approved in 1972. The Federal Reserve went to great lengths to eliminate all channels of influence which American General might exert over Texas Commerce before certifying that American General was no longer a bank holding company under the 1970 amendments. Under this agreement, American General agreed to convert its stock in Texas Commerce to a special Class B nonvoting common stock and to divest itself of its holding by 1980. The Federal Reserve also demanded that no "director, officer, or policymaking employee of Company [American General] serves or will serve in a similar capacity with TCB or any of its subsidiaries." Other stipulations of the agreement included assurances by American General that no combination of its officers or directors owning more than 25 percent of the company also owned or controlled "directly or indirectly" 25 percent or more of the voting shares of TCB or any of its subsidiaries. To cover any other possible means of control, the Federal Reserve included the final stipulation that American General would "not control in any manner the election of a majority of the directors, or exercise a controlling influence over the management or policies of TCB or any bank or company that controls a bank." During the 1970s, American General fulfilled the terms of this agreement by avoiding any semblance of involvement in the management of TCB while steadily divesting itself of its stock in the bank by issuing shares as stock dividends to its own shareholders and by selling of debentures that could be exchanged for Texas Commerce Bancshares stock.[15]

The dispersal of American General's large block of Texas Commerce stock into the hands of numerous smaller investors marked another significant step in the ongoing transition from control of the bank by owner-managers to control by professional managers. By

1972 a bank whose stock had been concentrated in a few hands as recently as 1964 suddenly had no minority interest clearly capable of controlling its management. The way was clear for the emergence within the bank of the sort of managerial control which had developed in most American manufacturing industries earlier in the twentieth century.

The choice of the manager to guide the bank in this new era remained open in the late 1960s. John Whitmore had successfully guided the bank through a series of dangerous straits in the difficult years following the bloody merger. Under his leadership Texas Commerce had shaken off the ill-effects of the events of 1964 and 1965 and embarked on an impressive period of growth which vaulted it past the one-billion-dollar mark in deposits in 1970. Whitmore had also forcefully addressed the problem of management succession by enforcing mandatory retirement at sixty-five and by advancing within the bank and recruiting from outside several excellent prospects to succeed him.

The influx of young managers from the training program of Texas National Bank never quite materialized, since many of these managers left the merged bank during the bitter conflicts which followed the 1964 merger. Several men who had joined National Bank of Commerce before the merger emerged as potential top managers in the 1960s. Robert Gerrard, who ultimately left Texas Commerce to become the chief executive officer of Continental Bank in Fort Worth, played a prominent role in Texas Commerce's management in the years after the merger. Also important was John Cater, who came to work in the credit training program at NBC in 1959 and subsequently played the leading role in managing the installation of a new generation of data processing equipment. Cater served as president of Texas Commerce from 1972 to 1976, when he resigned and moved to Bank of the Southwest. When that Houston-based bank holding company merged with Mercantile National Bank of Dallas to form MCorp in 1984, Cater became the president of the new holding company.

Emerging from this group of managers was Benton F. Love, who joined the bank in 1967. Having spent much of his business life in industry before becoming a banker at the age of forty-three, Love came to Texas Commerce with attitudes and ideas about management which differed from those of traditional bankers. At Texas Commerce, Love found an organization still recovering from the bloody merger in an industry poised on the brink of far-reaching changes. His training and temperament matched the needs of the bank, and he quickly moved up to become president in 1969 and chairman in 1972.

Ben Love and the Coming of Industrial Management

Ben F. Love

Born in 1924, Benton F. Love grew up in Paris, Texas. After flying twenty-five bombing missions over Europe as a captain in the Eighth Air Force during World War II, he graduated from the University of Texas in 1948. Love entered business as the cofounder of Gift-Rap, Inc., a company which manufactured and distributed specialized wrapping papers nationally. In building this business, he learned quickly the value of careful budgeting, the need for effective internal control systems, and the necessity of a systematic call program to expand markets. After thirteen years, he merged the company with Gibson Card Company. CIT Financial Corporation acquired Gibson one year later. In that highly organized large corporate structure, Max Weaver, president of Gibson Card, impressed upon Love the importance of the use of quantifiable measures of performance in establishing planning goals and in evaluating managers in a decentralized management system. These lessons from industry were not forgotten by Love when he became in 1965 the chief executive of River Oaks Bank and Trust, a suburban Houston bank on whose board he had served for much of his business career. There he applied to the banking industry the management philosophy he had developed in industry, and the results were immediate and impressive. As his bank's deposits and profits grew, the larger downtown Houston banks took notice, and Love moved on to Texas Commerce Bank in 1967 as senior vice-president of the metropolitan division, which included most of the bank's commercial accounts in the Houston area other than energy and real estate loans.

Having successfully tested his ideas about bank management at the laboratory provided by River Oaks Bank and Trust, Love now faced the challenge of adapting them to fit the needs of a much larger downtown bank. His primary goals remained the same: (1) asset profitability, (2) asset growth, and (3) asset quality. These were essentially the same goals which had guided traditional bank management, but in a new order of priority. Profitability moved from near the bottom of the old list of goals to the top of the new list, and the ramifications for the management of the bank were far-reaching. In pursuit of greater profitability, Love hastened an ongoing transformation from traditional to modern management at the bank. The highly personal and centralized approach characteristic of the bank in the Jesse Jones-Robert Doherty years gave way to a market-oriented system of decentralized management with strong reliance on statistical measures of financial performance to coordinate the bank's management. Love adapted concepts of accountability and marketing initially developed in industry and in business schools. This modern managerial approach proved suited to the times, much as the traditional personal approach had matched the needs of an earlier, less competitive era in banking.

SOURCES: Interviews with Ben Love by Joseph A. Pratt, June 10, 1983, June 25, 1983, July 30, 1983; Interviews with John E. Whitmore by Walter L. Buenger and Joseph A. Pratt, August 17, 1982, September 17, 1982, June 15, 1983, December 16, 1985; TCB Archives.

Love's approach to bank management reflected a growing concern among bank managers for profitability. Underlying that concern were basic changes in stock ownership. The old owner—Jesse Jones—had put little pressure on his managers to show greater profits. The new owners—the thousands of shareholders and potential investors—paid considerable attention to various measures of financial performance, especially after Texas Commerce Bancshares was listed on the New York Stock Exchange in 1974. The opinions and recommendations of financial analysts became a matter of intense concern to bank managers in this era of dispersed stock ownership. Return on assets, return on equity, and the price-earnings ratio replaced a pat on the back by Jesse Jones as the measure of performance of managers at Texas Commerce.

While communicating the status of Texas Commerce to investors in the universal language of financial markets, such statistics also served as the starting point for planning under Love. In summarizing his ideas on management, Love concluded that "to organize human resources in the pursuit of statistical objectives is uppermost in my philosophy of management." [16] Short-term and long-term operational objectives were defined after analysis of historical performance and current market conditions. These goals then were publicly announced, primarily in terms of targets of quarterly and yearly profitability. Once announced, broad organizational goals could be broken down into statistical goals for the various aspects of the bank's operations. The publication each month of a detailed analysis of the bank's financial performance encouraged the comparison of the results produced in all divisions of the organization. Called "Blue Books" because of the color of their binding, these monthly reports featured detailed comparisons of actual performance with budgeted goals, a comparison which forced those responsible for every specific aspect of the bank's operations to evaluate regularly their success in fulfilling planned objectives. Such statistical measures of performance had not been an important part of the traditional management system of the predecessor banks of Texas Commerce, but in the new system called forth by the increasing size and complexity of banking, these numbers played the critical role of tying together an expanding organization with common goals defined in a common language.

The transition from traditional to industrial management at Texas Commerce required the development of a more formal organizational chart with more clearly delineated lines of authority and responsibility. Only then could accurate statistics be produced for the use of top management. Also required was a more formal budget to allocate resources based on responsibilities. The ongoing efforts to make these statistical measures more accurate helped pinpoint previously unrecognized opportunities for profits. That these performance goals could be applied to appropriate positions throughout the organization made them a tool for the comparison and evaluation of managers. Finally, the public announcement of the goals and the great importance they were accorded by top management meant that they became a driving force pushing individuals and the organization as a whole toward maximum effort in increasing profitability.

Nowhere was the difference in the traditional and the modern bank more evident than in the approach to calls on customers and potential customers. Under traditional management, officers serviced their existing accounts and pursued leads on new accounts from a variety of sources, but there was little coordination of the efforts of the individual officers and no system for evaluating the overall effectiveness of the calling program. Love's approach to calling on customers reflected his earlier experience in founding and expanding a new manufacturing company. An effective understanding of the market, he felt, required systematic canvassing. Beginning with his first job at Texas Commerce in the metropolitan division, Love transformed the existing calling program by breaking down the potential customers into standard industrial classifications and assigning accounts in related industries to the same officer, who could then build a specialized knowledge of a segment of the market. He also emphasized the importance of systematic calling by budgeting the number of calls expected of individual officers and by requiring formal call reports to summarize the nature of calls made and the business conducted at each stop. The increasingly competitive banking market of the 1960s and 1970s required a highly organized approach to business development. Love summarized the results as follows: "We stir up enough lending opportunities in the marketplace so that we don't have to grab at every opportunity we uncover. If we see a potential problem with a prospect, we will let some other bank make that loan." [17]

Nonetheless, as the bank became more aggressive in the marketplace, it faced greater risks. Traditionally, the predecessors of Texas Commerce had maintained asset quality by dealing primarily with proved businesses and individuals and by relying heavily on the personal knowledge of its top managers in evaluating risk. Love sought to build on this tradition while adapting to changing conditions in the banking industry. One high priority was to retain the blue-chip accounts traditionally served by Texas Commerce while expanding its presence in the more diverse middle market of smaller companies. Another was to bring to bear the most advanced tools of financial analysis to augment the personal knowledge of bank officers in evaluating potential creditors. The final adjustment was the most difficult. In the traditional world of Houston banking before the 1960s, the ultimate assurance of asset quality was careful evaluation of each major loan by a small loan and discount committee made up of top bank officers. Amid the faster pace of modern banking, Texas Commerce constructed a quality-control system of checks and balances and internal audits designed to maintain traditional standards of loan quality while making many more loans in an increasingly competitive environment. The growing scale and complexity of TCB's business required the creation of a bureaucratic system of controls not needed in previous eras. This included the decentralization of both authority and responsibility for evaluating loans with the final decision being assigned to a committee system in which an executive committee of senior officers ultimately approved all large loans. In combination with expanded calling to generate business opportunities, this quality-control system produced an excellent record of loan quality amid rapid growth in lending (see Table 11.2).[18]

Crucial to the bank's performance in the marketplace was the increasingly aggressive approach of its specialized lending groups. The five basic groups—metropolitan, oil, real estate, national, and international—had developed steadily since World War II in response to the evolution of specialized needs of particular sectors of a diversifying economy. Love's transformation of the metropolitan division pointed the way to similar changes in the other lending groups. Staffed by numerous specialized officers making regular calls throughout the re-

Table 11.2 Loan Growth and Quality at Texas Commerce Bancshares, 1971–85

Year	Total Loans at Year End (in millions)	Loan Losses as Percent of Loans [a]	Loan Loss Reserve as Percent of Loans [b]
1971	$ 659	0.07%	1.87%
1972	833	.10	1.98
1973	1,384	.15	1.65
1974	1,649	.24	1.80
1975	2,111	.31	0.97
1976	2,385	.42	.96
1977	3,103	.27	.96
1978	4,130	.12	.98
1979	4,940	.15	1.04
1980	5,730	.23	1.12
1981	7,773	.13	1.16
1982	9,760	.33	1.18
1983	11,664	.38	1.11
1984	13,412	.44	1.13
1985	13,368	1.39	2.10

SOURCE: Annual Reports of Texas Commerce Bancshares.

[a] Loan losses each year as a percentage of the average loans outstanding during the year.

[b] Reserve set aside for possible loan losses as a percentage of the average loans outstanding for each year.

gional economy, the lending groups gave Texas Commerce a systematic presence throughout the major sectors of its banking markets.

These groups quite naturally became the center of the bank's planning. The overall goals determined by top management could be quantified and reduced to goals for each lending group. The performance of each could then be evaluated at two levels: relative to the other groups and relative to the historical performance of the department in question. Weekly reports on the performance of each department became a Friday morning ritual which kept officers from all specialized areas informed of the overall performance of their organization. Resources and personnel for the bank as a whole could then be focused on those areas with demonstrated needs. Officers could be evaluated in the context of the progress of their departments. The organization of the company's lending activities into specialized groups thus served the management

functions long served by decentralized management structures in industries other than banking. In the early 1960s, the organization chart
of National Bank of Commerce could be described as a circle with
Robert Doherty in the middle and everyone reporting directly to him.
A decade later, this traditional banking version of centralized management had been replaced by a decentralized management structure in
which a strong chief executive sat atop a pyramid constructed of specialized lending groups with considerable autonomy.[19]

To increase profitability and size while simultaneously maintaining strict loan quality standards required capable officers, and Texas
Commerce's hiring and promotion practices under Ben Love reflected
this need. Whereas Jesse Jones's bank had been staffed largely with
loyal men who had impressed Jones in some other endeavor, the far
more numerous management positions in the modern bank were filled
with young men and women who had graduated near the tops of their
classes from an increasingly widespread array of the nation's most respected business schools. Top management at Texas Commerce believed that those who had demonstrated academic excellence as recorded in quantitative measures such as grade-point averages were
most likely to respond well to the pressures to produce in an organization which emphasized statistically measured performance. Reinforc-
ing the message that Texas Commerce expected its officers to compete
aggressively was the announced policy of paying above the market rate
for quality managers willing and able to accept greater responsibilities
than those of their counterparts in competing banks. Those who accepted jobs at TCB chose to enter an intensely performance-oriented
system quite different from the world of traditional banking.

From the late 1960s through the early 1980s, this system produced excellent results amid a rapidly growing economy. In these
years Texas Commerce regularly ranked as one of the most profitable
and fastest-growing banking organizations in the nation, with similar rankings in asset quality. In the decade from 1973 to 1983, for
example, Texas Commerce Bancshares, the bank holding company
created in 1971 to contain Texas Commerce–Houston and member
banks throughout the state, posted financial results which brought
considerable note in the financial community. In that period it posted
an annual compound growth rate in earnings per share of approximately 17 percent; a more than 20 percent compound annual growth
rate in assets; a 1 percent average return on assets; an 18 percent
average return on equity; and a 0.24 percent ratio of loan losses to
loans. These results ranked as either first or second among the nation's
twenty-five largest banks in this decade. The regional and national
prestige which accompanied frequent favorable newspaper and maga-

zine articles about the performance of Texas Commerce fostered a sense of pride and accomplishment among its employees.[20] Replacing the organizational bond traditionally supplied by the personal commitment of employees to Jesse Jones and his bank was a bond created by a shared sense of accomplishment in a much larger organization. A record of shared success combined with salaries higher than the industry's norms provided the glue which bound together the rapidly growing organization.

This sustained growth was at once the cause and the result of the coming of industrial management to Texas Commerce in the years after the 1964 merger. The steady expansion of the predecessors of Texas Commerce before that time had already challenged the continued viability of traditional management practices and attitudes developed to run a relatively small institution which could be managed effectively through the close attention of several high officers. Loosening regulatory constraints increased competitive pressures in banking, further undermining the inherited traditions of bank management. Finally, the rapid dispersal of the bank's stock after 1964 encouraged a shift from control by a few owners to control by professional managers in the interest of an increasing diverse collection of stockholders. Commercial banks in Texas and throughout the nation were entering a new era in which profitability and the interests of shareholders replaced stability and the security of deposits as the overriding concerns of bank managers.

CHAPTER 12

From Bank to Bancshares, 1971–85

The holding-company movement in Texas presented demanding challenges to the management of Texas Commerce in the 1970s and 1980s. Indeed, the transition from Texas Commerce Bank—a unit bank doing business from a single location in downtown Houston—to Texas Commerce Bancshares—a holding company with seventy member banks throughout the state (see Table 12.1)—absorbed much of the attention of the bank's top management in the years after 1971. In this period, the evaluation of potential acquisitions, the negotiations of agreements of consolidation, and the integration of member banks into an effective management system were the top priorities of those in charge of Texas Commerce. At the same time, they sought to retain the standards of loan quality and profitability traditionally set by Texas Commerce–Houston. The geographical expansion made possible by the new holding-company structure produced a much larger organization with a physical presence in the major banking markets of Texas, allowing Texas Commerce to compete more effectively with other Texas banks and with larger financial institutions based outside the state.

A variety of regulatory changes in the late 1960s and early 1970s made possible the bank holding company movement in Texas. Multibank holding companies had perhaps been legal in Texas since the Bank Holding Company Act of 1956, which established rules governing bank holding-company activities and required them to register with the Federal Reserve.[1] But bankers in Texas proved unwilling to test these new rules. Their conservatism was not surprising given their cautious approach to the banking business and their understandable reluctance to challenge the strong political sentiment against branch banking in Texas. Not until fundamental questions about bank structure throughout the nation were raised in the 1960s did bankers in

Texas follow the lead of bankers in numerous other traditional unit banking states in exploring the possibility that bank holding companies might provide a legal alternative to branching.

A crucial impetus to the spread of bank holding companies was the passage in 1970 of significant amendments to the Bank Holding Company Act of 1956. In the late 1960s, banks throughout the nation had begun to take advantage of a section in the 1956 act which allowed one-bank holding companies to own a single bank plus a variety of other enterprises without being subject to registration and regulation as a bank holding company. Congress closed this loophole in 1970 by ending the exemption of one-bank holding companies while taking steps to allow bank holding companies more freedom to conduct bank-related activities. The signing of these amendments by President Richard M. Nixon in December, 1970, set off a wave of adjustments among banks throughout the nation the following year, as each bank moved to assure that its traditional operations and structure were legal under the new law.[2]

The 1970 amendments presented Texas Commerce with immediate problems as well as long-term opportunities. Under the new law, American General Insurance faced the choice of giving up its controlling interest in Texas Commerce or submitting to regulation by the Federal Reserve as a banking holding company. As previously discussed, American General arranged to sell its holdings gradually, preparing the way for the organization of Texas Commerce Bancshares as a multibank holding company. Under the leadership of Chairman of the Board John Whitmore, Texas Commerce then moved quickly, forming Texas Commerce Bancshares and bringing Texas Commerce Bank–Houston into this new holding company in July, 1971. Along with the Houston bank came Texas Commerce Shareholders Company and its minority interests in six suburban banks. Because it moved quickly in the wake of the legal changes in the status of bank holding companies after 1970, Texas Commerce placed itself in an excellent position to take advantage of the proliferation of mergers in 1971 and 1972 which heralded the beginning of the bank holding company movement in Texas.[3]

An obvious early move for Texas Commerce Bancshares was the strengthening of existing links with its suburban chain banks. In September and October, 1971, merger agreements were announced with Airline, Reagan State, North Freeway Bank, and MacGregor Park National (which had strong ties to Airline). Like most of Texas Commerce's subsequent acquisitions, these mergers involved the exchange of common stock. Full ownership of these former affiliates meant closer coordination of policies between them and Texas Commerce. It

Table 12.1 Member Banks of Texas Commerce Bancshares, with Assets and Dates of Acquisition

Date	Name at Merger	Present Name	Assets (12/31/85)
1971	Texas Commerce Bank, N.A.	TCB-Houston	$11,969,956
1972	North Freeway State Bank	TCB-North Freeway	69,828
1972	American National Bank of Beaumont	TCB-Beaumont	305,808
1972	Reagan State Bank	TCB-Reagan	314,374
1972	Airline Bank	TCB-Airline	125,792
1973	Citizens National Bank	TCB-Lubbock	156,585
1973	American Bank of Commerce of Odessa	TCB-Odessa	163,509
1973	San Angelo National Bank	TCB-San Angelo	250,318
1973	Lakeside Commerce Bank*	TCB-Lakeside	104,241
1973	Plaza del Oro Commerce Bank*	TCB-Del Oro	70,936
1973	Inwood Commerce Bank*	TCB-Inwood	46,457
1973	Irving Bank & Trust	TCB-Las Colinas	227,296
1974	Kingwood Commerce Bank*	TCB-Kingwood	74,063
1974	Westwood Commerce Bank*	TCB-Westwood	57,047
1974	Texas Commerce Medical Bank*	Texas Commerce Medical Bank	187,537
1974	Plaza Commerce Bank*	TCB-Greenway Plaza	110,269
1974	Guaranty National Bank & Trust of Corpus Christi	TCB-Corpus Christi	182,787
1974	Southeast Bank	TCB-Southeast	81,775
1974	Union Bank of Fort Worth	TCB-Fort Worth	162,059
1974	First National Bank of Hurst	TCB-Hurst	164,002
1974	Arlington Bank & Trust	TCB-Arlington	369,973
1974	Highland Park State Bank	TCB-San Antonio	212,691

Year	Acquired Bank	Texas Commerce Bank	Amount
1975	Pan American Bank of Brownsville	TCB-Brownsville	412,992
1975	Northwest Bank of Dallas	TCB-Northwest	60,263
1975	Casa Linda National Bank of Dallas	TCB-Casa Linda	86,357
1975	Royal National Bank of Dallas	TCB-Preston Royal	55,350
1975	Fidelity National Bank of Dallas	TCB-Park Central	79,002
1975	Village National Bank Association of Dallas	TCB-Campbell Centre	98,524
1975	Commerce National Bank of Conroe*	TCB-Conroe	52,961
1976	First National Bank of New Braunfels	TCB-New Braunfels	105,133
1976	Longview National Bank	TCB-Longview	213,255
1977	Southern Bank & Trust	TCB-Garland	138,553
1977	BanCapital Financial Corp. (Capital National Bank)	TCB-Austin	1,402,067
1977	Tanglewood Commerce Bank*	TCB-Tanglewood	128,631
1977	Main Street National Bank	TCB-Dallas	478,795
1978	First National Bank of McAllen	TCB-McAllen	442,909
1979	Richmond Commerce Bank*	TCB-Richmond/Sage	45,722
1979	TCB-Katy Freeway*	TCB-Katy Freeway	41,807
1979	TCB-Southbelt*	TCB-South Belt	39,940
1980	TCB-CyFair*	TCB-CyFair	23,256
1981	Banc-Southwest Corporation, Amarillo	TCB-Amarillo	116,732
1981	Gulfway National Bank of Corpus Christi	TCB-Gulfway	58,980
1981	Friendswood Bank	TCB-Friendswood	57,028
1981	TCB-Quorum*	TCB-Quorum	37,221
1981	First National Bank of Stafford	TCB-Stafford	148,667
1981	Hillcrest State Bank, University Park	TCB-Hillcrest	103,184
1982	TCB-Barton Creek*	TCB-Barton Creek	28,013
1982	Stone Fort National Bank, Nacogdoches	Stone Fort National Bank	113,916

Table 12.1 *(continued)*

Date	Name at Merger	Present Name	Assets (12/31/85)
1982	TCB-Clear Lake *	TCB-Clear Lake	32,412
1982	TCB-Cypress Station *	TCB-Cypress Station	45,937
1982	El Paso National Corporation		
	Border City Bank	TCB-Border City	27,769
	East El Paso National Bank	TCB-East	41,664
	El Paso National Bank	TCB-El Paso	804,408
	El Paso National Bank-Chamizal	TCB-Chamizal	23,747
	First State Bank	TCB-First State	73,287
	Northgate National Bank	TCB-Northgate	50,497
	West El Paso National Bank	TCB-West	28,135
1982	Chemical Bank & Trust, Houston	TCB-Chemical	115,186
1983	TCB-Westlake Park *	TCB-Westlake Park	49,694
1983	TCB-Champions Park *	TCB-Champions Park	22,708
1983	TCB-Greens Crossing *	TCB-Greens Crossing	27,931
1983	TCB-West Oaks *	TCB-West Oaks	15,374
1983	Bank of Pasadena	TCB-Pasadena	25,890
1983	TCB-Sugar Land *	TCB-Sugar Land	22,348
1984	TCB-Northcross *	TCB-Northcross	30,921
1984	TCB-Midland *	TCB-Midland	57,275
1984	TCB-Irving Boulevard *	TCB-Irving Boulevard	68,036
1985	TCB-San Antonio Northwest *	TCB-San Antonio Northwest	15,387
1985	TCB-River Oaks *	TCB-River Oaks	28,375
1985	TCB-Brookhollow *	TCB-Brookhollow	3,998

SOURCE: Financial Accounting Files, TCB Archives.
* de novo charters

also meant that the legal lending limit of the holding company as a whole became the lending limit of each individual member bank. The regulatory approval process required considerable time and was unpredictable. The Reagan State and Airline merger agreements were announced in October, 1971; received the approval of the Federal Reserve in September, 1972; and were completed in October, 1972. The MacGregor Park merger was not approved.[4]

As the acquisition of these previously affiliated suburban Houston banks moved forward, Texas Commerce Bancshares also became involved in its first merger with a bank outside the Houston area. After extensive negotiations, Texas Commerce announced in July, 1971, a merger agreement with American National Bank of Beaumont. Because this merger was one of the first cases of a major bank holding company in Texas entering a banking market outside its traditional home city, the Federal Reserve's decision was of considerable interest to banks throughout the state. Indeed, this merger merits detailed study because it raised many issues encountered by Texas Commerce in subsequent acquisitions.

American National was the second-largest bank in Beaumont, the largest city in a heavily industrialized section of the Texas Gulf Coast, approximately 90 miles east of Houston in Jefferson County. In 1970 almost 250,000 people lived in this county, drawn primarily by employment opportunities in three of the largest petroleum refineries in the nation and numerous large petrochemical plants. Founded in 1901, the year the discovery of oil at Spindletop near Beaumont introduced a new era in oil production in the state and the nation, American National had subsequently grown with its region. The bank had prospered for decades by doing business with the local refineries of such major oil companies as Mobil Oil, Gulf Oil, and Sun Oil; oil-related manufacturers; rice growers and millers; Gulf States Utilities, which served a broad area of southwestern Louisiana and southeastern Texas from its headquarters in Beaumont, and local retailers. With assets of $125 million in 1971, American National was a substantial bank in an important second-tier banking market in Texas.[5]

American National also faced an uncertain future. In the late 1960s, several groups of investors outside Beaumont expressed interest in purchasing the bank. The management of American National discouraged these inquiries, but the possibility that outside investors would acquire the bank created an air of uncertainty which hampered the recruitment and retention of young officers. The bank's options were much the same as those facing banks of similar size in small cities throughout the state. It could attempt to create its own holding company and expand with its region. Affiliation with Beaumont State Bank in the city's suburbs was a step in this direction. But American National's managers doubted their bank's ability to prosper—or even to survive—in competition with the much larger Houston- and Dallas-based bank holding companies. Another choice available to them was to become a part of a bank holding company with members in other small-to-medium-sized cities. Indeed, a holding company based in the central Texas city of Waco offered American National an opportunity to join such an endeavor, but the bank's management declined, fearing that a small city holding company presented insufficient promise of future growth. A third option for the Beaumont bank was to seek the best available merger with one of the major bank holding companies. Finally, the bank's managers could choose to do nothing for the time being, wagering that their options and bargaining position would improve with the passage of time as the holding company movement increased in intensity.[6]

In deciding whether or not to join a holding company, a prime consideration of both the bank's managers and its stockholders was to obtain the best possible exchange value for their stock. Perhaps more than stockholders, top management took a long-run view when evaluating the best exchange. The bank's president, William Phillips, was convinced that affiliation with a major holding company could improve the long-term profitability of his bank by providing resources and specialized personnel beyond the means of a small city bank. He believed that early entry into a major holding company would supply his bank with a much-needed boost in its increasingly competitive regional banking market. Further, he believed that geographical and historical ties dictated association with a holding company based in Houston, not in Dallas. Texas Commerce seemed a logical choice, since its wholesale focus, intense professionalism, and expertise in energy, real estate, and international lending all matched the vision he had for American National.[7]

A primary incentive for the bank's major stockholders to support such a merger was their desire for a market in which to trade their stock. Traditionally, the stock of American National was tightly held by a relatively small group of owners, much as had been the case at National Bank of Commerce in the days of Jesse Jones. By the early 1970s, however, Texas Commerce shares were traded on the New York Stock Exchange, while those of smaller banks such as American National still changed hands primarily through a network of personal contacts including present and former directors and officers and large customers and friends of the bank. In such closed and often quite limited markets, large stockholders often experienced difficulties selling their stock. A merger with a publicly traded concern promised shareholders the oppportunity to liquidate their investments with the greatest profit and least inconvenience.

Phillips had approached Texas Commerce about the possibility of a merger even before the formal creation of Texas Commerce Bancshares. Officers of Texas Commerce quickly recognized that American National was an excellent merger prospect, if it could be purchased at a price compatible with its earnings. These officials had an informal contact at the Beaumont bank in the person of John Blaffer, whose family had strong ties with Texas Commerce through the old Texas National Bank. Blaffer had invested in American National stock in the 1960s and 1970s, and he helped bring the two banks together for exploratory discussions.[8]

Not surprisingly, price was the key issue. Tom McDade, the executive vice-president for investments at Texas Commerce, took a leading role in negotiations with American National over the proper exchange value of the stocks of each bank, a role he subsequently repeated in each major merger. McDade sought to determine an acquisition price which would avoid dilution of the value of the stock of Texas Commerce Bancshares while at the same time persuading American National to complete the transaction. This endeavor took McDade into detailed calculations of earnings per share of each bank and of estimates of the future earning power of the acquired bank as a member of the holding company.[9] It also forced him to come up with ways to "sell" his findings to officers of the potential merger partner, who almost inevitably sought to receive more for their bank than the figure projected by McDade. Several prominent American National stockholders opposed the merger with Texas Commerce on the grounds that the price offered was insufficient, but the bank's managers delivered a strong majority vote of the stockholders with compelling arguments that the long-term payoffs to investors who owned stock in a rapidly growing, Houston-based holding company exceeded those to be gained from owning stock in an independent Beaumont bank.

Stockholders' approval was not even half the battle, for the proposed merger was guaranteed to attract intense scrutiny by the Federal Reserve officials, eager to establish guidelines for acquisitions by big-city banks in smaller markets in Texas. In April, 1972, the Federal Reserve Board announced its decision to deny approval of the merger on the grounds that it would be anticompetitive. The board feared that the merger would decrease the likelihood of future banking competition in the Beaumont market. If Texas Commerce desired to enter Beaumont, the board suggested, it should do so by creating a de novo bank; that is, it should build a new bank. The decision gave Texas Commerce one other choice: it would be allowed to acquire Beaumont State Bank, the suburban affiliate of American National, but not the downtown bank itself. Taken as a whole, this decision put all Texas banks on notice that the Federal Reserve Board would not lightly dismiss competitive factors in rulings on mergers between major holding companies and large banks in second-tier markets.[10]

Just four months later, however, in August, 1972, the board reversed its decision by approving the acquisition of American National by Texas Commerce Bancshares. In justifying its reversal, the board cited new evidence which suggested that American National was unlikely to compete effectively with the largest bank in Beaumont. But more important in influencing the board was that potential competition had become quite real in Beaumont in the months since the denial of the original application. As the holding-company movement intensified throughout the state, three bank holding companies outside the Beaumont region had either reached agreements to merge with or applied for Federal Reserve approval to acquire the third-, fourth-, and fifth-largest banks in this market. In an interesting twist on its earlier decision, the board made permission for Texas Commerce to acquire American National contingent on the latter's divestiture of its stock in Beaumont State Bank, which subsequently was acquired by InterFirst Corporation of Dallas.[11]

The implications of these two contradictory decisions had to be absorbed quickly by officers of Texas Commerce Bancshares who were trying to anticipate the Federal Reserve's reactions to potential acquisitions under consideration in other parts of the state. This initial regulatory skirmish revealed that the doctrine of potential competition was a regulatory minefield still to be traversed. Until regulators had established a coherent set of guidelines laid down in a consistent body of decisions, Texas Commerce could not be certain which mergers would be approved. It had little recourse except to push forward with new acquisitions, uncertain when it might stray over the vaguely defined and shifting line which separated legal from illegal acquisitions.

The next step in the expansion of Texas Commerce Bancshares took the bank away from its traditional home base on the Texas Gulf Coast. In acquiring three West Texas banks—Citizens National Bank of Lubbock, American Bank of Commerce of Odessa, and San Angelo National Bank—Texas Commerce established a presence five hundred miles from Houston in an area which long had looked primarily to

Dallas for banking services. The negotiations leading to the purchase of these three banks revealed much about the competitive and regulatory climates facing the major bank holding companies as they sought to enter banking markets throughout a large, diverse state.

Binding these three banks was the ownership of a controlling interest in each by a group of West Texas businessmen active primarily in that region's oil and gas industries. W. D. (Bill) Noel, E. G. Rodman, and M. H. McWhirter had been partners in a variety of oil-related concerns before investing in banking. Their interests included producing wells in West Texas and New Mexico, drilling operations, gasoline plants which extracted gasoline and other products from natural gas, and oil-field supply companies. McWhirter was also an experienced banker. These men invested in West Texas banks as a natural outgrowth of their broad involvement in the region's economy. Beyond serving as directors, they did not become deeply involved in the daily operations of the banks.[12]

The three banks had distinct histories, and they served three quite different regional economies. The largest of the three was the Citizens National Bank of Lubbock, which had approximately $100 million in assets when it was absorbed by Texas Commerce early in 1973. Lubbock was one of the major metropolitan areas in West Texas, with a population approaching 180,000 in 1970 and strong ties to the region's cotton-based economy. Originally organized in 1906, Citizens National was the smallest of the city's four major banks. In 1961 the Noel-Rodman group acquired a controlling interest in this bank. The group previously had acquired control of the San Angelo National Bank, which traced its origins back to 1884. The economy of San Angelo, about 200 miles southeast of Lubbock, shared with its larger neighbor strong ties to agriculture. In the post–World War II era, San Angelo attracted a variety of manufacturing enterprises, ranging from the production of clothing and ceramic tiles to the manufacture of petroleum equipment. At the time of its acquisition by Texas Commerce, San Angelo National Bank had approximately $50 million dollars in deposits and was the largest bank in its city. The final member of the trio of West Texas banks acquired by Texas Commerce in 1973, the American Bank of Commerce in Odessa, had been organized by the Noel-Rodman group in 1956. The twin cities of Odessa and Midland had grown with the development of the vast oil reserves of the Permian Basin, and their economies reflected the importance of oil and natural-gas production, the manufacture of oil-field tools and supplies, and the production of chemicals and petrochemicals. With deposits of about $50 million in 1973, American Bank of Commerce ranked as the second-largest bank in Odessa, although it was considerably smaller than the dominant oil lending bank in its region, First National Bank of Midland.[13]

More than common ownership explains why three diverse banks entertained the desire to merge with a larger holding company in the early 1970s. As had been the case in Beaumont, a strong incentive for such a merger was the desire of major stockholders in all the banks to have ready access to an established market for their securities. To investors interested in shifting part or all of their holdings out of banking, acquisition by a larger bank promised financial benefits, particularly if competitive conditions persuaded the acquiring bank to pay a premium for their stock. From the perspective of the bank's managers, a merger into a major bank holding company offered immediate assistance in meeting two critical needs of a growing regional economy: an infusion of managerial resources and the immediate and dramatic expansion of the legal lending limit of their banks.

Throughout West Texas, such potential benefits of mergers with larger bank holding companies based in Dallas and Houston were the source of much debate. In a region characterized by long distances between cities and towns, close-knit communities, and a tradition of frontier independence, many feared the impact of outside control of local banks. This sentiment helps explain why West Texas remained a bastion of independent banks in comparison to other sections of Texas. Indeed, throughout much of the state, the bank holding-company movement produced fears that the big-city banks would prove less sensitive to the needs of outlying regions than had the locally owned unit banks which traditionally had dominated the financial affairs of small towns and cities.

The Noel-Rodman group did not share such qualms. They believed instead that ties to a major holding company would allow their banks to bring more resources into West Texas. The choice of the best available holding company remained. On the basis of past patterns in West Texas, the RepublicBank Corporation of Dallas was a logical choice. Republic had a long and active history as the major correspondent bank of many banks in the region, including those in the Noel-Rodman chain. It also had a long tradition of lending to independent oil producers in the Permian Basin. Finally, Dallas was closer than Houston to West Texas. Yet in the early years of the bank holding-company movement in Texas, Republic moved more slowly than did its primary competitors as it sought to reorganize around its subsidiary, the Howard Corporation. This shareholders' company held valuable and profitable properties for the benefit of the bank, but its also posed organizational problems. The grandfather provisions of the 1970 Bank Holding Company Amendments allowed Republic to retain ownership of the Howard Corporation because its nonbank activities had been acquired well before the deadline for such acquisitions set by the new law. Yet a critical decision remained. If Republic reorganized under a new charter for a bank holding company, it might lose its exemption for continued control of the Howard Corporation. As Republic contemplated various possible solutions to its dilemma, banks such as those controlled by the Noel-Rodman group began evaluating other alternatives.

Their attention soon focused on Texas Commerce, which had indirect ties to the Noel-Rodman group through its strong historical connections with El Paso Natural Gas. Texas Commerce also had direct lending ties with both Noel and his banks, primarily through its aggressive energy lending department. The head of this department, E. O. Buck, had strong personal ties dating back to the 1930s to many of the oilmen active in the Permian Basin. Thus when Noel and his colleagues explored their options, they found an eager potential merger partner in Texas Commerce. Ben Love, the bank's new chief executive officer, took a leading role in the negotiations leading to the merger agreement. In January, 1972, an announcement of an agreement to merge between Texas Commerce and the three West Texas banks controlled by Noel's group heralded the creation of a banking organization which reached across a broad expanse of Texas, strengthening traditional commercial ties forged by the cotton and oil trade between Houston and West Texas.

The initial reaction of representatives of the Federal Reserve Board to Noel's inquiries regarding the potential merger was not promising. The board suggested that the West Texas group should form a regional holding company to compete with the Houston and Dallas banks. Noel's answer echoed that of the management of American National in Beaumont: his banks simply did not have the financial or managerial resources to compete effectively against the much larger banks of Dallas and Houston. He argued further that the Federal Reserve's disapproval of the mergers would not encourage the growth of a strong regional holding company but would ensure instead that much of the banking business of major West Texas concerns would continue to flow out of state, to the large money-center banks. Ben Love joined Noel and his colleagues in a trip to Washington to discuss the matter with representatives of the Federal Reserve. In this meeting, as in the formal application to merge, the group offered concrete reasons why the proposed mergers would benefit the West Texas economy. They argued that the resources and expertise of Texas Commerce would enable the three West Texas banks to compete more effectively for business in their respective cities. They also offered specific evidence that the largest of the three, Citizens National Bank of Lubbock, required significant changes before it was likely to emerge as an effective competitor to its larger competitors in Lubbock. Such arguments ultimately proved convincing, and in January 1973, the Federal Reserve Board formally approved the mergers.[14]

In its first year and a half of existence, Texas Commerce Bancshares had absorbed Texas Commerce–Houston, four former chain banks in the Houston suburbs, a major bank in Beaumont, and three substantial concerns in diverse sections of West Texas. Numerous other mergers were in various stages of completion as the bank aggressively pursued other opportunities to expand. In this initial phase of the holding-company movement, Texas Commerce had simply responded quickly and aggressively to several excellent opportunities for mergers, but as the pace of acquisitions quickened, the bank's management devised ways to respond more systematically to rapidly changing competitive and regulatory conditions. The critical need was to balance several quite different sets of considerations in evaluating a potential merger: Which banking markets in Texas should be given top priority? Within each market, what were the financial costs of acquiring each bank, and could such costs be justified in terms of the long-term performance of the holding company as a whole? Finally, what was the likely regulatory response to each merger proposal?

To answer these questions, Texas Commerce created an executive committee made up of officers drawn from the holding company's lead bank, Texas Commerce–Houston. This committee, called the Acquisitions/Strategy and Screening Committee, took much of the responsibility for overseeing the process by which new member banks were identified, evaluated, acquired, and absorbed into Texas Commerce Bancshares. At regular meetings during the era of rapid holding-company expansion in the mid-1970s, this committee sought to define and implement a coherent long-run strategy amid considerable regulatory uncertainties and competitive pressures. Because of the far-reaching implications of acquisitions and the need for quick decisions on mergers involving competing bids, the Mergers and Acquisitions Committee of the board of directors was also organized to review, analyze, and approve management's proposals for new mergers.

The overall strategy defined by the acquisitions committee was straightforward. Texas Commerce sought to grow into a balanced statewide organization with a strong presence in the six major banking markets in Texas—Houston, Dallas, Fort Worth, Austin, San Antonio, and El Paso. It focused on banks with the potential to grow into substantial concerns ultimately approaching $100 million in assets, thus excluding most small-town banks except those near a major metropolitan region. Finally, it sought to acquire such banks while avoiding dilution of the value of its stock. All of its primary competitors no doubt shared this last strategic objective, but none placed more practical importance on the question of dilution than did Texas Commerce. While several of its primary competitors seemed to value size over profitability, Texas Commerce generally placed a higher value on continued profitability than on absolute growth in assets.

To assist in identifying the best potential merger partners in the state, the Acquisitions/Strategy and Screening Committee employed the assistance of the bank's professional economists, who conducted regular surveys of economic conditions in the major Texas cities. These studies became more systematic in the mid-1970s, when the potential merger opportunities were placed in order of priority. As of May, 1976, for example, the "Review of TCBK Merger Opportunities" presented to the Acquisitions/Strategy Committee discussed the prospects for further expansion in areas where the bank already had subsidiaries before reviewing in more detail the desirability of expansion into the fourteen Standard Metropolitan Statistical Areas in Texas in which the holding company did not yet have a member bank. Included was information about possible merger partners in various cities and summaries of information about the activities of other bank holding companies in several of these areas. The prospects for each area were summarized under two separate categories, "economic" and "regulatory." In subsequent years the bank's economists regularly prepared two lists for the acquisitions committee. The first presented the economists' opinion of the five most promising markets in Texas in which the bank had no member bank; the second listed the most promising locations for expansion in areas which already had a member bank. These two lists often served as starting points for the committee's deliberations. Economists also prepared numerous more detailed studies of banking conditions, including, for example, lists showing the sizes, the affiliations, and the most likely merger prospects of the three hundred largest banks in the state. Such systematic reviews were critically important in keeping decision makers abreast of rapidly changing conditions in markets throughout Texas.[15]

These analyses of merger partners frequently referred to the probable reaction of regulatory authorities to each potential acquisition, reflecting the Acquisitions/Strategy and Screening Committee's need to anticipate the Federal Reserve Board's response to potential mergers. If the bank consistently misread the regulatory environment, it would waste time and resources in the futile pursuit of acquisitions ultimately denied by the Federal Reserve. Texas Commerce Bancshares and the other major bank holding companies had a small measure of influence over the approval process. The banks could ensure that their applications fully stated the case for approval, and their representatives also often could set up personal conferences to press their cases with the board of governors and its staff. But in most instances, bank managers sought not to influence the board's decisions but to anticipate them. To do so, they analyzed the board's decisions on bank-merger applications in Texas while at times seeking the informal reaction of Federal Reserve officials to acquisitions under consideration.

Yet frequent shifts in the Federal Reserve Board's interpretation of the law and the numerous exceptions granted to general rules ensured that much regulatory uncertainty would remain no matter how well holding-company managers did their homework. In regulating bank holding companies, the Federal Reserve had a mandate to prevent undue concentration and to enhance competition in banking. Its greatest difficulty was in predicting the competitive impact of potential bank mergers. Before the 1970s, when banks in Texas had competed primarily against other banks in the same city, the impact of a proposed merger on competition in that city could be estimated by adding together the market shares of the two banks involved. Most of the early holding-company mergers, however, did not alter existing concentration ratios as traditionally measured in citywide markets, since they involved banks based in different cities. Some critics argued with considerable logic that concentration should be measured at the state level, where by any available comparison with other industrial states Texas had a relatively unconcentrated banking industry. Still others suggested that the breakdown of traditional local markets in banking had progressed so far that the Federal Reserve Board should consider the implications of bank mergers in Texas for the market structure of the national banking industry. This argument held that, in order to compete effectively with expansive money center banks, the major Texas holding companies must be allowed to grow through merger. Yet in its practical, day-by-day casework in the 1970s, the board continued to undertake the painstaking—and at times frustrating—work of seeking to calculate the competitive impact of each particular merger on each regional bank market affected.[16]

An important turning point in the early regulatory history of the bank holding company in Texas came with the Federal Reserve Board's announcement of the so-called Tyler doctrine. In December, 1973, after two years of rapid expansion by Texas bank holding companies, the Board refused the application of Dallas-based First International Bancshares (InterFirst) to acquire Citizens First National Bank of Tyler, the largest bank in that East Texas city. In explaining its decision, the board argued that the merger would have possible adverse effects on potential competition in the Tyler banking market. The board implied that competition could be enhanced in Tyler by the entry of InterFirst "underneath" the city's dominant bank, through either purchase of a smaller bank or de novo entry. The practical meaning of this much-discussed decision was clarified by subsequent rulings of the Federal Reserve. A pattern emerged—with numerous exceptions—which Texas Commerce's internal planning documents summarized as follows: "It is assumed . . . that absence of entry by one of the major five bank holding companies in one of the principal banks (in a specific market under study) precludes entry by TCBK in the largest bank in the city or the largest two if both are near the same size." [17] Even this rule of thumb often proved unreliable in predicting specific rulings of the Federal Reserve Board, and regulatory uncertainties accompanied most mergers considered by Texas Commerce in the 1970s. Not until a series of court decisions in the early 1980s severely limited the board's legal authority to continue to apply its theory of potential competition were such uncertainties eased.

With or without the Tyler doctrine, intense competitive pressures shaped the actions of the major bank holding companies in Texas as they sought to acquire member banks throughout the state, often in head-to-head bidding. Banks attractive to Texas Commerce were also likely to be attractive to its major competitors, and the large holding companies scrambled to secure the best available entry into desirable markets. At times Texas Commerce had an inside track in acquiring a specific bank because of strong correspondent banking ties or personal connections with the bank's officers, board members, or primary owners. But more often than not, Texas Commerce was one of several suitors in the courtship of a prospective partner. The bank's reputation as a well-managed, profitable organization would gain its representatives a seat on the front porch, but when it came time to talk to the father— in this case the major stockholders—the discussion invariably focused on price. Officers at Texas Commerce took pains to determine with precision what a particular bank was worth in terms of its probable future contributions to the earnings of the holding company, but they were well aware that a solid bank in a desirable market might fetch a handsome premium in the active bidding for bank acquisitions. Perhaps more than its major competitors, Texas Commerce Bancshares tried to hold the line on paying such premiums, but on occasion its managers were forced to swallow hard and up the ante or risk losing important merger prospects. Size alone obviously was of little value without profitability. Yet Texas Commerce Bancshares might harm its future prospects for long-run profitability if it fell too far behind its major competitors in size.

As the Acquisitions/Strategy and Screening Committee pursued its strategy of expansion into the major banking markets in the state, measures of profitability were far from being the only factors considered in evaluating a potential acquisition. Location, quality of management, and lending philosophy also influenced choices. The value of a bank's stock to competing holding companies also inevitably entered into the committee's decisions, as did analysis of the comparative cost of the alternatives available to Texas Commerce in a particular banking market. Personal ties between officers and directors at Texas Commerce Bancshares and colleagues and friends at other banks could also influence the choice of a particular merger partner. As they sought to balance all of these various considerations while also trying to understand an often confusing regulatory environment, those in charge of acquisitions at Texas Commerce were well aware that their options in specific banking markets were neither perfect nor infinite. A merger forgone for one reason or another was often not available for reconsideration. Even major markets such as San Antonio often contained only a few logical merger candidates, a situation which produced a sellers' market. Attractive banks often could negotiate simultaneously with numerous suitors, secure in the knowledge that the pressure to pay a premium for entry into a desirable market would likely increase as other possible merger partners in the market were acquired. A brief account of the efforts of Texas Commerce to establish a strong presence in the state's six major banking markets shows how its managers sought out the best available option amid considerable regulatory uncertainty and intense competitive pressures.

Houston remained the bank's primary market, and TCB–Houston became the hub of a growing system of member banks throughout the metropolitan area. In 1982, after more than a decade of acquisitions around the state by Texas Commerce Bancshares, the downtown Houston flagship bank still accounted for approximately 58 percent of the holding company's assets. The addition of the assets of the more than twenty-five member banks in the Houston region boosted this figure to almost 70 percent of the bank's total assets. In the holding-company era, expansion in Houston came in three ways: the continued growth of TCB–Houston, which became the largest bank in Houston in the 1980s; the acquisition of the remaining links in TCB's chain-banking network; and the construction of numerous de novo banks in promising areas throughout the growing Houston area.[18]

After the initial move in 1971 to acquire three affiliates in this chain-banking network, Texas Commerce remained a part owner of two rapidly growing Houston-area banks, the First National Bank of Stafford, a growing community southwest of Houston, and Chemical Bank & Trust, situated between the affluent suburbs of River Oaks and West University Place. Both of these banks had been established by friends of the National Bank of Commerce, and both had maintained close contacts with Texas Commerce. Texas Commerce Shareholders Company owned more than a 20 percent interest in each, and a strong minority owner with ties to Texas Commerce bolstered the bank's influence at each. For almost a decade after the creation of Texas Commerce Bancshares, all parties seemed willing to continue their historical relationships without moving toward formal merger. But in the early 1980s, Texas Commerce and these two affiliated banks had incentives to merge. Two large, profitable banks would solidify Texas Commerce's position in attractive Houston-area markets. Because of the strong traditional ties between Texas Commerce and these affiliated banks, regulatory approval for the merger was likely, which was not necessarily the case for other independent banks in the Houston market. The management at both the Stafford and the Chemical bank also had good reasons to merge. Stafford in particular was chronically short of capital as it sought to keep pace with rapid, sustained economic growth in its region. The specialized services which would be offered through TCB–Houston and the much higher loan limit available in a major bank holding company promised to assist those banks in servicing their customers. Finally, as in most of the other mergers of the 1970s and 1980s, major stockholders in the two banks had a strong incentive to own stock in a company listed on the New York Stock Exchange.[19]

In other areas around Houston, expansion generally took place through the creation of de novo banks. This involved identifying an area likely to grow rapidly, acquiring a suitable site, obtaining a charter for a new bank, constructing a building, and then developing business. During the oil-led boom of the 1970s, Texas Commerce believed strongly that the Houston area was one of the most attractive banking markets in the state and, indeed, in the nation. In combination with the continued expansion of its lead bank, de novo expansion throughout the region was an essential part of Texas Commerce's strategy of building a strong statewide holding company.

In identifying promising locations for de novo banks, advice came from many directions. The members of the Acquisitions/Strategy Committee were, of course, deeply involved. Directors and customers, particularly developers, at times suggested new sites, as did officers from member banks. If a site appeared promising, the bank's economics staff conducted a field study to determine the area's stage of development and its prospects for future growth. Texas Commerce favored sites on major transportation corridors in areas with considerable residential development and clear indications that commercial growth would follow. If preliminary studies of a location proved encouraging, the results were then presented to the Acquisitions/Strategy and Screening Committee. The most promising of the sites generally found their way onto the company economists' regular list of the most attractive sites for future expansion. If the committee agreed on the desirability of a general location, the bank's real estate development managers were given the authority to seek the best available property for the construction of a new bank.

Before construction began, however, a new charter had to be obtained from the Office of the Comptroller of the Currency or from the Banking Commission. The application for a charter required an economic study of the area, and that study had to demonstrate the need for a new bank. Although the granting of a new charter was far from automatic, the rapid growth of the Houston area in the 1970s and 1980s meant that Texas Commerce generally could make a convincing argument for the issuance of new charters to build de novo banks in suburban Houston. Once a charter was granted, Texas Commerce Bancshares then had to apply to the Federal Reserve Board for permission to merge the new bank into the holding company. This required convincing evidence that the proposed merger had no anticompetitive implications. As long as the new bank was a sufficient distance from existing member banks, winning the board's approval seldom proved difficult, since its prevailing policy on mergers generally favored de novo expansion over the acquisition of existing banks.[20]

Planning for construction of the new bank generally proceeded after the granting of a new charter but before the Federal Reserve's decision. Because Texas Commerce emphasized de novo expansion during the period of its most rapid growth in the 1970s, Texas Commerce Bancshares developed its own team of specialists to design and supervise the construction of its many new buildings. While the building was going up, the holding company's personnel specialists were busy putting together a staff, and top management helped assemble a board of directors generally composed of a liaison director from the holding company, the top managers of the new bank, and prominent businessmen with ties to the area surrounding the new bank. Capital for the de novo bank came from the single shareholder, Texas Commerce Bancshares.

Building new businesses was no easier than building a new facility, but here again de novo banks drew on the resources of the holding company. Because the new bank gained immediate identification as part of an established and highly advertised concern, it had a head start in gaining credibility in the surrounding community. For business development, it could draw on the contacts of the holding company, as well as the connections of member banks throughout the Houston area. For specialized services to customers, it had access to the advice and assistance of the holding company's experts in various types of lending and in trust services. It could also rely on the holding company for capital, for managers, and for participation in loan packages. In short, affiliation with a major holding company gave the new bank numerous advantages not available to a newly chartered independent bank. Such advantages, combined with the careful planning which went into the initial selection of site, generally translated into rapid growth, and the de novo banks founded by Texas Commerce often quickly grew into substantial concerns capable of supplying capital for development in fast-growing sections of Houston.[21]

Several of these new banks gave Texas Commerce direct access to particularly fast-growing areas of Houston. TCB–Greenway Plaza expanded along with the mixed-use development of which it was a part. As Greenway Plaza developed into a major commercial complex between the central business district and the west loop around the city, it became the home of a variety of businesses and their employees, and the bank which served this market quickly had more than $100 million in assets. Texas Commerce Medical Bank enjoyed similar success in the burgeoning area surrounding the Texas Medical Center and Rice University. In serving the high-technology medical facilities and the professionals who staffed them, Texas Commerce developed strong connections in an important segment of the Houston economy with excellent long-run potential for expansion. Twenty miles southeast of the city, TCB–Clear Lake sought to establish the same sort of presence in the area surrounding the Lyndon B. Johnson Space Center of the National Aeronautics and Space Administration, another dynamic center of high technology in the Houston region.

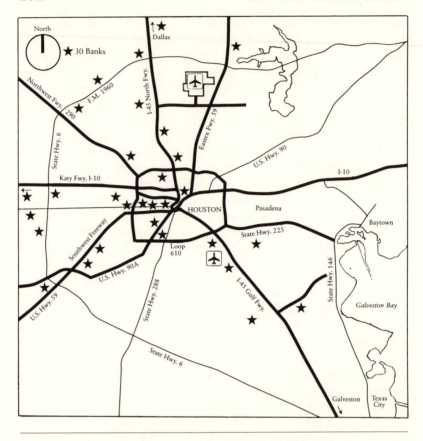

Map 12.1. Texas Commerce Banks in the Houston Area, 1986.

New banks in Clear Lake and other suburbs, such as Conroe, Pasadena, and Sugarland, embodied in bricks and mortar a new economic reality, the integration of an ever-growing section of southeast Texas into the regional economy of Houston. Texas Commerce and other holding companies with systems of banks throughout the area hastened this process of integration by providing financial services to companies and individuals active throughout the region. The de novo banks which played such a prominent role in Texas Commerce's expansion in the Houston area—and, less prominently, in other metropolitan areas—helped ensure that capital and other developmental resources would be readily available to finance the continued expansion of Houston's suburbs. Critics correctly noted that these de novo banks were, in important respects, difficult to distinguish from branches, which remained illegal in Texas. If so, their performance provided strong evidence that the big-city banks had been correct in their unsuccessful lobbying efforts in the 1950s and 1960s to persuade the Texas legislature to allow limited branching within a single metropolitan area. When combined with the continued growth of the previously absorbed chain banks and of TCB–Houston, the development of de novo banks enabled Texas Commerce to keep pace with the rapid growth in its largest market, Houston.

As Texas Commerce sought to retain its historical leadership in the Houston-area banking market, it encountered considerable difficulties in breaking into the other major market in Texas, the Dallas–Fort Worth area. Here Texas Commerce faced a stiff competitive challenge as it invaded the home territory of the large Dallas-based holding companies, RepublicBank Corporation, InterFirst Corporation, and Mercantile Texas Corporation. These concerns fought hard to maintain their traditional dominance in Dallas as they expanded into other markets throughout the state. At least in the early stages of the holding-company movement, these large banks had no interest in merging with the major Houston banks. Aside from the big three in Dallas, however, there were few banks with the location, size, and prestige to give Texas Commerce an immediate and significant entry into downtown Dallas. Lacking the option to jump into direct competition with Republic, InterFirst, and Mercantile through the acquisition of a large, established bank in downtown Dallas, Texas Commerce chose instead to move forward in shorter hops by acquiring a group of smaller banks spread throughout the Dallas–Fort Worth area.

The approach taken came to be known by management as "the metroplex strategy." Texas Commerce initially sought to establish a presence in the Dallas–Fort Worth market by acquiring well-established banks in the rapidly growing suburban communities around and between the two cities. From this base of operations, Texas Commerce sought to build banks in downtown Dallas and Fort Worth capable of growing into prominent concerns. Management, marketing, and business development drew on the holding company's much larger operations in Houston. Gradually, Texas Commerce hoped to encircle the downtown areas and then use its strength throughout the region to help build strong downtown banks. Whereas the bank had grown from the center of the city outward into the suburbs in Houston, it would attempt the opposite in Dallas–Fort Worth.[22]

This decision reflected the reality that strong outlying banks proved more readily available than did downtown banks. Early in its

history, Texas Commerce Bancshares acquired four banks in the metroplex, including a small bank in downtown Fort Worth and three
others between Dallas and Fort Worth. In April, 1973, Texas Commerce merged with Union Bank in downtown Fort Worth and with the
First National Bank of Hurst, a growing town just west of Fort Worth's
loop. Both banks were controlled by Gene Engleman, a Fort Worth
banker and entrepreneur who had worked at American Airlines before
founding a finance company and a casualty insurance company. Later
that year, Texas Commerce Bancshares acquired Irving Bank & Trust,
the largest bank in Irving, a booming area on the western edge of
Dallas. The addition of Arlington Bank and Trust, the largest bank in
a growing city roughly halfway between Dallas and Fort Worth, provided a link in a chain which reached from Fort Worth to Hurst to

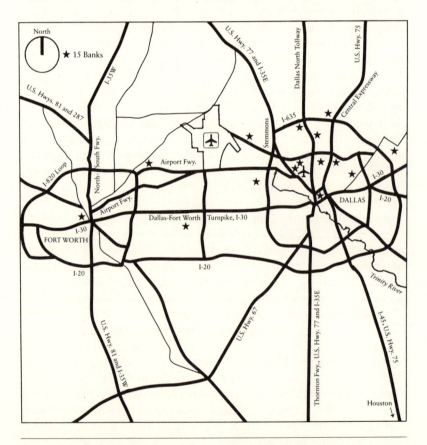

Map 12.2. Texas Commerce Banks in the Dallas–Fort Worth Area, 1986.

Arlington to Irving, giving Texas Commerce a position of strength in an area likely to grow for decades.[23]

Texas Commerce continued its strategy of encirclement in 1975, when it acquired five small banks in north Dallas. These five locations offered the opportunity to expand in good suburban sites close in to the city. Their control by one man, Dallas banker Cam Dowell, meant that they could be brought into the holding company as a package, and the announcement of this multiple acquisition in October, 1975, gave Texas Commerce an excellent opportunity to advertise its growing presence in the metroplex. As these banks grew, Texas Commerce acquired another area bank, Southern Bank & Trust of Garland. Taken as a whole, these acquisitions gave Texas Commerce numerous excellent banks in the suburbs surrounding Dallas and Fort Worth.

As of 1975, however, Texas Commerce still had not moved into the downtown area of Dallas, though not for lack of effort. The Acquisitions/Strategy and Screening Committee explored numerous potential pathways into Dallas, but the major thoroughfares remained blocked. A wide gap in resources separated the big three in Dallas and the next largest group of banks. First City Bancorporation further limited Texas Commerce Bancshares's choices by acquiring the fourth-largest bank in Dallas, Texas Bank and Trust. The few remaining downtown Dallas banks of substantial size were not yet prepared to merge or appeared to fall short of Texas Commerce's loan quality criteria.

In January, 1977, Texas Commerce established a presence in downtown Dallas through the acquisition of Main Street National Bank of Dallas, a small bank incorporated in 1964. Main Street National offered several attractions to Texas Commerce. Despite its small size relative to the dominant banks in the city, it had a charter for a downtown location and a flexible lease to allow for easy relocation should a promising site become available. To bolster Texas Commerce's Dallas operations, the National Division of Texas Commerce–Houston stepped up its calling program in the metroplex. Then in 1978, TCB–Houston established a loan-production office in Dallas to develop business for itself, for the member banks in the metroplex, and for the downtown Dallas member bank, now called Texas Commerce–Dallas. As business grew, so did the impulse to create a more visible headquarters for the holding company's lead bank in the second-largest bank market in Texas. This was accomplished in the late 1970s, when TCB–Dallas moved into a new downtown Dallas development, the Plaza of the Americas. This move, along with a $3 million infusion of capital and lending specialists from the holding company, pushed TCB–Dallas to a new stage in its development. To proclaim this change to the people of the metroplex, Texas Commerce held a gala grand opening, complete with more than 2,000 guests and supported by an intensive advertising campaign to proclaim the arrival of Texas Commerce as a major competitor in the metroplex.

The bank had pursued a similar course several years earlier in downtown Fort Worth. In 1977, Texas Commerce–Fort Worth, formerly Union Bank, moved to a prominent new address, Tandy Center, a twin-towered development which housed the headquarters of the Tandy Corporation in downtown Fort Worth. The move was accompanied by a highly publicized reception for business and civic leaders, the presentation by Ben Love of an economic study of the area prepared by the bank's economists, an advertising campaign aimed at calling the attention of those in Fort Worth to the growing banking organization in their midst, and an intensified program of calling on existing and potential customers.[24]

Such efforts to encircle the metroplex and then to develop highly visible banks in downtown Dallas and Fort Worth firmly established Texas Commerce in a highly competitive market. Yet by the mid-1980s, the bank still could not claim parity with its major competitors in the metroplex. Texas Commerce's major rival in Houston, First City, had established a larger presence by early acquisition of a second-tier downtown Dallas bank. The largest Dallas-based holding companies, RepublicBank and InterFirst, had acquired downtown Houston banks large enough to provide solid cores around which to compete in the region. Thus Texas Commerce trailed the other members of the big four in Texas banking in moving toward substantial positions in both Houston and Dallas. Steady growth of the sort pursued in the 1970s might ultimately redress this imbalance, but for a company engaged in heated competition with other equally expansive concerns, only one alternative promised immediate results: a merger with a bank with substantial holdings in the metroplex.[25]

From its earliest entry into the Dallas–Fort Worth area, Texas Commerce had explored every merger prospect in the metroplex which seemed capable of gaining the approval of the Federal Reserve Board. Throughout the 1970s, however, such regulatory considerations had excluded mergers between Texas Commerce and the largest downtown banks in both Dallas and Fort Worth. This constraint loosened in the early 1980s, as a series of decisions by the Federal Reserve and successful challenges of two of its decisions in court opened the way for a wave of mergers involving the acquisitions of one large holding company by another. Texas Commerce sought to use this new flexibility to expand decisively in the metroplex, but several substantial mergers pursued by Texas Commerce did not come to fruition.

One attractive option for Texas Commerce was to acquire one of the two large bank holding companies anchored by large downtown Fort Worth banks, First United Bancorporation and Texas American Bancshares. A strong lead bank in Fort Worth could then become the center of Texas Commerce's Dallas–Fort Worth operations. Both banks ranked among the ten largest bank holding companies in Texas, but neither had emerged as an effective competitor to the much larger Dallas- and Houston-based banks. Texas Commerce found First United to be an attractive merger candidate because of its traditional strength in Fort Worth, its rate of growth, its quality of assets and earnings, and its management philosophy. Indeed, Ben Love summarized the sentiment of Texas Commerce when he wrote to Paul Mason, First United's chairman, "There are no other banking organizations in my opinion which are more complementary or compatible than First United and Texas Commerce." [26] Texas Commerce made its first unsolicited merger offer in the spring of 1980. First United chose not to accept the offer, citing the opinion of its general counsel that the proposed merger would probably violate existing antitrust guidelines and was thus unlikely to gain regulatory approval. Although disagreeing with this assessment, Texas Commerce had little choice but to withdraw the offer. Two years later, after several Federal Reserve Board decisions indicated that regulatory approval for the merger could be obtained, Texas Commerce renewed is efforts to merge with First United. In an attempt to persuade First United's management of the benefits of affiliation with Texas Commerce and to calm fears that the smaller bank would lose its historical identity in becoming one part of a Houston-based holding company, Love offered to work out a "merger founded on the principle of merging *results* more than merging *operations* where one organization abandons a proven and successful management philosophy." [27] First United responded by weighing its options, comparing the offers of merger which it was receiving from several large bank holding companies. In 1983, it announced its intent to merge with InterFirst, becoming the center of that expansive Dallas-based bank's activities in Fort Worth rather than the center of Texas Commerce's operations in the entire metroplex.

Texas Commerce then examined the prospect of a merger with the remaining large Fort Worth–based holding company, Texas American Bancshares, which was at that time the seventh-largest bank in Texas with assets approaching $5 billion. In July, 1983, Texas Commerce submitted an unsolicited merger offer to the chairman of Texas American. This offer set off a flurry of activity and publicity which made headlines but did not produce the strong presence in the metroplex long sought by Texas Commerce. In presenting the merger proposal to Lewis Bond, chairman of Texas American, Ben Love stressed the vast ongoing changes in the structure of the financial services industry and suggested that a bank the size of Texas American would have difficulty surviving in the coming era of intense competition involving banks and new competitors such as Sears. He promised that "the integrity and history of both organizations would be preserved and enhanced by a logical division of managerial authority. This concept entails your assuming senior responsibility for all banks in the northern part of Texas . . . anchored by your flagship bank in Fort Worth." [28]

Bond's response was quick and direct. He notified Love that the Texas American Board rejected this "unsolicited and unwanted offer" as "inadequate." At the same time, Bond issued a press release announcing his bank's rejection of Texas Commerce's offer and reaffirming its intentions to remain an independent bank. The release concluded with the statement that "the present is not the optimum time to merge with a larger Texas holding company," suggesting that Texas American's stockholders might receive higher offers for their shares in a future which seemed to hold increasingly intense intrastate and interstate competition. Coming at the same time that First City announced an agreement to merge with Cullen/Frost Bankers, Inc., a San Antonio–based holding company similar in size and market position to Texas American, the much publicized rejection by Texas American of the merger offer by Texas Commerce represented a discouraging and even embarrassing setback in the organization's efforts to strengthen its position in the metroplex. [29]

The management of Texas Commerce had no time to dwell on the Texas American episode, however, for in the summer and fall of 1983 events were moving rapidly in Texas banking. The approval of the merger between the third-largest bank in Dallas, Mercantile Texas Corporation, and the third-largest in Houston, Southwest Bancshares, suggested that the Federal Reserve would no longer block mergers in Texas of any size, as long as potential anticompetitive impacts in specific bank markets could be resolved by the divestiture of competing member banks from the holding companies involved. The path for mergers between the major Houston and Dallas banks was no longer blocked by insurmountable regulatory barriers. In response, the two largest Houston-based bank holding companies, Texas Commerce and First City, and the two largest in Dallas, RepublicBank and InterFirst, eyed each other warily. Texas Commerce and RepublicBank made a particularly interesting potential match, and published reports speculated about the prospects of a merger between the two, which would have created the dominant bank in Texas and the twelfth-largest in the nation. In mergers involving banks of roughly equal size by a variety of measures of size and profitability, agreement on the exact exchange value would present complex, yet surmountable, problems. More difficult, however, would be the organization of a management structure and the division of authority among existing executives in each organization. Such potential problems were serious, but the potential benefits of a major merger between Texas Commerce and Republic or Inter-First were also great. From the perspective of Texas Commerce, these included a dramatic solution to its long quest for a stronger presence in Dallas as well as the attainment of a higher national profile. Exploratory discussions between representatives of Texas Commerce and of RepublicBank and InterFirst did not lead to an agreement to merge, however, and Texas Commerce was forced to abandon the dream of vaulting forward in Dallas and in the state as a whole and return to the ongoing reality of building strength gradually in the Dallas–Fort Worth market. An important step in this direction came in January, 1986, with the announcement of plans for the Texas Commerce Tower, a major downtown-Dallas office building to be constructed by Trammell Crow Company as the headquarters for the operations of Texas Commerce in the Dallas–Fort Worth area.[30]

The bank's experiences in the Central Texas markets of Austin and San Antonio illustrate the impact of the regulatory process on holding-company expansion. In the early 1970s, Texas Commerce had what it thought was a ready entry into Austin, since members of the bank had a long and close relationship with those in control of Austin National Bank, the largest bank in the state capital. Former Governor Allan Shivers, who served on the boards of National Bank of Commerce from 1957 to 1963 and of Texas Commerce from 1964 to 1976, was the chairman of Austin National in the early 1970s. Thus when Texas Commerce sought to acquire a member bank in Austin, it approached Austin Bancshares Corporation, the holding company of Austin National and two much smaller suburban Austin banks. Negotiations went forward smoothly, and in August, 1973, the two banks announced a preliminary agreement to merge, pending approval by Austin Bancshares' stockholders and regulatory authorities.

From the earliest contact between the banks, all parties knew that regulatory approval was far from certain, but the Federal Reserve's approval of a variety of mergers in diverse markets throughout the state from 1970 to 1973 offered hope that this hurdle could be cleared. Realizing, however, that the acquisition of the largest bank in

Austin by one of the major Houston holding companies would be intently scrutinized, Texas Commerce carefully and thoroughly prepared its formal application for permission to merge. The bank's economists presented studies to show the need for larger banks in Texas to meet the competitive challenge of out-of-state banks. These studies sought to show that the economy of the Austin area would benefit greatly from the resources of a large holding company. The application argued further that Texas Commerce had few realistic alternatives for entering Austin through the acquisition of an existing bank and that de novo entry was impractical. Finally, spokesmen from both banks sought to convince the Federal Reserve that Austin Bancshares' three-member holding company was unlikely to grow into an organization large enough to compete effectively against the largest holding companies in the state. In support of the application, the two banks mustered an impressive array of informal contacts between friends of the bank and government officials with potential influence.[31]

Unfortunately for the banks, timing proved more important than either specific arguments or influence. The shareholders of Austin Bancshares approved the merger in May, 1974. Eight months later, in January 1975, the Federal Reserve Board announced denial of permission to complete the merger. Between the preliminary announcement of the intent to merge in August, 1973, and the board's decision, the rush of mergers which had marked the rapid emergence and spread of bank holding companies in the years before 1974 was slowed considerably by the impact of the Tyler decision. The regulatory environment had changed, challenging the plans of Texas Commerce for a decisive early entry into Austin.

The Federal Reserve Board's denial of Texas Commerce's acquisition of Austin Bancshares echoed the words of the Tyler decision: "Applicant's acquisition of the Austin Bank would have significantly adverse effects on the concentration of banking resources and on potential competition with respect to the Austin banking market."[32] The board supported its decision with the assertion that future competition in Austin would be encouraged by the entry into this market of the major bank holding companies through the acquisition of relatively small area banks or through the construction of de novo banks. Texas Commerce and similar large statewide concerns would then be forced to compete aggressively to expand; the large Austin banks such as Austin Bancshares would be forced to compete aggressively to defend their traditional positions, and in so doing, these banks might be expected to grow into regional or even statewide holding companies.

Such a theory of potential competition required at least two prerequisites to work in practice: the existence of banks in Tyler, Austin, Fort Worth, or El Paso capable of growing into competitive parity with the major Dallas and Houston-based holding companies and the systematic enforcement over the long run of regulatory policy which fostered the growth of such banks. Neither prerequisite existed in Texas in the 1970s. The Houston and Dallas economies remained the center of economic activity in the state, and the largest banks in those cities had overwhelming advantages in size, location, and tradition over the banks in smaller cities. Perhaps such advantages could have been overcome through decades of sustained growth; perhaps not. For its part, the Federal Reserve Board did not allow much time for its theory of potential competition to work, since frequent exceptions and periodic shifts in policy undermined the systematic, consistent enforcement of the Tyler doctrine.

Texas Commerce's entry into Austin after the denial of its application to merge with Austin Bancshares embodied this inconsistency. Forbidden its first choice by the Federal Reserve, Texas Commerce began exploring alternative routes into Austin. After meetings with officers and directors of numerous banks in Austin and much internal discussion of the options available to it in that city, Texas Commerce focused its efforts on negotiations with Capital National Bank, the second-largest bank in Austin with assets nearly as large as those of Austin National. In 1976 the two banks reached an agreement to merge; in the next year, the Federal Reserve Board granted its approval, and the merger was completed. Capital National's assets of $490 million made it second in size within the holding company to Texas Commerce–Houston, and its acquisition established Texas Commerce in Austin.[33]

The Federal Reserve's approval of this acquisition was the exception that disproved the rule. Clearly the merger of Texas Commerce with one of the two largest Austin banks was not consistent with the Federal Reserve Board's previous application of the concept of potential competition in denying Texas Commerce Bancshares's application to merge with Austin Bancshares. As the board wavered in its commitment to a strict interpretation of the Tyler doctrine, banks succeeded in obtaining approval for numerous mergers which probably would not have been approved several years before. Once the board made an exception which allowed a major bank holding company to acquire one of the largest banks in a market—as in the merger of Texas Commerce and Capital National—competitive considerations then dictated the approval of other, similar mergers. Independent banks in a market such as Ausitn could not realistically compete as equals after the largest banks traditionally active in their market began pairing off with the large Houston- or Dallas-based bank holding companies. The Federal Reserve's tortuous quest for competition, real and potential, proceeded gradually on a case-by-case basis in each market. Nowhere were the results more striking than in Austin, where, in 1982, the board allowed Austin Bancshares to merge with InterFirst Corporation in a union of the largest bank in the city and the largest bank holding company in the state. So much for the theory of potential competition in practice.

Federal Reserve decisions combined with the particular nature of the economy and the banking industry in San Antonio to hamper the growth of Texas Commerce in that central Texas city. Early in the holding-company era, Texas Commerce moved aggressively into the third-largest city in Texas by acquiring in 1974 the Highland Park State Bank, a well-established, profitable organization in southeastern San Antonio. Three years later, First National Bank of New Braunfels joined Texas Commerce Bancshares, giving it a strong member bank in a small city some thirty miles northeast of San Antonio. These two banks gave the holding company a foothold in the region, but neither was well situated to serve the substantial banking needs of the central business district of San Antonio. Texas Commerce sought to address this problem through the acquisition of Bexar County National Bank, a major downtown bank which announced its intention to join Texas Commerce in 1976. As in Austin, however, the Federal Reserve blocked this merger, basing its decision on the tortured logic that New Braunfels and San Antonio were part of a single banking market. The board reasoned that the proposed acquisition would give Texas Commerce too large a share in this market. Bexar County National ultimately was acquired by RepublicBank, and Texas Commerce continued to expand its existing locations in the San Antonio area while exploring every available option for increasing its presence in the city's central business district.[34]

To the south of San Antonio stretched a broad area of increasing importance to the Texas economy in which Texas Commerce steadily built a network of member banks. Its entry into the port city of Corpus Christi came in 1974 with the acquisition of Guaranty National Bank and Trust, and the addition of other locations subsequently strengthened its operations in this region. Further south in the Rio Grande valley, Texas Commerce acquired Pan-American Bank of Brownsville in 1975. As one of the major Texas cities bordering Mexico, Brownsville promised to contribute to the holding company's operations in South Texas while also facilitating transactions involving trade with Mexico.

The addition in 1978 of First National Bank of McAllen—another growing South Texas city west of Brownsville—expanded Texas Commerce's presence in this area.[35] This member bank also brought into the holding company the Bentsen family, which had long played a leading role in the development of the Rio Grande Valley.

As Texas Commerce pursued expansion throughout the state, the pace of change in Texas banking accelerated in the early 1980s. With their stock values buoyed by an oil-led economic boom in the Southwest, the major bank holding companies in Houston and Dallas accelerated the pace of their acquisitions. Regulatory constraints previously posed by the Tyler doctrine had been weakened by a series of decisions by the Federal Reserve Board, which now seemed willing to approve large mergers previously rejected under the doctrine of potential competition. Meanwhile, the competitive pressures on the largest bank holding companies intensified as the list of attractive merger targets in the state's important banking markets declined with each successful merger. As Texas Commerce and its chief rivals surveyed the field in the early 1980s, the time seemed ripe for decisive action. By 1981, the decade-long contest to create profitable statewide bank holding companies had entered its most intensive phase, as each large holding company sought to improve its competitive position in a rapidly changing industry by increasing the number and size of acquisitions.

In this highly charged period, one focus of attention for Texas Commerce Bancshares was El Paso, the fifth-largest banking market in Texas. There the bank's options were distinctly limited. In the 1970s, First City and InterFirst had acquired second-tier banks in El Paso before the Federal Reserve had become willing to approve the acquisition by a major holding company of one of the largest banks in a market. In the early 1980s, neither Texas Commerce nor Republic had a member bank in El Paso, and both sought to enter the city through the purchase of one of its two dominant banking organizations. The largest of these was El Paso National Corporation (previously Trans Texas Bancorporation), a holding company headed by the largest bank in the city, El Paso National Bank. Close behind in size was Pan National Group, Inc., a holding company headed by the city's second-largest bank, State National. The lead banks of these two holding companies were roughly the size of Capital National Bank of Austin, and the acquisition of either would establish Texas Commerce as a leader in this significant banking market while also giving an impressive boost to its aggregate size.

Since the mid-1970s, Texas Commerce had considered El Paso National Bank the most attractive potential merger partner in El Paso.

Indeed, as the acquisitions committee of the holding company sought to determine the proper strategy toward El Paso in this era, it faced a difficult choice. Merger with El Paso National was blocked, since that bank's principal owners were not interested in selling their stock. In addition, the committee assumed that a merger with the largest bank in El Paso would not be approved by the Federal Reserve. As competing holding companies entered El Paso through the purchase of smaller banks, those in charge of acquisitions at Texas Commerce chose instead to postpone entry. One strong motivation for delay was the fear that the purchase of a second-tier competitor of El Paso National might endanger a substantial and profitable correspondent relationship with that bank. By postponing direct entry into El Paso, Texas Commerce might become a perpetual outsider with little direct access to an important market in Texas; conversely, patience might prove beneficial in the long run, since it would leave Texas Commerce unrestrained by previous commitments if changing regulatory interpretations allowed the acquisition of one of the two largest banks in the city.[36]

El Paso National Bank seemed worth the wait. Founded in 1925 by local businessman Charles Harvey and Sam D. Young, who had come to El Paso as a receiver for a failed bank, El Paso National grew steadily with the economy of the El Paso–Juárez, Mexico, metropolitan area. By 1980, the population of the region approached one million, with about half of this number residing in El Paso, the fifth-largest metropolitan area in Texas. The city's banks served a regional economy dominated by the apparel industry, copper and lead smelting, and several large military installations. As the second-oldest bank in the region, El Paso National took advantage of its long-run growth to become the largest bank, with more than 30 percent of deposits. In 1971, El Paso National moved to solidify its position through the creation of a regional holding company which included six El Paso–area banks by 1980, when total assets of approximately $727 million ranked this organization as the fifteenth-largest bank holding company in Texas.[37]

Yet the future prosperity of even a large El Paso–based bank holding company was uncertain. The city's remoteness from other major urban centers made continued rapid growth of its banks unlikely. The nearest large city was Phoenix, Arizona, which was separated from El Paso banks by approximately 400 miles and two state boundaries. Dallas was 600 miles away, and Houston was 700 miles from the border city. Besides its remoteness, in the late 1970s, El Paso National faced increasing competitive pressures from local member banks of

First City and InterFirst, which could use the resources of their parent banks in Houston and Dallas to expand. The bank was living proof of the difficulties facing bank holding companies based in the smaller cities as they competed directly with much larger Dallas- and Houston-based banking organizations.

When El Paso National Corporation began to explore its options, it found two willing suitors, Texas Commerce Bancshares and RepublicBank Corporation. Texas Commerce had begun to discuss seriously this acquisition in 1978, after the Federal Reserve's approval of its merger with Capital National of Austin offered hope that a merger with one of the two largest El Paso banks could gain regulatory approval. In its earliest calculations in 1978, however, Texas Commerce's managers concluded that the best offer it could tender without unacceptable dilution of its stock was insufficient to persuade the owners of El Paso National to merge.[38] The increased competition among the major bank holding companies in the years that followed raised second thoughts among Texas Commerce's top managers. Concern that the growth of its chief rivals might "be leading toward repositioning of Texas Commerce among our three principal competitors in terms of size" led Ben Love to caution the acquisitions committee that "if the resultant psychology . . . began to envelop this organization, it would be difficult to reverse at some future time."[39] Such sentiments shaped subsequent negotiations with El Paso National. Amid the intense competitive pressures of the early 1980s, Texas Commerce became willing to pay a significant premium for the acquisitions of a desirable bank in a desirable banking market in which other options for entry were quite limited.

El Paso National's principal owners and managers, Sam Young and his son, Sam Young, Jr., were the focus of negotiations. The Youngs held an excellent bargaining position, since they could entertain offers from Texas Commerce and Republic while also seeking to put together a group of local investors to purchase their bank. The declining performance of the bank relative to its more aggressive rivals in El Paso did little to dampen the enthusiam of its suitors, who greatly valued the bank's location and size. Indeed, the management of Texas Commerce steadily increased its estimate of the intangible value of El Paso National as it watched its rivals move forward with large mergers throughout the state.

By 1981, Texas Commerce was willing to increase its offer for El Paso National, in part on the assumption that the integration of the bank into a statewide holding company could, in time, improve its financial performance. In the summer of 1981, the management of Texas

Commerce sought the approval of its board for the largest merger in its history. The importance of this acquisition to Texas Commerce was reflected by the fact that, for the first time, its management sought approval of an acquisition at a price "that will result in significant earnings dilution." [40]

After additional bargaining throughout that summer, Texas Commerce and El Paso National announced their intention to merge. Regulatory approval was forthcoming, and in September, 1982, the merger took effect. With the completion of the acquisition of El Paso National Corporation's assets of almost $850 million, Texas Commerce Bancshares temporarily became the largest bank holding company in Texas.

The merger with El Paso National marked the end of an era in the evolution of Texas Commerce Bancshares. As the Texas economy absorbed the impact of declining oil prices after 1983, the enthusiasm for bank holding-company expansion waned. Weaker stock prices for the major holding companies made large acquisitions relatively more expensive and thus less attractive. The state's largest bank holding companies had entered a period of consolidation as they sought to coordinate more fully their existing operations while defining appropriate strategic responses to the downturn in the Texas economy after the waning of the oil-led boom of the 1970s. The giant mergers which had characterized the early 1980s disappeared from the headlines. For Texas Commerce, the symbolic end of this era of rapid expansion came with the rejection of its unsolicited offer to buy Fort Worth–based Texas American Bancshares. For the Texas holding-company movement as a whole, the climax of the era of acquisitions was the merger of the third-largest Dallas-based bank holding company, Mercantile Texas Corporation, with the third-largest Houston bank, Southwest Bancshares, announced in June, 1983, and completed the following year. Perhaps more indicative of future trends was the ultimate fate of a much-publicized announcement in July, 1983, of an intent to merge First City Bancorporation of Houston and Cullen/Frost Bankers, Inc., the ninth-largest bank holding company in Texas. A year later spokesmen for the two banks announced that the merger would not be pursued. As in numerous potential mergers which might have been attractive in the heady days for Texas banks in the early 1980s, the First City–Cullen/Frost proposal ceased to make sense in the sluggish Texas economy of the mid-1980s. [41]

Yet before the downturn in acquisitions after 1983, the bank holding-company movement had fundamentally altered the position of Texas Commerce in the state and national economies. Between 1971

Figure 12.1. Increase in legal loan limit at Texas Commerce Bancshares, 1971–85.

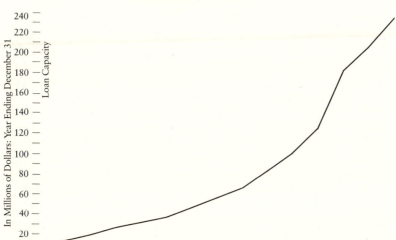

and 1984, its assets grew thirteen times, from $1.6 billion to more than $20.7 billion, a figure which made it the twenty-first largest commercial bank in the nation in 1984. The dramatic increase in assets produced by the acquisition of member banks and the simultaneous expansion of the Houston flagship bank gave Texas Commerce resources with which to compete more aggressively with banks of all sizes. The holding company's legal ability to combine the lending limit of all of its members gave the bank the capacity it had previously lacked to extend much larger loans to major customers (see Figure 12.1). At the same time, the bank's geographical expansion enabled it to participate directly in major Texas banking markets outside Houston, where the experience and traditional ties to the communities of the various member banks made possible involvement on a level which would have been most difficult for a Houston bank to achieve. All in all, the size and geographical diversity resulting from the holding-company movement greatly enhanced the competitive position of Texas Commerce in its traditional region, in Texas as a whole, and in markets beyond the state's boundaries.

Historical statistics on the bank's assets relative to those of the

Table 12.2   Texas Commerce in the Nation's Banking Hierarchy,
1930-84

Year	Assets[a] (billions)	Rank[b]	Average Assets of Top 5 (billions)[b]	Percentage Texas Commerce of Top 5 Average[c]	Percentage Texas Commerce of Largest[d]
1930	$ 0.014		$ 1.815	0.8	.5
1940	0.068	124	2.615	2.6	1.8
1948	0.201	87	3.815	5.3	3.6
1954	0.331	72	4.956	6.7	4.0
1964	0.979	44	10.834	8.0	5.6
1973	2.828	44	33.100	8.5	5.7
1974	3.684	33	42.586	8.7	6.1
1975	4.524	26	44.030	10.3	6.8
1976	5.196	27	48.816	10.6	7.0
1977	6.643	24	55.947	11.9	8.1
1978	8.027	24	64.482	12.4	8.5
1979	8.260	24	74.126	12.5	8.5
1980	11.286	21	82.048	13.8	9.8
1981	14.512	21	86.172	16.8	12.0
1982	17.217	19	91.144	20.0	14.0
1983	19.499	20	92.021	21.2	14.5
1984	20.732	21	98.998	20.1	13.0
1985	20.076	22	105.145	19.1	11.6

SOURCE: *Moody's Bank and Finance Manual; Fortune; Business Week.*
[a] Before 1964, the assets are those of National Bank of Commerce.
[b] Position of Texas Commerce in the nation's banks by total assets.
[c] Assets of Texas Commerce as a percentage of the average of the assets of the five largest banks in the nation.
[d] Assets of Texas Commerce as a percentage of the assets of the largest bank.

nation's largest banks give one indication of the extent to which it closed the gap in resources which had long marked its relationship to the major money center banks. Table 12.2 demonstrates that, as of 1930, the distance between the National Bank of Commerce and the major money-center banks was as wide as Texas. As NBC grew steadily, this gap closed somewhat, but as recently as the 1950s, the Bank of America—then the largest bank in the nation—remained twenty-five times larger than NBC. The merger of 1964 boosted Texas Commerce slightly, making it 5 to 6 percent the size of Bank of America, where it remained on the eve of the holding company movement. Against this backdrop, the move up to around 14 percent of the assets of the nation's largest bank between 1971 and 1984 represented a great leap forward in the evolution of Texas Commerce toward greater competitiveness with the money-center banks.

The 1970s also brought a marked improvement in the bank's competitive position in Texas. Indeed, Table 12.3 suggests that Texas Commerce benefited more than any other major Texas bank from the era of rapid expansion unleashed by the coming of the bank holding company. From the 1920s to the 1970s, the two leaders in Texas banking had been from Dallas: RepublicBank Corporation of Texas and First National Bank of Dallas. These banks remained roughly twice as large as NBC until the 1964 merger, which increased the size of Texas

Table 12.3   Assets of Largest Bank Holding Companies
in Texas, 1971–85 (in millions of dollars)

End of Year	TCBK[a]	FCBC[b]	RBT[c]	IFC[d]	MCorp[e] MTX[f]	SWB[g]
1971	$ 1,609	$ 1,883	$ 2,894	$ 2,612	—	—
1972	2,077	2,638	3,649	3,485	—	—
1973	2,829	3,581	4,215	5,052	—	—
1974	3,684	4,067	4,382	5,792	$ 1,016	$ 1,911
1975	4,524	4,577	5,215	6,356	1,296	2,121
1976	5,196	5,256	6,521	7,167	2,820	2,292
1977	6,643	6,274	7,526	8,307	3,417	2,619
1978	8,027	7,569	9,225	10,025	4,094	3,076
1979	9,260	9,505	10,798	11,504	4,709	3,558
1980	11,287	11,275	11,867	13,781	5,460	4,158
1981	14,512	14,291	14,441	17,318	6,870	5,253
1982	18,217	16,567	17,218	21,030	10,190	6,927
1983	19,499	17,263	19,082	21,736	11,884	7,989
1984	20,732	17,319	21,595	21,617	20,697	
1985	20,076	16,460	23,205	22,071	22,586	

SOURCE: *Business Week*, Annual Scorecard of 200 Banks.
[a] Texas Commerce Bancshares (Houston)
[b] First City Bancorporation (Houston)
[c] RepublicBank Corporation (Dallas)
[d] InterFirst Corporation (Dallas)
[e] MCorp (Dallas), created in 1984 through the merger of Mercantile Texas (Dallas) and Southwest Bancshares (Houston)
[f] Mercantile Texas (Dallas)
[g] Southwest Bancshares (Houston)

Commerce relative to its Dallas rivals without fundamentally altering the competitive balance. The largest Houston banks constituted a second tier of Texas banking until the 1970s, when they challenged the Dallas banks' traditional advantage in size. In 1984, MCorp joined the ranks of the state's largest banking organizations through the merger of the third-largest bank holding companies based in Dallas and Houston. Perhap the clearest indication of the importance of the holding-company era to Houston's banks is that, as early as 1961, Republic was the twentieth-largest bank in the nation at a time when no Houston bank made the top fifty. In this sense, the Dallas banks solidified their traditional standing in the national banking industry in the 1970s, while the Houston banks fundamentally altered their positions. In the 1960s, Houston's largest banks had yet to become the equals of their counterparts in Dallas; by the 1980s, the major bank holding companies based in the two cities competed as equals in markets throughout the state.

This is not to say that Texas Commerce was equally strong throughout Texas. Indeed, Texas Commerce–Houston remained far and away the largest bank in Texas Commerce Bancshares, accounting for more than 50 percent of the holding company's assets at the end of 1984. The additional twenty-nine Houston-area member banks pushed the total assets of all of the bank's Houston-area operations to more than 70 percent of the holding company's total. Even the two largest member banks—Texas Commerce–Austin, with $1.4 billion in assets, and the complex of seven El Paso–area banks organized around El Paso National, with total assets of approximately $1 billion—remained substantially smaller than the flagship bank in Houston. This meant that in the overall operations of the holding company, TCB–Houston often fulfilled a variety of staff functions as well as services in specialized lending areas, investments, and trusts. During the years of transition from a unit bank toward a multibank holding company in the 1970s, Texas Commerce–Houston also provided most of the officers for the holding company, many of whom fulfilled dual responsibilities in TCB–Houston and the holding company.[42]

Efforts to create a unified, effective management system for the holding company inevitably collided at times with the traditional tone of operations and the managerial autonomy of individual member banks. Such tensions reflected in part the natural concern of smaller organizations acquired by a larger one; in some member banks, they arose from the resistance of traditional bankers to the introduction of techniques drawn from industrial management, a process which was particularly difficult to accept when imposed by outsiders. For their part, the managers of the holding company faced a difficult challenge. They had to build a unified organization from once separate member banks while retaining the support of the key managers who had built these banks before their acquisition by Texas Commerce. This task was complicated by the widespread image of Texas Commerce among the state's bankers as a hard-driving organization strongly committed to quantitative measures of performance. Bank presidents, long accustomed to independence and authority within their organizations, were seldom eager to have their performance scrutinized by their new superiors in the Houston offices of Texas Commerce.

The holding company's management under Ben Love attempted to gain acceptance of unifying reforms in a manner suggested by the slogan "sell, don't tell," an approach employed by an earlier master of management in a decentralized structure, Alfred D. Sloan, chairman of General Motors in the mid-twentieth century. The idea was to educate key managers of the member banks concerning the potential benefits of new policies, not to force their acquiescence. In the holding company's formative years, however, a somewhat hard-sell approach was at times required to assure the acceptance of changes from the traditional practices of some member banks. In an intensely competitive industry in which fluctuations in stock value could shape future plans for acquisitions, the luxury of management by consensus was not always available. In this early stage in the evolution of a decentralized management system, the centralization of certain powers was a prerequisite for the subsequent dispersal of authority back down into the organization. Overall goals had to be defined and shared procedures installed. Only then could effective decision-making powers be pushed back down into the organization. Until such lines of authority and communications were in place, the holding company was likely to remain less than the sum of its individual parts. Afterward, it could become more.

One centrally important task was the adoption of the same accounting and reporting procedures by all the member banks. Unified operations of a holding company could not go forward without a commonly accepted financial language. Uniformity was needed to allow for the adoption of the most effective computing system. A common method of reporting also facilitated the evaluation of managers. Monthly publication of statistics analyzing the financial performance of each member bank served to define standards of performance for the holding company as a whole. Such comparisons encouraged competition among the member banks while also identifying successful banking practices employed by one bank which might prove beneficial to others.

The management of the holding company found numerous ways to foster a shared identity. Included was the creation of a new Texas Commerce logo, a flag much like that of Texas. This common symbol was prominently displayed in all institutional advertising, as well as in the signs and letterheads of the individual banks. Regular meetings of the top managers of all the member banks likewise fostered a sense of unity while also providing for the flow of information and ideas down into the organization from the holding company and up from the individual banks. Finally, the holding company built a concrete symbol of its permanence and its aspirations, the Texas Commerce Tower, a seventy-five-story skyscraper which was the tallest building in Texas and the sixth tallest in the nation when it opened in 1981. The planning, construction, and occupation of the tower provided the member banks with a sense of shared accomplishment while also creating new office space which allowed the holding company's management to move out of its old offices in the Gulf Building.

Such efforts fostered the growth of organizational bonds within the holding company, but perhaps the most important element in the evolution of numerous once-separate organizations into a unified whole was simply the passage of time. As years passed, those most wedded to traditional practices retired, often to be replaced by managers who had risen to prominence within the holding-company structure. The transfer of managers throughout the entire holding-company system also tended to promote unity of outlook. The passage of time contributed to the instititionalization of paths of input up from the member banks to the holding company officers, an important step in allowing a decentralized organization to stay in touch with varied markets. But from 1971 forward, the strongest of all glues binding the holding company together was the shared experience of competing in one of the most dynamic and demanding banking markets in the nation. Fluctuations in the Texas economy in the 1970s and 1980s provided challenges sufficient to test any banking organization's mettle, and the successes and failures of Texas Commerce banks in meeting these challenges forged a shared sense of identity and history throughout the holding company.

CHAPTER 13

Banking Amid Boom and Bust

The years 1971 to 1986 witnessed sharp fluctuations in the Texas economy. The growing economic diversity which had been apparent in the 1950s and 1960s was temporarily submerged under a wave of oil-related activities brought by extraordinary increases in the price of oil. In the decade after 1971, the real price of oil in the United States quadrupled in response to the success of the Organization of Petroleum Exporting Countries in raising the world price of oil. As a major oil-producing state, Texas benefited greatly from the sustained and at times frenzied expansion of oil-related industries in the 1970s. Houston, the self-proclaimed oil capital of the nation, surged forward to become the fourth-largest city in the United States, behind only New York, Los Angeles, and Chicago. Then in the 1980s the weakening of OPEC's power sent the price of oil sliding downward, jolting the Texas economy out of the boom mentality of the previous decade. Although other industries continue to contribute significantly to the growth of the state in the years after 1971, the cycle of boom and bust in oil had far-reaching impacts on the overall development of Texas and its financial institutions.*

While adjusting to fluctuations in the Texas economy, the management of Texas Commerce also had to adjust to the sweeping of regulatory changes brought by the deregulation of financial institu-

---

*The perils of including an overview of current events in a historical account are all too evident as this is written in February, 1986. In the first two months of the year, oil prices have dropped precipitously, with no evidence yet in sight of the end of the recent era of sharp fluctuations in oil prices. The long-range impact of such ongoing changes is impossible to predict. We have chosen to avoid the role of seers into the future, attempting instead to summarize events since 1971 in the context of Texas Commerce's previous history.

tions. As the security-based rules inherited from the 1930s steadily gave way in the 1970s and 1980s, a new wave of competition forced bankers to reexamine all phases of their traditional operations. The process of regulatory change proved difficult to monitor, much less to manage, since numerous laws enforced by various agencies were involved. Thus in the 1970s and 1980s, bank managers in Texas faced the stiff challenge of simultaneously adjusting to far-reaching economic and regulatory changes.

The boom of the 1970s presented Texas Commerce with excellent opportunities for expansion. Texas Commerce–Houston, the lead bank of the growing bank holding company, was firmly positioned in one of the fastest growing banking markets in the nation. It had in place the experience, personnel, and established contacts to take full advantage of the oil-led boom without sacrificing its traditional, conservative lending practices. At the same time, the expansion of the activities of member banks throughout the state also fed the growth of Texas Commerce Bancshares. The combination of the oil boom and the bank holding-company movement after 1971 produced a heady era of expansion. As it grew, Texas Commerce joined its major Texas competitors as the darlings of Wall Street by outperforming and outgrowing the traditionally stronger money-center banks. Throughout the 1970s, Texas Commerce invited the attention of the nation's financial community by publicly announcing its quarterly and annual earnings goals and then proudly proclaiming its success in meeting or bettering them. Most notable was the record of growth of quarter-to-quarter earnings for 65 consecutive quarters or more than 16 years. By aggressively proclaiming success as measured by statistics on financial performance, its management sought to solidify its reputation and enhance its stock value.[1]

When the boom finally subsided after 1981, however, Texas Commerce faced several difficult adjustments. Bank managers moved to consolidate and protect the dramatic gains of the previous decade and braced for the impact of the boom-to-bust cycle on the loan portfolio of the individual member banks. Since fewer loans could be made in the oil industry, Texas Commerce's bankers sought alternative markets. Management also had to adjust to less flattering treatment in the financial press, including the wide publicity given to the end of the streak of growth in quarter-to-quarter earnings in the spring of 1985 and the announcement of the first quarterly loss in the bank's modern history in the winter of 1985.[2]

One suggestive measure of Texas Commerce's overall record in this volatile era is Table 13.1, which summarizes the growth of the

Table 13.1 Loans by Lending Groups at Texas Commerce–Houston, 1970–84

End of the Year	Metropolitan	International	Lending Group Real Estate	Energy	National
1970	$ 255,183,221	$ 15,153,420	$ 147,941,885	$ 60,327,661	$ 103,538,022
1971	285,369,606	48,381,394	162,200,509	71,949,658	85,503,926
1972	325,053,000	45,836,000	159,115,000	91,352,000	100,966,000
1973	443,896,365	62,834,539	249,936,599	113,678,943	158,272,935
1974	460,026,596	69,759,129	306,581,397	191,910,665	213,558,401
1975	443,896,365	73,384,501	306,652,215	303,323,391	197,332,683
1976	449,387,145	76,449,888	338,817,702	373,243,765	234,101,960
1977	569,858,507	45,765,932	428,663,833	394,262,179	271,917,871
1978	681,654,412	93,863,737	517,097,250	583,578,751	353,481,139
1979	669,257,400	352,140,398	829,148,709	736,355,073	596,242,733
1980	791,525,552	416,187,262	883,734,240	919,439,932	747,597,978
1981	1,116,691,426	596,927,704	1,252,620,645	1,573,359,283	858,367,096
1982	1,239,813,427	650,152,319	1,546,816,049	1,852,615,638	1,172,920,509
1983	1,431,486,396	801,586,332	1,764,515,970	2,005,056,035	1,447,696,612
1984	1,538,096,952	751,194,494	2,238,276,756	1,969,711,540	1,824,391,252

SOURCE: End of Year Balance Sheets, Financial Accounting, TCB Archives.

various lending divisions of TCB–Houston after 1970. The marked
expansion of all the major lending areas of the bank is evidence of its
broad involvement in a dynamic economy with strengths in areas
other than oil-related activities. In the decade after the oil embargo of
1973, the bank's energy lending grew twenty times, but this specialized area was simply one center of growth in an organization expanding vigorously throughout its operations. Indeed, with the elimination
of all lending by the energy group, the remainder of the bank's loan
portfolio grew by a factor of twelve in the years from 1970 to 1984.

Oil lending, of course, remained an important part of the business of Texas Commerce, and the level of lending in this vital sector of
the economy mirrored the level of activity in the oil fields of the southwest. The impact of changing oil prices on drilling is best indicated by
the standard measure of drilling activity, the Hughes Tool rig count.
Taken together, Figures 13.1 (below), 8.1 (p. 140), and 10.1 (p. 212)
place recent trends in a long-run perspective. After a steady decline
from 1955 to 1973, drilling recovered dramatically throughout the remainder of the 1970s before peaking in 1981 at more than four times

**Figure 13.1. Rotary-rig count in Texas, the Southwest (Texas,
Oklahoma, Louisiana), and the United States, 1973–85.**

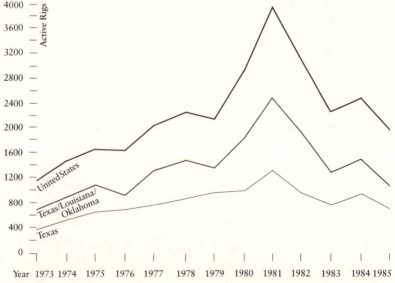

SOURCE: Hughes Tool Company, Rotary Rigs Running—by States, Annual Averages.

the low point of 1970. The fall from these heights was equally spectacular. When oil prices softened after 1981, the rig count plummeted back to levels more in keeping with the long-run trend established from 1970 to 1979.[4] The rig count obviously is not a comprehensive measure of oil-related activity in Texas or in the Houston area, but the direct and indirect impacts of drilling on broad sectors of the economy make it one useful indicator of the trends in the oil industry which shaped the business of Houston's major banks in the years after 1971.

As in the past at Texas Commerce–Houston, in the 1970s loans secured by oil production continued to account for roughly half the bank's total energy loan portfolio. In expanding its commitments to traditional customers among the large oil companies to the higher levels allowed by its growing legal lending limit and in seeking the business of new accounts, Texas Commerce sought to apply its historical strengths in energy lending to the new situations created by the oil boom and bust. The bank's energy lending officers continued to be predominantly petroleum engineers having previous experience with the major oil companies. Their technical expertise in reservoir engineering was reinforced by the knowledge of financial analysts recruited from the bank's credit training program. A strong, active board of directors with numerous ties to the petroleum industry supported the efforts of the energy lenders, while the approval of all large loans by a committee of senior officials of the bank served as a safeguard against problems which might arise if individual lending officers became overzealous in their pursuit of loans. As Texas Commerce entered the 1970s, it thus

---

Oil Prices

Since 1971 changes in the price of oil have directly affected banking in Texas more than any other factor. Figure 13.2 shows the trends in oil prices since World War II with two measures, the price of oil in current dollars and the price of oil adjusted for inflation. The roller-coaster ride of the Texas economy since 1971 has closely followed the pattern suggested by this chart, and all the major bank holding companies in the state faced both extraordinary opportunities and severe challenges in this economy in flux.

The abrupt changes in oil prices after 1971 were especially demanding because they came at the end of the longest era of relative price stability in the history of the petroleum industry. For almost a quarter of a century after World War II, the oil regulatory system put in place during the Great Depression in the United States worked to limit the supply of oil, thereby stabilizing the price and promoting conservation (see text). By the early 1970s, the major foreign producers managed to gain control over the international price of oil through concentrated actions within the Organization of Petroleum Exporting Countries. Since that time, price changes by OPEC have shaped the world petroleum industry while also greatly affecting the world economy. These price fluctuations had a direct impact on all major oil-producing regions both inside and outside OPEC, and the oil-rich Texas economy was particularly influenced by such wide variations in the price of its primary raw material.

The timing of the post-1971 price changes are thus of direct relevance to the history of Texas Commerce, since much of the bank's business in its major markets directly or indirectly responded to oil price fluctuation. The 38-cents-per-barrel jump in the price of OPEC oil in 1971—which seemed of historical proportions at the time—reflected the ability of Libya to extract a higher price for its oil followed by the demand of other OPEC producers for similar increases. The winter of 1973–74 then marked the beginning of a new era in the pricing of oil, as the growing dependence of the industrialized nations on OPEC oil and the embargo of Arab oil to the United States and other supporters of Israel helped more than quadruple the price of oil charged by mem-

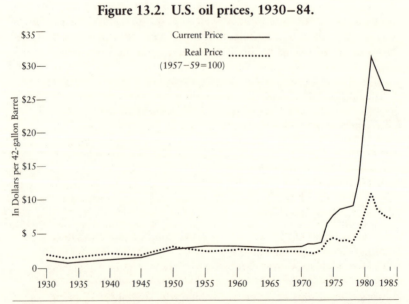

Figure 13.2. U.S. oil prices, 1930–84.

SOURCE: James M. Griffin and Henry B. Steele, *Energy Economics and Policy*, 2nd ed., 16.

bers of OPEC, which by that time were supplying more than half the world's production of oil. The price established during this embargo remained relatively stable and even declined slightly in real dollars until 1979, giving the world economy a brief era in which to adjust to the much higher prices. Then in 1979–81, the prevailing price again more than doubled as disruptions of supply caused by the Iranian revolution and by a simultaneous cutback in production by Saudi Arabia threw oil markets into a panic, driving prices as high as $40 per barrel before OPEC officially established a new price of $34 in October, 1981. This second round of price increases set off a frenzy of activity in the world petroleum industry, with various experts vying to project just how high oil prices would rise in the coming decades.

The 1981 price, however, proved unsustainable, as both conservation and the development of alternative, non-OPEC sources of production decreased the demand for OPEC oil. A price slide then began as OPEC cut its price in 1983 and again in the next two years. Then in early 1986, the gradual decline of the previous years accelerated sharply in response to OPEC's decision to suspend its efforts to sustain oil prices through production quotas. By February of 1986, contract prices for Texas oil had fallen as low as $20 per barrel, with bids for oil on the New York Mercantile Exchange dipping down toward $17 per barrel. No one can say with certainty at this time whether or where the world price of oil will stabilize in coming years, although many of the experts who in 1981 projected a steady movement upward in price over the next two decades are now projecting a price decline over the same period.

Because of the major role of oil-related activity in the Texas economy, such price changes have significant implications for the state as a whole. The state's economic boom of the 1970s was produced by the combination of the ongoing maturation of the Texas economy and the added impetus of oil price increases. The downturn of the 1980s reflects primarily rapid adjustments to much lower oil prices. One much-publicized study released in early 1986, for example, suggested that the decline in oil prices cost the Texas economy approximately 113,000 jobs in manufacturing and mining-related business from 1981 to 1985 and concluded that each additional decline of one dollar per barrel in the price of Texas oil would cost the state 25,000 additional jobs and $100 million in state and local tax revenue.

SOURCES: Peter Odell, *Oil and World Power: A Geographical Interpretation*; Steven Schneider, *The Oil Price Revolution* (Baltimore, Md.: Johns Hopkins University Press, 1983); James Griffin and David Teece (eds.), *OPEC Behavior and World Oil Prices* (London: George Allen & Unwin, 1982); "Study Warns Oil Slump Could Cost 25,000 Jobs," *Houston Chronicle* (February 9, 1986): section 1, page 1.

had in place a system of energy lending developed and tested over several decades and guided by experienced oil lenders.[5]

In evaluating potential loans on oil production, the bank's energy lending officers applied an approach originally developed in the 1950s and tested in the downturn in the domestic oil industry after 1956. The key variables examined were the current and projected future price of oil, the projected interest rates, and the estimate of proved reserves recoverable from a producing property. After conservative calculations of each of these variables, further safety was ensured by making loans up to only one-half of the future net revenues projected for a producing property.[6]

Before the 1970s, relatively stable prices and interest rates meant that engineering evaluations were the primary source of uncertainty in extending credit against producing properties. Because of this, Texas Commerce had developed technical personnel and a tradition of close involvement in reservoir evaluation which stood it in good stead in the boom years of the 1970s. As the rig count and the bank's production loan portfolio grew steadily after 1973, the staff of five petroleum engineers employed by TCB–Houston tripled by the early 1980s. During the rapid expansion of drilling between 1973 and 1979, this growing staff allowed Texas Commerce to keep pace with the new demands for reservoir estimates needed to support loan approvals. But the flurry of drilling set off by the second price shock in 1980 placed even greater demands on a technical staff already stretched thin. With old and new companies seeking to finance the highest level of drilling recorded in the United States since the compilation of reliable statistics, keeping pace proved difficult for the bank's technicians. Additional staff was needed, but petroleum engineers with the applied experience desired by the bank proved difficult to find, hire, and train amid an industry-wide scramble for qualified personnel. In the short but intense drilling boom of 1980–82, the bank's engineers made more evaluations, often based on less producing history for a property than had been the case traditionally, and their estimates of potential production became somewhat less accurate.[7]

Price was a second area of considerable uncertainty to oil lenders as they supplied the massive financing needs of the domestic industry. After 1973, the old guides to the price of oil no longer worked. They were replaced by widespread confusion over the long-run fate of OPEC, whose power over oil prices rested on a narrow economic identity of interest among quite diverse producing nations united only by their common interest in establishing and maintaining a higher world price for oil. OPEC's decisions were not easily predictable with the tools of economic analysis, since—at least in the short run—political forces often outweighed supply and demand in the setting of levels of production and thus of price. At no time was this uncertainty as painfully evident as in the wake of the second price shock in 1981. In response to spiraling oil prices, many experts inside and outside the oil industry came to the conclusion that the price of oil had reached a new plateau from which it would gradually increase to as much as $80 per barrel by the end of the century. Texas Commerce joined most of the rest of the oil fraternity in accepting this view, though it continued to design its loans with a considerable safety factor and what seemed at the time to be conservative estimates of future oil price rises. To bankers, the price of oil did not seem to be the major consideration in oil lending as of 1981, since normal production loans generally were fully amortized by the fifth or sixth year of production from a property, a period in which expert opinion almost universally projected a stable to steadily rising oil price. When the experts proved wrong and prices began to slide down after the winter of 1981, Texas Commerce's conservative assumptions regarding price projections and its inclusion of a safety factor proved important in limiting the damage done by falling oil prices to its oil production loans.[8]

Declining oil prices in the 1980s had a positive effect on the third and final variable in the formula used by Texas Commerce in calculating the terms of oil-production loans: projected interest rates. In discounting future earnings to current value, the bank's experience in the 1970s dictated the use of high interest-rate projections, which decreased the current value attributed to the oil reserves for lending purposes. As oil prices climbed, so did interest rates. When prices turned down, interest rates followed, thereby improving the discounted value of the borrower's property and absorbing some of the impact of the falling price of oil on outstanding loans.

In this and other cases, changes in oil prices were a two-edged sword even in Texas. As a major producing state, Texas greatly benefited from OPEC's ability to raise oil prices; but along with the United States economy as a whole, Texas also suffered from the high inflation and higher prices paid by consumers of energy within the state. On balance, Texas and Texas Commerce clearly stood to gain more than they lost from oil price increases. But the existence of broad economic benefits from lower energy prices cushioned a small part of the shock of price declines on the Texas economy in the 1980s. One example of this cushioning effect was even apparent in the energy group at TCB–Houston, where loans to petrochemical companies expanded in response to falling oil prices. Petrochemical plants, which were energy-intensive and used large amounts of hydrocarbons in their production processes, joined other energy-intensive regional industries in responding favorably to a drop in oil prices.

In response to changed conditions in the oil industry in the mid-1980s, Texas Commerce reassessed its energy lending procedures, introducing several modifications of its traditional practices. First, in response to increasing uncertainties associated with price, interest rates, and recoverable reserve estimates, TCB–Houston instituted sophisticated computer-based analyses of the sensitivity of individual loans to ranges of potential value for each of these variables. A second modification reflected ongoing changes in oil financing. Whereas before about 1981 petroleum engineers had been the crucial technical contributors to oil lending, after that time financial analysts took on a greater importance as the financial balance sheets of producing companies became more complicated with the advent of new methods of financing and the consolidation of the accounts of various merged companies. A broader strategic lesson of these years was that Texas Commerce was best prepared to serve the financial needs of the largest oil companies or those with the demonstrated capacity to grow into large companies. As National Bank of Commerce and Texas National Bank had done in the early 1950s, Texas Commerce responded to the new opportunities presented by the oil boom of the 1970s by expanding its business with independent oil producers. In the period of consolidation in the oil industry after the early 1980s, TCB–Houston responded much as its predecessors had during the downturn in drilling after 1956. It focused its attentions on the financial needs of the most secure, predictable cluster of energy concerns, the major vertically integrated companies and the largest regionally based independents.[9]

Within the half of the energy loan portfolio not secured by oil production, the cycle of boom and bust in the oil industry after 1971 also presented both great opportunities and risks. Loans to petroleum service and supply companies made up as much as one-third of all of the energy-related loans of Texas Commerce. These companies profited greatly from the boom in drilling after 1973 and suffered equally dramatic problems in the downturn after 1981. Texas Commerce enjoyed historically strong working ties with several of the largest service and supply companies in the industry, notably Hughes Tool Company and Cameron Iron Works, and such companies remained the focus of the bank's lending to this important regional industry. Such substantial, experienced companies had greater staying power during hard times than did most of their smaller competitors, particularly the newcomers who entered the industry in response to the surge in drilling from

1979 to 1981. Although the serious economic problems in the oil service and supply industries after that date affected all companies in the industry, smaller and less experienced concerns proved especially vulnerable. Texas Commerce experienced problems with oil service and supply loans as the declining price of oil severely curtailed drilling, but its historical focus on the largest, most experienced companies in the industry helped cushion its losses. The ongoing difficulties faced by all segments of these important regional industries nonetheless remain a concern for all of the major Texas banks.

Amid the fluctuations in the oil industry, drilling companies active both on and offshore also offered energy lenders the possibility of great profits and debilitating losses. From the 1930s forward, Texas Commerce had been cautious in making loans secured by drilling rigs, since rigs idled by changing conditions in the industry were of little value. The wisdom of this position had been demonstrated quite clearly during the long downturn in drilling after the mid-1950s. The head of energy lending at Texas Commerce as the boom of the 1970s began was John Townley, whose conservative approach was shaped by the fact that during his first fifteen years at the bank he had lived through an extended and largely unpredicted downturn in drilling. Despite strong competitive pressures to become more aggressive in extending loans to drilling companies, Texas Commerce held to its traditional conservative standards. As had been the case since the early days of energy lending at the National Bank of Commerce, TCB–Houston continued to do business primarily with established drillers with records of success and the personal confidence of the bank's officers. The bank further minimized risks by lending mainly to companies which utilized at least 50 percent of their rigs in their own operations. Finally, the ultimate safeguard against serious problems in this area was simply to keep loans to drilling companies to a relatively small percentage of the entire energy-related portfolio. Thus when the severe downturn in drilling came in 1982, Texas Commerce's energy-related loan portfolio included only about 6 percent in rig loans, most of which were to large companies best positioned to withstand an extended downturn in the industry. In comparison to many other energy lenders, Texas Commerce's losses in this volatile area have been relatively small, with the notable exception of the highly publicized write-off in 1985 of much of a $34 million loan to the drilling company of Pat Rutherford, Jr., a second-generation director and a large depositor of the bank. Even such long-lived and seemingly secure banking relationships could pose risks in the deepening depression in the oil industry.[10]

Problems of the oil industry in the 1980s sharply reduced the de-

mand for bank financing for expansion while at the same time encouraging the rapid growth of another sort of lending, the financing of the
wave of acquisitions which spread through all levels of the petroleum
industry in the 1980s. Acquisition financing was not new to Texas
Commerce or to the oil industry. Indeed, as early as the 1950s, the
bank had participated in the financing of the expansion and diversification of Tenneco, one of the first of the conglomerates. Throughout
the history of the industry, independent oil companies regularly had
been acquired by major oil companies and larger independents. But a
more fundamental restructuring of the industry began in response to
the widespread problems of the 1980s, setting off an unprecedented
wave of acquisitions which involved many traditional customers of
Texas Commerce, and its participation in the financing of mergers and
acquisitions increased. Texas Commerce traditionally had shied away
from the financing of unfriendly acquisitions. But in the 1980s, it
joined most other financial institutions in evaluating applications for
such loans on the basis of the projected financial performance of the
company seeking financing, without regard for the tone of the proposed transaction. Controversy often surrounded this type of lending,
particularly in Houston, where for a time most major petroleum companies were potential participants in life-or-death struggles for corporate survival. This wave of acquisitions in oil appears to have crested in
the mid-1980s, with the mergers of Standard Oil of California and
Gulf Oil, Mobil and Superior, and Texaco and Getty. Numerous other
acquisitions and near acquisitions, notably those of then Texas Commerce director T. Boone Pickens, of Mesa Petroleum of Amarillo,
boosted the bank's energy-related loan portfolio while also embroiling
the bank at least indirectly in the controversy inevitably accompanying
such highly publicized and bitterly contested transactions.[11]

Until a longer historical perspective is possible, one available context for evaluating the history of energy lending at Texas Commerce
during the hectic years in the oil industry since the early 1970s is a
brief comparison of its record with those of other energy lenders. All of
the major Texas bank holding companies took advantage of the economic boom of the 1970s and the opportunities afforded by the acquisition of member banks to enjoy sustained expansion and high profitability in that decade. In the 1980s, however, all have been battered
by the downturn in oil-related activities in the Southwest, some more
severely than others. InterFirst Corporation and First City Bancorporation thus far have experienced the most publicized problems, but
no major energy lender in Texas or throughout the nation can be com-

pletely insulated from the mounting uncertainties in oil-related industries in the 1980s.

In Texas banking, InterFirst's problems first received public scrutiny. In the third quarter of 1983, this Dallas-based holding company announced what at that time were the largest quarterly losses in U.S. banking history. These losses come from a variety of sources, notably loans to companies drilling deep wells in search of natural gas in the Anadarko Basin in Oklahoma, to large West Texas independents, and to numerous small and medium-sized oil service companies. Texas Commerce did not share the troubles experienced by InterFirst in Oklahoma deep-gas ventures, at least in part because it was not as close to Oklahoma and had no traditional customers who entered these fields. First City also encountered much-publicized problems, as a result of the post-1981 difficulties of small to medium-sized oil field supply and service companies, contract drillers, and small petroleum refiners, markets traditionally more important to that bank than to Texas Commerce. As these two companies experienced difficulties, Texas Commerce moved aggressively to expand its market share at their expense. This decision reflected Texas Commerce's assumption that the downturn in the state's oil-related industries was temporary; the accuracy of this assumption, as well as the timing and magnitude of future oil price changes, will determine the long-term success of this strategy. Although Texas Commerce initially avoided most of the adverse publicity generated by worsening conditions in the oil-related sectors of the Texas economy, its poor financial results in 1985 received considerable publicity in business publications.[12]

No discussion of the performance of Texas Commerce and its major Texas competitors would be complete, however, without at least noting the fates of several less fortunate energy lenders. The rush by banks throughout the nation to expand energy loans peaked after the second oil price shock produced a scene reminiscent of jazz banking in the 1920s. The national symbol of this oil-induced insanity became Penn Square National Bank, a small bank in a shopping center in Oklahoma City. Penn Square grew spectacularly during the oil boom of the late 1970s by syndicating packages of energy loans to much larger banks. When boom turned to bust in the early 1980s, Penn Square was closed by federal regulators amid mounting problems with questionable loans. The fallout from Penn Square's activities severely damaged several once-proud major banks, notably Seafirst (Seattle) and Continental Illinois of Chicago. The major Texas banks managed to avoid this fiasco, in part because their experience indicated that

Penn Square was not a reliable energy lender and in part because they had all the business they could handle without buying loans prepared by a little-known smaller bank.[13]

A less publicized but much more sobering crash closer to home affected all the major Texas banks, some more severely than others. The failure in 1983 of the First National Bank of Midland, which had a long and well-deserved reputation as one of the best energy lending banks in Texas, touched the business and the exposed nerves of all energy lenders. Attempting to build on its long tradition as the local bank of oilmen in the prolific Permian Basin producing region, First Midland pursued a policy of aggressive expansion throughout the 1970s based on the assumption of continued increases in oil prices. When prices turned down in the early 1980s, First Midland had neither the capital base nor the diversified loan portfolio needed to withstand the mounting pressures on its operations produced by the problems of many of its major accounts and of the regional economy as a whole. The large Dallas and Houston banks traditionally had served as major correspondents for First Midland, and they absorbed substantial losses on loans originated by First Midland. After the bank's failure, parts of its loan portfolio and its franchise were purchased by RepublicBank. The closing chapter in the history of this major West Texas oil lender stands as lasting testament to the force of the tornado which raged through the state's oil industry in the early 1980s.[14]

The ability of Texas Commerce to weather this storm reflected the effectiveness of its traditional lending philosophy and control systems and the experience of its top managers. It also reflected the bank's balanced growth during the boom years of the 1970s. As Table 13.1 above shows, energy lending was not the only source of lending expansion in this period. Indeed, all of the major lending groups of the bank posted substantial gains in the years after 1971. As a result, both lending and deposits became more diversified, even as the attention of the nation remained focused on the impact of changes in oil prices on the Texas economy. Of course, much of the nonenergy business of Texas Commerce was indirectly affected by changes in the oil industry, which remained a central part of the Texas economy as a whole. But while coping with the extreme fluctuations in the oil industry in this era, Texas Commerce was able to build on traditional strengths of TCB–Houston outside petroleum while also incorporating additional strengths from member banks in new markets throughout Texas.

Nonenergy lending in the Houston metropolitan area had surged in the late 1960s, and it expanded even more rapidly in response to the overall growth of the region induced by the oil boom of the 1970s. In this decade, the market facing Texas Commerce's metropolitan group became larger and more diversified with the rapid growth of the Houston-area economy. It also became more competitive, as banks based in Houston, Dallas, and other regions of the nation and in foreign countries increased their activities in one of the fastest-growing banking markets in the nation. In response, the metropolitan group further refined its calling program by segmenting the market into smaller groupings most effectively served by specialized lending officers. The division of accounts by Standard Industrial Classification set up in the late 1960s was supplemented by the further division of the responsibilities for accounts by the size of the company and by its location within the Houston area. In dividing the booming metropolitan area market by industry, size, and geography, the bank defined the responsibilities of individual officers so as to continue to build the expertise needed to meet the specialized needs of different segments of the market.[15]

Included in the accounts of the metropolitan group were numerous locally based companies whose businesses were directly or indirectly affected by conditions in the oil industry. Such business was a source of great strength for Texas Commerce during the 1970s, but many of these accounts also subsequently proved particularly vulnerable during the economic downturn of the early 1980s. Beginning in the 1960s, Texas Commerce had sought to expand its presence in the so-called middle market in the Houston area while retaining the large commercial accounts which had long been the mainstay of its business. This strategy paid dividends, as Texas Commerce became more broadly involved in a regional economy that was expanding at all levels in the 1970s. When companies in segments of this middle market most severely hurt by declining oil prices began experiencing severe problems after 1981, Texas Commerce had to work through a cluster of problem loans. The potential rewards of the middle market were accompanied by risks which were much more apparent in the downturn of the 1980s than they had been in the sustained expansion of the previous decade.

The most impressive gains registered by Texas Commerce in the period after 1971 came in an area not directly affected by fluctuations in the price of oil. The business of TCB–Houston's national group expanded dramatically in the 1970s and 1980s as more and more companies from other sections of the nation entered the thriving markets created by the sustained development of Houston and of Texas as a whole. The growth in lending by the national group from approximately $100 million in 1972 to almost $2 billion by the mid-1980s reflected the bank's growing commitment of resources to this area and the marked impact of a steadily increasing legal lending limit on the size of loans to major corporations. By the 1980s an area which only decades before had been the domain of A. D. Simpson and a few assistants had come to include more than fifty lending officers. The primary mission of this greatly expanded group, however, remained the same: to establish banking relationships with companies from outside the region which had significant operations or a substantial customer base in the bank's traditional markets. Yet the expanding list of potential accounts and the entry of Texas Commerce into major markets throughout Texas through its member banks made necessary the reorganization and reorientation of the national group.[16]

The burst of economic activity in Texas in the 1970s ensured that most large companies active in the United States would ultimately become involved in the state. Instead of waiting for an indication of an impending move into Texas by a specific company, the national group of TCB–Houston intensified a systematic calling program directed at the *Fortune* 1000 list of the nation's largest industrial corporations. Such a program was accompanied by the creation of geographical divisions within the national group, with individual lending officers assigned to a specific section of the nation. This change facilitated both traveling arrangements and the development of a specialized knowledge of the sectional markets.

The bank made a particularly strong, concerted effort to build on its traditional ties in the five-state "Southwestern Division," which included Texas, Louisiana, Oklahoma, Arkansas, and New Mexico. Within this broad section of the nation, Texas Commerce had extensive business experience developed through decades of previous involvement in correspondent banking and in the financing of oil, cotton, and other commodities. The growth of its network of member banks in Texas placed Texas Commerce even nearer to markets in surrounding states, and the Houston-based national group systematically coordinated their activities and those of lending officers in the member banks by sharing information about companies contemplating moves into various parts of Texas and by making joint calls on potential new accounts of the member banks.[17]

The activities of member banks also strengthened the ties of Texas Commerce to Mexico. Texas Commerce's representative office in Mexico City facilitated transactions with major accounts, and large member banks in three border cities, El Paso, Brownsville, and McAllen, placed Texas Commerce in an excellent position to expand its business in Mexico. In international banking, Texas Commerce continued to follow the basic philosophy which had guided its activities outside the United States since the early days of its foreign Department: lend only in areas with significant economic ties to Texas. This made Mexico the focus of much of the expansion of the international group. Japan's strong trade ties to the port of Houston also made it a natural area of expansion. In addition to these two primary foreign markets, Texas Commerce also developed a growing business in Brazil and Venezuela, in Korea in the Far East, in Saudi Arabia, and in the United Kingdom, the Netherlands, and Germany. The growing loan portfolio of the international group in the 1970s was heavily weighted toward the financing of energy and agriculture. Roughly half of these loans were trade-related, and generally financed traffic shipped through Texas Gulf Coast ports.

One particularly important segment of this business involved government-owned oil companies in Latin America. Such banking relationships obviously were affected by the ups and downs of oil prices after 1971. Mexico and its national oil company, PEMEX, were most significantly affected, since large deposits of oil and natural gas were discovered in Mexico in the mid- to late 1970s. These giant new fields promised to make Mexico a major force in the international petroleum industry while providing much-needed exports, and banks throughout the United States and the world found good reason to help finance a variety of projects in Mexico in the years before the downturn in oil prices. A debt crisis developed in Mexico in the summer of 1982, when loans designed in the expectation of rising oil revenues proved troublesome as prices began to decline. Texas Commerce, which had an overall exposure of approximately $300 million in loans to Mexico at that time, joined in the prolonged negotiations which led to the restructuring of much of Mexico's debt to foreign banks.[18]

The exposure of Texas Commerce in international lending was small relative to that of many of the larger money center banks, many of which encountered continuing uncertainties in developing nations in the 1980s. In this area, Texas Commerce's small size relative to the money center banks and its traditional policy of lending primarily in areas and to individuals and institutions with strong personal or trade ties with Houston-area businesses proved fortunate. Unwilling and unable to risk the extreme exposure taken on by many larger money-center banks in potentially volatile international markets, Texas Commerce avoided most of the serious problems which have hampered the repayment of the giant international loans outstanding at the largest American banks.

Of all areas of growth in its primary markets during the economic boom of the 1970s, Texas Commerce was perhaps best positioned to take advantage of the surge in construction. Texas Commerce Bancshares had a growing presence in most of the state's major cities, and the real estate group of the Houston flagship bank had excellent traditional relationships with most of the largest mortgage companies in its region. In addition, the banking organization built strong working ties with three premier Texas-based developers, Kenneth Schnitzer and Gerald Hines, of Houston, and Trammell Crow, of Dallas. As the construction boom of the 1970s began, Texas Commerce had an established market position and experienced personnel in real estate lending, and it capitalized on these strengths to build this segment of its loan portfolio from $162 million in 1971 to more than $2.2 billion in 1984.

Texas Commerce remained particularly active in the Houston area, where the construction of downtown office buildings after 1970 redrew the city's skyline. Table 13.2 shows the outlines of the construction boom in Houston, with downtown construction expanding rapidly from 1970 to 1974, pausing as the new office space was absorbed, and then again growing dramatically after 1980. While a new generation of downtown office buildings was being built, several "mini-downtowns"—notably the Galleria, Greenway Plaza, and the American General complex—grew outside the traditional central business district, so that by 1985 more than 70 percent of the general office space in the Houston area was in the suburbs. Office buildings were not the only construction undertaken in this era; expenditures on all types of construction in Harris County (Houston) grew from approximately $435 million in 1960 to more than $4 billion in 1984. Clearly, those well positioned to make sound construction loans to major Houston-area developers had plenty of opportunities to do so in this era.

Opportunities for real estate lending certainly were not confined to Houston. Although Texas Commerce—Houston originated approximately two-thirds of the total real estate loans of the holding company (as of 1982), about 30 percent of these were outside the Houston area, with Dallas accounting for most of the loans. The member banks outside Houston and Dallas were active in real estate lending in their markets, giving Texas Commerce good knowledge of local conditions in major population centers throughout the state. Finally, although Texas

Table 13.2 Major New Buildings in Houston, 1972–85
(500,000 square feet or more gross area)

Year Completed	Name	Square Footage	Floors
Central Business District:			
1972	One Allen Center	1,093,100	34
1973	1100 Milam Building	1,417,634	47
1973	Dresser Tower	1,137,000	40
1974	Two Houston Center	1,394,127	40
1975	Pennzoil Place (2 buildings)	1,815,379	36
1978	One Houston Center	1,288,960	46
1978	Two Allen Center	1,274,634	36
1980	InterFirst Plaza	1,411,725	55
1980	MCorp Plaza	1,500,196	50
1981	First City Tower	1,449,397	49
1981	Texas Commerce Tower	1,983,234	75
1982	Texas Commerce Center	1,100,000	18
1982	Gulf Tower	1,335,110	52
1983	The Park in Houston Center	687,000	16
1983	RepublicBank Center	1,515,103	53
1983	United Bank Plaza	802,560	45
1983	Four Allen Center	1,361,656	50
1983	Allied Bank Plaza	2,098,440	71
1984	First City Financial Center	1,154,400	24
1984	1600 Smith Street	1,192,649	52
Suburban Areas:			
1972	Kellogg Building	550,000	21
1973	Shell Oil Information Center	545,350	10
1973	Geosource Plaza	507,000	25
1973	Five Greenway Plaza	950,000	31
1976	Texaco, Inc.	500,000	10
1977	Union Texas Petroleum Building	595,000	25
1977	Gulf West Belt Center	586,689	3
1978	The Coastal Tower	550,000	21
1979	Summit Tower	800,000	31
1979	Brown & Root	605,000	3
1981	Weslayan Tower	541,094	17
1981	Bechtel Incorporated	683,000	9
1981	Shell Woodcreek (7 bldgs.)	839,358	5
1982	Sage Plaza	555,176	25
1982	MCO Plaza	517,259	22

Table 13.2   Major New Buildings in Houston, 1972–85, (*cont.*)
             (500,000 square feet or more gross area)

Year Completed	Name	Square Footage	Floors
1982	One Westchase Center	500,000	17
1982	Kaneb Building	510,000	10
1982	The Amoco Center (2 bldgs.)	1,005,000	28
1983	The American Tower	1,070,593	42
1983	Allied Bank in Four Oaks Place	589, 531	28
1983	Weatherford Tower in Four Oaks Place	528,574	25
1983	Central Tower in Four Oaks Place	528,574	25
1983	Interfin Building in Four Oaks Place	647,324	30
1983	Marathon Oil Tower	1,250,000	41
1983	Transco Tower	1,640,000	64
1983	Parkwest Tower One	603,917	25
1984	San Felipe Plaza	1,064,519	45
1984	Fluor Corp.–Houston (4 bldgs.)	1,263,167	7
1984	Woodcreek Plaza–Conoco (17 bldgs.)	1,200,000	2
1985	Arco Oil & Gas	596,222	6

SOURCE: Property Research and Investment Consultants, Inc., "Houston's Office Space Market" (June 1985).

Commerce remained committed to its traditional philosophy of concentrating on local markets which it knew best, it made significant exceptions for trusted, proved developers who undertook major projects outside Texas.

Texas Commerce placed great emphasis on the development of lasting relationships with the strongest builders in each market. This was a desirable goal for any bank, but Texas Commerce enjoyed notable success in achieving this goal with seasoned Lloyd Bolton and Stephen Field managing its real estate lending. The bank further protected its loans by lending only on an individual-project basis, by conducting its own cost analyses before approving a project, and by periodically inspecting construction sites. Acknowledging the historical risks associated with real estate construction lending, Texas Commerce went to considerable lengths in designing such loans to make them as secure as possible. But the ultimate source of security remained the experience and the financial strength of the primary developer. In a cyclical industry traditionally characterized by periods of rapid construction followed by periods of absorption, Texas Commerce sought major developers with the ability to weather both the inevitable downturns in the industry and unpredictable interest rates and overall economic conditions.[19]

One such account was that of Kenneth Schnitzer, whose Century Corporation was active in numerous significant commercial developments and a variety of supporting industries, including equipment leasing, land development, property management, and title insurance. Schnitzer's involvement in major construction projects in Houston began in the early 1950s, and his activities expanded steadily. After the successful completion in the 1960s of numerous projects, notably the Houston Natural Gas Building, in the central business district, Schnitzer embarked on the planning of Greenway Plaza, an ambitious mixed-use development southwest of downtown Houston. The choice of Texas Commerce as the local lead bank for this project reflected strong business and personal ties between Schnitzer and TCB–Houston. Indeed, Schnitzer's friendship with Ben Love dated from 1943, when Love had undergone Army Air Force cadet training with Ralph Schnitzer, Jr., the older brother of the future developer. Greenway Plaza grew steadily to encompass approximately 4.5 million square feet of office space, a luxury hotel, condominiums, and the Summit, an 18,000-seat sports and entertainment arena. Texas Commerce participated with several large life insurance companies in the financing of Greenway Plaza. The tie between Texas Commerce Bancshares and this major development was strengthened by the success of TCB–Greenway Plaza, a thriving member bank which grew with the plaza itself into a substantial bank with more than $100 million in assets. Texas Commerce also provided a portion of the financing of numerous other projects of the Century Development Corporation, including Allen Center—a mixed-use development in Houston's central business district—and the two-million-square-foot Allied Bank Plaza office tower in downtown Houston.[20]

Although based in Dallas, the Trammell Crow Company also grew into a major customer of Texas Commerce during the 1970s. From early successes in constructing warehouses in and around Dallas, Trammell Crow steadily built his operation to become one of the largest private real estate developers in the United States. Given his strong ties to Dallas, it was not surprising that Crow became a member of the board of one of the largest banks in that city, InterFirst Corporation. But as his business expanded throughout the state and as his interests in Houston grew, Crow also established banking ties with Texas Commerce. These ties were greatly strengthened in the mid-1970s, when Texas Commerce stood by Crow during a period of financial diffi-

culties. The growing significance of this account to Texas Commerce
was best symbolized by the inclusion on the board of TCB–Dallas and
then of Texas Commerce Bancshares of Harlan Crow, the son of
Trammell Crow and a partner in Trammell Crow Company.[21]

Also among the "big three" real estate accounts of Texas Commerce was Gerald Hines Interests, whose ties to predecessor banks of
Texas Commerce originated in the 1950s. The personal relationship of
Hines and Ben Love dated from 1950, when Hines was embarking on
his career as a developer and Love was in the manufacturing business.
Indeed, in the years before Love entered banking, Hines built a manufacturing plant for Love's company. Hines built a succession of major
office buildings in Houston beginning with One Shell Plaza and includ-
ing the Pennzoil Building, the Transco Tower, the Texas Commerce
Tower, InterFirst Plaza, and the RepublicBank Building. His projects
also took him to most major cities in the nation, notably New York,
Chicago, San Francisco, Seattle, Miami, Atlanta, and New Orleans,
and Texas Commerce served as Hines's lead bank in financing his
Houston-area projects as well as many of his out-of-state projects.[22]
The higher legal lending limit produced by the steady growth of Texas
Commerce Bancshares enabled TCB–Houston to increase its parti-
cipation in these projects, which were far larger than construction
projects traditionally financed by Texas banks before the 1970s.

Texas Commerce's real estate loans did not, of course, go exclusively to the big three, Hines, Crow, and Schnitzer. Through its member banks, Texas Commerce sought to identify developers with staying
power throughout its markets in Texas. Austin-based John Byram, who
sat on the board of Texas Commerce Bancshares in the 1980s, was an
experienced and successful developer with a track record established
over a twenty-year period. Among such accounts, Texas Commerce developed a profitable business, providing financing for the construction
of the varied projects needed by a booming state economy while seeking to develop working relationships with younger developers capable
of maturing into the next generation's big three.

Until the late 1970s, Texas Commerce, like most other banks,
made construction loans contingent on commitments for long-term
underwriting from other financial institutions such as major insurance
companies. Such "takeout" commitments meant that banks generally
provided only short-term construction financing, ending their involvement with the completion of a project. After 1979, however, changing
market conditions caused by high interest rates led many developers to
seek open-end construction loans without permanent takeout com-

The Texas Commerce Tower

The completion of the seventy-five-story Texas Commerce Tower in 1981 was a major event in the modern history of Texas Commerce Bancshares. At the time of its completion, it was the tallest building in Texas, the tallest building in the United States outside New York City and Chicago, and the tallest bank building in the world. Constructed at a cost of approximately $140 million and containing more than two million square feet of office space, the tower provided office space and a sense of identity to the holding company while also serving as a symbol of the banking organization's commitment to the region and the state.

Ironically, the construction of the Texas Commerce Tower was delayed by the work of Jesse Jones, who had died more than twenty years before the construction of the building began. The original preferred site for the new building was a block across Capitol Street from the Gulf Building. But Jones had feared that this block might be used to construct a building which would stand between his two prized possessions, the Gulf Building and the Rice Hotel, and he had helped split the ownership of the block among numerous individuals to prevent the purchase of the entire block for the construction of a major development which might rival his own buildings. After several years of effort to put the block back together, the management of Texas Commerce finally decided to build the tower across the street on a more easily acquired block. The bank later succeeded in purchasing the block it originally desired, which became the site of the Texas Commerce Center, a companion building to the tower which added more than one million square feet of gross area upon its completion in 1982.

The developer of the Texas Commerce Tower was Gerald Hines Interests. After a competition among several of the nation's premier architects, the design was awarded to I. M. Pei & Partners of New York and 3D International of Houston. The entrance to the building was set

back from the street to form United Energy Plaza, so named after the
largest single tenant. The landscaped street level plaza provided the
setting for a 55-foot sculpture by Joan Miró. The result was an elegant
building which dominated the northern edge of Houston's downtown
business district.

Interview with Gerald Hines by Joseph A. Pratt, February 22, 1985,
TCB Archives; John Bloom, "Three Gentlemen, One Ghost, and a Skyscraper," *Texas Monthly* (May 1980): 117–24; 242–62.

mitments. Texas Commerce moved into this new type of financing in
part to retain the business of valued customers who were being offered
open-end loans by money-center banks. As it sought to learn how to
evaluate the market risks of long-term involvement in real estate projects, the bank solicited the advice of experts among its established customers in the commercial mortgage business. The move into open-end
construction lending was a significant departure in the history of the
bank's real estate lending, and it attempted to minimize long-term risks
in this new market by adhering to concepts which traditionally had
guided its short-term construction lending: "We are selective about the
developer, his track record, capabilities and current exposure; we are
selective about the location; and we require equity either in the form
of cash contributed or the pledging of acceptable additional collateral.
We do not lend 100 percent of cost looking only to the project being
financed for value."[23] By 1982, open-end construction loans made up
approximately 25 percent of the real estate group's outstanding loans.
These long-term commitments embodied confidence in the future of
Texas and particularly of Houston, as well as its confidence in the judgment and staying power of the major developers served by Texas Commerce. As has so often been the case in the bank's history, long-term
trends in a currently depressed real estate market will ultimately determine the success or failure of open-end real estate lending.

In the mid-1980s, government regulators and segments of the financial press began to take a hard look at the real estate loan portfolios of the major Texas bank holding companies, including Texas
Commerce. As occupancy rates in downtown office buildings in Houston's central business district plunged from around 97 percent in 1978–
82 to approximately 80 percent in 1984 and 1985, concern grew that
problems in the region's economy would create real estate loan problems similar to those previously suffered by many energy lenders.[24]
This fear was fed by the knowledge that energy-related firms leased a

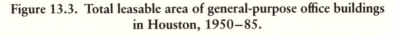

Figure 13.3. Total leasable area of general-purpose office buildings in Houston, 1950–85.

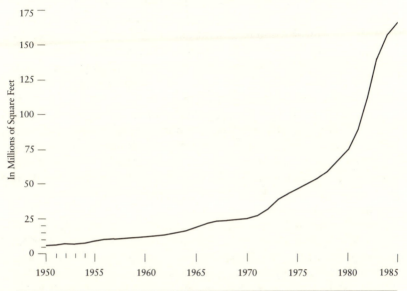

SOURCE: Property Research and Investment Consultants, Inc., "Houston's Office Space Market" (June 1985).

substantial percentage of the total office space in Houston and Dallas. Such fears were heightened by the fact that buildings completed in Houston between 1980 and 1985 more than doubled the total available office space in the city at a time when the downturn in economic activity was diminishing the demand for such space (see Figure 13.3).

Texas Commerce could do little to allay such fears, since even the effort to discuss the strengths of its real estate loan portfolio only fed further speculation about possible problem loans. One area of particular concern was the impact of the falling value of real estate projects on outstanding loans which had been designed on the assumption of the higher values prevailing in the late 1970s and early 1980s. The real estate lending group at TCB–Houston was included in an audit of major real estate lenders by the Office of the Comptroller of the Currency in 1985, and shortly thereafter the bank's management moved to strengthen its capacity to withstand potential future problems by substantially increasing its loan loss reserve.

Problems in the mid-1980s need not obscure the overall record of real estate lending at TCB–Houston. During the building boom in the decade after 1972, it recorded a tenfold increase in lending activity while suffering charge-offs for bad loans which averaged less than 0.1 percent annually. Such a record could not be expected to continue during a sharp downturn in construction which witnessed by 1985 a decline in new construction of general-purpose office buildings in Houston to the lowest levels in fifteen years. A return to economic growth in the region and the absorption of the office space completed in the massive wave of construction in the early 1980s will be required before an upturn in construction and construction lending is likely in Houston.

A final evaluation of the performance of Texas Commerce during the post-1971 cycle of boom and bust in its primary markets also must await the passage of time, as ongoing changes become absorbed by the regional and state economies. Yet standard measures of financial performance help place both the boom of the 1970s and the subsequent downturn in a longer perspective. Table 13.3 shows an organization sustaining a vigorous, profitable surge of expansion in the 1970s which pushed it to a new level of activity and made it a much more prominent force in the state and national financial communities. The table also suggests the slowing down of expansion amid the economic downturn of the 1980s, a process starkly symbolized by the posting of a loss in the final quarter of 1985. Despite this loss, which was caused in part by the desire to build loan loss reserves and forestall future problems, Texas Commerce Bancshares's overall net income for the entire year of 1985 was at a level not reached by the organization until 1978. The record of growth in Texas Commerce's past has set high standards against which to compare its present and future performance. Its ability to match these standards in the future will be shaped by the evolution of the Texas economy and its capacity to adjust to ongoing changes in its major markets.

As Texas Commerce sought to interpret and respond to changes in its primary markets in the 1970s and 1980s, it also faced fundamental changes in its regulatory environment. Competitive boundaries defined for over a quarter of a century by security-based regulations broke down rapidly in a wave of far-reaching regulatory reforms in the late 1970s and early 1980s. The ongoing movement to deregulate banking by removing many of the restrictions placed on commercial banks during the 1930s was as unpredictable and therefore unmanageable as it was significant. To be effective, bank managers had to monitor legislative and regulatory initiatives in an effort to anticipate future changes. They then had to make strategic choices on the basis of their best guesses about the pace, timing, and direction of regulatory

Table 13.3   Measures of Financial Performance by
Texas Commerce, 1973–85

Year	ROA TCBK[a]	ROA Top 25[b]	ROE TCBK[c]	ROE Top 25[d]
1973	0.90	0.62	13.37	12.35
1974	.87	.58	14.80	12.80
1975	.91	.58	15.47	12.31
1976	.89	.59	15.33	11.91
1977	.88	.61	15.76	12.65
1978	.93	.65	17.06	13.91
1979	1.00	.67	17.95	14.88
1980	1.11	.68	19.04	15.05
1981	1.20	.67	20.82	14.66
1982	1.15	.64	21.31	13.53
1983	1.09	.55	18.76	11.38
1984	.98	.38	16.79	7.04
1985	.27	.54	4.40	11.48
13-Year Average	0.94	.60	16.22	12.60

SOURCE: Statistics compiled from the Bank Scoreboard published annually in *Business Week*.

[a] Return on average assets of Texas Commerce Bancshares.

[b] Return on average assets of the twenty-five largest banks in the United States (as of December 31, 1984).

[c] Return on equity of Texas Commerce Bancshares.

[d] Return on equity of the twenty-five largest banks in the United States (as of December 31, 1984).

reform. The ground rules governing the operation of banks were being revised, and the lack of any consensus on the rules which would apply in the future created considerable uncertainty for bank planners.

Deregulation altered many aspects of commercial banking while blurring the lines that had separated various types of financial institutions into largely noncompeting industries since the 1930s. The impulse to deregulate the financial services industries generally reflected the impact of at least three long-term trends: (1) the introduction of ever-more-sophisticated information-processing equipment, allowing almost instantaneous posting of financial transactions and facilitating the calculation of the relative yield of various uses of money over short periods; (2) growing competition from other financial institutions in areas traditionally considered the domain of commercial banks; and (3) the general political movement of the recent past toward less gov-

ernment involvement in many areas of the economy. These trends culminated in a wave of regulatory changes which dramatically altered
the existing security-based banking system, pushing the pendulum
abruptly toward greater competitiveness in the ongoing effort by
bank regulators to balance the competing goals of security and
competitiveness.[25]

Texas Commerce and other regional banks primarily reacted to
deregulation; they had little control over the process of change. They
were not alone. At most times it seemed that no individual, organization, or interest group had much control over the process of deregulation. The result was a manager's nightmare: a series of fundamental
alterations in the rules of the game that sprang forth unpredictably,
filled with uncertainty and ambiguity. Even the designation of these
changes as "deregulation" exaggerates their overall coherence, since all
of the existing banking regulatory agencies remained intact and eager
to pursue their particular goals, often at the expense of coherent policy
within the regulatory system as a whole. As illustrated by the previously recounted history of the bank holding-company movement in
Texas, individual policy changes generally came in a haphazard, piece-
meal fashion. While regulators and legislators debated numerous alternatives, various financial services companies impatiently probed existing laws for loopholes which would allow them greater flexibility to
compete more aggressively.

One common justification for deregulation by both bankers and
regulators was that financial industries had been overprotected by
regulation at the cost of efficiency and that increased competition
would restore innovation and greater risk taking to these industries.
Yet when the risks became uncomfortably real in a wave of bank problems, culminating in the near collapse of the giant Continental Illinois
National Bank in 1984, regulators sought to pull in the reins on competitive practices by tightening the rules governing loan loss reserves
and the classification of problem loans. Because of the deep involvement of major Texas banks in two lending areas deemed particularly
risky in the mid-1980s, energy and real estate, they came in for special
attention from regulators in this period.[26]

In seeking to control the impact of deregulation on their organization, the managers of Texas Commerce and other banks had to respond to at least three general types of regulatory change: (1) the
loosening of geographical restrictions on competition among banks,
(2) the allowance of increased competition in the setting of interest
rates paid on deposits in financial institutions; and (3) the weakening
of traditional constraints or product competition among the various
types of financial services companies.

The bank holding-company movement which allowed Texas Commerce to build a statewide banking organization was no doubt the most significant regulatory change in this era of the bank's history, but a still broader movement toward interstate banking was potentially even more significant to the bank's future. Commercial banks had been limited to a single state in the 1920s and 1930s to safeguard against concentration of power over the credit system and to encourage local control of banks. The Bank Holding Company Act of 1956 effectively extended this geographical restriction to holding companies by allowing each state to define the rules governing bank holding companies within its boundaries. In recent decades, however, banks and regulators alike have sought pathways around this traditional restriction, which nonetheless remains a part of the nation's banking law in the mid-1980s.[27]

This did not mean, however, that banks were not active across state lines. Indeed, Texas Commerce faced direct competition in Houston and Dallas from numerous money-center banks, such as Citicorp, BankAmerica Corporation, and Chase Manhattan, which built substantial staffs in loan-production offices in Texas during the 1970s and 1980s. Such offices provided loans and services for large corporate clients, and they thus often directly competed with Texas Commerce. Banks from throughout the United States also established Edge Act offices in major Texas cities to handle international transactions. Additional competition came from the representative offices of foreign banks, which grew in number in Houston from 5 to 63 in the years from the early 1970s to the mid-1980s. Although out-of-state banks could not move into Texas and offer full banking services in a single location, they could and did establish offices to handle every specific banking transaction allowed by law.[28]

In the early 1980s, many banks began venturing into new territory beyond loan-production offices, and in so doing, they moved into a gray area of legality. With interstate banking seemingly on the horizon in these years, numerous banks sought head starts in building interstate systems by creating so-called nonbank banks outside their home states. The language of the 1970 amendments to the Bank Holding Company Act defined a bank as an institution that accepts demand deposits and makes commercial loans, leaving a loophole for interstate expansion for "consumer banks," which take deposits and make consumer, but not commercial, loans. When combined with the commercial-lending activities of a separately organized loan-production office, such nonbank banks could offer most of the services of traditional commercial banks. With its large population and bank deposits, Texas became a prime target of many of the money-center banks for the expansion of this new type of subsidiary. Despite the support of the comptroller of the currency, the growth of nonbank banks was sidetracked at least temporarily by a court decision in 1985 which blocked banks from collecting deposits outside their home states without regulatory permission from the state the bank was entering.[29]

Texas Commerce Chairman Ben Love lobbied against this variant of loophole banking, arguing that there were better, more rational alternatives, notably reciprocal regional interstate banking. The creation of banking organizations active in a multistate region could be accomplished with the permission of the states involved, since each state has the power to make laws governing branching and holding-company activities by banks within its boundaries. Thus if a cluster of states passed laws granting banks from all of the states reciprocal rights to conduct business throughout the multistate region, a regional banking system could be legally established. This path was first taken in New England and later in the southeastern United States, and Love joined others in Texas in arguing for the creation of a regional system including Texas and surrounding states. As Love and other bank spokesmen worked for the passage of enabling legislation in the states involved, Texas Commerce moved to establish a presence in surrounding states by purchasing holdings in attractive out-of-state banks up to the maximum 5 percent permitted by law in Louisiana, Oklahoma, New Mexico, Colorado, Arizona, and Wyoming. The management of Texas Commerce felt strongly that this collection of states—supplemented by Arkansas and Kansas—represented a natural region bound by traditional economic ties in energy and agriculture. They felt equally strongly that regional banking was a logical step in the evolution toward interstate banking, since regional banks would have an opportunity to grow stronger before facing unrestricted interstate competition from larger money-center banks.[30]

This concern for the competitive implications of interstate banking on Texas Commerce was not a reaction to the events of the mid-1980s but rather reflected a long-standing commitment of the bank's management to chart a strategy that would allow for the survival of the organization in competition with banks throughout the nation. As early as 1978, Love sought to encourage his top officers to think through the ramifications for Texas Commerce of interstate banking, which Love predicted would come within ten years. After asking for comments on several possible strategies to establish entry points in prime markets outside Texas, Love closed with the following statement: "Some day I suspect that some management at Texas Commerce and some Board at Texas Commerce will be confronted with the very

serious question as to whether this organization is to be acquired or is
to continue to be an acquirer. My suggestion is to construct strategy
which would forestall the former and assure the latter." [31] Central to
this strategy was the creation of a strong, large banking organization
with a stock value high enough to forestall acquisition by money-
center banks in the event interstate banking becomes a reality.

Along with the loosening of geographical restrictions on competition among banks, deregulation also encouraged competition on interest rates by removing government ceilings on such rates which had
been in effect since the 1930s. For a time, the prohibition of interest on
demand deposits and the relatively low ceiling on interest on demand
deposits were little debated, since commercial banks continued to attract sufficient deposits to fund their lending activities. Beginning in
the early 1960s, however, the ceiling on interest rates was gradually
modified so that banks could stop the migration of funds out of banks
in search of higher yields. Certificates of deposits allowing higher interest rates for very large depositors led the way. Then throughout the
1960s and 1970s, competition for deposits grew, with higher interest
rates for other categories of time deposits and finally the allowance of
interest on checking accounts. In 1980, Congress recognized the logic
of this long trend toward greater competition on interest rates by including in the Depository Institutions Deregulation and Monetary
Control Act arrangements for the gradual phase-out of all remaining
interest rate ceilings on bank deposits.

The impact of the growing competition for deposits can be seen
in Figure 13.4, which summarizes the decline of deposits as a source
of funding for Texas Commerce. In the world of traditional banking,
deposits had provided relatively inexpensive, reliable funding for banking activity. A secure, predictable deposit base set the tone of commercial banking. As deposits declined and as banks began paying competitive interest rates to attract deposits, bank managers were forced to
look for other sources of funds such as Eurodollars and to accept a
declining margin between the cost of money and the return on its use.
In short, bankers had to become more aggressive in securing funding,
a fact which heightened the competitiveness of banking while also
making the industry as a whole more volatile. Texas Commerce responded to these changes by entering the competitive search for funding and by pushing down noninterest expenses as one method of protecting its profit margin. [32]

Still another source of new competition in banking arose from
the loosening of regulatory boundaries between the various financial
services industries. The decade after the mid-1970s witnessed the

Figure 13.4. Source of funds of Texas Commerce, 1969–84.

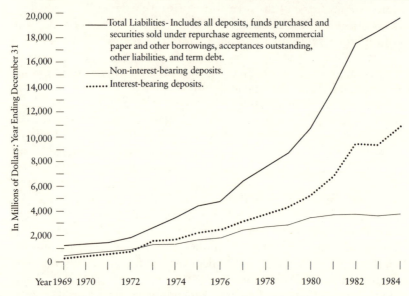

*Texas Commerce Bank before 1971; Texas Commerce Bancshares from 1971 forward.

emergence of a cluster of companies which sought to become "financial services supermarkets." Such companies as Citicorp, BankAmerica, Sears, and Merrill Lynch sought to diversify out of their traditional industries into a variety of closely related financial services, thus evolving into national firms capable of serving most of the financial needs of individuals and corporations. The exact mix of services to be provided differed within specific companies, but all seemed to share a long-run strategy of accumulating the resources and market position to survive as the major national concerns active in what they viewed as a unified emerging financial services industry.[33]

While monitoring these developments, the managers of Texas Commerce did not commit their organization to rapid diversification into a variety of financial services. Instead, they moved slowly into these unfamiliar areas, which were quite different from the corporate banking which had been TCB–Houston's historical strength. This posture was not new for Texas Commerce. When most of its major competitors had moved into the bank credit-card business and then established systems of automatic tellers in an effort to secure an increased share of the consumer market in the late 1960s and 1970s, Texas Commerce had not rushed into these ventures. After examining the potential profits and risks, it instead decided to invest its energies and resources in its traditional strength, wholesale or commercial banking for corporate accounts. It had built a thriving, profitable enterprise as a wholesale bank in a growing region, and it saw no reason to change this historical emphasis. Rapid changes in the emerging financial services industry in the 1980s nonetheless have raised far-reaching questions about the ability of Texas Commerce to remain profitable and competitive in its traditional niche as a commercial bank specializing in corporate accounts. With the growing attractiveness of consumer deposits in the 1980s as an alternative to more volatile sources of funding, Texas Commerce explored for ways of competing more effectively for such deposits.[34]

Far-reaching changes confronted Texas Commerce after 1971. As its managers sought to build an effective bank holding company and respond to basic regulatory reforms, they also had to contend with an intense cycle of boom and bust in the Texas economy. Texas Commerce surged forward on numerous fronts in the heady expansion brought by the oil-led boom of the 1970s. In the process, it solidified its traditional standing as one of the major financial institutions in Texas while also moving rapidly up the hierarchy of the nation's largest banks. As the Texas economy readjusted to falling oil prices in the 1980s, the expansion of the previous decade slowed dramatically. If viewed as a single—as yet unfinished—era in the history of Texas Commerce, the years from 1971 to 1986 stand out as a time of adjustment to sharp fluctuations in the oil-related sectors of the Texas economy. Although these fluctuations have not yet abated, it seems safe to assert that on balance this era brought much more good than harm to Texas Commerce.

CHAPTER 14

Conclusion: Banking and Regional Development

This book has focused on the role of Texas Commerce in financing development in Houston and a broad section of Texas and the Southwest. The title, *But Also Good Business,* reflects this focus by suggesting the close tie between the long-term profitability of the bank and the region's welfare. The title does not imply that what was good for the bank was good for the region; rather, it points to a broader identity of interest recognized by most bankers: what was good for the region ultimately contributed to the growth and profits of its banks.

This connection between Texas Commerce and regional development began with the founding of Commercial National in 1886. In the late nineteenth and early twentieth centuries nationally active companies with credit needs far in excess of the capacities of the young Houston banks were important initiators of regional growth. By integrating the region into the modern industrial economy, such concerns hastened development. The Southern Pacific and other major railroads tied the region into the national transportation system while also taking significant roles in the early histories of its banks. Anderson, Clayton and other nationally prominent cotton trading firms utilized Houston banks for the local credit needed to facilitate the flow of cotton from the interior through Houston. Major international oil companies such as Gulf Oil Corporation, the Texas Company, and Humble Oil and Refining Company also made use of local banks, primarily as convenient depositories for funds used in their local operations. In this role, the predecessors of Texas Commerce helped capture a measure of the resources used by these large concerns for regional development.

These resources were then available to numerous local entrepreneurs and the companies they built. Case studies of ties between Texas

Commerce and such regional concerns make up a significant portion of this book. The early histories of American General Insurance; various local cotton trading firms; Hughes Tool Company, Cameron Iron Works, and other large oil tool and service companies; numerous substantial independent oil producers such as R. E. (Bob) Smith; petroleum-related operations such as that of E. C. Scurlock; and Houston-based developers such as Gerald Hines and Kenneth Schnitzer provide evidence of the importance of Texas Commerce and its predecessors in supplying loans and other financial services to a variety of locally based concerns which ultimately grew into companies of national importance. These companies and many others found credit in their formative years at South Texas Commercial National, Union National, or National Bank of Commerce. They contributed to the growth and maturity of Texas Commerce by involving it in the most dynamic areas of the economy.

The most dynamic sector of the economy changed over time. In the late nineteenth century, the railroads provided much of the impetus for the growth of Houston's banks by facilitating the expansion of the businesses of lumbermen, wholesale dry goods merchants, and cotton merchants. The cotton trade through Houston became increasingly important to the major banks in the city after the turn of the century, and the opening of the ship channel in 1914 heralded a boom in the cotton trade which further enhanced the importance of cotton in the affairs of banks such as South Texas Commercial National. This boom was accompanied by a burst of building in the maturing region. With the exception of the interruption in building caused by the Great Depression and World War II, the financing of various types of real estate development remained an important component of the region's economy and its banking business through 1986.

The cotton trade, however, has not enjoyed such continued prominence. By the late 1920s, several of the predecessors of Texas Commerce were more highly dependent on cotton and real estate lending than Texas Commerce subsequently became on energy and real estate. When the Great Depression disrupted the existing patterns of trade and finance, these banks faced far-reaching adjustments. Fortunately for Houston and for Texas Commerce, oil-related lending provided a ready alternative to the declining cotton-related activities after about 1935. For the next half-century, oil remained quite important to Texas Commerce, a fact all too evident in the cycle of boom and bust in petroleum since 1973.

Yet as Texans and their banks contemplate the waning of the economic dynamism of the petroleum industry, history offers a measure of reassurance. The decline of cotton and the pause in construction in the 1930s were at once more abrupt and less predictable than the decline in petroleum and the downturn in real estate in the 1980s. Yet the region ultimately adjusted by finding alternative activities to replace the cotton trade. Unlike cotton, petroleum promises to diminish gradually over decades, giving the economy an extended era of transition in which to develop new industries or expand existing ones. Oil and natural gas have spawned a diverse complex of industrial activity in Texas and particularly along the Gulf Coast, and even as these raw materials are steadily exhausted, they will continue to provide the economy with a source of strength well into the future.

As a result of the oil-led boom of the 1970s and the impact of the bank holding company movement, the state's major banks in the 1980s have much greater resources with which to pursue such opportunities. Coming after decades of steady growth, the rapid expansion of the 1970s and early 1980s helped alter the competitive balance between the major Texas banks and the banks in the traditional money centers of the nation. Table 12.1 and Figure 1.2 highlight this change. In 1930 National Bank of Commerce was less than 1 percent the size of the nation's largest bank; by the 1980s, Texas Commerce Bancshares was approximately 12 percent the size of the largest bank. Although Texas Commerce obviously had not reached competitive parity, it nonetheless had grown large enough to be considered among the nation's major regional banks, and its lending limit had become great enough to allow it to compete for the business of many large corporations which had looked elsewhere for credit throughout much of the century.

In this sense, the bank holding company represented the climax of an almost century-long quest for the size required to meet the needs of the largest firms active in a growing region and state. Greater size not only was necessary to serve major customers, it also generally brought greater long-term profit and prestige. To stay small ran the risk of losing the business of rapidly growing regional companies, of being forced to pay salaries and advertising equal to larger banks while lending with a greater risk and less profit, of being unable to survive downturns in the economy, and of being unable to attract new business from major corporations coming into the region.

Within Texas, the combination of the increasing size of the Houston and Dallas banks and the holding-company movement transformed the banking system by altering the relationship between the big city banks and those in smaller cities and towns and by dramatically increasing the concentration of banking resources. During most of its modern history, the Texas banking system was among the least

concentrated in the nation, with thousands of independent banks insulated from competitive pressures from the Dallas and Houston banks
by the unit banking law and the broad geographical expanse of the
state. Correspondent ties bound the state's banking industry together
as the big city banks performed vital services for their smaller neighbors in return for fees and compensating balances. The decades after
World War II witnessed the growth of chain banking, in which partial
ownership of stock in small banks by prominent individuals active in
the big city banks allowed for a measure of coordination and control.
But not until the coming of the bank holding-company movement did
many of the previously independent banks become formally absorbed
into the operating structures of the big city banks such as Texas Commerce. While retaining separate boards of directors as required by law,
member banks were nonetheless operated as parts of state-wide organizations for many purposes. By the mid-1980s, five major bank holding companies controlled about 60 percent of bank assets in Texas, a
figure that represented a marked departure from the long-standing
Texas tradition of local markets served by unit banks. Ironically, as the
bank holding-company movement in Texas eased the traditional fears
of the dominance of eastern banks in Texas, it also heightened concern
about the power of the Dallas and Houston banks in the smaller cities
and towns in the state.

The transformation of Texas banking encouraged by the holding-
company movement well illustrates the importance of government regulation in shaping the size and number of banks and the nature of the
banking industry. Through its elected and appointed officials, the pol-
ity has sought to balance a variety of often competing demands. The
desire for an efficient, innovative, and competitive banking system has
often conflicted with the equally strong desire for a secure banking system, and the pendulum of public opinion regularly has swung between
these two goals as conditions changed. Bank deregulation in the last
decade is simply the latest adjustment in the quest for an efficient yet
secure banking system. In historical perspective, it should not be surprising if the pendulum swings at least temporarily toward the modern
equivalent of the jazz banking of the 1920s with the breakdown of the
security-based regulatory system constructed in response to the banking crisis of the Great Depression.

Understanding bank regulation in Texas requires going back to
the nineteenth century and examining Texans' skepticism of big business. Texans never opposed business or entrepreneurs. Instead, they
feared large economic institutions capable of controlling crucial sectors of the economy, and therefore politics. They also opposed any in-

stitutions that would unduly risk their money. Banks were a favorite target in both cases. Large banks lacking significant competition could determine who got credit and who did not. They could vary the price of credit for reasons other than the degree of risk of the loan. Banks through their connections to the business world and through the financial support of certain candidates could influence the political process. Banks in the nineteenth century had a relatively high failure rate and could cost depositors and shareholders their money. Given these attitudes and their grounding in reality, it is not surprising that the state constitutions of 1845 and 1876 banned banks incorporated by Texas. Private banks and, after 1865, national banks did come into existence, but with the exception of the brief period in which Texas operated under the constitution of 1869, no state-chartered bank existed until 1905. In that year the constitution was amended, but Texas lawmakers were careful to ban branch banking and in other ways to limit the size and increase the number of independent banks in Texas. This general thrust of state regulation has remained the same throughout much of the twentieth century, with gradual accommodations to the changing needs of business.

Federal regulations have had a more ambiguous impact. Federal regulation also required unit banking until 1927, when federal law allowed branch banking by national banks in those states where state-chartered banks could branch. Requirement of a larger amount of capital to start up a national bank than was required by the state tended to limit the number of national banks and increase their size. Regulations and the actions of federal agencies in the 1930s also tended to limit entry into the industry and to increase the size of the larger banks. Federal laws governing holding companies and the loosening of interpretations of those laws has allowed the growth of Texas holding companies, while the enforcement of the ban against interstate banking has insulated these holding companies from direct competition with money-center banks. Thus while federal banking regulators have often echoed the injunctions of state regulators against great size and undue influence, their actions have usually facilitated the growth of the major Texas banks. As the federal government has gradually assumed greater control over banking from the states, regulation has tended to become more uniform throughout the nation, further dampening the impact of traditional Texas attitudes concerning bigness on the state's banking system.

The effects of changes in regulation have been most apparent in the history of bank mergers. Because the unit banking law prevented branch banking and because loan limits made it difficult to meet the need of major customers, the quickest way to increase size and loan limit was to merge with another established bank. Changes in regulation affected the timing and pace of these mergers. Union National, for example, converted to a national bank and merged with Merchants in 1910 because the state put into place the Guaranty Fund. Mergers and acquisitions by the holding company in the 1970s and 1980s were shaped by changing interpretations of existing laws by federal regulators.

In addition to government regulation, changes in the banking industry and the search for management succession also shaped the merger process. A significant merger by one of the major Houston banks often affected the overall pace of mergers. Once a competitor had merged and changed the market structure of the Houston banking industry, as happened in 1910 with the creation of Union National and in 1956 with the creation of First City, other banks often sought mergers to reestablish their previous positions. The nature of the industry also influenced mergers because of its close ties to the ups and downs of the economy. The mergers of 1907 and of the late 1920s and early 1930s occurred in times of economic depression which put great stress on banks. Rather than fail or liquidate, banks merged.

In the 1912 merger between South Texas National and Commercial National, the 1953 merger between Union and South Texas, and the 1964 merger between Texas National and National Bank of Commerce, one of the goals of the merger was to replace aging managers and infuse new vigor into the merging banks. This was also true of the 1956 merger between First National and City National.

Growth through merger or internal expansion called forth the adoption of new approaches to management, since increased size placed greater demands on bank managers. Turn-of-the-century banks needed managers who could evaluate credit risks, keep the bank employees operating efficiently and economically, and serve as a symbol of prosperity, as visible representatives of the strength of the bank. These functions were usually carried out by two individuals. The bank president was seldom a full-time banker but helped evaluate loan customers and served as the symbol of the bank. The cashier ran the bank and also helped evaluate credit. Bank directors lent a hand in the evaluation of loan customers and also helped shore up the image of the bank. As the scope and complexity of business increased, it became impossible for two officers and the directors to manage the bank. Gradually more and more professional bankers, who became experts in a particular phase of banking, were added to the staff. During the 1920s, a new position of chairman of the board was added to most banks, and the chairman assumed the old functions of the president while the president became a full-time officer responsible for the day-to-day activities of the bank. The post–World War II era witnessed the extension of such trends, with the introduction of more systematic management training programs, the increasing specialization of lending in areas such as oil and real estate, and the expansion of marketing through more comprehensive, well-organized calling programs. These trends culminated in the 1960s and 1970s at Texas Commerce with the adoption of the banking equivalent of the decentralized management systems long utilized by industrial corporations.

The growing professionalization of bank management was aided by the dilution of ownership and the divorce of ownership and control. At the turn of the century, the primary bank officers and directors were also the major owners of the bank. At South Texas National, for example, President Charles Dillingham and Cashier J. E. McAshan both were major owners from the organization of the bank in 1890 to its consolidation with Commercial National in 1912. Jesse Jones owned a majority of the stock of NBC, and Captain Baker was the second largest stockholder of STCNB in the 1930s. Mergers tended to dilute the control of bank stock. After the 1912 merger no single person, family, or institution owned more than 20 percent of STCNB's stock. Mergers tended to add to Jesse Jones's share of NBC and Union stock because he usually owned stock in the banks acquired by those two. Jones's sale of his Union stock to the Carter family also increased their control of Union after 1917. But both NBC and Union would eventually follow the pattern of STCNB. Ownership was diluted at Union when it merged in 1953 and at NBC when it merged in 1964. The distribution of American General's stock in TCB, which was Jones's former share, further diluted ownership. By the mid-1970s ownership and control of the bank were separate.

When the owners were also the managers of the bank it was easier for them to accept a possible short-term loss in the interest of the long-term health of their bank and their city. The classic example, of course, was the 1931 bank crisis, in which most of the major banks absorbed losses to protect the Houston banking industry from bank failures. The managers, who even at STCNB were still at that time large stockholders, could take such an action without much concern about the reactions of a myriad of stockholders interested in their next dividend or for the short-term implications of this decision on the value of their stock. Subsequent changes in management and ownership structure forced managers to give greater weight to such considerations, making it more difficult to put aside concerns about short-term profitability in the interest of the long-term objectives.

Indeed, with the advent of the holding company and the growth of international and national business, the interests of Texas Commerce are no longer so exclusively tied to a clearly identifiable regional interest. In financing the flow of trade through Houston as well as the expansion of the city's industry and commerce, the predecessors of Texas Commerce were among the major banks in the city. They helped assure that Houston would be the financial center for a broad section of the state. As this region became more thoroughly integrated into the national and international economies, these banks took advantage of opportunities to follow Houston-based companies into broader markets; at the same time, they came to provide the local needs of a variety of nationally active concerns which were drawn to Houston by the city's sustained growth. With the creation of a state-wide holding company in the 1970s, Texas Commerce Bancshares gained a physical presence in major markets throughout the state, further extending its involvement outside of the Gulf Coast. As it became less tied to a single region, Texas Commerce became less vulnerable to economic changes in that region. This geographical diversification seems healthy for the bank, since it provides greater chances to take advantage of the variety of opportunities offered by a diverse, growing state, in the process making Texas Commerce less dependent on a single region or industry.

This change alters the traditional identity of interest between the bank and its region. It is not yet clear how this identity of interest might apply to the various regions served by a state-wide holding company, since the holding-company structure remains relatively new and since, to a degree uncommon among the major Texas banks, Texas Commerce remains concentrated in one geographic area. Despite having a large presence in various markets, some 70 percent of its assets are in Houston-area banks. The desire for profit, the chance to compete on more equal terms with the nation's largest banks, the need for new managers, or the coming of interstate banking could lead to a merger that would end this concentration along the Gulf Coast. Barring that, however, Texas Commerce will probably stay within the deeply etched patterns of the past. It will continue its quest for greater size in order to match the needs of a growing economy, maximize profit, and better survive downswings in the economy. Changing regulations, evolving managerial practices, and the pace of the merger process in Texas will affect this quest for size. Despite its increased size and geographical diversity, concern for the betterment of its ever-expanding region as well as for the state as a whole will continue to color decisions because the economic health of the region and the state will continue to shape the profitability and growth of Texas Commerce.

Appendices

Bank Directors

Directors, Commercial National Bank, 1886–1912

Name	Years	Occupation
Baker, James A.	1896–1912	Attorney, Baker, Botts
Bering, Conrad	1886–1900 1906–12	Lumber, Hardware
Chew, William B.	1886–1912	Banker, Cotton
Clay, Adam	1886 1889–92 1894–95	Dry Goods Merchant
Coombs, Eden L.	1886	Merchant
Currington, W. A.	1891	Cotton
Dawson, James D.	1906–12	President, Fidelity Cotton Oil and Fertilizer
Dorrance, John M.	1905–1908	Bank officer, cotton
Eldridge, H. R.	1906–1907	Bank officer
Ewing, Presley K.	1893–1900	Attorney
Fay, Thornwell	1905–12	President, Southern Pacific lines in Texas and Louisiana
Gardes, Henry	1886–88	Bank president, New Orleans investor
Hill, Edward P.	1886–96	Bank officer, attorney
Jones, Martin Tilford	1886–90	Lumber; Dry Goods Merchant
Lovett, Robert Scott	1900–12	Attorney, chairman of the board, Union Pacific Railroad and Southern Pacific Co.
Markham, C. H.	1903–12	President, Illinois Central Railroad Co.
Neuhaus, J. V.	1901–12	Vice-president, South Texas Grain Co.
Parker, Edwin B.	1906–12	Attorney, Baker, Botts, Parker & Garwood
Read, William M.	1889–99	Cotton
Red, S. C.	1892–1909 1911–12	Physician
Rice, J. S.	1903–1906	Lumber, railroads
Rice, Will	1903–1906	Lumber
Sewall, Cleveland	1906–12	Attorney, cotton
Sewall, E. W.	1897–1905	Cotton, wholesale groceries
Stuart, Dr. D. Frank	1887–97	Physician
Wells, Oscar	1909–11	Bank officer

Directors, South Texas National Bank, 1890–1912

Name	Date	Occupation
Allen, Samuel	1890–96	Rancher
Binz, Jacob	1901–1907	Cotton
Blaffer, R. L.	1911–12	Oil
Brashear, H.	1890–1911	Attorney
Breyer, A.	1908–10	Cotton
Bryan, Chester H.	1910–12	Banker
Campbell, J. I.	1899–1904	Cotton
Carter, S. F.	1901–1907	Lumber
Carter, W. T.	1904–1908	Lumber
Dillingham, Charles	1890–12	Railroads, cotton
Dillingham, E. K.	1909–12	Investments
Dorrance, John M.	1909–12	Cotton
Freeman, Thomas J.	1910–12	Lawyer
Harris, B. D.	1909–12	Banker
Heitmann, F. A.	1894–1904 1906–12	Hardware
Holt, O. T.	1890–95	Attorney
House, H. C.	1897–1901	Lumber
Jones, M. T.	1890–98	Lumber
Lombardi, C.	1890–1912	Cotton, lumber
McAshan, J. E.	1890–1904 1906–12	Bank officer
MacGregor, H. F.	1890–1912	Real estate, street railway
Miller, J. Z., Jr.	1908–10	Investments
Rice, Will	1896–1900	Lumber
Ripley, Daniel	1909–12	Cotton broker, shipping
Sanborn, H. B.	1890–93	Rancher

Directors, Union National Bank, 1910–53

Name	Years	Occupation
Anderson, Dillon	1948–53	Attorney, Baker, Botts
Anderson, James	1926–33	Investments
Anderson, Thomas D.	1948–53	Bank officer
Andrews, E. H.	1926–42	
Andrews, Frank	1910–36	Attorney
Baker, R. H.	1910–31	Railroads
Ball, Thomas H.	1910–22	Attorney
Bath, A. A.	1927–53	President, Houston Cotton Mills Co.
Binz, Norman A.	1945–53	Insurance
Bonner, J. S.	1916–39	Oil

Directors, Union National Bank, 1910–1953, *continued*

Name	Years	Occupation
Bowers, A. L.	1918–26	
Brooks, R. E.	1910–26	Attorney
Brown, E. W.	1915	
Bullington, John P.	1940–47	Attorney, Baker, Botts
Caldwell, T. J.	1926–43	
Carroll, J. J.	1922–38	Physician
Carter, A. L.	1921–53	Lumber
Carter, C. L.	1919–36	Attorney
Carter, W. T.	1910–21	Lumber
Carter, W. T., Jr.	1918–53	Investments
Carter, Winston	1936–53	Investments
Christie, George R.	1923–30	
Collier, R. H.	1925	
Connelly, W. L.	1919–21	
Cooley, D. W.	1913–24	Bank officer
Davis, W. F. N.	1910–17	Lumber
Dunlap, C. K.	1910–11	
Dunn, DeWitt C.	1913–24	Bank officer
Dunn, T. C.	1910–28	Bank officer
Dwyer, C. A.	1925–53	Business manager, William M. Rice Institute
Farish, S. P.	1926–39	Oil
Farrar, R. M.	1924–43	Bank officer, Lumber
Finch, H. B.	1921–35	Bank officer
Giles, William	1926–28	
Gilmer, B. B.	1918–43	President, Southern Drug Co.
Gordon, R. M.	1928–46	Cotton
Hamblen, W. P.	1947–53	Attorney
Hamman, George	1911–53	Bank Officer, Oil
Hamman, John, Jr.	1948–53	Oil
Heard, Bryan	1910–12	
Horne, Henry C.	1941–50	
Ilfrey, F. W.	1944–53	Bank officer
Jones, Jesse H.	1910–17	Lumber, Real Estate
Kelley, G. A.	1918–31	Lumber
Kelley, Robert H.	1937–47	
Kurth, Melvin E.	1947–53	Attorney, Andrews, Kurth
Lane, Jonathan	1910–14	Attorney
Levy, Haskell	1925–26	
Link, J. W.	1911–18	
Lummis, F. R. (Fred)	1921–53	Physician
McDonald, Arch	1910–17	Editor, *Houston Chronicle*
Michaux, Frank W.	1947–53	Oil

Directors, Union National Bank, *continued*

Name	Years	Occupation
Moore, Dallas H.	1944–47	
Nazro, Underwood	1924	
Neuhaus, C. L.	1910–30	
Neuhaus, W. O.	1910–43	
Otto, D. A.	1928–33	
Pillot, C. G.	1910–53	Wholesale grocer
Pillot, Norman V.	1922–47	Wholesale grocer
Randolph, R. D.	1922–53	Bank officer
Reynolds, J. W.	1925–31	Lumber
Rice, J. S.	1910–31	Lumber, railroads, bank officer
Rice, Will	1910–39	Lumber, oil
Robins, J. W.	1912–21	President, Trinity and Brazos Valley Railroad Co.
Rockwell, J. M.	1910–17	Cotton, lumber
Ross, J. O., Jr.	1910–18	
Schuhmacher, H. C.	1925–40	Banker, merchant
Sharp, W. B., Jr.	1940–49	Oil
Stevenson, Louis A.	1944–53	Insurance
Stuart, J. R.	1910–12	Physician
Sweeney, J. J.	1910–25	
Taylor, Judson L.	1939–44	Physician and surgeon
Thompson, J. Lewis	1910–11	
Tinker, H. N.	1910	Bank officer
Wells, Oscar	1912	Bank officer
West, J. Marion	1910	Oil
Wier, R. W.	1924–36	Lumber
Yoakum, B. F.	1913–20	Railroads

Directors, South Texas Commercial National Bank, 1912–53

Name	Years	Occupation
Anderson, James	1948–53	Investments
Baker, James A.	1912–41	Attorney, Baker, Botts; Bank officer
Baker, James A., Jr.	1920–53	Attorney, Baker, Botts
Baker, W. Browne	1945–53	Bank officer
Beatty, Amos L.	1914–22	President, Texas Co.
Bering, Conrad	1912–15	Lumber, hardware
Blaffer, John H.	1947–53	Oil
Blaffer, R. L.	1912–33 1942	Oil, Humble

Directors, South Texas Commercial National Bank, *continued*

Name	Years	Occupation
Booth, Horace	1912–14	
Bradley, Luke C.	1917–25	
Bryan, Chester A.	1912–16	Banker
Buckner, E. H.	1927–33	
Cargill, Ennis	1916–48	Bank officer
Chew, W. B.	1912–14 1924–31	Bank officer, cotton
Craft, E. A.	1946–53	Executive vice-president, Southern Pacific
Dawson, James D.	1912–24	President, Fidelity Cotton Oil and Fertilizer Co.
Decker, Harold	1950–53	President, Houston Oil Co.
Dillingham, Charles	1912–17	Attorney
Dillingham, Charles, Jr.	1939–42 1949–53	Cotton, bank officer
Dillingham, E. R.	1912–34	Investments, cotton
Dorrance, John M.	1912–31	Cotton
Evershade, P. J.	1916–27	Bank officer
Fay, Thornwell	1912–29	Southern Pacific
Freeman, Thomas J.	1912–17	Attorney
Godwin, Herbert	1924–33	
Gossett, E. F.	1922–53	Bank officer
Graves, M. M.	1925–31	Cotton, M. M. Graves Co.
Harris, B. D.	1912–15	Bank officer
Heitmann, F. A.	1912–53	Wholesale hardware
Heitmann, Fred W.	1949–53	Wholesale hardware
Hogan, E. L.	1939–53	Chairman, Hogan-Allnoch Dry Goods Co.
Holt, O. T.	1912	Attorney
Hoopes, J. W.	1919–21	
Horton, George	1952–53	President, Horton and Horton, Inc.
Hudson, E. J.	1949–53	President, Hudson Engineering Co.
Lawder, Sam R.	1944–50	Bank officer
Lovett, H. Malcolm	1942–53	Attorney, Baker, Botts
Lovett, R. S.	1912–16	Chairman, Union Pacific
Lull, H. M.	1923–45	Railroads
McAshan, Harris	1942–53	Bank officer
McAshan, J. E.	1912–16	Bank officer
McAshan, S. M.	1916–41	Bank officer
McAshan, S. M., Jr.	1947–53	Vice-president, Anderson, Clayton & Co.

Directors, South Texas Commercial National Bank, *continued*

Name	Years	Occupation
MacGregor, H. F.	1912–23	Real estate, streetcars
Markham, C. H.	1912–15	Railroads
Meachum, McDonald	1943–50	President, Houston Production Co.
Moore, Preston	1938–45	
Neuhaus, J. R.	1912–48	Grain
Parker, Edwin B.	1912–29	Attorney, Baker, Botts, Parker & Garwood
Patton, William S.	1922–40 1943–53	Bank officer
Pondrom, J. A.	1915–20	
Proctor, F. C.	1917–24	
Radford, John S., Jr.	1920–53	Vice-president, Oriental Textile Mills
Ralston, Ben W.	1922–24 1926	
Red, George P.	1933–53	Attorney
Red, S. C.	1912–40	Physician, surgeon
Ripley, Daniel	1912–21	Cotton, shipping
Ripley, Mrs. Daniel	1922–34	Cotton, shipping
Scott, W. R.	1922–26	
Sewall, Cleveland	1912–42	Cotton, attorney
Settegast, C. E., Jr.	1924–27	Real estate
Settegast, J. J., Jr.	1912–18	Real estate
Simpson, C. P.	1949–53	Simpson and Gillman Pontiac Co.
West, J. Marion	1946–53	Oil
Wiess, H. C.	1923–28	Oil, Humble
Wilson, E. Clifton	1949–53	President, Wilson Stationery and Printing Co.
Womack, K. E.	1921–46	Cotton, Sanders and Co.

Directors, National Bank of Commerce, 1912–64

Name	Years	Occupation
Abercrombie, J. S.	1946–63	Oil, Cameron Ironworks
Adair, J. H.	1912–14	President, Houston Cotton Exchange
Anderson, M. D.	1916–23	Cotton, Anderson, Clayton
Austin, P. R.	1921–22	

Directors, National Bank of Commerce, *continued*

Name	Years	Occupation
Ayers, Fred W.	1951–60	Senior vice-president and general manager, Hughes Tool Co.
Bates, F. W.	1953–58	Senior executive assistant, Missouri-Pacific Lines
Bellows, W. S.	1947–53	W. S. Bellows Construction Corp.
Blount, E. A.	1912–14	Capitalist
Buck, E. O.	1954–58	Bank officer
Burt, R. E.	1916–19	
Butler, George A.	1934–56	Attorney, Butler, Binion, Rice and Cook
Carlton, L. A.	1915–22	
Chase, Stephen, Jr.	1959–61	Vice-president, Champion Paper and Fire Co.
Chew, J. H.	1917–18 1922–31	Cotton
Clifford, G. H.	1926	
Collie, Marvin K.	1958–60	Bank officer
Collins, R. D.	1912–14	Bank officer
Coombs, E. H.	1920–29	Real estate
Coon, R. S.	1922–40	Ranching, real estate
Cotter, George F.	1916–17	
Cram, Ira. H.	1953–63	Senior vice-president, Continental Oil Co.
Dietrich, Noah	1938–56	Executive vice-president, Hughes Tool Co.
Doherty, R. P.	1925–63	Officer
Dunlap, C. K.	1924–27	
Dyche, W. E., Jr.	1963	Dyche, Wheat, Thornton and Wright
Elkins, J. A.	1918–28	Attorney
Farrar, R. M.	1915–20	Bank officer, lumber
Filson, H. S.	1912–19 1925–32	General manager, Alexander Gilmer Lumber Co.
Fisher, A. F.	1927–40	Bank officer
Fisher, H. E.	1961–63	President, Pipe Line Technologists, Inc.
Flaxman, Thomas	1912–14	Wholesale dry goods
Flowers, H. Fort	1955–63	Investments
Fondren, W. W.	1918–37	Oil, Humble

Directors, National Bank of Commerce, *continued*

Name	Years	Occupation
Fondren, Walter W., Jr.	1955–60	Oil
Foster, C. W.	1918–19	Bank officer
Foster, M. E.	1914–25	Editor, *Houston Chronicle*
Fraley, F. W.	1912–20	Manager, Pierce-Fordyer Oil Association; bank officer
Garrett, J. H.	1929–63	Bank officer
Giles, William	1913–14	
Gray, Ralph L.	1947–63	Chairman, Armco Steel Corp.
Griffith, I. C.	1925	Bank officer
Hamilton, Charles W.	1954–58	Bank officer
Hamilton, T. A.	1924–25	
Harrison, D. J.	1926	
Heyne, F. J.	1917–23	President, Bankers
	1925–33	Mortgage Co.
	1944–63	
Hill, J. C.	1916–26	
Hobby, Edwin	1912–13	Cashier, Guaranty State Bank and Trust Co., Dallas
Holmes, A. M.	1918–24	Bank officer
Holt, O. T.	1912–13	Attorney
Holt, O. T., Mrs.	1914	Investments
House, H. C.	1913–16	Lumber
Hoverstock, Newton K.	1963	General manager, South Texas Area, Southwestern Bell Telephone Co.
Hudgins, J. L.	1912	Manager, Industrial Cotton Oil Co.
Huggins, W. O.	1916–34	Attorney; editor, *Houston Chronicle*
Hulen, John A.	1912–17	General freight and passenger agent, Trinity and Brazos Valley Railroad Co.
Hutcheson, J. C., Jr.	1914–17	Attorney
Hutcheson, W. Palmer	1918	Attorney
Ireland, C. F.	1915–25	
Japhet, C. B.	1933–39	Investments
	1943–65	
Japhet, Dan A.	1921–25	Oil, cotton
Jones, A. C.	1946–57	Banker and rancher
Jones, Gainer	1954–58	Bank officer
Jones, Jesse H.	1914–16	Bank officer, real estate
	1920–55	

Directors, National Bank of Commerce, *continued*

Name	Years	Occupation
Jones, John T.	1921–33	Investments
Jones, John T., Jr.	1950–63	President, Houston Chronicle Publishing Co.
Jones, M. Tilford	1934–61	Investments
Jones, W. W.	1919–28	Rancher
Jones, W. W. II	1958–63	Rancher, banker
Kayser, Paul	1927–28	Attorney; president, El Paso
	1946–63	Natural Gas Co.
Kelley, G. A.	1912–13	Lumber
Kerr, C. L.	1917–31	
Kneebone, Robert W.	1954–58	Bank officer
Leach, J. S.	1940–63	Vice-president, Texaco
Levy, A. M.	1915–16	Levy Brothers Dry Goods Co.
Liddell, Frank A.	1944–63	Attorney, Kayser, Liddell, Benbow and Austin
Lindholm, W. L.	1960–63	General Manager, South Texas Area, Southwestern Bell Telephone Co.
Lindsay, S. A.	1921–25	Bank officer
Link, J. W., Jr.	1928–33	Lumber
Logan, J. M.	1912–13	Bank officer
Longnecker, O. M.	1932–33	
Lucia, V.	1914–26	
Lyons, Richard T.	1955–61	President, Union Oil and Gas Corp. of Louisiana
McCarthy, J. T.	1914–16	Bank officer
MacDonald, Arch	1912–15	Editor, *Houston Chronicle*
McFadden, A. M.	1912–25	Rancher
McMurray, John	1915–22	
Manley, F. T.	1924–39	President, Union Texas Petroleum, Division of Allied Chemical Corp.
Marshall, J. Howard, II	1957–63	President, Union Texas Petroleum, Division of Allied Chemical Corp.
Meador, N. E.	1912	Vice-president, Bankers Trust
	1914–25	Co.; bank officer
	1927–32	
Mecom, John W.	1951–63	Oil
Merchant, A.	1926	
Miller, Jeff N.	1912–14	Capitalist
Miller, Will F.	1920–31	

Directors, National Bank of Commerce, *continued*

Name	Years	Occupation
Mistrot, G. A.	1913–14	
Montrose, M. E.	1961–63	President, Oil Tool Division, Hughes Tool Co.
Moore, W. W.	1947–49	Vice-president, Bankers Mortgage Co.
Moran, Don	1938–39	Oil
Mosbacher, Robert	1959–63	Oil
Murphy, F. W.	1915–20	
Neff, P. J.	1948–56	Executive vice-president, Missouri Pacific Lines
Norwood, Ewing	1924	Bank officer
Parr, P. S., Jr.	1916–17 1920	Bank officer
Prather, Ed	1923–24	Oil
Pyeatt, J. S.	1913–20	Bank officer
Pyron, W. B.	1938–46	Vice-president, Gulf Oil Corp.
Rawcliffe, J. B. F.	1925–32	
Reed, Charles F., Jr.	1947–63	Dow Chemical Co.
Rehrauer, P. C.	1934–63	Bank officer
Rettig, Penn	1929–32	
Reynolds, J. W.	1912–24	Lumber
Rockwell, James W.	1921–58	Lumber
Rutherford, P. R.	1951–63	Oil
Ryder, W. F.	1913–14	
Sakowitz, Tobias	1928–32	Sakowitz Brothers
Samuels, S.	1912	Cotton, S. Samuels and Co.
Schreiner, Charles	1912–22	Banker, rancher
Scoggins, T. M.	1915–17	
Scurlock, E. C.	1959–63	Oil, Scurlock Oil Co.
Shivers, Allan	1957–63	Attorney; former governor of Texas
Simpson, A. D.	1919–60	Bank officer
Smith, J. H.	1923–30	
Smith, R. E.	1954–63	Oil
Stark, W. H.	1913–14	Lumber
Strake, G. W.	1938–43	Oil
Street, G. C.	1913–17	Cotton-oil merchant, bank officer
Streetman, Sam	1927–32	
Symonds, Gardiner	1947–63	President, Tennessee Gas and Transmission Co.

Directors, National Bank of Commerce, *continued*

Name	Years	Occupation
Taub, Ben	1930–33 1957–63	Tobacco wholesaler, real estate
Taub, Sam	1915–33 1940–55	Tobacco wholesaler, bank officer
Thompson, J. L.	1917	
von Rosenberg, C. J.	1912 1915–19	Capitalist
Waples, Paul	1913	
Watson, Roy G.	1917–18	
West, J. Marion	1929–33	President, South Texas Hardwood Manufacturing Co.
Whited, A. H.	1912–13	Houston East and West Texas Railroad
Whitmore, John E.	1954–58	Bank officer
Wingfield, B. Magruder	1944–54	Bank officer
Winters, W. G.	1929–33	
Wolfenstein, J.	1926–32	
Wood, W. E.	1924	
Wortham, G. S.	1928–63	President, American General Insurance Co.
Young, John R.	1919–20	

Directors, Texas National Bank, 1953–63

Name	Years	Occupation
Anderson, Dillon	1953–54 1957–63	Attorney, Baker, Botts
Anderson, James	1953–56	Investments
Anderson, Thomas D.	1953–59	Bank officer
Baker, James A., Jr.	1953–63	Attorney, Baker, Botts
Baker, W. Browne	1953–63	Bank officer
Bath, Albert A.	1953–63	Investments
Bendetson, Karl R.	1953–63	Manager, Texas Division, Champion Paper and Fibre Co.
Binz, Norman A.	1953–63	Insurance
Blaffer, John H.	1953–63	Oil

Directors, Texas National Bank, _continued_

Name	Years	Occupation
Burrow, Harold	1959–63	Executive vice-president, Tennessee Gas Transmission Co.
Carter, A. L.	1953–56	Lumber
Carter, Thomas L.	1957–63	Lumber
Carter, W. T., Jr.*	1953–56	Investments
Carter, Winston*	1953–63	Investments
Craft, E. A.	1953	Executive vice-president, South Pacific Lines in Texas and Louisiana
Cravens, Rorick	1957–63	Partner, Cravens, Dorgan and Co.
Decker, Harold	1953–63	President, Houston Oil Co. of Texas
Dillingham, Charles	1953–63	Attorney, Dillingham, Warner and Schleider
Dillingham, E. K.	1953–69	Investments
Doherty, W. T.	1957	President, Mound Co.
Dwyer, C. A.	1953	Business manager, Rice Institute
French, Richard W.	1961–63	President, United Carbon Co.
Gillingham, W. J.	1961–63	President, Schlumberger Well Surveying Corp.
Gossett, E. F.	1953	Bank officer
Hamblen, W. P.	1953–63	Attorney
Hamman, George	1953	Bank officer
Hamman, John, Jr.	1953–63	President, Hamman Oil and Refinery Co.
Heitmann, F. A.	1953–55	Chairman, F. W. Heitmann Co.
Heitmann, Fred W.	1953–63	Vice-president, F. W. Heitmann Co.
Hogan, E. L.	1953–63	Chairman, Hogan-Allnoch Dry Goods Co.
Horton, George	1953–63	President, Horton and Horton, Inc.
Hudson, E. J.	1953–57	President, Hudson Engineering Co.
Ilfrey, F. W.*	1954–59	Bank officer
Kurth, Melvin E.	1954–63	Attorney, Andrews, Kurth, Campbell and Bradley
Lockwood, Mason G.*	1960–63	Partner, Lockwood, Andrews, and Newman

* Associate director.

Directors, Texas National Bank, *continued*

Name	Years	Occupation
Lovett, H. Malcolm	1953–63	Attorney, Baker, Botts
Lummis, Dr. Fred R.	1953–59	Physician
Lybrand, Fred S.*	1960–63	Bank officer
MacGregor, Donald*	1959–63	Bank officer
McAshan, Harris	1953–59	Bank officer
McAshan, S. M., Jr.	1953–59	Vice-president, Anderson, Clayton and Co.
McGee, Kline*	1957–61	Bank officer
McLean, J. W.	1959–63	Bank officer
Michaux, Frank W.	1954–63	Oil
Mudd, Henry H.*	1960–63	Officer, South Texas Area Southwestern Bell Telephone Co.
Patton, William*	1953–61	Bank officer (retired)
Payne, Leon M.*	1959–63	Attorney, Andrews, Kurth
Radford, John S., Jr.	1953–59	Vice-president, Oriental Textile Mills
Randolph, R. D.	1953–63	Bank officer
Red, George	1953–63	Attorney
Settegast, Lester	1961–63	Trustee, Robert A. Welsh Foundation
Shamblin, L. S.	1961–63	Treasurer and Business Manager, Rice University
Sharp, Dudley C.	1961–65	Simpson Gillman Printing Co.
Sines, Bernard S.	1955–63	Executive vice-president, Pacific Lines in Texas and Louisiana
Stewart, Ross	1959–63	Oil
Stevenson, Louis A.	1954–60	Houston, Stevenson, and Cummings Insurance Co.
Tarkington, A. W.	1959–62	Senior vice-president, Continental Oil Co.
Van Wart, Walter B.	1963	Chairman, Wyatt Industries, Inc.
Vaughen, K. C.	1952–63	Vice-president, Union Oil Co., California
West, J. Marion	1953–57	President, West Production Co.
Wilson, E. Clifton	1953–63	President, Wilson Stationery and Printing Co.

* Associate director.

Directors, Texas Commerce Bank–Houston,* 1964–86

Name	Years	Occupation
Abercrombie, J. S.	1964–72 †1972–73	Oil and gas producer
Adams, John L.	1983–86	President, TCB–Houston
Alexander, Stanford J.	†1976–78	President, Weingarten Realty
Allen, Herbert	1966–78 †1979–86	Former Chairman, Cameron Iron Works
Anderson, Dillon	1964–65	First vice chairman, Texas National Bank of Commerce
Baker, James A., Jr.	†1964–65	Attorney, Baker, Botts, Shepherd & Coates
Baker, James A., III	†1969–74	Attorney, Andrews, Kurth, Campbell & Jones
Baker, W. Browne	1964–65 †1966–67	Executive vice president, Texas National Bank of Commerce
Bath, Albert	†1964–70	Investor
Barnett, E. W.	1984–86	Managing partner, Baker & Botts
Barrow, Thomas D.	1971–86	Investments, former vice chairman, Standard Oil Co. (Ohio)
Beall, Charles C., Jr.	†1976–77 1978–86	Chairman, TCB–Houston
Beck, John A.	1965–73	Investments
Bendetsen, Karl R.	†1964–65	President, Champion Papers
Binz, Norman A.	†1964–86	Investments
Blaffer, John H.	1964–73	Investments
Blaffer, Mrs. John H.	†1973–77	Investments (see Trammell, Camilla)
Blanton, Jack S.	1977–85 †1985–86	Chairman, Scurlock Oil Co.
Bolton, Lloyd L.	†1976–86	Vice chairman, TCB–Houston
Boyd, Howard	1967–78 †1979–86	Chairman, El Paso Natural Gas Co.
Buck, E. O.	1965–68 †1969–82	Investments, former vice chairman, Texas National Bank of Commerce
Carter, Thomas L.	†1964–65 1965–86	Investments
Carter, Winston	†1964–65	Investments
Cater, John T.	1972–76	President, TCB–Houston

* Formerly, Texas National Bank of Commerce
† Advisory director.

Directors, Texas Commerce Bank–Houston,* *continued*

Name	Years	Occupation
Choate, William R.	†1967–83	Attorney, Baker & Botts
Clark, Edward A.	1977–78	Senior partner, Clark, Thomas,
	†1979–86	Winters & Newton
Cram, Ira H.	†1964–65	Senior vice president, Continental Oil Co.
Cravens, Rorick	†1964–65	Chairman, Cravens,
	1965–76	Dargan & Co.
Creekmore, J. H.	1965–86	President, Houston Endowment, Inc.
Croshaw, Fred E.	1986	Attorney, Liddell, Sapp & Zivley
Davis, Roy B., Jr.	†1977–85	Chairman, TESCO
Decker, Harold	1964–65	Oil
Dillingham, Charles	†1964–86	President, Charles Dillingham, P.C.
Doherty, Robert P.	1964–67	Chairman, Texas National Bank of Commerce
Duncan, Charles W., Jr.	†1975–77	Chairman, Rotan, Mosle Financial Corp.
Duncan, John H.	1974–86	Investments
Dwyer, C. A.	†1964–78	Business manager, Rice University
Dyche, W. E., Jr.	†1964–74	President, Houston First Financial Group
Erwin, Jim E.	†1976–80	Executive vice president, Cameron Iron Works
Fisher, Herbert E.	†1964–69	Chairman, Pipe Line
	1970–82	Technologists
	†1983–85	
Flour, Peter J.	†1984–85	President, Texas Crude
	1985–86	Exploration, Inc.
Flowers, H. Fort	†1964–65	Chairman, Differential Corp.
	1965–71	
	†1972–74	
Garrett, J. H.	†1964–65	Senior vice president, Texas National Bank of Commerce
Gerrard, Robert W.	1969	Executive vice president, Texas National Bank of Commerce
Gillingham, W. J.	†1964–65	President, Schlumberger Well Surveying Corp.

* Formerly, Texas National Bank of Commerce
† Advisory director.

Directors, Texas Commerce Bank—Houston, * *continued*

Name	Years	Occupation
Gordon, Aron S.	†1977–86	President & co-chairman, Gordon Jewelry Corp.
Hamblen, W. P.	†1964–65	Attorney
Hamman, John, Jr.	†1964–65	President, Hamman Oil and Refining Co.
Hansen, George W.	1976–84	Area vice president, Armco, Inc.
Heiligbrodt, L. William	1976–81 †1982–86	Vice chairman, WEDGE International; former chairman, TCB–Houston
Heitmann, Fred W.	†1964–77	President, Heitmann Bering–Cortes Co.
Herbert, Ira C.	1980–86	President, Foods Business Sector of the Coca-Cola Company
Herring, Robert R.	1970–81	Chairman, Houston Natural Gas
Heyne, F. J.	1964 †1965	Chairman, Bankers Mortgage Co.
Hibbert, Robert E.	†1970–71 1972–79 †1980–86	Oil and gas producer
Hogan, E. L.	†1964–69	Chairman, Hogan-Allnoch Co.
Holliday, Raymond M.	1968–80	Chairman, Hughes Tool Co.
Horner, Jack A.	†1970–86	Former vice chairman, TCB–Houston
Horton, George	†1964–65	President, Horton and Horton
Hoverstock, Newton K.	1964–65	General manager, South Texas Area, Southwestern Bell Telephone Co.
Japhet, C. B.	1964–70 †1971–79	Investments
Japhet, E. C.	1965–78 †1979–86	Investments
Johnson, Mrs. Lyndon B.	1977–84 †1985–86	Investments
Jones, John T., Jr.	1964–65	President, Houston Chronicle Publishing Co.
Jones, W. W., II	†1964–86	Rancher and banker

* Formerly, Texas National Bank of Commerce
† Advisory director.

Directors, Texas Commerce Bank–Houston,* *continued*

Name	Years	Occupation
Kayser, Paul	†1964–79	Founder and chairman, El Paso Natural Gas Co.
Kirkley, Terry A.	1981–86	President, Esso Eastern, Inc.
Kurth, Melvin E.	†1964–68	Attorney, Andrews, Kurth, Campbell & Jones
LaBoon, R. Bruce	†1975–83 1984–86	Attorney, Liddell, Sapp, Zivley, Brown & LaBoon
Lane, William H.	†1967–69 1970–79	President, Riviana Foods
Lesch, James R.	†1977–79 1980–86	Chairman, Hughes Tool Company
Lockwood, Mason G.	†1964–65	President, Lockwood, Andrews & Newman
Loughnane, B. P.	†1976–78	President, Geosource, Inc.
Love, Ben F.	1969–86	Chairman, Texas Commerce Bancshares
Lovett, H. Malcolm	1964–65	Attorney, Baker, Botts, Shepherd & Coates
Marshall, J. Howard, II	1964–70 †1970–82	Investments
McCabe, John B.	1976–77	Vice president, Getty Oil Co.
McDade, Thomas B.	†1969–86	Vice chairman, TCB–Houston
McLean, J. W.	1964–65	President, Texas National Bank of Commerce
Mecom, John W.	1964–68	Oil
Michaux, Frank W.	†1964–65	Oil producer
Miller, Charles	1985–86	President, Criterion Group
Montague, Kenneth E.	1975–79	President, General Crude Oil Co.
Montrose, M. E.	1964–67 †1968–79	Senior vice president, Hughes Tool Co.
Morrison, Gary E.	†1974–86	Investments
Morse, Clinton F.	†1982–86	Attorney, Andrews & Kurth
Mosbacher, Robert	†1964–68 1969–86	Oil and gas producer
Newton, Carl D., III	1982–86	President, Fox-Stanley Photo Products
Nicandros, Constantine S.	†1984 1985	President, Petroleum Operations for Conoco, Inc.

* Formerly, Texas National Bank of Commerce
† Advisory director.

Appendix A

Directors, Texas Commerce Bank–Houston, * *continued*

Name	Years	Occupation
O'Donnell, William S.	†1971–86	Partner, Suburban Homes
Ohmstede, Gene E.	1972–73	President, Ohmstede Machine Works
Onstead, Robert R.	1985–86	Chairman, Randall's Food Markets
Payne, Leon M.	†1964–65	Attorney, Andrews, Kurth, Campbell & Jones
Peacock, Leslie C.	†1974–78	Vice chairman, TCB–Houston
Pfeiffer, Carl E.	1982–83	President, Quanex Corp.
Phillips, William W., Jr.	1972–73	Chairman, TCB–Beaumont
Platt, John D.	1980–86	Investments
Proler, Izzie	†1976–85	Chairman, Proler International
Randolph, R. D.	1964–70 †1971–86	Former vice chairman of Executive Committee, Texas National Bank of Commerce
Red, George	1964–71	Attorney, Red, Kemp & Wyckoff
Reed, Charles F.	†1964–65	Dow Chemical Co.
Rehrauer, P. C.	†1964–65 1966–68 †1969–70	Executive vice president, Texas National Bank of Commerce
Rupp, George	1986	President, Rice University
Rutherford, Pat R.	1964–76 †1977–83	Oil and gas producer, rancher
Rutherford, Pat R., Jr.	†1977 1978–85	President, Rutherford Oil Co.
Sands, Thomas Eugene	1980–86	Financial vice president, Big Three Industries
Sapp, Charles	†1965–75	Attorney, Liddell, Sapp, Zivley & Brown
Schwend, Fred S.	1971–76 †1977–86	Petroleum consultant, former chairman, Gulf Oil Company–U.S.
Scurlock, E. C.	1964–76 †1977–86	Chairman, Eddy Refining Company
Settegast, Lester	†1964–65	Attorney
Shamblin, L. S.	†1964–79	Treasurer, Rice University
Shapiro, Marc J.	†1982–86	Vice chairman, TCB–Houston
Sharp, Dudley C.	1964–65	Chairman, Mission Manufacturing Co.
Shelton, Robert R.	1973–85	Petroleum & ranching

* Formerly, Texas National Bank of Commerce
† Advisory director.

Directors, Texas Commerce Bank–Houston,* *continued*

Name	Years	Occupation
Shivers, Allan	1964–77	Investments; banking; former governor of Texas
Simmons, Thomas D., Jr.	1984	Senior partner, Trammell
	1985–86	Crow Co.
Sines, Bernard S.	1964–65	Vice president, Southern Pacific
Slocum, George S.	1985–86	President, Transco Energy Company
Smith, Harry K.	1966–80	Chairman, Big Three Industries
Smith, R. E.	†1964–73	Oil producer and rancher
Stewart, C. Jim	†1975–79	Chairman, Stewart &
	1980–86	Stevenson Services
Stewart, Ross	†1964–74	Chairman, Stewart & Stevenson Services
Taub, Ben	1964–72	J. N. Taub & Sons; chairman,
	†1972–82	Texas National Bank of Commerce
Taylor, T. O.	†1965–68	Senior vice president, Texas National Bank of Commerce
Townley, John P.	†1981–86	Vice chairman, TCB–Houston
Trammell, Camilla D.	†1978–79	Investments (former Mrs. John
	1979–83	H. Blaffer, see above)
	†1984–86	
Van Wart, Walter B.	†1964–65	Chairman, Wyatt Industries
Whitmore, John E.	1965–78	Former chairman, Texas
	†1979–86	Commerce Bancshares
Wilson, E. Clifton	†1964–65	President, Wilson Stationery and Printing Co.
Winstead, Ray L.	†1965–86	Former vice chairman, TCB–Houston
Wolf, Erving	†1978–79	Chairman, Inexco Oil Co.
	1980–85	
Woodson, Benjamin N.	†1969–70	President, American General Insurance Co.
Wortham, Gus	1964–70	Chairman, American General Insurance Co.

NOTE: Occupation listed is the position of the director at the time he left the board of directors of TCB–Houston.

Dates are taken from the bank's annual reports, which are published several months after the end of each year.

* Formerly, Texas National Bank of Commerce
† Advisory director.

Directors, Texas Commerce Bancshares, 1971–86

Name	Years	Occupation
Abercrombie, J. S.	1971 * 1972–73	President, J. S. Abercrombie Mineral Co.
Allen, Herbert	1971–79	Chairman, Cameron Iron Works
Anthony, Garner	1975–79	Chairman, Cox Enterprises
Atalla, Jorge Rudney	1978–86	Vice president, Usina Central do Paraña, S.A.
Ayoub, Sam	1982–85	Chief financial officer, the Coca-Cola Co.
Baker, James A., III	* 1971–74 1977–81	Attorney, Andrews, Kurth, Campbell & Jones; secretary of the treasury of the U.S.
Barrow, Thomas D.	1971–86	Investments; former vice chairman, Standard Oil Co. (Ohio)
Beall, Charles C., Jr.	1980–86	Chairman, TCB–Houston
Beck, John A.	1971–73	Investments
Bentsen, Donald L.	1977–86	President, Tide Products, Inc.
Binz, Norman A.	* 1971–74	Investments
Blaffer, John H.	1971–73	
Blaffer, Mrs. John A.	* 1973–74	Investments
Blanton, Jack S.	1977–86	Chairman, Scurlock Oil Co.
Boyd, Howard	1971–79	Chairman, El Paso Natural Gas Co.
Buck, E. O.	* 1971–74	Investments, former vice chairman, Texas National Bank of Commerce
Butt, Charles E.	1973–86	President, H.E.B. Foods/Drugs
Byram, John D.	1983–86	Investments, real estate development
Carter, Thomas L.	1971–86	Investments
Cater, John T.	* 1972–73 1974–76	Vice chairman, TCBK
Choate, William R.	* 1971–74	Attorney, Baker & Botts
Clark, Edward A.	1977–78 * 1979–86	Senior partner, Clark, Thomas, Winters & Newton
Cook, C. W.	1977–80	Former chairman, General Foods Corp.
Cox, Berry R.	1982–86	Investments

¹ Advisory director.

Directors, Texas Commerce Bancshares, *continued*

Name	Years	Occupation
Cravens, Rorick	*1971–75	Chairman, Cravens, Dargan & Co.
Creekmore, J. H.	1971–86	President, Houston Endowment, Inc.
Crow, Harlan R.	1981–86	Partner, Trammel Crow Co.
Dillingham, Charles	*1971–74	Attorney, Dillingham and Schleider
Dowell, Cam F., Jr.	*1975–85	Banker, Dallas
Duncan, Charles W., Jr.	*1975–77 1981–84 *1985–86	Investments, former secretary of energy of the U.S.
Duncan, John H.	1974–86	Investments
Dwyer, C. A.	*1971–74	Business manager, Rice University
Dyche, W. E., Jr.	*1971–74	President, Houston First Financial Group
Engleman, G. E.	1974–81	Chairman, Union Bank–Fort Worth and First National Bank of Hurst
Fisher, Herbert E.	1971–82	Founder and chairman, Kaneb Services, Inc.
Flowers, H. Fort	*1971–74	Chairman, Differential Corp.
Flour, J. Robert	1973–84	Chairman, Flour Corp.
Ford, Gerald R.	*1981–86	Former president of the U.S.
Garza, Eugenio Laguera	1976–86	Chairman, Valores Industriales, S.A.
Goodson, James B.	1981–86	Vice chairman, TCBK
Haas, Paul R.	*1974–80 1981–86	Chairman, Corpus Christi Oil and Gas Co.
Harvin, William C.	1975–86	Senior partner, Baker & Botts
Heiligbrodt, L. William	1976–83	Chairman, TCB–Houston
Heitmann, Fred W.	*1971–74	President, Heitmann Bering–Cortes Co.
Herring, Robert R.	1971–81	Chairman, Houston Natural Gas
Hibbert, Robert E.	1971–80	Oil and gas producer
Hoglund, Forrest E.	1982–86	President, Texas Oil & Gas Corp.
Holliday, Raymond M.	1971–80	Chairman, Hughes Tool Co.
Hook, Harold S.	1982–86	Chairman, American General Corp.

* Associate director.

Directors, Texas Commerce Bancshares, *continued*

Name	Years	Occupation
Horner, Jack S.	*1971–74	Executive vice president, TCBK
Japhet, C. B.	*1971–74	Investments
Japhet, E. C.	1971–79	Investments
Jarvie, Charles L.	1981–82	President, Dr Pepper Co.
Johnson, Mrs. Lyndon B.	1977–85 *1985–86	Investments
Jones, W. W., II	*1971–74	Rancher, banker
Jordan, Barbara	1978–86	Professor, LBJ School of Public Affairs; former congresswoman
Jordan, Don D.	1980–86	President, Houston Industries
Kayser, Paul	*1971–74	Chairman, El Paso Natural Gas Co.
Keogh, David R.	1985–86	President, the Coca-Cola Co.
King, Henry H.	1985–86	Vice Chairman, Texas Eastern Corp.
Kirkley, Terry A.	1985–86	President, Esso Eastern
LaBoon, R. Bruce	1986	Vice chairman, TCBK
Lane, William H.	1971–79	President, Riviana Foods, Inc.
Lay, Kenneth L.	1985–86	Chairman, Enron Corp.
LeMieux, Henry F.	1977–85	Chairman, Raymond International
Lesch, James R.	1980–86	Chairman, Hughes Tool Co.
Love, Ben F.	1971–86	Chairman, TCBK
Marshall, J. Howard	*1971–74	President, United Texas Petroleum
McCabe, John P.	1978–81	Group vice president, Getty Oil Co.
McDade, Thomas B.	*1971 1972–84 *1985–86	Vice chairman, TCBK
Moncrief, R. W.	1981–86	Oil and gas producer
Moncrief, W. A., Jr.	1976–80	Oil and gas producer
Montrose, M. E.	1971–74	Senior vice president, Hughes Tool Co.
Morrison, Gary E.	*1973–74	Investments
Mosbacher, Robert	1971–86	Oil and gas producer
Newton, Jon P.	1985–86	Attorney, Clark, Thomas, Winters & Newton

* Associate director.

Directors, Texas Commerce Bancshares, *continued*

Name	Years	Occupation
Nicandros, Constantine S.	1985–86	President, Petroleum Operations, Conoco, Inc.
Noel, W. D.	1973–86	Oil and gas producer
O'Donnell, William S.	*1971–74	Partner, O'Donnell Interests
Ohmstede, Gene E.	1973–74	President, Ohmstede Machine Works
Peacock, Leslie C.	1974–78	Vice chairman, TCBK
Petty, Travis H.	1982–86	Vice chairman, Burlington Northern
Phillips, William W., Jr.	1972–84	Chairman, American National Bank–Beaumont
Pickens, T. Boone	1979–85	Chairman, Mesa Petroleum Corp.
Powell, James L.	1981–86	Livestock producer and investor
Randolph, R. D.	*1971–73	Consulting vice president, TCB–Houston
Rawl, Lawrence	1979–80	Exxon Corp.
Red, George	1971 *1972–74	Attorney, Red, Kemp & Wyckoff
Reese, Kenneth W.	1980–86	Executive vice president, Tenneco
Roff, J. Hugh, Jr.	1981–86	Chairman, United Energy Resources
Rutherford, Pat R.	1971–76	Oil and gas producer
Rutherford, Pat R., Jr.	1983–85	Chairman, Rutherford Oil Co.
Sapp, Charles	*1971–74 1975–86	Senior partner, Liddell, Sapp & Zivley
Schneider, Fred S.	1982–86	Chairman, Great Western Management & Realty Co.
Schwend, Fred S.	1971–75	President, Gulf Oil Co., U.S.
Scurlock, E. C.	1971–76	Chairman, Scurlock Oil Co.
Shamblin, L. S.	*1971–74	Treasurer, Rice University
Shapiro, Marc J.	1983–86	Vice chairman, TCBK
Shelton, Robert R.	1973–85	Petroleum and ranching
Shivers, Allan	1971–76	Banker, former governor of Texas
Smith, Harry K.	1971–84	Chairman, Big Three Industries
Smith, R. E.	*1971–72	Oil and gas producer

* Advisory director.

Directors, Texas Commerce Bancshares, *continued*

Name	Years	Occupation
Stewart, Ross	*1971–74	Chairman, Stewart and Stevenson Services
Taub, Ben	1971–72	J. N. Taub and Sons; former
	*1972–74	chairman, TNBC
Wagner, Cyril, Jr.	1985–86	Oil and gas producer
Walker, Edward B., III	1978–84	President, Gulf Oil Corp.
Whitmore, John E.	1971–79	Former chairman, TCBK
Wilemon, C. Howard, Jr.	1974–83	Chairman, Arlington Bank and Trust
Winstead, Ray L.	*1971–74	Vice chairman, TCB–Houston
Young, Sam D., Jr.	1982–84	Chairman, El Paso National Corp.

* Advisory director.

APPENDIX B

Bank Executive Officers:
Biographical Sketches

John L. Adams

John L. Adams was born in 1946 in Nacogdoches, Texas. He became president of Texas Commerce Bank–Houston in 1983 after managing both the Metropolitan and National groups of the bank. In addition, he serves on the boards of TCB–Houston and two member banks in Dallas.

Adams graduated from the University of Texas at Austin with a B.B.A. in Finance and a J.D. from the School of Law. He joined Texas Commerce in 1973. He is on the board of the Texas Research League in Austin, and he has served as president of the Houston Clearing House Association. In 1968, he married Suzanne Baker, and they have two children.

Source: Biographical sketch provided by Texas Commerce Bank–Houston.

Dillon Anderson

Dillon Anderson, a director of Union National Bank from 1948 to 1953, served Texas National Bank as chairman of the board from 1958 to 1963 and its successor, Texas National Bank of Commerce, as vice-chairman of the board in 1964 and 1965.

Born in Prosper, Collin County, Texas in 1906, Anderson attended Texas Christian University, the University of Oklahoma, and Yale University Law School, where he received his law degree in 1929. He was admitted to the Texas bar in the same year, and entered the law firm of Baker, Botts, Parker & Garwood, in which he became a partner in 1940.

During World War II, Anderson served as major and colonel in the U.S. Army in the Middle East and on the War Department General Staff in Washington, for which he was awarded the Legion of Merit and the Army Commendation Ribbon. Later government service included terms as civilian consultant to the National Security Council (1953–55); special assistant to the president for national security affairs (1955–56), and member of the U.S. delegation to the Summit Conference at Geneva in July, 1955.

Anderson was also director of Houston Transit Company, Houston Fund Management Company, Westinghouse Electric Corporation, and Federated Department Stores.

A critically acclaimed writer (the author of *I and Claudie* [Boston, Little, Brown & Co., 1951] and *Claudie's Kinfolks* [Boston, Little, Brown & Co., 1954] and a contributor to serious magazines), Anderson was elected to membership in the prestigious Texas Institute of Letters. He also served as president of the Texas Philosophical Institute.

Dillon Anderson died on January 28, 1974, leaving his wife, Lena Carter Carroll Anderson, whom he had married in 1931, and three daughters.

SOURCES: *Houston Chronicle*, January 29, 1974; Biographies, TCB Archives.

James Addison Baker (see pp. 82–83)

James Addison Baker, who served the South Texas Commercial National Bank as president (1914–22) and chairman of the board (1923–41), was born in Huntsville, Texas, in 1857, to James Addison Baker and Rowena Crawford Baker.

After graduation from the Texas Military Academy in Austin, Baker was admitted to the bar and joined his father's law firm, Baker & Botts. Because of his post in the Houston Light Guard, a military and social organization, he acquired his lifelong title Captain Baker.

In 1883, Baker married Alice Graham, of Waco, Texas; their five children included James Addison Baker, Jr. (see below), and Walter Browne Baker, both of whom were active in the South Texas Commercial National Bank and the Texas National Bank of Commerce.

James A. Baker, Jr., served as vice-chairman of the board of South Texas Commercial National Bank from 1949 to 1952. He continued in that position in the successor Texas National Bank until 1958, when he was appointed chairman of the executive committee. After the merger with National Bank of Commerce in 1964, Baker served as chairman of the executive committee of the new Texas National Bank of Commerce for two more years. Throughout the years from 1920 to 1965, he served as a director of predecessors of Texas Commerce, a position subsequently held by his son, James Baker III, who has served as secretary of the treasury under President Ronald Reagan.

SOURCES: J. T. McCants, *Some Information Concerning the Rice Institute*, 80; Meiners, *Rice University*, 14–15; Clark, *Texas Gulf Coast* 3, 203–204; TNB Press Releases, TCB Archives.

Charles C. Beall, Jr.

Charles Beall was born in Oxford, Mississippi, in 1935. He graduated from the University of Mississippi with a B.B.A. in 1957, after which he served as an officer in the U.S. Air Force. After his discharge, he returned to the University of Mississippi and received his M.B.A. in finance in 1961.

Beall joined National Bank of Commerce as a management trainee in 1961. His career at Texas Commerce includes periods in the Credit Department and the Commercial Loan Department, and he managed both the national and metropolitan divisions of TCB–Houston. He was elected president of the bank in January, 1978, and chairman in February, 1983. In addition, he became vice chairman of Texas Commerce Bancshares in July, 1982, and he is also a director of both TCB–Houston and TCBK.

During his years with Texas Commerce, Beall has served on the boards of numerous civic organizations, including M.D. Anderson, the Institute for Rehabilitation & Research, the American Red Cross–Houston, the Houston Symphony, and INROADS (an organization which co-sponsors minority students and helps them work through school).

In 1956 he married Anne Watts from Houston.

SOURCES: Biographical sketch provided by Texas Commerce Bank–Houston; Interview with Charles Beall by Joseph A. Pratt, July 3, 1985, TCB Archives.

Robert Lee Blaffer

Robert Lee Blaffer, elected chairman of the board of South Texas Commercial National Bank in 1942, was born in 1875 in New Orleans, where his father, J. A. Blaffer, was involved in brick, lumber, and banking businesses. After Blaffer's graduation from Tulane University in 1897, he entered the coal business in New Orleans, supplying the Southern Pacific Railway Company and the American Sugar Refinery.

In 1902, he moved to Beaumont, Texas, where he was briefly involved in supplying Southern Pacific with crude oil for fuel and in organizing the Rio Bravo Oil Company, in which the railroad had an interest. Later in the same year, he joined W. S. Farish in operating his Spindletop and Coastal oil fields. In 1917, Blaffer and Farish, along with others, formed the Humble Oil and Refining Company, which Blaffer served as vice-president and treasurer and later president.

In 1909, Blaffer married Sarah T. Campbell, daughter of W. T. Campbell, one of the originators of the Texas Company and the Hogg-Swayne Syndicate. Blaffer died in 1942.

SOURCES: *New Encyclopedia of Texas*, 1:326; *Who's Who in Texas*, 44; Clark and Halbouty, *Spindletop*, 183.

John Thomas Cater

John Cater was born in Temple, Texas, in 1935. He earned three degrees from the University of Texas at Austin: a B.B.A. in 1958, an LL.B. in 1959, and a B.A. in 1959. In 1970 he graduated from the Stonier Graduate School of Banking at Rutgers University.

Cater went to work for National Bank of Commerce in 1960. In December, 1972, he became president of Texas Commerce Bank–Houston and a member of the bank's board. In 1973 he was elected vice chairman of Texas Commerce Bancshares and a member of the board. After leaving Texas Commerce, Cater became president of Bank of the Southwest and of Southwest Bancshares in 1976. When that bank holding company merged with Mercantile Texas Corporation, a Dallas-based bank holding company, in 1984 to form MCorp, Cater became president and chief operating officer of the holding company and chairman of the executive committee of MBank–Houston.

Cater serves as a director of Anderson, Clayton & Company, Houston Industries, Houston Lighting & Power Company, and Master-Card International, Inc. He is also on the board of the Texas Medical Center. He is married and has two children.

SOURCE: Biography provided by MBank–Houston.

W. B. Chew (see pp. 28–29)

W. B. Chew served as vice-president of the Commercial National Bank from 1889 to 1890, as president from 1891 until its consolidation with the South Texas National Bank in 1912, and for two more years as president of the resulting South Texas Commercial National Bank.

At the time of his retirement in 1914, Chew was a director of the Houston Electric Company, the Houston & Texas Central Railroad Company, the South Texas Implement & Vehicle Company, the Standard Printing & Lithographing Company, and the Security Trust Company. He was vice-president of the Hogan-Allnoch Dry Goods Company, president of the Merchants Compress Company, president of the

Houston Cotton Exchange, and vice-president of the Driskill Hotel Company of Austin.

Chew returned as a director of South Texas Commercial National Bank in 1924 and served until 1931. He died in 1932.

SOURCE: *Houston Post*, January 4, 1914, August 18, 1932.

Marvin K. Collie

Marvin K. Collie, president of the National Bank of Commerce from 1958 through 1960, was born in San Antonio, Texas, in 1918. He attended Washington and Lee University and the University of Texas Law School, joining the Houston law firm of Vinson, Elkins, Weems & Searles in 1941.

During World War II, Collie served as a lieutenant in military intelligence, attached to the U.S. Army Air Corps.

Back at Vinson & Elkins after the war, Collie rose rapidly from trial lawyer to partner. Appointed as president of NBC without previous banking experience, Collie was one of the youngest bank presidents in the United States.

Collie's bank associations included service as a director of the First City Bancorporation of Texas; membership on the council of the Taxation Section of the American Bankers Association; and the presidency of the ABA's Real Estate, Probate, and Trust Section. Among his other activities were service on the advisory group of the U.S. House Ways and Means Committee, the Houston Business and Estate Planning Council, and committees of the American Law Institute and the Houston Chamber of Commerce.

Three children were born to Collie and his wife, the former Nancy Morriss, of Dallas.

SOURCE: Houston *Chronicle*, January 21, 1958, February 10, 1971.

Denton W. Cooley

Denton W. Cooley, one of the organizers of the Marine Bank and Trust Company in 1925, served as its first and only president. After his death in 1928, the bank was reorganized as Marine Banking and Trust Company, which was acquired by National Bank of Commerce in 1930.

Cooley was born in Ashland, Nebraska, in 1885, where his father, D. D. Cooley, was a banker. Seven years later, his parents moved to Houston, where his father entered the insurance business. After graduation from high school, Cooley became a messenger for the South Texas National Bank. From 1913 to 1924, he was an officer of the Union National Bank.

Cooley's other business interests included the Houston Lighting & Power Company, of which he was a director, and the Houston Fair & Exposition. He also served a term as vice-president of the Texas Division of the American Bankers Association during 1921–22. He was married to Val Lock Cooley, the daughter of pioneer Houston resident W. H. Lock.

SOURCE: *New Encyclopedia of Texas*, 2:1170, 1173.

Charles Dillingham

Charles Dillingham, one of the incorporators of the South Texas National Bank in 1890, served as the bank's vice-president from 1890 through 1898 and as president from 1899 through 1912.

Born in Waterbury, Vermont, in 1837, Dillingham was the son of Vermont Governor Paul Dillingham. The younger Dillingham, who was practicing law when the Civil War broke out, organized the Eighth Vermont Volunteers, of which he was successively captain, major, and lieutenant colonel. He did not return north after the war but settled in New Orleans, where he was appointed collector of the port of New Orleans. In 1885, he moved to Houston as the receiver of the Houston and Texas Central Railroad.

In 1912, the South Texas National Bank merged with the Commercial National Bank to become the South Texas Commercial National Bank, where Dillingham served as chairman of the board from 1912 until his death in 1917. Dillingham was survived by his wife of forty-four years, the former Frances M. Cutter, of Cleveland, Ohio, and two children, Edwin Kirke Dillingham and Mary Pauline Dillingham.

SOURCE: *New Encyclopedia of Texas*, 2:1900–1901.

Robert Pace Doherty (see pp. 102–104)

Robert Pace Doherty served the National Bank of Commerce, later Texas National Bank of Commerce, for more than forty-eight years. He began as a teller in 1917 and rose through several ranks to become executive vice-president in 1935, president in 1952, chairman of the board and chief executive officer in 1958, chairman of the board and president in 1962, and honorary chairman of the board in 1966.

Born in Fort Worth in 1891, Doherty was the son of railroad executive William Doherty and Catherine Pace Doherty. His first bank position was with the First State Bank of Kingsville, Texas, from 1914 to 1917.

Doherty's other professional and business affiliations included the Rice University board of governors, the Baylor Medical Foundation, the Reserve City Bankers Association, the Texas Bankers Association, and the American Bankers Association.

Doherty died in 1967, leaving his wife of fifty-two years, the former Ada Mary Horan, and three children.

SOURCES: *Bankers' Hours* (January 1966); R. P. Doherty, Jr., to Mike Quinn, June 30, 1982, TCB Archives.

Roy Montgomery Farrar (see pp. 99–101)

Roy Montgomery Farrar served the National Bank of Commerce as vice-president in 1915 and as president from 1916 to 1920, and as president of the Union National Bank from 1924 to 1943.

Farrar, who was born in Saint Louis, Missouri, in 1870 to John H. Farrar and Sarah Rose Farrar, came to Houston in 1887, where he entered the lumber business. In 1902, he established, with Jesse H. Jones, the South Texas Lumber Company, which he operated for ten years before founding the Farrar Lumber Company in 1912.

Other business interests of Farrar's included the Missouri Pacific Lines, the Houston Compress Company, the Houston Textile Mills, the Houston Terminal Warehouse and Cold Storage Company, and the Silver Falls Timber Company of Silverton, Oregon, of which he was a director.

Farrar was also a director of the Houston branch of the Federal Reserve Bank of Dallas, a member of the Houston Port Commission for eleven years, president of the Houston Chamber of Commerce during two terms, and a member of the American Bankers Association.

Farrar was the father of one daughter by his first wife, Emily Taylor Farrar, of Houston, who died in 1902 after five years of marriage; and two daughters by his second wife, Margaret Campbell Farrar, of Waxahachie, Texas, whom he married in 1906. Farrar died on August 17, 1943.

SOURCES: *New Encyclopedia of Texas*, 1:254; *Who's Who in Texas*, 31; *Handbook of Texas*, 1:586–87.

Henry Gardes

Henry Gardes, the first president of Commercial National Bank (1886–89), was a New Orleans merchant. From 1876 to 1890, he was associated with Dymond & Gardes, commission merchants; Gardes & Wisdom, cotton merchants; and Holloway & Gardes, hardware merchants. He also served as president of American National Bank of New Orleans in 1890.

SOURCE: *New Orleans City Directory.*

E. F. Gossett

E. F. Gossett, born in Henderson County, Texas, in 1881, was an officer of South Texas Commercial National Bank for thirty-two years, beginning as second vice-president and cashier in 1922. He served as first vice-president, 1927–41; president, 1942–43; and chairman, 1944–53. For an additional year, he was chairman of successor Texas National Bank.

Gossett's banking career began at age twenty-two, when he went to work at Beaumont's Gulf National Bank, later First National Bank. After serving as state banking examiner and deputy state banking commissioner, he was appointed Houston manager of the Federal Reserve Bank of Dallas. Gossett died in November, 1954.

SOURCE: *Houston Chronicle*, November 6, 1954.

George Hamman

George Hamman, vice-president of the Union Bank and Trust Company from 1910 to 1943 and president from 1944 to 1951, was born in Calvert, Texas, in 1874, the son of William H. and Catherine L. Hamman. William Hamman was a general in the Texas state troops during the Civil War and a candidate for governor in 1878 and 1880 on the Greenback Labor ticket. His investments in mineral leases helped make his son very wealthy.

After graduation from the University of the South, in Sewanee, Tennessee, George Hamman worked at the Calvert Cottonseed Oil & Gin Company. In 1898, he entered the Planters and Mechanics National Bank, Houston, where he rose from clerk to cashier. After Planters and Mechanics' merger with the Union Bank and Trust, he was appointed vice-president of the latter institution. In the 1920s and 1930s, Hamman devoted much of his energy to the oil, gas, and sulfur industries.

Hamman was married in 1904 to Josephine Milby, daughter of Houston resident Charles Milby. He died in 1953, leaving most of his fortune to a charitable foundation set up in his name.

SOURCES: *Southeast Texas*, 508; *New Encyclopedia of Texas* 2, 2125; Webb, *et al.*, *Handbook of Texas*, 1: 762.

L. William Heiligbrodt

L. William Heiligbrodt was born in Bay City, Texas, in 1941. He received a B.B.A. in finance from the University of Texas at Austin in 1963. In 1964 he entered the training program of United California Bank, where he remained until he joined Texas Commerce Bank–Houston in 1967. He became manager of the bank's Loan Administration Division in 1969, president of TCB–Houston in 1976, and chairman of the bank in 1977. He also became vice chairman of Texas Commerce Bancshares in 1982.

In 1983 Heiligbrodt left Texas Commerce and became the vice chairman and chief executive officer of WEDGE Group, Inc., a Houston-based multi-industry holding company. He is a director of Fox Photo, Inc., Gordon Jewelry Corp., and Service Corporation International. He is an advisory director of TCB–Houston.

Heiligbrodt and his wife, Corinne, have two children. The Heiligbrodt family raises and breeds horses at their ranch in South Texas in Matagorda County.

SOURCE: Biography provided by WEDGE Group, Inc.

Edward Pinkney Hill

Judge Edward Pinkney Hill was born in Bastrop, Texas in 1838 and served as vice-president (1886–87, 1891–96) and president (1889–90) of the Commercial National Bank.

In 1875, Hill helped organize the Houston Land and Trust Company. For many years he was the Texas attorney for the Southern Pacific Company. Hill made a substantial fortune investing in Houston real estate, and in 1915 he founded the Houston Foundation. He willed most of his estate to the foundation to be used for the good of Houston and its people. He died in 1920.

SOURCES: Biographical file, Texas & Local History Department, Houston Public Library; *Houston Chronicle,* February 8, 1920, May 13, 1974; W. A. Kirkland to Kathy J. Whitmire, May 20, 1982.

Jesse Holman Jones (see pp. 75–77)

Jesse Holman Jones, president of the National Bank of Commerce from 1923 to 1929 and chairman of the board from 1929 to 1956, was born in Robertson County, Tennessee, on April 5, 1894, to William Hasque Jones and Laura Anna Holman Jones.

In 1844, young Jesse went to work for his uncle at the M. T. Jones Lumber Company in Dallas, where he subsequently became manager and general manager, moving to Houston in the interim. In 1902, Jones organized his own South Texas Lumber Company.

Jones's first venture in the investment-banking field came in 1905 when he founded the Southern Loan and Investment Company, later Jesse H. Jones and Company. In 1909, he organized the Texas Trust Company of Houston, which he served as president until its consolidation with Bankers Trust Company in 1911, after which he was chairman of the board of directors. In 1920, Bankers Trust was succeeded by the Bankers Mortgage Company, of which he was board chairman and president until 1930. By this time Jones had expanded his business interests to include real estate and commercial buildings, and he had become owner and publisher of the *Houston Chronicle*.

In 1932, President Herbert Hoover appointed Jones to the board of the Reconstruction Finance Corporation. In further federal appointments by President Franklin D. Roosevelt, he was chairman of the board of the Reconstruction Finance Corporation (1936–43), administrator of the Federal Loan Agency (1939–45), and secretary of commerce (1940–45). Jones resigned from his federal posts in 1945 and returned to Houston.

Jones' public service included such organizations as the International Red Cross, the Texas Centennial, the Texas Committee for the New York World's Fair of 1939 and the San Francisco Golden Gate Exposition. He held memberships on many public and private boards and commissions.

Jesse Jones and his wife, Mary Gibbs Jones of Mexia, Texas, whom he had married in 1920, established a charitable foundation, the Houston Endowment, Inc. Jones died in Houston on June 1, 1956.

SOURCES: *Handbook of Texas*, 3:454; *Who's Who in Texas*, 8; *New Encyclopedia of Texas*, 1:222.

Martin Tilford Jones

Martin Tilford Jones, president of the South Texas National Bank from 1890 to 1898, was born in Tennessee in 1842. He moved to Illinois sometime before the Civil War, in which he fought at the battles of Chickamauga and Nashville with the 115th Illinois Infantry. After his discharge in 1865, Jones married Louise Wollard and farmed in Illinois for ten years before moving to Texas in 1875. He opened a lumberyard in Terrell and then moved to Houston in 1883. The M. T. Jones Lumber Company soon expanded to several locations in Texas and included lumberyards and sawmills.

M. T. Jones died in 1898, naming his nephew Jesse Jones one of his five executors.

SOURCE: Timmons, *Jesse Jones*, 14, 28, 36–40, 44–46.

John Henry Kirby

John Henry Kirby, born in Tyler County, Texas, in 1860, served briefly at the turn of the century as second vice-president, and then president of Planters and Mechanics National Bank.

Kirby was admitted to the bar in 1882 and served as clerk of the Texas Legislature for the next two years. After winning a significant land case for Boston clients, he turned to lumber interests. He was involved successively in the Texas and Louisiana Land and Lumber Company, the Texas Pine Land Association, and the Gulf, Beaumont and Kansas City Railway. In 1901, he founded the Kirby Lumber Company.

Kirby's other interests included the Democratic party, the Order of Masons, Order of the Elks, and the Woodmen of the World. In 1883 he married Lelia Stewart; they had one daughter. Kirby died in 1940.

SOURCES: Houston Press Club, *Men of Affairs of Houston and Environs* (Houston, 1913): 20–21; *Handbook of Texas*, 1:966.

Benton F. Love (see pp. 255–56)

Ben Love was born in 1924 in Paris, Texas. His parents were Benton F. Love, Sr., and Nell Scott Love. His father was a cotton broker.

Love's banking career began at River Oaks Bank and Trust, where he became the chief executive in 1965. He moved to Texas Commerce as a senior vice-president in 1967. He became president of the bank in 1969 and chairman of the board in 1972, when he also became chairman and chief executive officer of Texas Commerce Bancshares.

Love serves on the boards of Burlington Northern, Inc.; Cox Enterprises, Inc.; Hughes Tool Company; and Proler International Corporation. He has served on the board of the International Monetary

Conference and as a director and president of the Association of Reserve City Bankers.

In 1947 he married Margaret McKean of Austin, and they have three children.

SOURCES: Interviews with Ben Love by Joseph A. Pratt, June 10, 1983, June 25, 1983, July 10, 1983, TCB Archives; Biographical Files, TCB Archives.

Harris McAshan

Harris McAshan, who served South Texas Commercial National Bank as first vice-president (1942–48), president (1949–58), and vice-chairman of the board (1959), was born in 1906 in Houston, as had been his parents, Samuel Maurice McAshan and Aline Harris McAshan. Both his father and his grandfather (J. E. McAshan) had served as officers of the South Texas National Bank and its successor, the South Texas Commercial National Bank; his father served as president of the latter from 1927 to 1941.

McAshan graduated from Princeton University in 1929 and returned to Houston to join the staff of South Texas National Bank as bookkeeper. During World War II, he served in the U.S. Army Anti-aircraft Corps in North Africa and Europe.

In 1933, he married Frances Corn, who bore him three daughters. McAshan died in 1962.

SOURCE: Clark, *Texas Gulf Coast* 3 : 13.

Samuel Maurice McAshan

S. Maurice McAshan was born in 1881 in Houston. He was married to Aline Harris McAshan. His parents were Elizabeth Smith McAshan and James Everett McAshan, who was one of the organizers of the South Texas National Bank in 1890 (see pp. 33–34).

Like his father and grandfather before him, McAshan became a banker. He started work in 1898 at his father's bank, South Texas National. In 1907 he began working for J. M. West at Lumbermans National Bank in Houston. In 1909 he moved to Waco where he was vice-president of Citizens National Bank. In August, 1914 he returned to Houston when ill health forced the early retirement of his father. He took his father's place as cashier of South Texas Commercial National. He soon became the chief operating officer and was named president in 1927.

Those that knew McAshan described him as blunt but fair. After his death on April 15, 1941, the Houston Clearing House Association passed a resolution in his memory which read in part, "Sham was a thing he abhorred and ostentation was anathema to him."

SOURCES: STCNB, *Directors' Minutes* 10 (May 29, 1941): 131. Also see Biographical files, TCB Archives; Interview with S. M. McAshan, Jr., by William Allison, January 28, 1972, Allison Papers, TCB Archives; J. T. McCants, *Some Information Concerning the Rice Institute*, 83; Biographical Files, TCB Archives.

N. E. Meador

N. E. Meador, vice-president of the National Bank of Commerce from 1925 to 1930 and president from 1930 to his death in 1933, was born in Atlanta, Georgia, in 1868. Meador's first location in Texas was at Mexia, where he was involved in mercantile, real estate, investment, and lumber interests beginning in 1886. In 1904, he moved to Houston as vice-president of the South Texas Lumber Company.

He was involved in the 1909 organization of the Texas Trust Company, which merged with Bankers Trust Company in 1911 to become the Bankers Mortgage Company, of which he was vice president. Meador also held at various times the positions of president of the Rice Hotel, a director of the Houston Chronicle Publishing Company, and vice-president of the Houston Hotel Association.

SOURCE: *New Encyclopedia of Texas*, 1:222.

Jonas Shearn Rice (see pp. 51–52)

Jonas Shearn Rice, president of Union Bank and Trust (1905–10), president of Union National Bank (1910–24), chairman of the board (1925–31), and director (1905–31), was born in Houston in 1855. He was one of the ten children born to Frederick A. Rice, who came to Houston from Massachusetts in 1850, and Charlotte M. Baldwin, daughter of former Houston Mayor Horace Baldwin. His father's brother, William Marsh Rice, was the founder of Rice Institute, in Houston.

After an education in the Houston public schools and Texas Military Institute, in Austin, he worked as a railroad clerk and a bank teller before going into the sawmill business in Tyler County with a brother, William M. Rice II. After working as a receiver of the Kirby Lumber Company from 1904 to 1909, he was elected to that company's vice-presidency.

Mary J. Ross, of Waco, who married Rice in 1887, bore him three daughters: Laura F. (Mrs. R. W. Neff), Lottie B. (Mrs. S. P. Farish), and Kate (Mrs. Hugo V. Neuhaus). Colonel Rice died on March 31, 1931.

SOURCES: *New Encyclopedia of Texas*, 1:230; Houston Press Club, *Men of Affairs*, 18; UNB, *Directors' Minutes* 2 (March 17, 1931): 172–73.

Albert Dee Simpson (see pp. 128–29)

Albert Dee Simpson served the National Bank of Commerce as an officer for thirty-seven years, as vice-president (1923–34), president (1935–51), vice-chairman of the board (1952–57), and honorary chairman of the board (1958–60).

The son of a Methodist minister, Simpson was born in Burnet County, Texas, in 1881. After an education in the Marble Falls public schools, Simpson worked in mercantile companies for a decade before taking his first bank job, at the First National Bank of Georgetown in 1907. From 1913 to 1917, he held the positions of university secretary and assistant to the president of Southwestern University at Georgetown.

After a year in the auditing department of the Texas Company in Houston, Simpson entered the National Bank of Commerce as a bookkeeper in 1919; he remained with the bank until his death in December, 1960.

Simpson served two terms on the executive council of the American Bankers Association and was an officer or director of the National Foreign Trade Council, the Houston Foreign Trade Association, the Houston Transit Company, Trans-World Airlines, the Radio-Keith-Orpheum Corporation, the Tennessee Gas Transmission Company, the Houston Community Chest, Jefferson Davis Hospital, and the Houston Chamber of Commerce. He was a member of the American Academy of Political and Social Science, the New York Southern Society, and the Pan-American Society.

Simpson was married in 1905 to Mamie Verna Tate, of Llano County; they were the parents of a daughter and three sons.

SOURCES: Clark, *Texas Gulf Coast*, 3:187; *New Encyclopedia of Texas*, 1:222; *Who's Who in Texas*, 56.

Gus C. Street

Gus C. Street, president of the National Bank of Commerce 1913 to 1915, was born in Charleston, South Carolina, in 1853. He worked in the cottonseed-oil business in New Orleans and then in Houston, where he formed his own cottonseed-oil manufacturing firm, G. C. Street and Company, in 1896.

Street served as an alderman during the administration of Houston Mayor O. T. Holt, who, coincidentally, preceded Street as president of the National Bank of Commerce.

Street became the father of three children by his first wife, Ella R. Richardson Street, who died in 1890, and of three more by his second wife, Emily Speed Street. Street died in 1948.

SOURCES: *New Encyclopedia of Texas*, 1:501; Houston Press Club, *Men of Affairs*, 105.

Ben Taub

Ben Taub, a native Houstonian, was a director of the National Bank of Commerce from 1930 to 1933, and of NBC and its successors, Texas National Bank of Commerce and Texas Commerce Bank, from 1957 until 1974. He served as TNBC board chairman from 1966 to 1968 and as TCB senior board chairman in 1969.

Taub, one of six children, was born in 1889 to Jacob Nathan Taub and Johanna Taub. His father, an Austrian immigrant, began a wholesale tobacco business the following year. Ben Taub was active in the business for most of his adult life, as was his brother Sam, who was a director and officer of the National Bank of Commerce for many years.

It would be difficult to overstate the importance of Ben Taub's role in the development of medicine and health care in Houston. He is credited with shaping the Harris County Hospital District, persuading key leaders to build the Texas Medical Center, and influencing the move of the Baylor College of Medicine to Houston in 1943. Houston's primary charity hospital is named for him. In addition, Taub had a crucial role in obtaining the land for the University of Houston's University Park campus.

Taub served as a member of the board of the Institute for Rehabilitation and Research, the Baylor Medical Foundation, the Texas Medical Center, the DePelchin Faith Home, the University of Saint Thomas, the Wolff Foundation, the Mading Foundation, and the Taub Foundation. He was board chairman of Jefferson Davis Hospital from 1935 until 1964, as well as honorary life chairman of the board of managers of the Harris County Hospital District. He died on September 9, 1982, at the age of ninety-three.

SOURCES: *Bankers' Hours* (June 1966); *Houston Post*, September 10, 1982.

John E. Whitmore (see pp. 161–62)

John E. Whitmore served the National Bank of Commerce as vice-president (1948–57), senior vice-president (1958–63), and senior vice-president and loan officer (1964). He served successor banks Texas National Bank of Commerce and Texas Commerce Bank as president (1965–67), president and chief executive officer (1968), chairman of the board (1969–71), and senior board chairman (1972–73). He also served as the first chairman of Texas Commerce Bancshares, 1971–72.

Born in Tucumcari, New Mexico, in 1907, Whitmore attended the University of Texas, the University of New Mexico, and Jefferson University School of Law. He was a regional executive with the Home Owners' Loan Corporation in Albuquerque and Dallas until 1942, when he came to Houston as a U.S. naval officer in charge of naval officer procurement. In 1945, he entered the National Bank of Commerce.

Whitmore's other associations have included the Reserve City Bankers Association, the Better Business Bureau of Houston, the Houston Chamber of Commerce, the Houston Mortgage Bankers Association, the Texas Mortgage Bankers Association, the Mortgage Bankers Association of America, the Small Business Administration Regional Advisory Board, the Baylor College of Medicine board of trustees, the Gordon Jewelry Corporation, the Guardian Bank of Houston, and the Houston Symphony Society.

Whitmore and his wife, the former Clara Bauman, of Dallas, have four children.

Sources: *Bankers' Hours* (January 1965); Biographical Files, TCB Archives.

Page One, Commercial National Bank
Directors' Minutes

1

Houston, Texas. May 19 1886

The first regular meeting of Board of Directors of
The Commercial National Bank of Houston was
held at office of Hutcheson & Carrington immediately after adjournment of Stockholders meeting,
with the following Directors present; H Gardes,
E P Hill, W B Chew, M T Jones, Adam Clay, and
E L Coombs. On motion of E P Hill, E L Coombs
was called to the chair, and W B Chew elected
Secretary. On motion, H Gardes was elected
President, and E P Hill, Vice Prest, of The
Commercial National Bank of Houston, to hold
the respective positions until first regular
annual meeting, in January next.
                              On motion, a
recess was taken until 4 o'clock p.m., when
the Board again met, with all the members present. Salary of the President was
fixed at rate of $5000⁰⁰ pr annum, and Salary
of Cashier at rate of $2400⁰⁰ pr annum, &
Salarys of each to begin when the Bank
is formaley opened for business. Bond of
Cashier fixed at $25000⁰⁰, to be given with
approved security. On motion, R H Giraud
was elected Cashier. On motion, the following resolution was adopted; Resolved, that
a call of 50% be made upon all subscribers
of stock, said amount to be paid on, or before,
May 28th 1886, and E P Hill, Vice Prest, is hereby
authorized to accept, and receipt for amounts
due by Subscribers in Texas, and H Gardes,
Prest, is authorized to accept, and receipt
for amounts due by subscribers in Louisiana
and Alabama. The meeting then adjourned.

approved.   E. L. Coombs
   W B Chew Secly.   President

Notes

Chapter 1

1. National Bank of Commerce of Houston, *Directors' Minutes* (November 10, 1931): 136.

2. Despite its recent rise to prominence as the nation's "energy capital" and fourth-largest metropolitan area in the United States, Houston has not been the focus of much historical study. The best existing account of its history is David McComb, *Houston: The Bayou City*. For particularly significant aspects of the economic history of the region, see Joseph A. Pratt, *The Growth of a Refining Region*; Marilyn McAdams Sibley, *The Port of Houston: A History*.

3. Economic growth and technological change often redefine the effective boundaries of a regional economy as new activities and areas are tied into an expanding urban economy. This presents challenges to historians. Which economic activities are and are not parts of a regional economy at different times? This issue is addressed from a variety of perspectives in Glenn Porter (ed.), *Regional Economic History: The Mid-Atlantic Area since 1700*. A useful introduction to the economic analysis of regions is Harry Richardson, *Regional Growth Theory*. In writing a history of the Texas Commerce Banks, we have tended to define the regional economy as that changing area in which the major Houston banks were active. This approach becomes most difficult when we discuss the 1970s, the decade in which Houston-based holding companies began to acquire other banks in regions throughout Texas.

4. For a history of the National Bank of Commerce—one of the most important predecessor banks of the Texas Commerce Bank—see Ben F. Love, "People and Profits: A Bank Case Study" (Thesis, Southwest School of Banking, 1967). Love, who is currently the chairman and chief executive officer of Texas Commerce Bancshares, completed "People and Profits" after joining the bank in 1967, and his account concludes in that year.

5. An overview of the regulation of state banks in Texas is presented in Joseph M. Grant and Lawrence L. Crum, *The Development of State-Chartered Banking in Texas: From Predecessor Systems until 1970*. A good introductory treatment of the regulatory systems with authority over banks in the United States is William Brown, *The Dual Banking System in the United States*. Also see Helen M. Burns, *The American Banking Community and New Deal Banking Reforms, 1933–1935*, 53–61. For an introduction to the literature on bank holding companies, see Michael Jessee and Steven Seelig, *Bank Holding Companies and the Public Interest*; *The Bank Holding Company Movement to 1978: A Compendium*, Staff Economic Study (Federal Reserve System); Charles Smaistrla and David Cordell, "Expansion and Performance of Multibank Holding Companies in Texas," *Voice*, Federal Reserve Bank of Dallas (April 1979): 1–10; S. Kerry Cooper and Donald Fraser, *Banking Deregulation and the New Competition in Financial Services*.

5

6. The basic source for information about the managerial revolution in America is Alfred D. Chandler, Jr., *The Visible Hand: The Managerial Revolution in Modern Business.* Chandler's work analyzes the development of professional management in industrial firms, with emphasis on the period from about 1880 to 1920. For much of its history, the commercial-banking industry in Texas experienced little of the rapid growth and technological change which fostered the rise of modern management in other industries. Amid the rapid changes of the recent past, however, modern banks have undergone their own version of a managerial revolution, which has seen them adapt many of the attitudes and techniques previously developed in other industries.

Chapter 2

1. For an example of the use of this quotation see S. Deane Wasson, *Fifty Years a Cotton Market: Houston Cotton Exchange and Board of Trade Brochure,* 1924, 64. On the beginnings of urbanization in Texas see Kenneth W. Wheeler, *To Wear a City's Crown: The Beginnings of Urban Growth in Texas, 1836–1865*; Susan Jackson, "Movin' On: Mobility through Houston in the 1850s," *Southwestern Historical Quarterly* [hereafter *SHQ*] 81 (January 1978): 251, 261.

2. For an excellent review of antebellum agriculture in Texas see Randolph B. Campbell and Richard G. Lowe, "Some Economic Aspects of Antebellum Texas Agriculture," *SHQ* 82 (April 1979): 351–78. Neither slavery nor commerce has received adequate study, but for an introduction to those topics see Abigail Curlee, "A Study of Texas Slave Plantations, 1822–1865" (Ph.D. dissertation, University of Texas, 1932); Vera Lea Dugas, "A Social and Economic History of Texas in the Civil War and Reconstruction Periods" (Ph.D. dissertation, University of Texas, 1963); Karl E. Ashburn, "Slavery and Cotton Production in Texas," *Southwestern Social Science Quarterly* 14 (December 1933): 257–71; Abigail Curlee Holbrook, "Cotton Marketing in Antebellum Texas," *SHQ* 73 (April 1970): 456–78; Raymond E. White, "Cotton Ginning in Texas to 1861," *SHQ* 61 (October 1957), 257–69. Also of interest are Randolph B. Campbell and Richard G. Lowe, *Wealth and Power in Antebellum Texas*; Harold D. Woodman, *King Cotton and His Retainers: Financing and Marketing the Cotton Crop of the South, 1800–1925,* 3–198; Stanley L. Engerman, "A Reconsideration of Southern Economic Growth, 1770–1860," *Agricultural History* [hereafter *AH*] 49 (April 1975): 343–61; Julius Rubin, "The Limits of Agricultural Progress in the Nineteenth-Century South," *AH* 49 (April 1975): 362–73; William N. Parker (ed.), *The Structure of the Cotton Economy of the Antebellum South.*

3. Andrew Forest Muir, "Railroads Come to Houston, 1857–1861," *SHQ* 64 (July 1960): 42–63; Andrew Forest Muir, "The Destiny of Buffalo Bayou," *SHQ* 47 (October 1943): 91–106.

4. Muir, "Railroads Come to Houston," 48–49. Brazoria County had more Texans with over $100,000 in property than did any other Texas county.

See Ralph A. Wooster, "Wealthy Texans, 1860," *SHQ* 71 (October 1967): 163–80. Also see James P. Baughman, "The Evolution of Rail-Water Systems of Transportation in the Gulf Southwest, 1836–1890," *Journal of Southern History* [hereafter *JSH*] 34 (August 1968): 357–61.

5. For an interesting review of profitability see Campbell and Lowe, "Economic Aspects of Antebellum Texas Agriculture," 374–78. Also see Hugh G. J. Aitken (ed.), *Did Slavery Pay? Readings in the Economics of Black Slavery in the United States*; James D. Foust and Dale E. Swan, "Productivity and Profitability of Antebellum Slave Labor: A Micro-Approach," *AH* 44 (January 1970): 39–62; Campbell and Lowe, *Wealth and Power*, 62–65. Although it seriously underestimates the level of commercial agriculture before 1875, the best review of economic development in late-nineteenth-century Texas is John Stricklin Spratt, *The Road to Spindletop: Economic Change in Texas, 1875–1901*. Also see Vera Lea Dugas, "Texas Industry, 1860–1880," *SHQ* 59 (October 1955): 151–83; Robert A. Calvert, "Nineteenth-Century Farmers, Cotton and Prosperity," *SHQ* 73 (April 1970): 509–30; Ralph A. Wooster, "Wealthy Texans, 1870," *SHQ* 74 (July 1970): 24–35. On the South in general see Harold D. Woodman, "Sequel to Slavery: The New History Views the Postbellum South," *JSH* 43 (November 1977): 523–54; Harold D. Woodman, "Post-Civil War Southern Agriculture and the Law," *AH* 53 (January 1979): 319–37; Pete Daniel, "The Metamorphosis of Slavery, 1865–1900," *Journal of American History* 66 (June 1979): 88–99.

6. Spratt is particularly useful on cotton and the railroads; see *Road to Spindletop*, 19–83. For an excellent discussion of the changes in the cotton industry and the need for cities see L. Tuffly Ellis, "The Revolutionizing of the Texas Cotton Trade, 1866–1885," *SHQ* 73 (April 1970): 478–508. Also see Gavin Wright, "Cotton Competition and the Post-Bellum Recovery of the American South," *Journal of Economic History* 34 (September 1974): 610–35; Roger Random and Richard Sutch, "The 'Lock-in' Mechanism and Overproduction of Cotton in the Postbellum South," *AH* 49 (April 1975): 405–26.

7. S. S. McKay, "Economic Conditions in Texas in the 1870s," *West Texas Historical Association Year Book* 15 (October 1939): 84–127; Edgar P. Sneed, "A Historiography of Reconstruction in Texas: Some Myths and Problems," *SHQ* 72 (April 1969): 435–48; Larry Earl Adams, "Economic Development in Texas During Reconstruction, 1865–1875" (Ph.D. dissertation, North Texas State University, 1980); Theodore Saloutos, "Southern Agriculture and the Problems of Readjustment: 1866–1877," *AH* 30 (April 1956): 58–76.

8. Milton Friedman and Anna J. Schwartz, *A Monetary History of the United States, 1876–1960*; *Proceedings of the Annual Convention of the Texas Bankers' Association, 1894*, 79–120; Edmund T. Miller, *A Financial History of Texas*.

9. Houston Cotton Exchange and Board of Trade, *Description of Harris County, Texas*, 6–8.

10. Houston Post, October 23, 1886. Also see Woodman, *King Cotton and His Retainers*, 346–59.

11. For a convenient summary of the changes in banking regulation be-

tween 1863 and 1913 and their impact see Benjamin J. Klebaner, *Commercial Banking in the United States: A History*, 1974): 53—102. Also see Avery L. Carlson, *A Monetary and Banking History of Texas*, 19—46; Grant and Crum, *State-chartered Banking in Texas*, 15—36; William A. Kirkland, *Old Bank—New Bank: The First National Bank, Houston, 1866—1956*, 1—21.

12. Carlson, *Monetary and Banking History of Texas*, 19—74; Grant and Crum, *State-chartered Banking in Texas*, 30—36, 163—64; Mrs. Henry Fall, *The Key to the City of Houston*, 187—89; Kirkland, *Old Bank—New Bank*, 1—48; Henry C. Grover, "The Dissolution of T. W. House and Company" (Master's thesis, University of Houston, 1962); *Texas Bankers Journal* 1 (October 1907): 6, 27.

13. On Texans' attitudes toward banks see Frederic L. Paxson, "The Constitution of Texas, 1845," *SHQ* 18 (April 1915): 397—98; Carlson, *Monetary and Banking History of Texas*; Grant and Crum, *State-chartered Banking in Texas*, 3—46; Margaret Swett Henson, *Samuel May Williams: Early Texas Entrepreneur*.

14. *Proceedings of the Fifth Annual Convention of the Texas Bankers' Association, Held at Dallas, Texas, May 8, 9, and 10, 1889*, 32, 68.

15. Gauging public attitudes toward banks and the reason for their persistence is an uncharted sea. Some insight can be gleaned from Grant and Crum, *State-chartered Banking in Texas*; Alwyn Barr, *Reconstruction to Reform: Texas Politics, 1876—1906*; Lawrence Goodwyn, *Democratic Promise: The Populist Movement in America*; Robert C. McMath, Jr., *Populist Vanguard: A History of the Southern Farmers' Alliance*; James R. Green, "Tenant Farmer Discontent and Socialist Protest in Texas, 1901—1917," *SHQ* 81 (October 1977): 133—54; Bruce Palmer, *Man over Money: The Southern Populist Critique of American Capitalism*.

16. Grant and Crum, *State-chartered Banking in Texas*, 26—30; Carlson, *Monetary and Banking History of Texas*, 31—39; *Houston Post*, April 25, 28, 1886; Thomas B. Love, "Banking Legislation in Texas—Past, Present and Future," address delivered before Texas Bankers' Association, June 5, 1908, 26—28; "Houston, South's Leading Banking Center," *Houston* (September 1941): 2—29.

17. On the dependent or colonial nature of the Houston area economy up to the 1890s see McComb, *Houston*, 19—51; Ellis, "Revolutionizing the Texas Cotton Trade," 506—508; Dewey W. Grantham, *Southern Progressivism: The Reconciliation of Progress and Tradition*, 99—103. On that topic for the South as a whole see Woodman, *King Cotton and His Retainers*, 243—360; Pete Daniel, "The Crossroads of Change: Cotton, Tobacco, and Rice Cultures in the Twentieth-Century South," *JSH* 50 (August 1984): 429—32; James C. Cobb, *Industrialization and Southern Society, 1877—1984*. For a description of Texas manufacturers' difficulties see Dugas, "Texas Industry, 1860—1880," 166—70. Also see *Houston Post*, March 10, 16, 19, 1890.

18. *Houston Post*, March 1, 1890.

19. *Houston Post*, April 25, 28, August 18, 22, 1886. On the bank situa-

tion at that time see McComb, *Houston*, 49–50; Kirkland, *Old Bank-New Bank*, 1–48.

20. Ellis, "Revolutionizing the Texas Cotton Trade," 492–94; Rupert N. Richardson, Ernest Wallace, and Adrian Anderson, *Texas: The Lone Star State*, 317–35.

21. Seymour V. Connor, *Texas: A History*, 267–73; Terry G. Jordan, "The German Settlement of Texas after 1865," *SHQ* 73 (October 1969): 193–212; Homer L. Kerr, "Migration into Texas, 1860–1880," *SHQ* 70 (October 1966): 184–216; Directors and Officers File, TCB Archives; Max H. Jacobs and H. Dick Golding, *Houston and Cotton: Commemorating Seventy-five Years of Leadership and Progress as a Cotton Market*, 15–28.

22. Interview with Tom Carter by Walter L. Buenger and Joseph A. Pratt, July 13, 1983; April 2, 1986; *The Industrial Advantages of Houston, Texas, and Environs*, 27–30.

23. *Industrial Advantages of Houston*, 11–30; Charles H. Dillon, "The Arrival of the Telegraph in Texas," *SHQ* 65 (October 1960): 200–11; McComb, *Houston*, 92–123.

24. McComb, *Houston*, 92–123; Sibley, *The Port of Houston*, 60–145. Vera Lea Dugas, "A Duel with Railroads: Houston vs. Galveston, 1866–1881," *East Texas Historical Journal* 2 (October 1964): 118–27; Michael T. Kingston (ed.), *Texas Almanac and State Industrial Guide, 1984–1985*, 349.

25. Sibley, *The Port of Houston*, 102–45; South Texas National Bank, *Directors' Minutes* 2 (October 26, 1911): 140.

26. Wasson, *Fifty Years a Cotton Market*, 52.

27. Ellis, "Revolutionizing the Texas Cotton Trade"; *Houston Post* (May 18–20, 22, 1886); Woodman, *King Cotton and His Retainers*; Carlson, *Monetary and Banking History of Texas*, 19–46.

28. This analysis is based on *Houston Post*; Commercial National Bank, South Texas National Bank, *Directors' Minutes*; Houston Cotton Exchange and Board of Trade, *Description of Harris County*; *The Industries of Houston: Her Relations as a Center of Trade, Business Houses and Manufacturing Establishments*; *Industrial Advantages of Houston*; Jacobs and Golding, *Houston and Cotton*, 15–28.

29. Carlson, *Monetary and Banking History of Texas*, 19–46; *Houston Post*, May 22, 1886; Ellis, "Revolutionizing the Texas Cotton Trade;" Grant and Crum, *State-chartered Banking in Texas*, 30–35; *Industrial Advantages of Houston*, 15–19; *The Industries of Houston*, 8–16; A. J. Peeler and Ingham S. Roberts (eds.), *The Standard Blue Book of Texas: Who's Who Edition de Luxe of Houston*, 17–18.

30. Kirkland, *Old Bank-New Bank*, 22–48; Bill Logan, *The Houston Heritage Collection of National Bank Notes, 1863 through 1935*, 38.

31. *Houston Post*, May 20, 1886.

32. *Houston Post*, May 20, 22, 1886, Commercial National Bank, *Directors' Minutes* 1 (May 19, 1886): 1–40; Logan, *Bank Notes*, 38–42; *In-*

dustries of Houston, 46–47; Houston Cotton Exchange and Board of Trade, *Description of Harris County*, 6–7.

33. Robert Craig West, *Banking Reform and the Federal Reserve, 1863–1923*, 15–34; *Houston Post*, October 23, November 12, December 9, 1886, January 6, 1901.

34. Interview with John G. Dreaper by William Allison, Allison Papers, TCB Archives. Also see *Houston Post*, May 22, 1886; Directors' Files, TCB Archives; Commercial National Bank, *Directors' Minutes* 1 (January 8, 1889): 73; (January 12, 1897): 183; *Houston Chronicle*, February 8, 1920; November 5, 1978.

35. *Houston Post*, May 20, 22, 1886, March 10, 1887, October 6, 1889; Commercial National Bank, *Directors' Minutes* 1 (May 19, 1886): 1–40.

36. Logan, *Bank Notes*, 38–59.

37. South Texas National Bank, *Directors' Minutes* 1 (May 10, 1890): 1–13; Robert S. Maxwell and Robert D. Baker, *Sawdust Empire: The Texas Lumber Industry, 1830–1940*, 20–50; *Industrial Advantages of Houston*, 63, 51; McComb, *Houston*, 112–13; Logan, *Bank Notes*, 47–51; Fall, *City of Houston*, 23.

38. *The Handbook of Texas*, ed. Walter Prescott Webb and H. Bailey Carroll, 2: 477–78; South Texas National Bank, *Directors' Minutes* 1 (March 21, 1890): n.p.; 2 (February 26, 1912): 170–71; South Texas Commercial National Bank [hereafter STCNB], *Directors' Minutes* 3 (September 29, 1921): 193–94; 8 (September 27,1934): 15–16; STCNB, *Stockholders' Minutes* 1 (January 9, 1934): 15–23; Directors' and Officers' Files, TCB Archives.

39. Planters and Mechanics National Bank Advertisements, TCB Archives; Logan, *Bank Notes*, 52–55; Fall, *City of Houston*, 67.

40. Logan, *Bank Notes*, 57–59; Marilyn McAdams Sibley, *George W. Brackenridge: Maverick Philanthropist*; *Texas Banker* 3 (December 1904): 28.

41. On the early development of the oil industry in Texas see Carl Coke Rister, *Oil! Titan of the Southwest*; John O. King, *Joseph Stephen Cullinan: A Study of Leadership in the Texas Petroleum Industry, 1897–1937*; Pratt, *The Growth of a Refining Region*. Also see McComb, *Houston*, 113–17; South Texas National Bank, *Directors' Minutes* 2 (January 10, 1911): 116–18; Interview with E. C. Japhet by Walter L. Buenger and Joseph A. Pratt, June 22, 1983, TCB Archives; *Houston Post*, April 5, 1901.

42. Henry C. Dethloff, "Rice Revolution in the Southwest, 1880–1910," *Arkansas Historical Quarterly* 20 (Spring 1970): 66–75; *Houston Post*, December 24, 25, 1900; January 3, March 31, 1901; Texas, *State Bank Law of the State of Texas as Passed by the 29th Legislature, Effective August 14, 1905*.

43. For an introduction to the extensive literature on populism in Texas and the South see Roscoe C. Martin, *The People's Party in Texas: A Study in Third Party Politics*; McMath, *Populist Vanguard*; Goodwyn, *Democratic Promise*; Lawrence Goodwyn, "Populist Dreams and Negro Rights: East Texas as a Case Study," *American Historical Review* 76 (December 1971): 1435–56; J. R. Norvell, "The Railroad Commission of Texas: Its Origin and History," *SHQ* 68 (April 1965): 465–80; Palmer, *Man over Money*.

44. Barr, *Reconstruction to Reform*, 229–42; Lewis L. Gould, *Progressives and Prohibitionists: Texas Democrats in the Wilson Era*, 25–26; Love, "Banking Legislation in Texas—Past, Present and Future;" Grant and Crum, *State-chartered Banking in Texas*, 37–46; *Proceedings of the Fifth Annual Convention of the Texas Bankers' Association, Held at Dallas, Texas, May 8, 9, and 10, 1889*, 14–20; *Houston Post*, August 27, 1905; Logan, *Bank Notes*, 78–82; Union Bank and Trust's Advertisements, TCB Archives.

45. *Houston Post*, January 6, 1901.

Chapter 3

1. Peeler and Roberts (eds.), *Blue Book of Texas*, 17–18; *Houston Post*, December 31, 1906; Logan, *Bank Notes*, 38–98; *Industries of Houston*, 14.

2. For a general overview of the economic boom in Houston from 1890 to 1930 see McComb, *Houston*, 92–123. Also see Elmer H. Johnson, *The Basis of the Commercial and Industrial Development of Texas: A Study of the Regional Development of Texas Resources*; 1–23. For a start on the study of banking and public attitudes see Bray Hammond, *Banks and Politics in America from the Revolution to the Civil War*; Gabriel Kolko, *The Triumph of Conservatism: A Reinterpretation of American History, 1900–1916*, 139–254; West, *Banking Reform and the Federal Reserve, 1863–1923*. On Texas see Grant and Crum, *State-chartered Banking in Texas*, 37–46. Love, "Banking Legislation in Texas," is a good example of the call in 1908 for banking reform to prevent a reoccurrence of the events of 1907. Also see *Proceedings of the 23rd Annual Convention of the Texas Bankers' Association, May 28, 29, 30, 1907*, 61–208.

3. Logan, *Bank Notes*, 56; Sibley, *The Port of Houston*, 136–38; *Houston Post*, October 1, 1890; November 5, 1911.

4. See, for example, *Texas Bankers' Journal* 1 (October 1907). Also see T. Harry Gatton, *The Texas Bankers' Association: The First Century, 1885–1985*.

5. Grant and Crum, *State-chartered Banking in Texas*, 99–103; Earl Bryan Schwulst, *Extension of Bank Credit: A Study in the Principles of Financial Statement Analysis as Applied in Extending Bank Credit to Agriculture, Industry, and Trade in Texas*, 237–80.

6. Grant and Crum, *State-Chartered Banking in Texas*, 71–116; Texas, *General Laws Texas, Thirty-first Legislature: Regular, First, and Second Called Sessions, 1909*, 406; Texas, *State Banking Laws: Digest 1909*.

7. Union National Bank [hereafter UNB], *Directors' Minutes* (November 8, 1924): 40; Frank W. Ilfrey, "A Thumbnail History of Union National Bank and Its Personnel," *Houston Banker* (September 1944): 4; Carlson, *Monetary and Banking History of Texas*, 56–67; Grant and Crum, *State-chartered Banking in Texas*, 171–91.

8. Grant and Crum, *State-chartered Banking in Texas*, 75–76.

9. Friedman and Schwartz, *A Monetary History of the United States*, 152–73; *Texas Banker* 6 (November 1907): 13; Grover, "The Dissolution of T. W. House and Company."

10. West, *Banking Reform*, 42—135; Robert H. Wiebe, *The Search for Order, 1877—1920*, 201.

11. *Texas Almanac, 1984—1985*, 348—49; McComb, *Houston*, 82—83.

12. *The Planters & Mechanics National Bank*, 2—3, 14. For a review of Houston banks in this period see J. Virgil Scott, "Houston Banks Grow," *Houston* 15 (September 1943): 6—7.

13. On John Henry Kirby see George T. Morgan, Jr., "The Gospel of Wealth Goes South: John Henry Kirby and Labor's Struggle for Self-Determination, 1901—1916," *SHQ* 75 (October 1971): 186—97; Maxwell and Baker, *Sawdust Empire*, 98—105; John O. King, *The Early History of the Houston Oil Company of Texas, 1901—1908*; Mary Lasswell, *John Henry Kirby: Prince of the Pines*. On the bank see Logan, *Bank Notes*, 52—54; *Industrial Advantages of Houston*, 15—16, 67; "Planters & Mechanics National Bank Minutes and Liquidation Contracts, 1906—1912," TCB Archives; "Planters & Mechanics National Bank, 1901," TCB Archives; Planters & Mechanics National Bank, Statement of Condition, 1907; *Texas Bankers' Journal* 1 (October 1907): 1, 6.

14. Logan, *Bank Notes*, 52—55; Directors and Officers File, TCB Archives.

15. For a comparison of Houston banks in 1894 see *Industrial Advantages of Houston*, 15—16. For 1907 see *Texas Bankers' Journal* 1 (October 1907): 28.

16. Logan, *Bank Notes*, 57—59. Also see Bascom N. Timmons, *Jesse H. Jones: The Man and the Statesman*, 72—87; Statements of Condition, TCB Archives.

17. Grant and Crum, *State-chartered Banking in Texas*, 44; Schwulst, *Extension of Bank Credit*, 166—67.

18. *Houston Post*, August 27, 1905; Directors' and Officers' File, TCB Archives.

19. *Union Bank and Trust Company of Houston, Texas*, 19; Grant and Crum, *State-chartered Banking in Texas*, 47—70.

20. *Union Bank and Trust Company*, 19.

21. Commercial National Bank, *Directors' Minutes* 2 (March 13, 1906); Love, "Banking Legislation in Texas"; UNB, *Directors' Minutes* 1 (November 8, 1924): 40; Ilfrey, "History of Union National Bank"; Contracts and Agreements concerning the Organization of Union National, TCB Archives; Interview with Earl V. Dreyling by William Allison, Allison Papers, TCB Archives.

22. Houston Post, December 31, 1910; Statements of Condition, TCB Archives; UNB, *Directors' Minutes* 1 (April 1, 1924): 21—27; Interview with Dreyling by Allison; Interview with James J. Clayton by William Allison, Allison Papers, TCB Archives.

23. UNB, *Directors' Minutes* 1 (October 4, 1910): 20; 1 (November 1, 1910): 38—39.

24. Interview with Dreyling by Allison. Also see Timmons, *Jones*, 61—96; J. Lester Jones, *W. T. Carter and Bro.*, 7—18; UNB, *Directors' Minutes* 1

(May 10, 1917): 187; 1 (October 9, 1917): 200; 1 (January 8, 1918): 205–208.

25. Love, "People and Profits," 15–17; Timmons, *Jones*, 85–96; National Bank of Commerce [hereafter NBC], *Directors' Minutes* 1 (October 13, 1914): 111; 2 (February 10, 1925): 197. For the earliest available list of stockholders see National Bank of Commerce, "Auditors' Report, August 30, 1919," 53–56, TCB Archives.

26. NBC, *Directors' Minutes* 1 (July 3, 1912): 1–2; 2 (February 10, 1925): 196–99; 2 (January 9, 1923): 127–28.

27. Logan, *Bank Notes*, 88–93; "The New Houston Bank," *Texas Bankers' Record* 1 (May 1912): 119–20; "The National Bank of Commerce, Silver Anniversary, 1912–1937"; J. Evetts Haley, *Charles Schreiner, General Merchandise*; Gene Hollon, "Captain Charles Schreiner, the Father of the Hill Country," *SHQ* 48 (October 1944): 145–168.

28. Love, "People and Profits," 17; Directors and Officers Files, TCB Archives; Timmons, *Jones*, 77, 120–23.

29. Sibley, *The Port of Houston*, 156–58; Love, "People and Profits," 12–14; NBC, *Directors' Minutes* (January 11, 1921): 45–51.

30. Texas Bankers' Record 1 (February 1912): 67. Also see "Report of Robinson and Masuelette at the Consolidation of Commercial National Bank and South Texas National Bank, March 2, 1912," TCB Archives; W. B. Chew, "To the Stockholders of the Commercial National Bank of Houston," February 26, 1912, TCB Archives.

31. Directors and Officers Files, TCB Archives; Sibley, *The Port of Houston*, 137–38.

32. Interview with John G. Dreaper by William Allison, Allison Papers, TCB Archives; Statements of Condition, TCB Archives; *Houston Post*, August 18, 1932; Commercial National Bank, *Directors' Minutes* 2 (December 31, 1907).

33. South Texas National Bank, *Directors' Minutes* 2 (December 29, 1910): 115.

34. 1912 Merger of Commercial National and South Texas National File, TCB Archives; South Texas National Bank, *Directors' Minutes* 2 (January 20, 1912): 160; "The New South Texas Commercial National Bank of Houston," *Texas Bankers' Record* 1 (February 1912): 58–59.

35. Interview with Dreaper by Allison; STCNB, *Directors' Minutes* 1 (February 24, 1912): 15–23; Statements of Condition, TCB Archives; Bank Histories of Predecessor Banks of Texas National Prepared by Marketing, TCB Archives.

36. Interview with Dreaper by Allison.

37. Schwulst, *Extension of Bank Credit*, 237–80; STCNB, *Directors' Minutes*, 2 (September 24, 1914): 281–95.

38. West, *Banking Reform and the Federal Reserve*, 52–230.

39. STCNB, *Directors' Minutes* 1 (January 13, 1914): 189–93; 1 (March 26, 1914): 197–216; 1 (April 30, 1914): 217–23.

40. STCNB, *Directors' Minutes* 1 (March 26, 1914): 201.

Chapter 4

1. Lamar Fleming, Jr., *Growth of the Business of Anderson, Clayton &
Co.*, ed. James A. Tinsley; McComb, *Houston*, 92–123; Sibley, *The Port of
Houston*, 121–70; STCNB, *Directors' Minutes* 6 (October 29, 1931): 195;
"Railroad Mileage in Texas, 1853–1980,"in Kingston (ed.), *Texas Almanac,
1984–1985*, 466.
2. Sibley, *The Port of Houston*, 160–61; Wasson, *Fifty Years a Cotton
Market*, J. V. Scott, "Cotton and the Port of Houston," *Houston Port and City*
(November 1930): 32–33; Louis Tuffly Ellis, "The Texas Cotton Compress In-
dustry: A History" (Ph.D. dissertation, University of Texas, 1964): 304–306.
3. Fleming, *Anderson, Clayton & Co.*, 1–35; STCNB, *Directors' Minutes* 4 (June 28, 1923): 83–91; NBC, *Directors' Minutes* 2 (November 8,
1921): 74–76, 2 (December 12, 1922): 117–20; UNB, *Directors' Minutes* 1
(January 9, 1923); 1 (February 3, 1925); Colonel William B. Bates, *Monroe D.
Anderson: His Life and Legacy.*
4. Richardson, Wallace, and Anderson, *Texas*, 322–24; Robert E. Snyder,
Cotton Crisis, 20–21; Karl E. Ashburn, "The Texas Cotton Acreage Control
Law of 1931–1932," *SHQ* 61 (July 1957): 116–24; Joseph A. Becker, "Regional Shifts Large in Major Crop Acreage during Decade 1919–1929," *Yearbook of Agriculture*, 1932, 485–86; "Value of Texas Cotton and Cottonseed,"
in Kingston (ed.), *Texas Almanac, 1984–1985*, 467; Daniel, "The Crossroads
of Change," 429–56.
5. Wasson, *Fifty Years a Cotton Market*; Fleming, *Anderson, Clayton
& Co.*, 1–35; Sibley, *The Port of Houston*, 160–61; Interview with S. M.
McAshan by Walter L. Buenger and Joseph A. Pratt, January 4, 1985, TCB
Archives.
6. Fleming, *Anderson, Clayton, & Co.*, 1–35; Woodman, *King Cotton*,
269–360; Ellis, "Texas Cotton Compress Industry," 250–360; Jacobs and
Golding, *Houston and Cotton*, 88–89.
7. Ellen Clayton Garwood, *Will Clayton: A Short Biography*; 97–101;
Fleming, *Anderson, Clayton & Co.*, 14n.; Schwulst, *Extension of Bank Credit*,
165–81.
8. Directors' Files, TCB Archives; Bank Families, TCB Archives; Interview with S. M. McAshan by Buenger and Pratt, January 4, 1985.
9. Stockholders' Files, TCB Archives; STCNB, *Directors' Minutes* 8
(September 27, 1934): 15–16.
10. STCNB, *Directors' Minutes* 4 (June 28, 1923): 89. A similar statement can be found in NBC, *Directors' Minutes* 1 (May 8, 1917): 199.
11. Fleming, *Anderson, Clayton, & Co.*; Interview with S. M. McAshan
by Buenger and Pratt, January 4, 1985.
12. Schwulst, *Extension of Bank Credit*, 166–67; STCNB, *Directors'
Minutes* 3 (June 30, 1921): 171–81; Interview with S. M. McAshan by
Buenger and Pratt, January 4, 1985.
13. STCNB, *Directors' Minutes* 4 (June 28, 1923): 83–91; Directors'
Files, TCB Archives; Kirkland, *Old Bank–New Bank*, 68.

14. STCNB, *Directors' Minutes* 4 (June 28, 1923): 83–85.

15. Ibid., 85–89. Also see Directors' Files, TCB Archives.

16. *Texas Bankers' Record* 4 (September 1914): 47–49; STCNB, *Directors' Minutes* 3 (September 29, 1921): 195–205; 4 (September 24, 1925): 255–57.

17. NBC, *Directors' Minutes* 2 (November 8, 1921): 75. Anderson, Clayton also was a substantial borrower from Union National. See, for example, UNB, *Directors' Minutes* 2 (January 12, 1926): 1; 2 (February 8, 1927): 90.

18. *Texas Bankers' Record* 12 (January 1923): 36; Maxwell and Baker, *Sawdust Empire*, 155–202; Jones, *W. T. Carter & Bro.*.

19. Some indication of the role of oil in the industrialization of Texas can be gained from Pratt, *The Growth of a Refining Region*. On calls for industrialization and the level of industrialization see Spratt, *The Road to Spindletop*; Cobb, *Industrialization and Southern Society*.

20. For an in-depth look at one of the most prominent Texas oilmen see King, *Joseph Stephen Cullinan*.

21. Directors' and Officers' Files, TCB Archives; Henrietta Larson and Kenneth Porter, *History of Humble Oil and Refining Company: A Study in Industrial Growth*; Wasson, *Fifty Years a Cotton Market*, 56–57; Interview with John Blaffer by William Allison, May 11, 1972, Allison Papers, TCB Archives.

22. Schwulst, *Extension of Bank Credit*. For alternatives to bank lending used by oilmen, see Roger Olien and Diana Olien, *Wildcatters: Texas Independent Oilmen*, 80, 92, 122–26, 145–54, 167–68.

23. Directors' and Officers' Files, TCB Archives; Bank Families, TCB Archives.

24. *The Handbook of Texas*, 2: 668–69; STCNB, *Directors' Minutes* 6 (October 29, 1931): 193–203.

25. Auditors' Reports, National Bank of Commerce, TCB Archives; Timmons, *Jesse H. Jones*; NBC, *Directors' Minutes* 3 (February 14, 1929): 37–38.

26. McComb, *Houston*, 142–43; King, *Cullinan*, 97–135; Writers' Program, WPA, *Houston: A History and Guide*, 258–84.

27. NBC, *Directors' Minutes* 3 (December 18, 1928): 27–28; 3 (October 9, 1934): 269–70; Statements of Condition, TCB Archives.

28. UNB, *Directors' Minutes* 1 (December 21, 1925); Also see STCNB, *Directors' Minutes* 4 (June 28, 1923): 73; UNB, *Directors' Minutes* 1 (January 9, 1923); 2 (February 8, 1927): 91.

29. *The Handbook of Texas*, 2: 86–87; Directors' and Officers' Files, TCB Archives; Jesse Andrews, "A Texas Portrait: Capt. James A. Baker, 1857–1941," *Texas Bar Journal* (February 1961): 111, 187.

30. Interview with H. Malcolm Lovett by Walter L. Buenger and Joseph A. Pratt, June 24, 1983, TCB Archives; Interview with Thomas Carter by Walter L. Buenger and Joseph A. Pratt, July 13, 1983, TCB Archives.

31. McComb, *Houston*, 118–20; Susan Estabrook Kennedy, *The Banking Crisis of 1933*, 5–21.

32. STCNB, *Directors' Minutes* 5 (April 29, 1926): 29. These conclusions are drawn from a systematic reading of the three banks' minute books.

33. Klebaner, *Commercial Banking*, 111–30.

34. STCNB, *Directors' Minutes* 5 (January 11, 1927): 81–83; UNB, *Directors' Minutes* 2 (April 7, 1926): 72–73; 2 (July 6, 1926): 76. For a brief but informative discussion of the U.S. banking industry in the 1920s see Klebaner, *Commercial Banking*, 111–30.

35. STCNB, *Directors' Minutes* 5 (January 8, 1929): 275.

36. Statements of Condition, TCB Archives; Grant and Crum, *State-chartered Banking*, 117–91; R. V. Shirley and Bernard Nichols, *Trends of Development of Texas Financial Institutions*, 2–11.

37. Marine Bank Files, TCB Archives.

38. Marine Bank, *Directors' Minutes*; Marine Bank Files, TCB Archives; Statements of Condition, TCB Archives.

39. UNB, *Directors' Minutes* 1 (April 1, 1924): 21–27; 2 (December 28, 1931): 191–92; Interview with Dreyling by Allison.

40. Statements of Condition, TCB Archives; Love, "People and Profits," 18–20.

41. Statements of Condition, TCB Archives; Timmons, *Jones*, 34–98; Jesse H. Jones to Cordell Hull, January 5, 1949, Jesse H. Jones Papers, Library of Congress.

Chapter 5

1. Statements of Condition, TCB Archives.

2. On the effects of the Depression in Houston see Marsha Grant Berryman, "Houston and the Early Depression: 1929–1932" (Master's thesis, University of Houston, 1965); William Edward Montgomery, "The Depression in Houston during the Hoover Era, 1929–1932" (Master's thesis, University of Texas, Austin, 1966). For an understanding of the banking problems in Houston and elsewhere see Kennedy, *The Banking Crisis of 1933*; Timmons, *Jones*, 153–61; McComb, *Houston*, 167–71; Elmus R. Wicker, *Federal Reserve Monetary Policy, 1917–1933*, 129–96.

3. STCNB, *Directors' Minutes* 5 (August 26, 1926): 47. For deposit information see Table 4.2. Also see Statements of Condition, TCB Archives; STCNB, *Directors' Minutes* 6 (December 12, 1929): 23. For information on how the bank was operated, see S. M. McAshan to William S. Patton, January 11, 1922, STCNB Papers, TCB Archives.

4. UNB, *Directors' Minutes* 1 (November 8, 1924): 39. Also see R. M. Farrar to Our Stockholders, December 28, 1931, UNB, *Directors' Minutes* 2 (January 12, 1932): 191; Interview with Dreyling by Allison.

5. NBC, *Directors' Minutes* 2 (March 14, 1922): 97–99; 2 (December 12, 1922): 115–20; Love, "People and Profits," 15–22; Statements of Condition, TCB Archives.

6. Marine Banking and Trust, *Directors' Minutes* 1 (January 14, 1930): 96–97; People's State Bank Files, TCB Archives; Marine Bank Files, TCB Archives; Statements of Condition, TCB Archives; Grant and Crum, *State-chartered Banking in Texas*, 117–91.

7. Logan, *Bank Notes*, 95–100; Public National Files, TCB Archives. On the number of banks in Houston see Table 3.1.

8. *Houston Post*, June 10, 1928; Marine Bank and Trust, *Directors' Minutes* 1 (June 15, 1928): 14–15; Denton W. Cooley et al. to Charles O. Austin, Commissioner, Department of Banking, October 6, 1925, Marine Bank Files, TCB Archives; Denton W. Cooley to the Board of Directors, Marine Bank and Trust, January 8, 1926, Marine Bank Files, TCB Archives; UNB, *Directors' Minutes* 1 (October 14, 1924).

9. Examiners' Report of Marine Bank and Trust, August 27, 1925, Marine Bank Files, TCB Archives. Also see Cooley to the Board of Directors, January 8, 1926; Expense Account, 1928, Marine Bank Files, TCB Archives.

10. Cooley to Austin, October 6, 1925. Also see Marine Banking and Trust, *Directors' Minutes* 1 (June 15, 1928): 15; (March 12, 1930): 104–105; (May 27, 1930): 107–16.

11. Timmons, *Jones*, 85–161; Marine Banking and Trust, *Directors' Minutes* 1 (March 12, 1930): 104–106; 1 (May 27, 1930): 107–108.

12. Interview with Gainer B. Jones by William Allison, Allison Papers, TCB Archives. Also see Public National Bank and Trust Company, Loans over $1,000,000, Jones Papers; STCNB, *Directors' Minutes* 6 (October 29, 1931): 195–207.

13. Jesse Jones to A. D. McDonald, October 29, 1931, Jones Papers.

14. S. M. McAshan to Jesse Jones, October 29, 1931, Jones Papers; Memorandum for Mr. Dreaper, Jones Papers; Jones to McDonald, October 29, 1931.

15. Jones to McDonald, October 29, 1931; STCNB, *Directors' Minutes* 6 (October 29, 1931): 195–207. Also see Albert U. Romasco, *The Poverty of Abundance*, 39–96.

16. William E. Leuchtenburg, *Franklin D. Roosevelt and the New Deal*, 71–79.

17. S. M. McAshan to James A. Baker, October 27, 1931, in STCNB, *Directors' Minutes* 6 (October 29, 1931): 197. Also see UNB, *Directors' Minutes* 2 (November 10, 1941): 185–90; Jones to McDonald, October 19, 1931; Jesse Jones to R. M. Farrar, October 27, 1931, Jones Papers; Jesse Jones to R. C. Holmes, November 14, 1931, Jones Papers; Jesse Jones to W. T. Kemper, November 14, 1931, Jones Papers.

18. McAshan to Baker, October 27, 1931.

19. R. M. Farrar to Our Board of Directors, November 5, 1931, in UNB, *Directors' Minutes* 2 (November 10, 1931): 189.

20. NBC, *Directors' Minutes* 3 (November 10, 1931): 136. Also see S. M. McAshan to Jones, October 29, 1931, Jones Papers; Jones to Holmes, November 14, 1931, Jones Papers; Jesse Jones to James A. Baker, October 29, 1931, Jones Papers; STCNB, *Directors' Minutes* 6 (October 29, 1931):

195–207; NBC, *Directors' Minutes* 3 (November 10, 1931): 135–37; Jesse Jones with Edward Angly, *Fifty Billion Dollars: My Thirteen Years with the RFC, 1932–1945,* 85–86.

21. McAshan to Baker, October 27, 1931; Jones to McDonald, October 29, 1931; R. H. Collier to Jesse H. Jones, October 28, 1931, Jones Papers.

22. UNB, *Directors' Minutes* 2 (November 10, 1931): 188; Jones to Mc-Donald, October 29, 1931; McAshan to Baker, October 27, 1931; Houston Land and Trust Company, Report of Condition, March 27, 1929, TCB Archives; Jones to Kemper, November 14, 1931.

23. McAshan to Baker, October 27, 1931. Also see Jones to Baker, October 29, 1931; Jesse Jones to A. B. Elias, November 7, 1931, Jones Papers; UNB, *Directors' Minutes* 2 (November 10, 1931): 187. On the role of the Southern Pacific see Jones to McDonald, October 29, 1931; Jesse Jones to Hale Holden, November 30, 1931, Jones Papers; H. W. DeForest to Jesse Jones, December 4, 1931, Jones Papers; Jesse Jones to H. W. DeForest, December 18, 1931, Jones Papers.

24. *Houston Post-Dispatch,* October 27, 1931; *Houston Chronicle,* October 27, 1931; McAshan to Baker, October 27, 1931; Jones to Holmes, November 14, 1931; Kirkland, *Old Bank–New Bank,* 75–91; McComb, *Houston,* 115–17.

25. Interview with Clayton by Allison. Also see R. M. Farrar to Jesse Jones, October 30, 1931, Jones Papers; R. M. Farrar to Jesse Jones, November 13, 1931, Jones Papers; R. M. Farrar to Jesse Jones, December 16, 1931, Jones Papers; R. M. Farrar to Jesse Jones, December 30, 1931, Jones Papers.

26. For a sampling of Jones's letters to executives of major financial institutions and corporations see Public National File, Jones Papers. Also see Love, "People and Profits," 20–22; McComb, *Houston,* 115–17; NBC, *Directors' Minutes* 3 (October 20, 1933): 205–206; 3 (October 27, 1933): 207–208; 3 (December 29, 1934): 277.

27. Jones to McDonald, October 29, 1931. Also see Leuchtenburg, *Roosevelt and the New Deal,* 71–72; Arthur M. Schlesinger, Jr., *The Coming of the New Deal,* 425–33.

28. December, 1935, Statements of Condition, TCB Archives; 1935 Annual Reports to the Boards of Directors, TCB Archives.

Chapter 6

1. For an overview of the changes in the regional economy see McComb, *Houston,* 92–205; Pratt, *The Growth of a Refining Region,* 61–122; Sibley, *The Port of Houston,* 146–92; Fleming, *Anderson, Clayton, & Co.,* 22–24; Jacobs and Golding, *Houston and Cotton,* 33–37.

2. Berryman, "Houston and the Early Depression"; Montgomery, "The Depression in Houston during the Hoover Era"; Kennedy, *The Banking Crisis of 1933,* 203–36; O'Connor, *The Banking Crisis and Recovery,* 14–84; Grant and Crum, *State-chartered Banking,* 204–96; STCNB, *Directors' Min-*

utes 6 (December 12, 1929): 23; STCNB, *Stockholders' Minutes* 1 (January 9, 1934): 13.

3. O'Connor, *The Banking Crisis and Recovery*, 63–64, 89; Grant and Crum, *State-chartered Banking*, 230–35; Burns, *New Deal Banking Reform*; Jones, *Fifty Billion Dollars*, 13–87; Kingston (ed.), *Texas Almanac, 1984–1985*, 407.

4. Fleming, *Anderson, Clayton, & Co.*, 24. Also see W. L. Clayton to *Houston Post*, October 23, 1934, reprint in Anderson, Clayton Archives.

5. Robert E. Snyder, *Cotton Crisis*; Fleming, *Growth of Anderson, Clayton, & Co.*, 22–25; Leuchtenburg, *Roosevelt and the New Deal*, 73–75; Statements of Condition, TCB Archives.

6. On cotton problems before 1930 see *Texas Bankers' Record* 4 (September 1914): 47–49; STCNB, *Directors' Minutes* 3 (September 19, 1921): 195–205; 4 (June 29, 1923): 82–91.

7. For a good summary of the problems facing all southern cotton growers and the reasons for this decline see Daniel, "The Crossroads of Change," 429–56.

8. S. M. McAshan to Captain James A. Baker, September 16, 1936, in STCNB, *Directors' Minutes* 8 (October 15, 1936): 295. Also see STCNB, *Directors' Minutes* 8 (June 27, 1935): 113–21; Union National Bank, *Directors' Minutes* 2 (January 8, 1935): 5–8; NBC, *Directors' Minutes* 3 (January 8, 1935): 285–86.

9. Loan and security figures are in Statements of Condition, TCB Archives. Liquidity is in STCNB, *Shareholders' Minutes* 1.

10. Anderson, Clayton, "Anderson Clayton: Eight Decades of Progress," *Annual Report*, 1984, 4–9; STCNB, *Directors' Minutes* 6 (May 26, 1932): 285; 8 (November 1934): 27.

11. Anderson, Clayton and Geo. McFaddin & Bros. continued to borrow from NBC through the 1940s. See NBC, *Executive and Discount Committee Minutes*, TCB Archives.

12. Pratt, *The Growth of a Refining Region*; Marquis James, *The Texaco Story: The First Fifty Years, 1902–1952*; King, *Joseph Stephen Cullinan*; Larson and Porter, *History of Humble*; John McLean and Robert Haigh, *The Growth of Integrated Oil Companies*; Craig Thompson, *Since Spindletop: A Human Story of Gulf's First Half-Century*; James A. Clark and Michael Halbouty, *Spindletop*; King, *The Houston Oil Company*.

13. Timmons, *Jones*, 77–78, 96, 118–19; Directors' Files, TCB Archives; R. L. Blaffer to Charles Dillingham, February 16, 1912, in South Texas National Bank, *Directors' Minutes* 2 (March 26, 1908–April 29, 1913).

14. Hugo Anderson, "A Banker's View of Oil Conservation," address before Independent Bankers' Association of Southern California, June 24, 1954, Los Angeles, California. A copy of the speech was supplied by the First National Bank of Chicago. Also see Schwulst, *Extension of Bank Credit*, 220–34; Harry Carothers Wiess, "The Banker and the Oil Man in Texas," address before Texas Bankers' Association, San Antonio, Texas, May 19, 1937, Eugene

C. Barker Texas History Center, Austin, Texas; Interviews with E. O. Buck by Joseph A. Pratt, Houston, August 8, 1982, July 8, 1983, TCB Archives.

15. Auditors' Report, National Bank of Commerce, July 31, 1921, Schedule No. 27, TCB Archives; Auditors' Report, National Bank of Commerce, July 31, 1922, Schedule No. 30, TCB Archives; Interview with Japhet by Pratt and Buenger, June 22, 1983.

16. H. Harold Wineburgh, *The Texas Banker: The Life and Times of Fred Farrel Florence,* 127–35; Nathan Adams, *The First National in Dallas,* 62–63; James Clark and Michel Halbouty, *The Last Boom.*

17. Interview with William A. Kirkland by Walter L. Buenger, July 3, 1985, TCB Archives.

18. These generalizations are drawn from a systematic study of the individual loans approved by the National Bank of Commerce in this era. The loan records are found in NBC, *Executive and Discount Committee Minutes.*

19. NBC, *Executive and Discount Committee Minutes* 1:1, 10.

20. Gerald Nash, *United States Oil Policy, 1890–1964;* Harold Williamson, Ralph Andreano, Arnold Daum, and Gilbert Klose, *The American Petroleum Industry: The Age of Energy, 1899–1959,* 535–66; David Prindle, *Petroleum Politics and the Texas Railroad Commission,* 19–69; August Giebelhaus, *Business and Government in the Oil Industry: A Case Study of Sun Oil, 1876–1945,* 198–240; Erich Zimmermann, *Conservation in the Production of Petroleum: A Study in Industrial Control;* Stephen McDonald, *Petroleum Conservation in the United States: An Economic Analysis;* Interview with J. Howard Marshall by Joseph A. Pratt, July 19, 1983, TCB Archives; Interviews with E. O. Buck by Joseph A. Pratt, August 8, 1982, July 8, 1983, TCB Archives.

21. Interviews with Buck by Pratt, August 8, 1982, July 8, 1983; Interview with John Sears by Joseph A. Pratt, July 17, 1983, TCB Archives.

22. NBC, *Executive and Discount Committee Minutes,* vols. 1–10; Statements of Condition, TCB Archives.

23. John Frey and H. Chandler Ide (eds.), *A History of the Petroleum Administration for War, 1941–1945;* Olien and Olien, *Wildcatters,* 67–86.

24. McComb, *Houston,* 80–81; Wasson, *Fifty Years a Cotton Market,* 56–64; *Houston Post,* July 19, September 1, 1914; June 25, 1916.

25. McComb, *Houston,* 128–32; Sibley, *The Port of Houston,* 188–98; Fleming, *Anderson, Clayton, & Co.,* 36–44; Jacobs and Golding, *Houston and Cotton,* 37–41, 61, 69.

26. Joseph L. Clark, *The Texas Gulf Coast: Its History and Development,* 2:151–72; R. H. Startzell, "Texas Steel," *Texas Journal of Science* 2 (December 20, 1950): 451–61; Pratt, *The Growth of a Refining Region,* 127–51; Interview with Herbert Allen by Walter L. Buenger and Joseph A. Pratt, August 7, 1985; *Twenty-five Years: Cameron Iron Works, 1920–1945,* 9–82.

27. McComb, *Houston,* 129–31.

28. NBC, *Executive and Discount Committee Minutes* 8 (January 7, 1944): 2353.

29. NBC, *Directors' Minutes* 3 (February 13, 1934): 240. Also see NBC, *Directors' Minutes* 3 (October 20, 1933): 205–206; 3 (October 27, 1933): 207–208; 3 (December 29, 1934): 277; NBC, *Executive and Discount Committee Minutes.*

30. STCNB, *Directors' Minutes*; UNB, *Directors' Minutes* 3 (August 23, 1943): 88–91; NBC, *Directors' Minutes* 3 (August 8, 1933): 196–97; (October 9, 1934): 270–71; (December 29, 1934): 277–79.

31. The move into international banking by NBC is discussed in Chapter 8. For the attitude of major corporations toward Union National in 1945 see Interview with R. D. Randolph by William Allison, February 10, 1972, Allison Papers, TCB Archives. John Whitmore described Union and STCNB as being "secondary or tertiary" banks when he arrived in Houston in 1945. See Interview with John E. Whitmore by Walter L. Buenger and Joseph A. Pratt, December 16, 1985, TCB Archives.

32. Kirkland, *Old Bank–New Bank*, 92–95; Statements of Condition, 1944–1946, TCB Archives.

Chapter 7

1. For an introduction to banking reform and its causes in the 1930s see Kennedy, *Banking Crisis of 1933*; James Stuart Olson, *Herbert Hoover and the Reconstruction Finance Corporation, 1931–1933*; William G. Sheperd, "The Banking Industry," in Walter Adams (ed.), *The Structure of American Industry*; Leonard L. Watkins, *Commercial Banking Reform in the United States*; James Francis Thaddeus O'Connor, *The Banking Crisis and Recovery under the Roosevelt Administration.*

2. "Regulation and Competition in Commercial Banking," Harvard Business School Case #0-385-247 (Draft), (HBS Case Services: 1985); Kerry Cooper and Donald Fraser, *Banking Deregulation and the New Competition in Financial Services*; Burns, *New Deal Banking Reforms.*

3. Grant and Crum, *State-chartered Banking*, 230–35; Kingston (ed.), *Texas Almanac, 1984–1985*, 407; Cooper and Fraser, *Banking Deregulation*, 50–56; David Alhadeff, *Monopoly and Competition in Banking.*

4. McComb, *Houston*, 115–17; also see William Hubert Baughn, *Changes in the Structure of Texas Commercial Banking, 1946–1956*, 2–7; Grant and Crum, *State-chartered Banking in Texas*, 193–242.

5. Statements of Condition, TCB Archives; Annual Reports, TCB Archives.

6. Interview with Clayton by Allison.

7. Union National Bank, *Directors' Minutes* 2 (January 8, 1935): 5.

8. Burns, *New Deal Banking Reforms*, 77–96; Kennedy, *The Banking Crisis*, 232–34; STCNB, *Directors' Minutes* 7 (September 28, 1933): 143–57; UNB, *Directors' Minutes* 2 (January 9, 1931): 243–49.

9. UNB, *Directors' Minutes* 2 (December 28, 1931): 191, 2 (May 9, 1933): 226; STCNB, *Directors' Minutes* 8 (March 25, 1935): 103. For an interesting treatment of the New Deal's effect on competition see Ellis W.

Hawley, *The New Deal and the Problem of Monopoly: A Study in Economic Ambivalence*.

10. Grant and Crum, *State-chartered Banking in Texas*, 193–242.

11. Statements of Condition, TCB Archives; STCNB, *Directors' Minutes* 8 (January 31, 1935): 81–87.

12. UNB, *Directors' Minutes* 2 (May 9, 1933): 225–25.

13. Quoted in James Stuart Olson, *Herbert Hoover and the Reconstruction Finance Corporation, 1931–1933*, 93. Also see STCNB, *Directors' Minutes* 7 (October 26, 1933): 165; UNB, *Directors' Minutes* 2 (November 14, 1933): 239; 2 (December 14, 1933): 240–41.

14. See "Original Disbursements to Banks," Texas, p. 4, Jones Papers; Jones, *Fifty Billion Dollars*, 33–34, 82–83.

15. "Original Disbursements to Banks," Texas, p. 4, Jones Papers; Kirkland, *Old Bank–New Bank*, 75–91.

16. NBC, *Directors' Minutes* 3 (October 20, 1933): 205–206; (October 27, 1933): 207–208; "Original Disbursements to Banks," Texas, p. 4, Jones Papers; Reconstruction Finance Corporation, *Minutes* (November 9, 1933): 891; (November 11, 1933): 1057–58; (November 17, 1933): 1600–1605; (December 16, 1933): 3721; Record Group 234, National Archives, Washington, D. C.

17. Lawrence L. Crum, *Transition in the Texas Commercial Banking Industry, 1956–1965* (Austin: 1970); Baughn, *Texas Commercial Banking, 1946–1956*; Klebaner, *Commercial Banking in the United States*, 145–86.

18. Statements of Condition, TCB Archives.

19. Interview with Allen by Buenger and Pratt, August 7, 1985.

20. Interview with Randolph by Allison, February 9, 1972.

Chapter 8

1. Economic Advisory Department of the National Bank of Commerce of Houston, "Strategic Houston: 6th City in the U.S.A." (Houston, 1960), p. 18; New York World-Telegram, *The World Almanac* (New York, 1941).

2. Economic Advisory Department of the National Bank of Commerce of Houston, "Strategic Houston," p. 18. For general background on the industrial growth of Houston after World War II, see Pratt, *The Growth of a Refining Region*, 87–122; Sibley, *The Port of Houston*, 171–214.

3. "Up from the Ground Came the Bubbling Crude," *Bankers' Hours* 1, no. 6 (1976): 10–12. Oil lending by banks has been little studied by scholars or journalists, and little secondary literature exists on the subject. Much of our history of oil lending thus has been constructed from interviews, internal bank reports, and the minutes of the loan committee of the National Bank of Commerce. Interviews with E. O. Buck by Joseph A. Pratt, August 8, 1982, June 8, 1983, TCB Archives; Interview with Kline McGee by Joseph A. Pratt, July 26, 1983, TCB Archives; Interview with Joseph Nalle by Joseph A. Pratt and Robert A. Calvert, July 26, 1983, TCB Archives; Interview with W. D. Noel by

Joseph A. Pratt, July 19, 1983, TCB Archives; Interview with J. Howard Marshall by Joseph A. Pratt, August 26, 1983, TCB Archives; Interview with John Sears by Joseph A. Pratt, August 8, 1983, TCB Archives; Interviews with John Townley by Joseph A. Pratt, June 24, 1983, June 4, 1985, TCB Archives. Interview with Ray Winstead by Joseph A. Pratt, August 4, 1983, TCB Archives. For information about oil lending in the Permian Basin by banks in and outside Texas, see Olien and Olien, *Wildcatters*, 75, 80, 92, 122, 124–26, 145, 153–54, 167–68.

4. Interviews with Townley by Pratt, June 24, 1983, June 4, 1985.

5. Generalizations about oil lending by the National Bank of Commerce are drawn primarily from the study of the minutes of the bank's executive and discount committee from 1944 to 1964. These bound volumes contain a brief description of every loan approved by the bank in those decades. We have used this source to reconstruct the major trends in all lending areas of importance to the National Bank of Commerce.

6. "Director Close-up," *Bankers' Hours* 2, no. 2 (1977), p. 2.

7. Interviews with Buck by Pratt, August 8, 1982, June 8, 1983; Interviews with Townley by Pratt, June 24, 1983, January 4, 1985.

8. Interview with Buck by Pratt, June 8, 1983. The arrangement with Bankers Trust Company of New York is evident in the Minutes of the Executive and Discount Committee of the National Bank of Commerce in the early 1950s. See, for example, Vol. 15 (1950): 4327, 4339, 4453; Vol. 16 (1950–51): 4567, 4607, 4677, 4732, 4822, 4865, 4878; Vol. 17 (1951–52): 4920, 4986, 5004, 5008, 5011, 5021, 5077. Such loans appear regularly in the Minutes of the Executive and Discount Committee of NBC, 1950–57.

9. Interview with E. C. Scurlock by Joseph A. Pratt, June 12, 1984, TCB Archives; Interview with Jack Blanton by Joseph A. Pratt, June 12, 1984, TCB Archives.

10. Interview with Nalle by Pratt and Robert A. Calvert, July 26, 1983; Interview with McGee by Pratt, July 26, 1983. For the early history of Zapata, see the thirtieth-anniversary issue of the company's newsletter, *Viva* (October 1984), insert. For a summary of Houston-based offshore activity, see Texas National Bank of Commerce, *Houston Business* 11, no. 4 (July 1967).

11. Frank Mangan, *The Pipeliners: The Story of El Paso Natural Gas* (El Paso, Texas, 1977). Interview with W. D. Noel by Joseph A. Pratt, July 19, 1983; Interviews with Buck by Pratt, August 9, 1982, June 8, 1983.

12. Rush Loring, Jr., "The View from Inside Hughes Tool," *Fortune* (December 1973): 106–109, 173–76; *Hughes Ridgway* 14, no. 3 (Fall 1976); Interview with Calvin Collier by Joseph A. Pratt, Houston, November 27, 1984, TCB Archives.

13. Interviews with Buck by Pratt, August 8, 1982, June 8, 1983.

14. The history of the lending of the National Bank of Commerce in oil, real estate, and other areas was reconstructed from the Minutes of the Executive and Discount Committee of the bank, 1934–64. These minutes record each loan approved by the bank.

15. McComb, *Houston*, 131–44.

16. Interview with John E. Whitmore by William Allison, October 4, 1972, Allison Papers, TCB Archives; Interviews with John Whitmore by Walter L. Buenger, August 17, 1982, September 17, 1982, and by Joseph A. Pratt, June 15, 1983, TCB Archives; Interview with Lloyd Bolton by Joseph A. Pratt, June 15, 1983.

17. Such loans begin to appear in significant numbers in 1947 in the Minutes of the Executive and Discount Committee of the National Bank of Commerce and they grow in numbers in the 1950s and 1960s.

18. The details on the role of the National Bank of Commerce in financing Gulfgate Shopping Center come from Minutes of Executive and Discount Committee, Vol. 20 (1957), p. 5849.

19. Loans to GMAC, International Harvester Credit Corporation, GE Credit Corporation, Chrysler Corporation, and Rheem Acceptance Corporation appear regularly in the Minutes of the Executive and Discount Committee of NBC in the decade after World War II.

20. Houston's rapid growth after World War II made it a magnet for nationally active firms of all kinds. Although comparative information about the lending activities of other Houston banks was not available to us, one competitive advantage of NBC over its Houston-based rivals in this era appears to have been the bank's success in attracting the business of national firms that migrated to Houston.

21. Interview with William L. Tandy by William Allison, Allison Papers, TCB Archives.

22. Interview with George Ebanks by Joseph A. Pratt, November 30, 1984, TCB Archives; Interview with Mike Gaetz by Joseph A. Pratt, February 27, 1985, TCB Archives. Interview with George Ebanks by William Allison, Allison Papers, TCB Archives.

23. Interview with Ebanks by Pratt, November 30, 1984. These letters of credit appear throughout the Minutes of the Executive and Discount Committee of NBC in the late 1950s.

24. Interview with Collier by Pratt, November 27, 1984.

25. Interview with Ebanks by Allison; Interview with Ebanks by Pratt, November 30, 1984.

26. Baughn, *Texas Commercial Banking, 1946–1956*, 54.

Chapter 9

1. NBC, *Directors' Minutes*.

2. Interviews with Whitmore by Buenger, August 17, 1982, September 17, 1982; NBC, *Directors' Minutes* (1956).

3. The portrait of Jones is built from several sources, including Timmons, *Jones*; Paul Wakefield, *Jesse Holman Jones* (Houston: n.d.); Jones with Angly, *Fifty Billion Dollars*; Ben Love, "People and Profits." Also instructive were interviews with several men who worked with Jones, most notably Howard

Creekmore, of the Houston Endowment. See Interview with Howard Creekmore by Walter L. Buenger, September 17, 1982, TCB Archives; Interview with Howard Creekmore by Joseph A. Pratt, March 6, 1985, TCB Archives.

4. Although he was active in the affairs of National Bank of Commerce for almost half a century, few of Doherty's letters or personal files remain from which to construct a portrait of him. We have thus of necessity relied heavily on interviews with numerous people who worked with him, including John Whitmore, E. O. Buck, Marvin Collie, Allan Shivers, and J. W. McLean. Also interviewed was Doherty's son, Robert P. Doherty, Jr. In addition, many of the interviews conducted by William Allison included impressions of Doherty.

5. Resolution in Memory of Sam Taub, NBC, Loan and Executive Committee Minutes (1956): 296−98; NBC, *Directors' Minutes* 7 (February 28, 1956): 296−97.

6. Interview with Maurice Butler by Barbara Eaves, November 11, 1982, Eaves Papers, TCB Archives.

7. STCNB, *Directors' Minutes* 13 (May 31, 1946): 11, 19.

8. Interview with W. A. Kirkland by Walter L. Buenger, July 3, 1985, TCB Archives; W. A. Kirkland, "Memories of Jesse H. Jones," undated typescript, TCB Archives; Interview with Allan Shivers by Joseph A. Pratt and Robert A. Calvert, August 10, 1983, TCB Archives.

9. Interview with Love by Pratt, February 27, 1985.

10. Details about this episode come primarily from, Interview with Shivers by Pratt and Calvert, August 10, 1983.

11. In seeking to reconstruct the events which led to Collie's brief tenure as the president of National Bank of Commerce, we have again relied primarily on interviews with various individuals who were active in the bank during these years, including Marvin Collie, Allan Shivers, John Whitmore, E. O. Buck, Ray Winstead, and John T. Jones.

12. Interview with Kirkland by Buenger, July 3, 1985.

13. Most of the information about the activities of Texas National Bank in the 1950s and early 1960s came from interviews of former employees of that bank, since few TNB records survived the merger of 1964 with the National Bank of Commerce. Of special usefulness were interviews with J. W. McLean, Norman Binz, Tom Carter, Jean Dupree, Kline McGee, and Joseph Nalle. Personal papers provided by J. W. McLean, now in the TCB Archives, included a group of memoranda on the affairs of TNB.

14. The best sources for an overview of these programs were the annual reports of the Texas National Bank and the minutes of the board of directors meetings. Both sources are now in the TCB Archives.

15. The analysis of the merger from the perspective of Texas National Bank's management is taken from J. W. McLean to Executive Committee, Memorandum on Consolidation, July 8, 1963, Personal Files of J. W. McLean.

16. Ibid. See also "Application for Approval to Consolidate," National Bank of Commerce and Texas National Bank to Office of Comptroller of the Currency, Treasury Department, September 6, 1963. A copy is filed with the minutes of the board of directors of each bank.

17. The nuts-and-bolts details of these discussions, as well as those of subsequent meetings between major participants in the merger, remain the subject of controversy. The best published account of the merger is Douglas Austin, "Proxy Contests and the Control of Commercial Banks," *Bankers' Magazine* (Winter 1966): 9–20. After interviewing survivors from both camps, uncertainty remains. Our task has been made easier, however, by the fact that we are primarily concerned with the broad trends affecting the history of the bank, not the role of specific individuals in specific incidents.

18. The primary source of information on the progress of the proposed merger through the regulatory system was a file on the merger in the records of Liddell, Sapp, the law firm of the National Bank of Commerce. See "The National Bank of Commerce of Houston Consolidation with Texas National Bank of Houston," File 4901, Liddell, Sapp, Houston.

19. For the details on the antitrust implications of the merger, see "NBC Consolidation with TBN-Antitrust Considerations," File 4691B, Liddell, Sapp, Houston.

20. For a detailed discussion of the justifications of the merger from the perspective of the banks' managers, see "Application for Approval to Consolidate," NBC and TNB to the Office of the Comptroller of the Currency, September 6, 1963. See p. 15 for a summary of the lending limit of the banks, both as separate institutions and as a single, merged bank.

21. Such attitudes of long-term officers of the National Bank of Commerce appear to have been hardened by their sense that the newcomers were a bit too eager to assert control. Such tensions accompany most major mergers between partners of roughly equal size; as in many similar instances, these tensions ultimately were resolved only by a clear assertion of control by one partner, in this instance, the National Bank of Commerce.

22. J. W. McLean to R. P. Doherty, March 5, 1965, Ben Love Papers, TCB Archives.

23. Doherty's explanation of events can be seen in R. P. Doherty to Norman Dunn (regional comptroller of the currency), January 25, 1965. This letter is in "Texas National Bank of Commerce of Houston—Corporate Matters," File 4692, Liddell, Sapp, Houston.

24. The vote of the executive committee embodied all of the growing tensions within the bank. Doherty later described this crucial vote as a vote to give McLean a newly created job as vice-chairman, thus removing him from the presidency and the line of succession to chairman. McLean, however, understood the issue in question as whether he should become the chief executive officer of the bank. Since minutes of the meeting are not available, the exact nature of the vote cannot be definitively described. What is certain is that the executive committee handed Doherty a defeat which he had not expected, setting the stage for the proxy battle which followed quickly. See, Interview with McLean by Pratt, August 3, 1984.

25. The collapse of this merger merited coverage in the *Wall Street Journal*, which rarely included much coverage of the major Texas banks in this era. This sort of publicity was not, of course, the sort preferred by the bank.

Chapter 10

1. For a brief overview of Houston's development after World War II, see Pratt, *The Growth of a Refining Region*, 89–119. See also Economic Advisory Department of the National Bank of Commerce, "Strategic Houston," copy in TCB Archives.

2. "U.S. Rotary Rig Count: Drilling Trends in the United States, 1949–1983," Hughes Tool Company, Houston, Texas.

3. For an overview of the developments in the international oil industry in this era, see Peter Odell, *Oil and World Power: A Geographical Interpretation*. For a broad view of federal oil policies in this era, see Richard Vietor, *Energy Policy in America since 1945*; for events in one important portion of the Texas industry, the Permian Basin, see Olien and Olien, *Wildcatters*.

4. The mix of loans within the petroleum division at TCB during the 1960s and early 1970s was summarized in charts compiled by lending officers of the period. See "Historical Folder—Petroleum Division," Gary Wright Files, TCB–Houston Records, TCB Archives.

5. Wallace Wilson, "Bank Financing of Oil and Gas Production Payments" (Thesis, Southwestern Graduate School of Banking, Dallas, July 1962); reprinted by Continental Illinois National Bank and Trust Company of Chicago, October 1962; G. S. Simpson, "ABC—How Deal Works, What Changes Would Do," *Independent Petroleum Monthly* (September 1961): 13–16; W. I. Spencer, J. R. Rowan, and L. F. Terry, "Bankers Like to Do Business with Oil Men," *Oil and Gas Journal* (November 21, 1955): 168–76; J. E. Warren, "Considerations concerning Bank Financing of Oil Properties," *Journal of Petroleum Technology* 8, no. 5 (May 1956): 11–14.

6. Interview with Townley by Pratt, June 24, 1983.

7. Interview with W. N. Davis by Joseph A. Pratt, August 26, 1983, TCB Archives; Interview with Townley by Pratt, June 24, 1983.

8. "Banks Offer Diversified Chemical Services," *Chemical and Engineering News* (April 29, 1968): 18–19.

9. Interview with Ebanks by Pratt, November 11, 1984; Interview with Collier by Pratt, November 27, 1984.

10. Interviews with Gaetz by Pratt, June 24, 1983, February 27, 1985.

11. Marcia Stigum, *The Money Market* (Homewood, Ill.: Dow Jones–Irwin, 1983): 129–92; "Texas Commerce Buys Interest in Major London Banking House," *Houston Chronicle*, August 8, 1968; "Texas National Bank of Commerce Purchases Interest in London Bank," *Wall Street Journal*, August 9, 1968; Interview with Ben Love by Joseph A. Pratt, July 30, 1983, TCB Archives.

12. "It's Official," *Bankers' Hours* (August 1969): 9.

13. "In Houston, In London, and in New York," *Bankers' Hours* (February–March 1969): 10–11.

14. Interview with Love by Pratt, July 30, 1983; Interview with Gaetz by Pratt, February 27, 1985.

15. "TCB in London—The City That Invented Banking," *Bankers'*

Hours (August–September 1973): 1–5; "Texas Commerce to Open Middle East Office," *Bankers' Hours* 1, no. 7 (1976): 2–5; "Spanning the Globe," *Bankers' Hours* 2, no. 7 (1977): 2–3.

16. Property Research and Investment Consultants, Inc., *Houston's Office Space Market* (Houston, 1985).

17. Interview with Bolton by Pratt, June 15, 1983; "T. O. Taylor Begins Leisure Time in March," *Bankers' Hours* (February–March 1969): 19, 32.

18. Interview with Gerald Hines by Joseph A. Pratt, February 22, 1985, TCB Archives; Interviews with Stephen Field by Joseph A. Pratt, June 6, 1983, February 2, 1985, TCB Archives; Interview with Jim Lowrey by Joseph A. Pratt, August 18, 1982, TCB Archives; Interview with Whitmore by Pratt, June 16, 1983.

19. For general information about American General, see Andrew C. Brown, "The Profitable Pariah of Insurance," *Fortune* (August 9, 1982): 60–63. For more specific ties to the Texas Commerce Bank, see "Gus Sessions Wortham, February 18, 1891–September 1, 1976," *Bankers' Hours* 1, no. 6 (1976): 3–4; Interview with Benjamin Woodson by Joseph A. Pratt, June 18, 1985, TCB Archives; Interview with Steven Walker by Joseph A. Pratt, June 17, 1985, TCB Archives.

20. Interview with Carl Galloway by Joseph A. Pratt, February 2, 1985, TCB Archives; Interview with John Adams by Joseph A. Pratt, August 6, 1982, TCB Archives; Interview with Love by Pratt, February 27, 1985; Interview with Charles Beall by Joseph A. Pratt, July 3, 1985, TCB Archives; "Houston/Southwest Commercial Division," *Bankers' Hours* (February–March 1970): 9–10; "Houston & Southwest Division," *Bankers' Hours* 8, no. 9 (1973): 32–34.

21. "Many Banks Benefit from Services of a Complete Correspondent Department," *Bankers' Hours* (March 1962): 1, 3; "Correspondent Banking Division," *Bankers' Hours* (February-March 1970): 11. The correspondent relationships among different banks varied considerably over time. Information on the existence of such relationships, but not on their magnitude, comes from an examination of banking directories, which generally list each bank's major correspondent ties.

22. John Stodden, "Their Small Size Costs Banks Business of Large Companies," *Business Review* (Federal Reserve Bank of Dallas) (October 1973): 6–7.

23. Background information about bank regulation in Texas in the decade before the holding company era was provided in the following interview: Interview with Charles Sapp by Joseph Pratt, August 9, 1982, TCB Archives.

24. Benjamin Klebaner, "The Bank Holding Company Act of 1956," *Southern Economic Journal* 24 (January 1958): 313–26.

25. The Federal Reserve Bank of Dallas compiled statistics on the percentage of deposits in chain banks in each major Texas market as of December 1, 1971. See Keefe, Bruyette and Woods, Inc., *Texas and Its Banks* (New York, n.d.): 50–54; copy of pamphlet in TCB Archives. See also John Stodden, "Multibank Holding Companies: Development in Texas, Changes in Recent Years," *Business Review* (December 1974): 1–10.

26. "Reagan State Bank, Airline Bank: Supplemental Information Supporting Applications to the Board of Governors of the Federal Reserve System," Reagan State Folder, Files of Financial Accounting Division, Texas Commerce Bancshares, TCBK Records.

27. "Reagan State: Application to the Board of Governors of the Federal Reserve System," Reagan State Folder, Files of Financial Accounting Division, TCBK Records.

28. Ibid.

29. The creation and early activities of the Texas Commerce Shareholders Company is summarized in the bank's annual report for 1970. See "Texas Commerce Bank, 1970 Annual Report" (Houston, 1971): 23.

30. Interview with Whitmore by Pratt, October 2, 1984.

Chapter 11

1. The managerial revolution which has transformed the management of many banks in recent decades is similar in many respects to the rise of modern management practices in major industrial corporations in the decades before World War I. For the basic historical treatment of the rise of the modern business enterprise, see Alfred D. Chandler, Jr., *The Visible Hand: The Managerial Revolution in Modern Business*. Also see Alfred D. Chandler, Jr., and Richard Tedlow, *The Coming of Managerial Capitalism*.

2. For background on the McAshan family, see Chapter 2 above.

3. Interviews with Buck by Pratt, August 8, 1982, June 8, 1983; Interview with Ebanks by Pratt, November 30, 1984; Interview with Whitmore by Pratt, June 15, 1983; Interview with Bolton by Pratt, June 15, 1983.

4. Interviews with Buck by Pratt, August 8, 1982, June 8, 1983.

5. Interview with Kline McGee by Joseph A. Pratt, July 26, 1983; Interview with Jean Dupree by Walter L. Buenger, Robert A. Calvert, and Joseph A. Pratt, August 5, 1983, TCB Archives.

6. Interview with Tandy by Allison.

7. Interview with Ben Kuenemann by Joseph A. Pratt, August 12, 1983, TCB Archives.

8. Interview with Woodson by Pratt, June 18, 1984, Interviews with Creekmore by Buenger, September 17, 1982, and by Pratt, March 6, 1985.

9. Interview with McLean by Pratt, August 13, 1984. For a fuller discussion of the events surrounding the proxy battle in January, 1965, see Chapter 9. Also see Douglas V. Austin, "Proxy Contests for Control of Commercial Banks," *Bankers' Magazine* (Winter 1966): 9–20.

10. Mecom's aborted deal with the Houston Endowment received heavy coverage in the regional and national media. A good summary of this episode is presented in Stanley Brown, "The Big Deal That Got Away," *Fortune* (October 1966): 164–66, 179–92. See also "Oilman Mecom Builds Fortune by Exploiting Chances Others Miss," *Wall Street Journal*, January 28, 1966; "John Mecom Heads Texas Commerce," *Houston Chronicle*, January 18, 1966); "A Deal Done In," *Time* (June 17, 1966): 62. Interview with Buck by Pratt, August 9, 1982.

11. For general background on Gus Wortham, see Dana Blankenhorn, "Gus Wortham: Insurance, Ranching, and Civic Trend-Setter Embodied Houston Establishment," *Houston Business Journal* (March 26, 1979): sec. 2, pp. 1–3; "Sphere of Gus Wortham Embraces Many Efforts," *Bankers' Hours* (March 1962): 1–2. For a chronology of the evolution of American General, see American General Corporation, 1982 Annual Report, p. 19.

12. Interview with Woodson by Pratt, June 19, 1985. "American General Buys 30 Pct. of TNBC Stock," *Houston Chronicle*, March 20, 1968.

13. "American General/Texas Commerce Bank Partners in Progress," *Bankers' Hours* (March 1968): 1–2.

14. Gerald Fischer, *Bank Holding Companies*; Gerald Fischer, *American Banking Structure: Its Evolution and Regulation*; Benjamin Klebaner, "The Bank Holding Company Act of 1956," *Southern Economic Journal* 24 (January 1958): 213–26; "One Bank Holding Company before the 1970 Amendments," *Federal Reserve Bulletin* 50 (December 1972): 999-1008.

15. Federal Reserve System, "American General Corporation: Final Certification Pursuant to the Bank Holding Tax Act of 1976," press release dated February 26, 1981, Files of Benjamin Woodson; Interview with Woodson by Pratt, June 19, 1985.

16. Interviews with Love by Pratt, June 10, 25, 1983, July 30, 1983.

17. "Texas Commerce: Master of Controls," *Dun's Business Month* 124, no. 6 (December 1984): 40–41. "Interview with Ben F. Love, Texas Commerce Bancshares," *United States Banker* (July 1981): 38–40.

18. Interview with Nelly by Pratt, August 9, 1982; Interview with Love by Pratt, June 25, 1983.

19. For the best historical account of the coming of decentralization to industrial management, see Alfred D. Chandler, Jr., *Strategy and Structure: Chapters in the History of the Industrial Enterprise*. For the observation by Doherty, see interview with Maurice Butler by Barbara Eaves, November 11, 1982, TCB Archives.

20. *Texas Commerce Bancshares: Basic Report*, Institutional Research pamphlet, Montgomery, Securities, February 22, 1984, TCB Archives. This pamphlet presents a two-page transcript of interviews with Ben Love, Chairman and Chief Executive Officer of Texas Commerce, and Marc Shapiro, Vice-Chairman and Chief Financial Officer of the bank by J. Richard Fredericks, of Montgomery Securities, TCB Archives.

Chapter 12

1. For background on bank holding companies and the Bank Holding Company Act of 1956, see Fischer, *Bank Holding Companies*; Fischer, *American Banking Structure*; Klebaner, "The Bank Holding Company Act of 1956," 213–26; "One Bank Holding Company before the 1970 Amendments," *Federal Reserve Bulletin* 50 (December 1972): 999-1008.

2. Jessee and Seelig, *Bank Holding Companies and the Public Interest*; Staff of the Board of Governors of the Federal Reserve System, *The Bank Holding Company Movement to 1978: A Compendium* (Washington, D.C.:

Government Printing Office, 1978); Association of Registered Bank Holding Companies, "The Regulation of Bank Holding Companies, 1971–1973" (Washington, D.C., 1974).

3. Interview with Whitmore by Pratt, October 2, 1984.

4. "Airline File" and "Reagan State Bank/Airline Bank File," Application to the Board of Governors of the Federal Reserve System by Texas Commerce Bancshares, Inc., for Prior Approval of Acquisition of Bank Shares, Files of Financial Accounting Division, TCBK Records.

5. The information on the acquisition of American National Bank of Beaumont by Texas Commerce Bancshares comes primarily from materials from the personal files of William Phillips, Jr. Copies of this material are in TCB Archives.

6. Phillips summarized the problems facing American National Bank in a letter to John Whitmore, Chairman of Texas Commerce Bancshares: Wm. W. Phillips, Jr., to John Whitmore, April 20, 1972, "Merger Files," TCB–Beaumont. See also William Phillips, Jr., Draft of Special to *Texas Bankers Record*, copy in "Merger Files," TCB–Beaumont.

7. Letters to Shareholders of American National Bank of Beaumont from Wm. W. Phillips, Jr., June 25, 1971, "Merger Files," TCB–Beaumont.

8. For Blaffer's role, see John Whitmore to George C. Cochran III (Federal Reserve Bank of Dallas), January 3, 1972, copy in "Merger Files," TCB–Beaumont.

9. Thomas McDade to Wm. W. Phillips, June 21, 1971, "Merger Files," TCB–Beaumont.

10. Federal Reserve System to Texas Commerce Bancshares, Inc., "Order Denying Approval for Acquisition of Bank," April 11, 1972, copy in "Merger Files," TCB–Beaumont.

11. "Fed Reconsiders Previous Denial, Approves Tex. Commerce HC Acquisition of American NB," *American Banker* (September 7, 1972); Federal Reserve System to Texas Commerce Bancshares, Inc., "Order Approving Acquisition of Banks, August 31, 1972, copy in "Merger Files," TCB–Beaumont.

12. Interview with Noel by Pratt, July 19, 1983. For a discussion of the history of each bank, its ownership, and its position in its regional economy, see the file of material on each bank in the Files of the Financial Accounting Division, TCBK Records.

13. "Half of San Angelo National Stock Sold," *San Angelo Evening Standard*, March 17, 1955; "Odessa Men Buy City Bank," *Lubbock Avalanche-Journal*, October 24, 1961; "Odessa to Get 14-Story Building," *Odessa American*, April 29, 1959. See also *Texas Commerce Bank–Lubbock, Texas, 1906–1984*, pamphlet published for the bank's seventy-eighth anniversary, TCB Archives; Minnie Conaway, "Forward with the San Angelo National Bank 1884–1959," manuscript, n.d., TCB Archives.

14. Interview with Noel by Pratt, July 19, 1983.

15. This summary of TCB's strategy comes from a variety of sources, including the following: Interview with Love by Pratt, July 30, 1983; Interview with Thomas McDade by Joseph A. Pratt, June 22, 1983, TCB Archives; Interview with May Chu by Joseph A. Pratt, June 3, 1983, TCB Archives. The de-

velopment of strategy is evident throughout the files of the Acquisitions/
Strategy and Screening Committee, TCBK Records. For an example of the
planning surveys compiled by TCBK to guide its acquisitions, see Thomas
McDade, "Review of TCBK Merger Opportunities," memo, May 10, 1976,
Minutes of Acquisitions/Strategy and Steering Committee, TCBK Records.
For general information about the bank holding-company movement in Texas
in the early 1970s, see William Broyles and Alex Sheshunoff, "How First
National Passed Republic," *Texas Monthly* 2 (May 1974): 44–54, 85–96;
William Kelly, "Consolidation of Banks Reshaping Texas Markets," *Texas
Business Review* (December 1974): 1–10; Fred Hays, "Multibank Holding
Companies: A Review of the 1970s," *Texas Business Review* (January–
February 1981): 30–33; John H. Lewis, "Bank Holding Company Acquisitions
in Texas," *Texas Business Review* (April 1978): 75–78; Charles Smaistrla and
David Cordell, "Expansion of Multibank Holding Companies in Texas," *Voice*
(April 1979): 1–10.

16. Interview with George Cochran III by Joseph A. Pratt, August 16,
1983, TCB Archives; Interview with Tim Irvine by Joseph A. Pratt, June 8,
1983, TCB Archives.

17. Anthony Winer, "Applying the Theory of Probable Future Competition," *Federal Reserve Bulletin* (September 1982): 527–33; Fred Hays, "The
Incipiency Doctrine and Potential Competition in Secondary Banking Markets
in Texas," *Texas Business Review* (March–April 1981): 70–74; Billy C. Hamil-
ton, "The Potential Competition Doctrine and Bank Holding Company Acquisitions in Texas," *Texas Business Review* (March–April 1981): 64–69;
Stephen Smith, "The History of Potential Competition in Bank Mergers and
Acquisitions," *Economic Perspectives* (Federal Reserve Bank of Chicago) (July–
August 1980): 16.

18. The assets of the member banks of the bank holding companies in
Texas are published in the holding companies' annual reports. For the figures
cited regarding TCB, see Texas Commerce Bancshares, *1982 Annual Report*
(Houston, 1983): 72–73.

19. Prospectus: Texas Commerce Bancshares, Inc., re Proposed Merger
of First National Bank of Stafford, July 15, 1981, Stafford National Bank
Folder, Files of Financial Accounting Division, TCBK Records; "Special Meeting of Shareholders of Chemical Bank & Trust Company—Proxy Statement,"
copy in Chemical Bank Folder, Files of Financial Accounting Division, TCBK
Records.

20. Interview with Irvine by Pratt, June 8, 1983; Interview with May
Chu by Pratt, June 3, 1983; "*De Novo* Banks," *Bankers' Hours* 20 (1982):
1–19.

21. Thomas McDade, "Evaluation of *De Novo* Results," memo dated
December 13, 1978, Acquisitions Strategy & Screening Committee, 1978
folder, Files of Thomas McDade, TCBK Records; Marc Shapiro, "Additional
De Novo Banks," memo dated May 12, 1976, Acquisitions Committee—
1976—Folder, Files of Thomas McDade, TCBK Records.

22. The clearest summary of TCB's metroplex strategy is presented in the
bank's in-house magazine. See "The Metroplex Strategy," *Bankers' Hours* 18

(1980): 1–13. Detailed discussions of aspects of this strategy and of the expansion of the bank's Dallas–Fort Worth operations are sprinkled throughout the Minutes of Acquisitions Strategy and Steering Committee, TCBK Records. Much of this material is contained in duplicate in folders labeled with the name of each bank involved in the files of Thomas McDade, TCBK Records.

23. "Director Closeup: Gene Engleman, Entrepreneur," *Bankers' Hours* 20 (1982): 20–22.

24. "The Metroplex Strategy," *Bankers' Hours* 18 (1980): 8–12.

25. The difficulties encountered by Texas Commerce Bancshares in establishing a major presence in downtown Dallas are suggested by comparative statistics. As of December 31, 1983, the assets of Dallas-based RepublicBank Corporation's major Houston bank were about $2 billion, which was more than 10 percent of the holding company's total assets. Dallas-based InterFirst Corporation's flagship bank in Houston had $1.6 billion in assets, or more than 7 percent of the total assets of the holding company. First City Corporation based in Houston had a Dallas bank with $1.1 billion in assets, which represented more than 6 percent of its total assets. Finally, Texas Commerce Bancshares' largest bank in Dallas at the time had only $341 million in assets, or less than 2 percent of the holding companies' total assets.

26. Thomas McDade, "Implications of Merger of First United Bancorporation and TCBK," February 6, 1980, Minutes of Acquisitions Strategy and Steering Committee, TCBK Records; Ben Love to Paul Mason, April 13, 1982, First United Bancorp folder, Files of Thomas McDade, TCBK Records.

27. Ben Love to Paul Mason, April 16, 1982, First United Bancorp folder, Files of Thomas McDade, TCBK Records.

28. James Pierobon, "TCB Makes Unsolicited Bid for Big Texas Banking Firm," *Houston Chronicle*, July 23, 1983; Ben Love to Directors of Texas Commerce Bancshares, July 27, 1983, Ben Love Files, TCBK Records.

29. "Texas American Rejects as Inadequate $50-a-Share Offer by Texas Commerce," *Wall Street Journal*, July 27, 1983; "Cullen/Frost to Be Acquired by a Texas Bank," *Wall Street Journal*, July 27, 1983, p. 6. Despite the optimism which accompanied the initial announcement of the proposed First City-Cullen/Frost merger, the two banking organizations subsequently called off the proposed merger, citing as the reason the uncertainties caused by regulatory delays.

30. Interview with Ben Love by Joseph A. Pratt, July 30, 1983, TCB Archives.

31. Interview with Shivers by Pratt and Calvert, August 10, 1983; "Austin National Bank—Preliminary Outline for Application to FRB," memo from Jody Grant to Messrs. Love, Cater, McDade and Sapp, August 27, 1973, Austin National Bank folder, Thomas McDade Files, TCBK Records. Included with this memo are numerous other documents concerning the proposed merger.

32. Federal Reserve System to Texas Commerce Bancshares, Inc., "Order Denying Acquisition of Banks," January 22, 1975, copy in Austin National Bank folder, Files of Thomas McDade, TCBK Records.

33. Capital National Bank–Austin folder, Files of the Financial Account-

ing Division, TCBK Records; Capital National Bank folder, Files of Thomas McDade, TCBK Records.

34. Merger files, Highland Park State Bank, Financial Accounting, TCBK Records.

35. Merger files, First National Bank of McAllen and Pan-American Bank, Financial Accounting, TCBK Records.

36. Thomas McDade to Acquisitions Strategy and Screening Committee, August 7, 1978, El Paso National folder, Files of Thomas McDade, TCBK Records.

37. The background history of El Paso National was taken from a pamphlet published by the bank on its fiftieth anniversary. See *50th Anniversary, 1925–1975*, El Paso National Bank, TCB Archives. See also "Summary of the El Paso Banking Study, 1974," Marshall Tyndall to Acquisitions Strategy and Screening Committee, June 26, 1979, Acquisitions Committee, 1979, folder, Files of Thomas McDade, TCBK Records.

38. Thomas McDade to Acquisitions Strategy and Screening Committee, August 7, 1978, El Paso National folder, Files of Thomas McDade, TCBK Records.

39. Ben Love to Tom McDade, June 23, 1979, Acquisitions Committee, 1979, folder, Files of Thomas McDade, TCBK Records.

40. Memo to File, July 22, 1981, Acquisitions Committee, 1981, folder, Files of Thomas McDade, TCBK Records.

41. "Cullen/Frost to Be Acquired by a Texas Bank," *Wall Street Journal*, July 27, 1983.

42. These figures are compiled from Texas Commerce Bancshares, *1984 Annual Report* (Houston, 1985): 72–73.

Chapter 13

1. The excellent national publicity generated by Texas Commerce Bancshares's excellent financial performance in the 1970s and early 1980s is exemplified by "Ben Love Conquers All in Houston," *Fortune* (November 19, 1979): 122–32.

2. "Profit at Texas Commerce Seen Dropping 35%," *Wall Street Journal*, March 18, 1985; "A Texas Bank That May Not Stay Tall in the Saddle," *Business Week* (January 28, 1985): 94; "The Pep Talk between Quarters," *Bankers' Hours* 23, no. 4 (May 1985): 1–3.

3. The literature on the deregulation of financial institutions in the United States in the recent past is vast. An excellent overview of this problem is Cooper and Fraser, *Banking Deregulation and the New Competition in Financial Services*.

4. "U.S. Rotary Rig Count," Hughes Tool Company, Houston, Texas (published quarterly).

5. For a broad discussion of energy lending, see Norman A. White, *Financing the International Petroleum Industry*. For TCB–Houston's philosophy of lending on oil properties, see *Remarks by Gary Wright*, presentation to

Bank Analysts' Forum, Houston, Texas, October 6, 1982, pp. 21–27. This bound booklet was prepared by officers of Texas Commerce Bancshares for use in addressing a group of financial analysts. Copies are filed in the TCB Archives. See also interview with Townley by Pratt, January 4, 1985.

6. A practical summary of the lending philosophy of TCB–Houston's Energy Group is found in "Remarks by Robert J. McGee to the Member Bank Seminar," Houston, February 3, 1983. TCB–Houston Records, TCB Archives. See also "Texas Commerce Bank Avoids Energy Pitfalls by Shunning Big Risks," *Wall Street Journal*, April 23, 1984.

7. Interview with Gary Wright by Joseph A. Pratt, July 22, 1985, TCB Archives.

8. For a retrospective discussion of the perils of predicting oil prices in the early 1980s, see Cambridge Energy Research Associates and Arthur Anderson & Co., "The Future of Oil Prices: The Perils of Prophecy," 1984. For the impact of changes in oil prices on the Texas economy, see "Winners and Losers from Cheaper Oil," *Fortune* (November 26, 1984): 81–82, 86, 88; "OPEC's Loss Is the Economy's Gain," *Business Week* (November 5, 1984): 28–29.

9. Interview with Wright by Pratt, July 22, 1985. The impact of changing conditions in the oil industry are clearly seen in a comparison of the three-year strategic plans prepared by TCB–Houston's Energy Division. See "Three-Year Strategic Plan," Petroleum and Minerals Division, Energy Department, TCB–Houston, 1984–1986, TCB–Houston Records, TCB Archives.

10. "Energy-loan Problems Touch Texas Commerce," *Dallas Morning News*, March 24, 1985. See also "Energy-Loan Losses Bigger Than Expected, Figure to Climb Higher," *Wall Street Journal*, November 14, 1983.

11. For an interview with Pickens on the need for restructuring the oil industry, see "Championship," *Texas Business* (May 1985): 36–42. For TCB–Houston's involvement in financing acquisitions, see interview with Wright by Pratt, July 22, 1985.

12. For the troubles at InterFirst, see "InterFirst Dismays Analysts," *Dallas Times Herald*, January 20, 1984; "Chairman of Dallas's InterFirst Corporation Quits," *Houston Chronicle*, January 19, 1984; "InterFirst Cites Bad Loans, Errors for Huge Losses," *Wall Street Journal*, October 10, 1983. The problems of First City are summarized in "First City Bancorporation Struggles to Regain Footing," *Dallas Morning News*, June 16, 1985). A summary of the financial performance in 1983 of the four largest Texas bank holding companies is presented in "The State of Texas Commerce," *Bankers' Hours* 23, no. 1 (1984): 1–4.

13. Mark Singer, *Funny Money*; "Continental Illinois: How Bad Judgments and Big Egos Did It In," *Wall Street Journal*, July 30, 1984; "Long before the 'Run' at Continental Illinois, Bank Hinted of Its Ills," *Wall Street Journal* (July 12, 1984): 1, 18; "The Nationalization of Continental Illinois," *Fortune* (August 20, 1984): 135–40.

14. "FDIC Takes Cautious Approach in Liquidating Midland Bank," *Dallas Times Herald*, October 21, 1984. For background information on the

purchase of First National Midland by RepublicBank Corporation, see "First National Midland," *Republication* 7, no. 1 (November 1983): 1–3.

15. Interview with Beall by Pratt, July 3, 1985; Interview with Galloway by Pratt, February 2, 1985.

16. Interview with Adams by Pratt, August 6, 1982.

17. "Remarks by John Adams," presentation to the Bank Analysts' Forum, Houston, Texas, October 6, 1982, pp. 53–56.

18. Interview with Gaetz by Pratt, February 27, 1985; "Remarks by Mike Gaetz," presentation to the Bank Analysts' Forum, Houston, Texas, October 6, 1982, pp. 57.–61.

19. "Remarks by Lloyd Bolton," presentation to the Board Analysts' Forum, Houston, Texas, October 6, 1982, pp. 35–38; Interview with Bolton by Pratt, June 15, 1983.

20. Interview with Kenneth Schnitzer by Joseph A. Pratt, August 19, 1985, TCB Archives; Susan Shullaw, "Century Development: Nowhere but Houston," *Buildings* (May 1980): 1–6; "Kenneth Schnitzer: Executive of the Year," *Houston Business Journal* (March 25, 1985): sec. 2, p. 1; "Greenway Plaza, Houston, Texas," Urban Land Institute—Project Reference File, vol. 6, no. 8 (April–June 1976).

21. Interview with Stephen Field by Joseph A. Pratt, February 22, 1985, notes in TCB Archives.

22. Interview with Gerald Hines by Joseph A. Pratt, February 22, 1985, TCB Archives.

23. "Remarks by Steve Field," presentation to the Bank Analysts' Forum, Houston, Texas, October 6, 1982, pp. 29–46.

24. Property Research and Investment Consultants, Inc., "Houston's Office Space Market . . . Up the Down Staircase," presented to developers of Houston, *Houstonian* (June 27, 1985): 1–4; "Energy Firms Use 34 Percent of Offices Leased in Houston," *Houston Chronicle*, February 26, 1984.

25. An excellent overview of banking deregulation is Cooper and Fraser, *Banking Deregulation*. See also Robert Craig West, "The Evolution and Devolution of Bank Regulation in the United States," *Journal of Economic Issues* 17, no. 2 (June 1983): 361–67.

26. In the wake of widespread problems with energy loans, Texas Commerce and other major energy lending banks were subjected to special audits by federal regulators. The U.S. comptroller of the currency also mandated increases in the bank's loan-loss reserve while applying stricter standards in identifying potential problem loans. The most broadly publicized result of the comptroller's investigation of Texas Commerce Bancshares was an allegation, subsequently dropped, that TCB–Houston had given two directors preferential treatment.

27. For a broad discussion of geographical restrictions on banks, see George Kaufman, Larry Mote, and Harvey Rosenblum, "Implications of Deregulation for Product Lines and Geographical Markets of Financial Institutions," *Proceedings of a Conference on Bank Structure and Competition*, Federal Reserve Bank of Chicago, April 12–14, 1982, 7–21.

28. Deborah Fowler, "Money Center Giants Staking Out Houston Market," *Houston Business Journal* (November 26, 1984): 1A, 11A.

29. An excellent summary of the history of the complicated issue of "nonbank banks" is found in Richard H. K. Vietor and Dekkers L. Davidson, "The Comptroller and Nonbank Banks," Harvard Business School Case 0–385,248, 1985. The periodical literature on interstate banking has become extensive. See, for example, Robert Eisenbeis, "Pressures for Interstate Banking," *Issues in Bank Regulation* (Summer 1981): 21–27; "Interstate Banking's Difficult Birth," *New York Times* (June 2, 1985): sec. 3, pp. 1, 13; "Interstate Banking: The Big Gamble That Congress Will Make It Legal," *Business Week* (June 24, 1985): 90–91; "Congress Edges toward Bank Bill to Clear Up Confusion in Industry," *Wall Street Journal*, April 23, 1984).

30. Ben Love to Executive Council Members of Texas Commerce Bancshares, May 21, 1984, "Regional Banking" folder, Ben Love Files, TCBK Records; "Interview with Ben F. Love, Texas Commerce Bancshares," *United States Banker* (July 1981): 38–40. Love has been an aggressive advocate of regional banking in public and political lobbying.

31. Ben Love to Tom McDade, November 4, 1978, Minutes of the Acquisitions/Strategy and Screening Committee, TCBK Records; Interview with Ben Love by Joseph Pratt, July 30, 1983, TCB Archives.

32. For an overview of changes in bank funding in the 1960s see Donald C. Miller, "Problems of Asset and Liability Management," address before Bank Administration Institute," Cleveland, Ohio, October 28, 1969; more recent developments are included in Ernest W. Swift, "Asset/Liability Management: History and Technique," *NABW Journal* (May–June 1981): 13–18; Stigum, *The Money Markets*. For the impact of these changes on Texas Commerce, see interview with Ben Cohen by Joseph A. Pratt, August 28, 1985, TCB Archives.

33. The new competition in financial services is discussed in Cooper and Fraser, *Banking Deregulation*. See also "Deregulation of Banks Stirs Confusion, splits Fed and White House," *Wall Street Journal*, July 1, 1983; Joseph F. Sinkey, Jr., "New Competition for Financial Services," *Economic Review* (Federal Reserve Bank of Atlanta) (August 1981): 4–35; "The Peril in Financial Services," *Business Week* (August 20, 1984): 52–57; "The Supercompanies Emerge," *Dun's Business Month* (April 1983): 44–50; "Banking Deregulation Benefits Many People but Stirs Some Worry," *Wall Street Journal*, September 30, 1985). For the impact of these changes in Texas, see Bernard Weinstein, "Monetary Mixmaster," *Texas Business* (October 1984): 80–110.

34. For an overview of the efforts of Texas banks to expand their involvement in consumer or retail banking, see "Texas Banks Resurrecting Retail Service," *Dallas Morning News*, May 13, 1984.

Bibliography

Primary Sources

Manuscript Collections

Anderson, Clayton Archives. Houston, Texas.
Federal Reserve Bank. Dallas, Texas.
Library of Congress. Washington, D.C.
    Jones, Jesse H. Papers.
Liddell, Sapp Records. Houston, Texas.
National Archives. Washington, D.C.
    Reconstruction Finance Corporation. Records.
Texas Commerce Bancshares (TCBK) Records. Houston, Texas.
    Acquisitions/Strategy and Screening Committee. Minutes.
    Financial Accounting Division. Files.
    McDade, Thomas. Files.
    Love, Ben. Files.
Texas Commerce Bank Archives. Houston, Texas.
    Allison, William. Papers.
    Cater, John T. Papers.
    Commercial National Bank. *Directors' Minutes.* 1886–1912.
    Eaves, Barbara. Papers.
    Love, Ben. Papers.
    Marine Banking and Trust Company. *Directors' Minutes.* 1928–36.
    Member Banks, TCBK. Papers.
        Phillips, William, Jr. Personal Papers.
    National Bank of Commerce. *Directors' Minutes.* 1912–64.
    National Bank of Commerce. *Executive and Discount Committee Minutes.* 1934–64.
    National Bank of Commerce. Records.
    Statements of Condition for Houston banks. 1925–66.
    South Texas Commercial National Bank. *Directors' Minutes.* 1912–54.
    South Texas National Bank. *Directors' Minutes.* 1890–1912.
    Tandy, W. L. Papers.
    Texas Commerce Bank-Houston. Records.
    Texas National Bank. *Directors' Minutes.* 1954–63.
    Texas National Bank. Records.
        McLean, J. W. Personal Papers.
    Texas National Bank of Commerce. Records.
    Union National Bank. *Directors' Minutes.* 1910–53.
Woodson, Benjamin. Personal Papers. Houston, Texas.

Oral Interviews

By Walter L. Buenger, Robert A. Calvert, and Joseph A. Pratt, housed in TCB Archives.

Herbert Allen. August 7, 1985.
John Adams. August 6, 1982.
Malcolm Baker. July 26, 1983.
Chester Arthur Barrett. August 19, 1982.
Charles Beall. July 3, 1985.
Norman Binz. July 26, 1983.
Jack Blanton. June 12, 1984.
Lloyd Bolton. June 15, 1983.
E. O. Buck. August 9, 1982; June 8, 1983.
Tom Carter. July 13, 1983; April 2, 1986.
Cater, John. August 19, 1985.
May Chu. June 3, 1983.
George Cochran III. August 16, 1983.
Ben Cohen. August 18, 1983.
Marvin Collie. August 12, 1983.
Calvin Collier. November 27, 1984.
J. Howard Creekmore. September 17, 1982; March 6, 1985.
W. N. Davis. August 26, 1983; September 19, 1983.
Robert P. Doherty, Jr. September 30, 1983.
Jean Dupree. August 5, 1983.
George Ebanks. November 30, 1984.
Harlord Elsom. August 12, 1983.
Stephen Field. June 6, 1983; February 2, 1985.
Mike Gaetz. February 27, 1985.
Carl Galloway. February 2, 1985.
Gerald Hines. February 22, 1985.
E. C. Japhet. June 22, 1983.
John T. Jones. August 21, 1982.
Tim Irvine. June 8, 1983.
Ben Love. June 25, 1983; July 30, 1983; February 27, 1985.
H. Malcolm Lovett. June 24, 1983.
J. Howard Marshall. August 26, 1983.
S. M. McAshan. January 4, 1985.
Thomas McDade. June 22, 1983.
Kitty McCord. October 21, 1983.
Kline McGee. July 26, 1983.
J. W. McLean. August 13, 1984.
Richard Melton. August 19, 1983.
Joseph Nalle. July 26, 1983.
W. D. Noel. August 19, 1983.
Charles Sapp. August 9, 1982.
Kenneth Schnitzer. August 19, 1985.
John Sears. August 8, 1983.
E. C. Scurlock. June 12, 1984.
Allan Shivers. August 10, 1983.
Harry Simms. October 14, 1983.
John Townley. January 4, 1985.

Steven Walker. June 17, 1985.
John West. August 30, 1983.
John Whitmore. August 17, 1982, September 17, 1982; June 15, 1983; October 2, 1984; December 16, 1985.
Ray Winstead. August 4, 1983.
Benjamin Woodson. June 18, 1985.
Gary Wright. July 22, 1985.

Newspapers

Houston Chronicle
Houston Post
Lubbock Avalanche-Journal
Odessa American
San Angelo Evening Standard
Wall Street Journal

Trade Journals

American Banker
Bankers' Hours
Bankers' Magazine
Houston Banker
Houston Business Journal
Hughes Ridgway
Texas Banker
Texas Bankers Journal
Texas Bankers' Record

Books

The Bank Holding Company Movement to 1978: A Compendium. Staff Economic Study. Washington, D.C.: Publication Services, Division of Administrative Services, Board of Governors of the Federal Reserve System, September, 1978.

Houston Cotton Exchange and Board of Trade. *Description of Harris County, Texas.* Houston: W. H. Coyle, 1886.

The Industrial Advantages of Houston, Texas, and Environs. Houston: Akehurst Publishing Co., 1894.

The Industries of Houston: Her Relations as a Center of Trade, Business Houses and Manufacturing Establishments. Houston: J. M. Elstner & Co., Publishers, 1887.

Fall, Mrs. Henry. *The Key to the City of Houston.* Houston: Federation of Women's Clubs, 1908.

General Laws of Texas, Thirty-first Legislature: Regular, First, and Second Called Sessions, 1909. Austin: State Printer, 1909.

Jacobs, Max H., and H. Dick Golding. *Houston and Cotton: Commemorating Seventy-five Years of Leadership and Progress as a Cotton Market.* Houston: Houston Cotton Exchange and Board of Trade, 1949.

Johnson, Elmer H. *The Basis of the Commercial and Industrial Development of Texas: A Study of Regional Development of Texas Resources.* Austin: Bureau of Business Research, 1933.

Jones, Jesse, with Edward Angly. *Fifty Billion Dollars: My Thirteen Years with the RFC, 1932–1945.* New York: Macmillan Publishing Co., 1951.

Kingston, Michael T., ed. *The Texas Almanac and State Industrial Guide, 1984–1985.* Dallas: A. H. Belo Corp., 1983.

Peeler, A. J., and Ingham S. Roberts, eds. *The Standard Blue Book of Texas: Who's Who Edition de Luxe of Houston.* Houston: Who's Who Publishing Co., 1907.

The Planters and Mechanics National Bank. Galveston: Clarke & Coupts, 1900.

Proceedings of the Annual Convention of the Texas Bankers' Association. Galveston: Clarke and Counts.

Schwulst, Earl Bryan. *Extension of Bank Credit: A Study in the Principles of Financial Statement Analysis as Applied in Extending Bank Credit to Agriculture, Industry, and Trade in Texas.* Boston and New York: Houghton Mifflin Co., 1927.

Shirley, R. V. and Bervard Nichols. *Trends of Development of Texas Financial Institutions.* Austin: Bureau of Business Research, The University of Texas, 1931.

Sweet, Alexander E., and J. Armoy Knox. *On a Mexican Mustang through Texas from the Gulf to the Rio Grande.* Hartford, Conn.: S. S. Seranton and Co., 1883.

Texas. *State Bank Law of the State of Texas As Passed by the 29th Legislature, Effective August 14, 1905.* Austin: State Printing Co., 1905.

Texas. *State Banking Laws: Digest 1909.* Austin: State Printing Co., 1909.

Union Bank and Trust Company, Houston, Texas. Houston, Privately Printed, 1908.

Wasson, S. Deane. *Fifty Years a Cotton Market: Houston Cotton Exchange and Board of Trade Brochure, 1924.* Houston: Houston Cotton Exchange and Board of Trade, 1924.

Yearbook of Agriculture, 1932. Washington, D.C.: U.S. Government Printing Office, 1932.

Addresses

Anderson, Hugh. "A Banker's View of Oil Conservation." Before Independent Bankers' Association of Southern California. Los Angeles, Calif., June 24, 1954.

Weiss, Harry Carothers. "The Banker and Oil Man in Texas." Before Texas Bankers' Association. San Antonio, Texas, May 19, 1937.

Articles

Brown, Stanley. "The Big Deal That Got Away." *Fortune* (October 1966): 164–92.

"Houston, South's Leading Banking Center," *Houston 12* (September 1941): 2–29.

Loring, Rush, Jr. "The View from inside Hughes Tool." *Fortune* (December 1973): 106–109, 173–76.

"One Bank Holding Company before the 1970 Amendments." *Federal Reserve Bulletin* 50 (December 1972): 999-1008.

Simpson, G. S. "ABC—How Deal Works, What Changes Would Do." *Independent Petroleum Monthly* (September 1961): 13–16.

Smaistrla, Charles, and David Cordell. "Expansion and Performance of Multibank Holding Companies in Texas." *Voice* (Federal Reserve Bank of Dallas) (April 1979): 1–10.

Smith, Stephen. "The History of Potential Competition in Bank Mergers and Acquisitions." *Economic Perspectives* (Federal Reserve Bank of Chicago) (July–August 1980): 16.

Spencer, W. I., J. R. Rowan, and L. F. Terry. "Bankers Like to Do Business with Oil Men." *Oil and Gas Journal* (November 21, 1955): 168–76.

Stodden, John. "Multibank Holding Companies: Development in Texas, Changes in Recent Years." *Business Review* (Federal Reserve Bank of Dallas) (December 1974): 1–10.

———. "Their Small Size Costs Banks Business of Large Companies." *Business Review* (Federal Reserve Bank of Dallas) (October 1973): 6–7.

"Texas Commerce: Master of Control." *Dun's Business Month* 124, no. 6 (December 1984): 40–41.

30th Anniversary issue of Zapata newsletter, *Viva* (October 1984): insert n.p.

Warren, J. E. "Considerations concerning Bank Financing of Oil Properties." *Journal of Petroleum Technology* 8, no. 5 (May 1956): 11–14.

Winer, Anthony. "Applying the Theory of Probable Future Competition." *Federal Reserve Bulletin* (September 1982): 527–33.

Secondary Sources

Books

Adams, Nathan. *The First National in Dallas.* Dallas: First National Bank, 1942.

Aitken, Hugh G. J., ed. *Did Slavery Pay? Readings in the Economics of Black Slavery in the United States.* Boston: Houghton Mifflin Co., 1971.

Alhadeff, David. *Monopoly and Competition in Banking.* Berkeley: Bureau of Business and Economic Research, University of California, 1954.

Barr, Alwyn. *Reconstruction to Reform: Texas Politics, 1876–1906.* Austin: University of Texas Press, 1971.

Bates, Colonel William B. *Monroe D. Anderson: His Life and Legacy.* Houston: Texas Gulf Coast Historical Association, 1957.

Baughn, William Hubert. *Changes in the Structure of Texas Commercial Banking, 1946–1956.* Austin: Bureau of Business Research, The University of Texas, 1959.

Bohi, Douglas, and Milton Russell. *Limiting Oil Imports: An Economic History and Analysis.* Baltimore, Md.: Resources for the Future, Johns Hopkins Press, 1978.

Brown, William. *The Dual Banking System in the United States.* New York: American Bankers Association, Department of Economics and Research, 1968.

Burns, Helen M. *The American Banking Community and New Deal Banking Reforms, 1933–1935.* Westport, Conn.: Greenwood Press, 1974.

Campbell, Randolph B., and Richard G. Lowe. *Wealth and Power in Antebellum Texas.* College Station: Texas A&M University Press, 1977.

Carlson, Avery L. *A Monetary and Banking History of Texas.* Fort Worth: Fort Worth National Bank, 1930.

Chandler, Alfred D., Jr. *Strategy and Structure: Chapters in the History of Industrial Enterprise.* Cambridge, Mass.: The Massachusetts Institute of Technology Press, 1962.

————. *The Visible Hand: The Managerial Revolution in Modern Business.* Cambridge, Mass.: Harvard University Press, 1977.

Chandler, Alfred D., and Richard Ledlow (eds.). *The Coming of Managerial Capitalism.* Homewood, Ill.: Richard D. Irwin, 1985.

Clark, James A., and Michael Halbouty. *The Last Boom.* New York: Random House, 1972.

————. *Spindletop.* New York: Random House, 1952.

Clark, Joseph L. *The Texas Gulf Coast: Its History and Development.* 2 vols. New York: Lewis Historical Publishing Co., 1955.

Cleveland, Harold van B., and Thomas Huertas. *Citibank, 1812–1970.* Cambridge, Mass. and London: Harvard University Press, 1985.

Cobb, James C. *Industrialization and Southern Society, 1877–1984.* Lexington: University of Kentucky Press, 1984.

Connor, Seymour V. *Texas: A History.* Arlington Heights, Ill.: AHM Publishing Corp., 1971.

Cooper, S. Kerry, and Donald Fraser. *Banking Deregulation and the New Competition in Financial Services.* Cambridge, Mass.: Ballinger Publishing Co., 1984.

Crum, Lawrence L. *Transition in the Texas Commercial Banking Industry, 1950–1965.* Austin: Bureau of Business Research, The University of Texas at Austin, 1970.

Fischer, Gerald. *American Banking Structure: Its Evolution and Regulation.* New York: Columbia University Press, 1967.

————. *Bank Holding Companies.* New York: Columbia University Press, 1951.

Fleming, Lamar, Jr. *Growth of the Business of Anderson, Clayton & Co.* Edited by James A. Tinsley. Houston: Texas Gulf Coast Historical Association, 1966.

Frey, John, and H. Chandler Ide, eds. *A History of the Petroleum Administration for War, 1941–1945.* Washington, D.C.: Government Printing Office, 1946.

Friedman, Milton, and Anna J. Schwartz. *A Monetary History of the United States, 1876–1960.* Princeton, N.J.: Princeton University Press, 1963.

Garwood, Ellen Clayton. *Will Clayton: A Short Biography.* Austin: University of Texas Press, 1958.

Gatton, T. Harry. *The Texas Bankers' Association: The First Century, 1885–1985.* Austin: Texas Bankers' Association, 1984.

Giebelhaus, August. *Business and Government in the Oil Industry: A Case Study of Sun Oil, 1876–1945*. Greenwich, Conn.: JAI Press, 1980.

Goodwyn, Lawrence. *Democratic Promise: The Populist Movement in America*. New York: Oxford University Press, 1976.

Gould, Lewis L. *Progressives and Prohibitionists: Texas Democrats in the Wilson Era*. Austin: University of Texas Press, 1973.

Grant, Joseph M., and Lawrence L. Crum. *The Development of State-chartered Banking in Texas: From Predecessor Systems until 1970*. Austin: Bureau of Business Research, University of Texas at Austin, 1978.

Grantham, Dewey W. *Southern Progressivism: The Reconciliation of Progress and Tradition*. Knoxville: University of Tennessee Press, 1983.

Griffin, James M., and Henry B. Steele. *Energy Economics and Policy*. New York: Academic Press, 1986.

Haley, J. Evetts. *Charles Schreiner, General Merchandise*. Austin: Texas State Historical Association, 1944.

Hammond, Bray. *Banks and Politics in America from the Revolution to the Civil War*. Princeton: Princeton University Press, 1957.

The Handbook of Texas. Vols. 1 and 2 edited by Walter Prescott Webb and H. Bailey Carroll. Austin: Texas State Historical Association, 1952. Vol. 3 edited by Eldon Stephen Branda. Austin: Texas State Historical Association, 1976.

Hawley, Ellis W. *The New Deal and the Problem of Monopoly: A Study in Economic Ambivalence*. Princeton: Princeton University Press, 1966.

Henson, Margaret Swett. *Samuel May Williams: Early Texas Entrepreneur*. College Station: Texas A&M University Press, 1976.

James, Marquis. *The Texaco Story: The First Fifty Years, 1902–1952*. New York: Texas Co., 1953.

Jessee, Michael, and Steven Seelig. *Bank Holding Companies and the Public Interest*. Lexington, Mass.: D. C. Heath and Co., 1977.

Jones, J. Lester. *W. T. Carter & Bro*. Houston: Privately printed, 1978.

Kennedy, Susan Estabrook. *The Banking Crisis of 1933*. Lexington: University Press of Kentucky, 1973.

King, John O. *The Early History of the Houston Oil Company of Texas, 1901–1908*. Houston: Texas Gulf Coast Historical Association, 1959.

———. *Joseph Stephen Cullinan: A Study of Leadership in the Texas Petroleum Industry, 1897–1937*. Nashville, Tenn.: Vanderbilt University Press, 1970.

Kirkland, William A. *Old Bank–New Bank: The First National Bank, Houston, 1866–1956*. Houston: Pacesetter Press, 1975.

Klebaner, Benjamin J. *Commercial Banking in the United States: A History*. Hinsdale, Ill.: Dryden Press, 1974.

Kolko, Gabriel. *The Triumph of Conservatism: A Reinterpretation of American History, 1900–1916*. New York: Free Press of Glencoe, 1963.

Larson, Henrietta, and Kenneth Porter. *History of the Humble Oil and Refining Company: A Study in Industrial Growth*. New York: Harper & Row, 1959.

Lasswell, Mary. *John Henry Kirby: Prince of the Pines*. Austin: Encino Press, 1967.

Leuchtenburg, William E. *Franklin D. Roosevelt and the New Deal*. New York: Harper & Row, 1963.

Logan, Bill. *The Houston Heritage Collection of National Bank Notes, 1863 through 1935*. Houston: D. Armstrong Co., 1977.

McComb, David G. *Houston: The Bayou City*. Austin: University of Texas Press, 1969.

McDonald, Stephen. *Petroleum Conservation in the United States: An Economic Analysis*. Baltimore, Md.: Resources for the Future, Johns Hopkins Press, 1971.

McLean, John, and Robert Haigh. *The Growth of Integrated Oil Companies*. Boston: Division of Research, Graduate School of Business, Harvard University, 1954.

McMath, Robert C., Jr. *Populist Vanguard: A History of the Southern Farmers' Alliance*. Chapel Hill: University of North Carolina Press, 1975.

Mangon, Frank. *The Pipeliners*. El Paso: Guynes Press, 1977.

Martin, Roscoe C. *The People's Party in Texas: A Study in Third Party Politics*. Austin: University of Texas Press, 1933.

Maxwell, Robert S., and Robert D. Baker. *Sawdust Empire: The Texas Lumber Industry, 1830–1940*. College Station: Texas A&M University Press, 1983.

Miller, Edmund T. *A Financial History of Texas*. Austin: University of Texas, 1916.

Muir, Andrew Forest. *William Marsh Rice and His Institute: A Biographical Study*. Edited by Sylvia Stallings Morris. Houston: Rice University Studies, 1972.

Nash, Gerald. *United States Oil Policy, 1890–1964*. Pittsburgh: University of Pittsburgh Press, 1968.

O'Connor, James Francis Thaddeus. *The Banking Crisis and Recovery under the Roosevelt Administration*. Chicago: Da Capo Press, 1938.

Odell, Peter. *Oil and World Power: A Geographical Interpretation*. New York: Taplinger Publishing Co., 1970.

Olien, Roger, and Diana Olien. *Wildcatters: Texas Independent Oilmen*. Austin: Texas Monthly Press, 1984.

Olson, James Stuart. *Herbert Hoover and the Reconstruction Finance Corporation, 1931–1933*. Ames: Iowa State University Press, 1977.

Palmer, Bruce. *Man over Money: The Southern Populist Critique of American Capitalism*. Chapel Hill: University of North Carolina Press, 1980.

Parker, William N., ed. *The Structure of the Cotton Economy of the Antebellum South*. Washington, D.C.: Agricultural History Society, 1970.

Porter, Glenn, ed. *Regional Economic History: The Mid-Atlantic Area since 1700*. Wilmington, Del.: Eleutherian Mills–Hagley Foundation, 1976.

Pratt, Joseph A. *The Growth of a Refining Region*. Greenwich, Conn.: JAI Press, 1980.

Prindle, David. *Petroleum Politics and the Texas Railroad Commission.* Austin: University of Texas Press, 1981.

Richardson, Harry. *Regional Growth Theory.* New York: Wiley Publishing Co., 1973.

Richardson, Rupert N., Ernest Wallace, and Adrian Anderson. *Texas: The Lone Star State.* Englewood Cliffs, N.J.: Prentice-Hall, 1981.

Rister, Carl Coke. *Oil! Titan of the Southwest.* Norman: University of Oklahoma Press, 1949.

Romasco, Albert U. *The Poverty of Abundance: Hoover, the Nation, the Depression.* New York: Oxford University Press, 1965.

Schlesinger, Arthur M., Jr. *The Coming of the New Deal.* Boston: Houghton Mifflin Company, 1958.

Schneider, Steven A. *The Oil Price Revolution.* Baltimore and London: Johns Hopkins University Press, 1983.

Sibley, Marilyn McAdams. *George W. Brackenridge: Maverick Philanthropist.* Austin: University of Texas Press, 1973.

———. *The Port of Houston: A History.* Austin: University of Texas Press, 1968.

Singer, Mark. *Funny Money.* New York: Alfred A. Knopf, 1985.

Skidmore, Thomas E., and Peter H. Smith. *Modern Latin America.* New York: Oxford University Press, 1984.

Snyder, Robert E. *Cotton Crisis.* Chapel Hill: University of North Carolina Press, 1984.

Spratt, John Stricklin. *The Road to Spindletop: Economic Change in Texas, 1875–1901.* Dallas: Southern Methodist University Press, 1955.

Stigum, Marcia. *The Money Market.* Homewood, Illinois: Dow Jones–Irwin, 1978.

Thompson, Craig. *Since Spindletop: A Human Story of Gulf's First Half-Century.* Pittsburgh: Gulf Oil Corp., 1951.

Timmons, Bascom N. *Jesse H. Jones: The Man and the Statesman.* New York: Holt Publishing Co., 1956.

Twenty-Five Years: Cameron Iron Works, 1920–1945. Houston: Privately Printed, 1946.

Vietor, Richard. *Energy Policy in America since 1945.* Cambridge: Cambridge University Press, 1984.

Watkins, Leonard L. *Commercial Banking Reform in the United States.* Ann Arbor: University of Michigan Press, 1938.

West, Robert Craig. *Banking Reform and the Federal Reserve, 1863–1923.* Ithaca, N.Y.: Cornell University Press, 1974.

Wheeler, Kenneth W. *To Wear A City's Crown: The Beginnings of Urban Growth in Texas, 1836–1865.* Cambridge, Mass.: Harvard University Press, 1968.

White, Norman A. *Financing the International Petroleum Industry.* London: Graham & Trotman Ltd., 1978.

Wicker, Elmus R. *Federal Reserve Monetary Policy, 1917–1933.* New York: Random House Publishing Co., 1966.

Wiebe, Robert H. *The Search for Order, 1877–1920*. New York: Hill and Wang, 1967.

Williamson, Harold, Ralph Andreano, Arnold Daum, and Gilbert Klose. *The American Petroleum Industry: The Age of Energy, 1899–1959*. Evanston, Ill.: Northwestern University Press, 1963.

Wineburgh, H. Harold. *The Texas Banker: The Life and Times of Fred Farrel Florence*. Dallas: H. H. Wineburgh, 1981.

Woodman, Harold D. *King Cotton and His Retainers: Financing and Marketing the Cotton Crop of the South, 1800–1925*. Lexington: University of Kentucky Press, 1968.

Writers' Program, WPA. *Houston: A History and Guide*. Houston: Anson Jones Press, 1942.

Zimmermann, Erich. *Conservation in the Production of Petroleum: A Study in Industrial Control*. New Haven, Conn.: Yale University Press, 1957.

Theses and Dissertations

Adams, Larry Earl. "Economic Development in Texas during Reconstruction, 1865–1875." Ph.D. dissertation, North Texas State University, 1980.

Berryman, Marsha Grant. "Houston and the Early Depression: 1929–1932." Master's thesis, University of Houston, 1965.

Curlee, Abigail. "A Study of Texas Slave Plantations, 1822–1865." Ph.D. dissertation, University of Texas, Austin, 1932.

Dugas, Vera Lea. "A Social and Economic History of Texas in the Civil War and Reconstruction Periods." Ph.D. dissertation, University of Texas, Austin, 1963.

Ellis, Louis Tuffly. "The Texas Cotton Compress Industry: A History." Ph.D. dissertation, University of Texas, 1964.

Grover, Henry C. "The Dissolution of T. W. House and Company." Master's thesis, University of Houston, 1962.

Love, Ben F. "People and Profits: A Bank Case Study." Thesis, Southwest School of Banking, Dallas, 1967.

Montgomery, William Edward. "The Depression in Houston during the Hoover Era, 1929–1932." Master's thesis, University of Texas, Austin, 1966.

Wilson, Wallace. "Bank Financing of Oil and Gas Production Payments." Thesis, Southwest School of Banking, Dallas, 1962.

Articles

Andrews, Jesse. "A Texas Portrait: Capt. James A. Baker, 1857–1941." *Texas Bar Journal* (February 1961): 110–11, 187–89.

Ashburn, Karl E. "Slavery and Cotton Production in Texas." *Southwestern Social Science Quarterly* 14 (December 1933): 257–71.

———. "The Texas Cotton Acreage Control Law of 1931–1932." *Southwestern Historical Quarterly* 61 (July 1957): 116–24.

Baughman, James P. "The Evolution of Rail-Water Systems of Transportation in the Gulf Southwest, 1836–1890." *Journal of Southern History* 34 (August 1968): 357–61.

Broyles, William, and Alex Shashunoff. "How First National Passed Republic." *Texas Monthly* 2 (May 1974): 44–54, 85–96.

Calvert, Robert A. "Nineteenth-Century Farmers, Cotton, and Prosperity." *Southwestern Historical Quarterly* 73 (April 1970): 509–30.

Campbell, Randolph B., and Richard G. Lowe. "Some Economic Aspects of Antebellum Texas Agriculture." *Southwestern Historical Quarterly* 82 (April 1979): 351–78.

Daniel, Pete. "The Crossroads of Change: Cotton, Tobacco, and Rice Cultures in the Twentieth-Century South." *Journal of Southern History* 50 (August 1984): 429–32.

———. "The Metamorphosis of Slavery, 1865–1900." *Journal of American History* 66 (June 1979): 88–99.

Dethloff, Henry C. "Rice Revolution in the Southwest, 1880–1910." *Arkansas Historical Quarterly* 20 (Spring 1970): 66–75.

Dillon, Charles H. "The Arrival of the Telegraph in Texas." *Southwestern Historical Quarterly* 65 (October 1960): 200–11.

Dugas, Vera Lea. "A Duel with Railroads: Houston vs. Galveston, 1866–1881." *East Texas Historical Journal* 2 (October 1964): 118–27.

———. "Texas Industry, 1860–1880." *Southwestern Historical Quarterly* 59 (October 1955): 151–83.

Ellis, L. Tuffly. "The Revolutionizing of the Texas Cotton Trade, 1866–1885." *Southwestern Historical Quarterly* 73 (April 1970): 478–508.

Engerman, Stanley L. "A Reconsideration of Southern Economic Growth, 1770–1860." *Agricultural History* 49 (April 1975): 343–61.

Foust, James D., and Dale E. Swan. "Productivity and Profitability of Antebellum Slave Labor: A Micro-Approach." *Agricultural History* 44 (January 1970): 39–62.

Goodwyn, Lawrence. "Populist Dreams and Negro Rights: East Texas as a Case Study." *American Historical Review* 76 (December 1971): 1435–56.

Green, James R. "Tenant Farmer Discontent and Socialist Protest in Texas, 1901–1917." *Southwestern Historical Quarterly* 18 (October 1977): 133–54.

Holbrook, Abigail Curlee. "Cotton Marketing in Antebellum Texas." *Southwestern Historical Quarterly* 73 (April 1970): 456–78.

Hollon, Gene. "Captain Charles Schreiner, the Father of the Hill Country." *Southwestern Historical Quarterly* 48 (October 1944): 145–68.

Jackson, Susan. "Movin' On: Mobility through Houston in the 1850's." *Southwestern Historical Quarterly* 81 (January 1978): 251–82.

Jordan, Terry G. "The German Settlement of Texas After 1865." *Southwestern Historical Quarterly* 73 (October 1969): 193–212.

Kerr, Homer L. "Migration into Texas, 1860–1880." *Southwestern Historical Quarterly* 70 (October 1966): 184–216.

Klebaner, Benjamin. "The Bank Holding Company Act of 1956." *Southern Economic Journal* 24 (January 1958): 313–26.

McKay, S. S. "Economic Conditions in Texas in the 1870s." *West Texas Historical Association Year Book* 15 (October 1939): 84–127.

Morgan, George T., Jr. "The Gospel of Wealth Goes South: John Henry Kirby and Labor's Struggle for Self-Determination, 1901–1916." *Southwestern Historical Quarterly* 75 (October 1971): 186–97.

Muir, Andrew Forest. "The Destiny of Buffalo Bayou." *Southwestern Historical Quarterly* 47 (October 1943): 91–106.

———. "Railroads Come to Houston, 1857–1861." *Southwestern Historical Quarterly* 64 (July 1960): 42–63.

Norvell, J. R. "The Railroad Commission of Texas: Its Origin and History." *Southwestern Historical Quarterly* 68 (April 1965): 465–80.

Paxson, Frederic L. "The Constitution of Texas, 1845." *Southwestern Historical Quarterly* 18 (April 1915): 397–98.

Random, Roger, and Richard Sutch. "The 'Lock-in' Mechanism and Overproduction of Cotton in the Postbellum South." *Agricultural History* 49 (April 1975): 405–26.

Rubin, Julius. "The Limits of Agricultural Progress in the Nineteenth-Century South." *Agricultural History* 49 (April 1975): 362–73.

Saloutos, Theodore. "Southern Agriculture and the Problems of Readjustment: 1866–1877." *Agricultural History* 30 (April 1956): 58–76.

Scott, J. Virgil. "Houston Banks Grow." *Houston* 15 (September 1943): 6–7.

Sheperd, William G. "The Banking Industry." In Walter Adams, ed. *The Structure of American Industry.* New York: Macmillan Publishing Co., 1977.

Sneed, Edgar P. "A Historiography of Reconstruction in Texas: Some Myths and Problems." *Southwestern Historical Quarterly* 72 (April 1969): 435–48.

White, Raymond E. "Cotton Ginning in Texas to 1861." *Southwestern Historical Quarterly* 61 (October 1957): 257–69.

Woodman, Harold D. "Post-Civil War Southern Agriculture and the Law." *Agricultural History* 53 (January 1979): 319–37.

———. "Sequel to Slavery: The New History Views the Postbellum South." *Journal of Southern History* 43 (November 1977): 523–54.

Wooster, Ralph A. "Wealthy Texans, 1860." *Southwestern Historical Quarterly* 71 (October 1967): 163–80.

———. "Wealthy Texans, 1870." *Southwestern Historical Quarterly* 74 (July 1970): 24–35.

Wright, Gavin. "Cotton Competition and the Post-Bellum Recovery of the American South." *Journal of Economic History* 34 (September 1974): 610–35.

Index